Waud's
EMPLOYMENT
LAW

**The Practical Guide for
Personnel Managers,
Trade Union Officials,
Employers, Employees
and Lawyers**

14th edition

PETER CHANDLER

RECOMMENDED BY

INSTITUTE OF DIRECTORS

**KOGAN
PAGE**

This book has been endorsed by the Institute of Directors.

The endorsement is given to selected Kogan Page books which the IoD recognises as being of specific interest to its members and providing them with up-to-date, informative and practical resources for creating business success. Kogan Page books endorsed by the IoD represent the most authoritative guidance available on a wide range of subjects including management, finance, marketing, training and HR.

First published in 1985 by Michael O'Mara Books Limited
Fourteenth edition published in 2003

Kogan Page Limited
120 Pentonville Road
London N1 9JN
United Kingdom
www.kogan-page.co.uk

© Peter Chandler, 1998, 2001, 2003

The views expressed in this book are those of the author and are not necessarily the same as those of the Institute of Directors.

British Library Cataloguing in Publication Data

A CIP record for this book is available from the British Library.

ISBN 0 7494 3888 6

Typeset by Saxon Graphics Ltd, Derby
Printed and bound in Great Britain by Clays Ltd, St Ives plc

Contents

3   Statutory employment rights (general)

8   A contract under the 'common law' 168

9   Contracts of employment 181

10   Restrictive covenants

About this book

In the two years since the 13th edition of this book was published a spate of new and amending legislation, heralded by the Government's *Work and Parents* White Paper and a number of EU Directives, has expanded the right of employees (and workers) and the duties and responsibilities of employers in a variety of areas.

As might be expected, this 14th edition of *Waud's Employment Law* has been updated to include new and amending legislation relating to • maternity leave and pay • adoption leave and pay • parental and paternity leave • flexible working • time off for dependents • part-time workers • fixed-term employees • working tax credits • equal pay • data protection • dismissal during 'protected industrial action' • increased compensation for unfair dismissal • new restrictions on the working hours and employment at night of young persons • the national minimum wage • holidays and holiday pay • workplace protection for children, young persons, and new and expectant mothers • guarantee payments; and so on.

Those readers who deal infrequently with employment-related issues should first read Chapter 1, and then glance through the other chapters to acquire a cursory knowledge of points for further reference. The book is fully cross-referenced throughout and there is a comprehensive index. Points of law are illustrated by decided cases, while abbreviations (see below) are used to identify relevant legislation.

GENDER BIAS IN THE ENGLISH LANGUAGE

Author's Note: Gender-bias in the English language has been the subject of debate for many years and is likely to be so for many years to come. Efforts to eliminate that bias have been largely unsuccessful as successive governments and their departments have long since acknowledged when drafting legislation and producing guidance notes and associated codes of practice.

The fact that our language has no common-sex personal pronoun in the singular does not, in my view, excuse the ungrammatical use of *their* in contexts (as Fowler* put it) that call logically for *his* or *his or her*. I am likewise unconvinced that the pronoun *it* is appropriate when referring to an *employer* already mentioned. Overuse of *he or she* (or *his or hers*), especially in paragraphs in which the nouns *employee* and *employer* compete for space is not only clumsy, but irritating and confusing, as is the practice, preferred by some authors, of repeating the nouns *employer* or *employee* in the same sentence or paragraph, seemingly to avoid the tedium of having to select a pronoun at all.

My solution (with apologies to those who do not share my views) is to use the masculine singular pronoun throughout the book when alluding to an *employer* and the phrases *he (or she)* or *his (or hers)* (once, and once only) in each paragraph in which the noun *employee* first appears. My intention in using these less than satisfactory devices is to (a) to produce a readable text; (b) to reassure readers that I am not unaware of the problems associated with gender bias in the English language; and (c) to remind them, as if they needed reminding, that employment legislation applies equally to men and to women.

* *Fowler's Modern English Usage*, 2nd Edition (*Oxford University Press*)

STATUTES, REGULATIONS AND ORDERS

Statutes, Regulations and Orders referred to only occasionally in this book (eg the Tax Credits Act 2002, or the Part-time Workers (Prevention of Less Favourable Treatment) Regulations 2000) are given their full titles in the accompanying text. The more dominant statutes and Regulations (such as the Employment Rights Act 1996) – which feature in almost every chapter of the book – are accorded the following abbreviations:

DDA 1995	Disability Discrimination Act 1995
EA 2002	Employment Act 2002
EPA 1970	Equal Pay Act 1970
ERA 1996	Employment Rights Act 1996
ER(DR)A 1998	Employment Rights (Dispute Resolution) Act 1998
ETA 1996	Employment Tribunals Act 1996
ETCRP Regs	Employment Tribunals (Constitution & Rules of Procedure) Regulations 1993
HASAWA 1974	Health & Safety at Work etc Act 1974
NMWA 1998	National Minimum Wage Act 1998
ROOA 1974	Rehabilitation of Offenders Act 1974
RRA 1976	Race Relations Act 1976
SDA 1975	Sex Discrimination Act 1975
TULRA 1992	Trade Union & Labour Relations (Consolidation) Act 1992
TUPE Regs	Transfer of Undertakings (Protection of Employment) Regulations 1981
WTR 1998	Working Time Regulations 1998 (as amended)

OTHER ABBREVIATIONS

The abbreviations used in this book (notably in cited cases) have the meanings given opposite:

Courts

HL	House of Lords
PC	Privy Council
CA	Court of Appeal
CS	Court of Session (Scotland)
ChD	Chancery Division of High Court
QB	Queen's Bench Division of High Court
QBD	*ditto*
DC	Divisional Court of High Court
EAT	Employment Appeal Tribunal
NIRC	National Industrial Relations Court
ECJ	European Court of Justice
ECHR	European Court of Human Rights
ET	Employment Tribunal

Law Reports

AC	Appeal Cases
AER	All England Reports
ChD	Law Reports, Chancery Division
CMLR	Common Market Law Reports
ECR	European Court Reports
ER	English Reports
ICR	Industrial Cases Reports
IRLR	Industrial Relations Law Reports
ITR	Industrial Tribunal Reports
LGR	Local Government Reports
TLR	Times Law Reports
QB/QBD	Law Reports, Queen's Bench Division
WLR	Weekly Law Reports

1

The law at work

GENERAL INFORMATION

1.1
The law governing the rights and duties of employers and employees is derived from three sources: the 'common law', UK legislation (mostly statutes and subordinate legislation introduced since 1963), and European Community Law. It is also influenced by the European Convention on Human Rights, recently given further effect in the UK by the Human Rights Act 1998 which came into force on 2 October 2000 (as to which, see Chapter 24).

1.2
This subject has become extremely complicated, not least because of the flood of decisions flowing from UK courts, the European Court of Justice (ECJ) and (to a lesser extent) from the European Court of Human Rights. Faced with this array of law, some of it highly technical, what is the ordinary employer or worker to do when faced with an employment problem? He (or she) may not want to incur the expense or go to the trouble of consulting a solicitor. And yet, if the wrong decision is made, the consequences can be very costly.

1.3
The purpose of this book is to explain the law in simple terms. It cannot hope to be more than a guide for employers in what is becoming an increasingly complex area of the law. Where the law is derived from Acts (or statutes), the intentions of Parliament are explained, as well as the principles to be applied. New legislation – supplementing, revoking or amending earlier statutes, regulations and orders – is appearing with almost undignified frequency. The reader will be familiar with (or, at the very least, be aware of) the Working Time Regulations 1998, the National Minimum Wage Regulations 1999, the Maternity & Parental Leave, etc Regulations 1999 (now significantly amended), the Public Interest Disclosure Act 1998 (whose provisions have been imported into the Employment Rights Act 1996), the Transnational Information & Consultation of Employees Regulations 1999, the Part-time Workers (Prevention of Less Favourable Treatment Regulations 2000, the Fixed-term Employees (Prevention of Less Favourable Treatment) Regulations 2002, and regulations made under the Employment Act 2002 giving eligible employees the right (*inter alia*) to adoption leave and pay, paternity leave and pay, the right to apply to their employers for more flexible

working arrangements, and the right to question their employers concerning any alleged breach of their rights under the Equal Pay Act 1970.

1.4
The impetus is likely to be maintained as even more European Union [EU] legislation appears. Lord Denning, MR saw the problem in this way: '[W]hen we come to matters with a European element, the Treaty is like an incoming tide. It flows into the estuaries and up the rivers. It cannot be held back. Parliament has decreed that the Treaty is henceforward to form part of our law. It is equal in force to any statute. The draftsmen of our statutes have striven to express themselves with the utmost exactness. They have tried to foresee all possible consequences and provide for them. They have foregone brevity. How different is this Treaty! It lays down general principles. It expresses its aims and purposes. All in sentences of moderate length and commendable style. But it lacks precision... All the way through the Treaty there are gaps and lacunae. They have to be filled in by the judges or by Regulations or directives. It is the European way' (*H P Bulmer Ltd. v J Bollinger SA* [1974] Ch. 401, CA).

TRIBUNALS OR COURTS – WHICH COURSE TO FOLLOW?

1.5
Nowadays, most complaints arising out of an employer's failure to acknowledge the statutory rights of employees are brought before the employment tribunals, where the proceedings are faster and less cumbersome. An employee may have little to gain by pursuing his (or her) claim before the civil courts, unless the compensation or damages sought are much higher than the tribunals are empowered to award; or unless there is some other aspect of the contractual relationship (eg breach of a restrictive covenant) which the tribunals are not yet empowered to deal with. The reader will note the reference to 'employment tribunals' rather than 'industrial tribunals'. The change of name was effected on 1 August 1998 by section 1 of the Employment Rights (Dispute Resolution) Act 1998, per Commencement No. 1 Order 1998 (SI 1998/1658).

Merits of each case

1.6
It should be borne in mind at this early stage that employment tribunals are not bound by their own decisions. The decision of a tribunal in a similar case elsewhere may appear to contradict a ruling by another tribunal in the same or a different location on almost identical facts (although the circumstances and dynamics of each case will never be identical). A tribunal comprises a legally qualified chairman and two lay members representing both sides of industry and having identifiable skills and experience in one or more aspects of the employer–employee relationship (such as race relations). There is

inevitably a 'grey area' in which one tribunal or court will take one view, and another, the opposite. Badly drafted legislation has been responsible for many seemingly strange decisions.

1.7
It should also be borne in mind that whereas one witness may impress, another giving identical evidence may not. This problem alone can (and has been known to) affect the outcome of a tribunal hearing.

RELATIONSHIP BETWEEN COMMON AND STATUTE LAW

1.8
When ascertaining the contractual rights and obligations of employers and employees, a tribunal will consider the 'common law' aspects of the relationship and the statutory provisions which apply to the particular facts. A lorry driver may, for instance, complain to an employment tribunal that he had been unfairly dismissed for refusing to drive on the Continent, contending that (under his contract of employment) he was only required to drive within the UK. Before determining the fairness or otherwise of the dismissal itself, the tribunal will look to the express and any implied terms in the driver's contract to establish whether he might on occasion (or as a matter of course) have been legitimately required to drive outside the UK. In other words, the ordinary common law canons of construction would be used to determine the extent of the driver's duties.

1.9
Some terms in a contract of employment will be *express*; others will be implied. The express terms will not generally cause any difficulty, so long as they are clear and unequivocal. The *implied* terms may be more difficult to establish. It is in this latter area that many disputes and differences of opinion will arise. Where there *is* ambiguity in a 'contract of employment' or in any accompanying or associated document (works handbook, collective agreement, policy document, etc) the general rule is that the ambiguity will be construed against the party seeking to rely on it. For instance, an employer facing a complaint of unfair dismissal brought by an employee who was sacked for refusing to transfer from one branch of the company to another, relying on a mobility clause in the employment contract which is not wholly clear, is likely to find that the lack of clarity will not work to his advantage (*Litster v Fram Gerrard Ltd* [1973] IRLR 302, NIRC).

Effects of difference

1.10
Under the common law, an employee has no legal redress if he (or she) is summarily dismissed for gross misconduct (or serious insubordination). An

employee who repudiates his employment contract thereby forfeits any and all rights under that contract. However, under the Employment Rights Act 1996, such a fundamental breach of contract would be one of the factors (albeit an important factor) which a tribunal will take into account when determining the fairness or otherwise of an employee's dismissal. A failure by an employer to follow the correct procedure (eg by not investigating the relevant circumstances fully, or by refusing to allow an employee to explain) could lead to a finding of unfair dismissal, although any award of compensation is likely to be reduced to the extent that the employee had contributed to his (or her) own dismissal (see Chapter 5, paras 5.146 to 5.154).

Common law concepts

1.11
Some common law concepts have been imported into the statutes. For example, the Employment Rights Act 1996 acknowledges the common law right of an employee to resign (with or without notice) if the employer's conduct is so gross as to amount to fundamental breach of the employment contract. One example of this would be an employer's unilateral decision to make a substantial cut in an employee's rate of pay. Under the 1996 Act, an employee left with no option but to quit in such circumstances may complain to an employment tribunal that he (or she) had been unfairly and 'constructively dismissed'. When examining the rights and wrongs of the situation, the tribunal would apply the normal common law rules to determine whether the employer's conduct was indeed tantamount to a fundamental breach of contract (going to the very root of the employment relationship) sufficient to justify the employee's decision to leave (see Chapter 8, paras 8.11 to 8.15).

DIVISION OF WORK

Employment tribunals

1.12
The jurisdiction of the employment tribunals is limited to those cases where jurisdiction is conferred on it by statute Most of the tribunals' workload relates to unfair dismissal and redundancy claims and complaints brought under (or by virtue of):

- the Equal Pay Act 1970;

- the Sex Discrimination Act 1975;

- the Race Relations Act 1976;

- the Trade Union & Labour Relations (Consolidation) Act 1992;

- the Disability Discrimination Act 1995;

- the Employment Tribunals Act 1996 ;

- the Employment Rights Act 1996;

- the National Minimum Wage Act 1998;

- the Employment Act 2002;

- the Tax Credits Act 2002;

- the Working Time Regulations 1998;

- the Part-Time Employees (Prevention of Less Favourable Treatment) Regulations 2000;

- the Fixed-term Employees (Prevention of Less Favourable Treatment) Regulations 2002;

as well as certain appeals under the Health and Safety at Work etc Act 1974, and appeals in respect of training levies, awards of compensation for loss of office, and so on.

1.13
There are, for the most part, statutory limits on the amount of compensation that the tribunals can award. For example, for 2003/04, the maximum statutory redundancy payment that can be awarded is £7,800. The maximum basic award of compensation for unfair dismissal (calculated in much the same way as the statutory redundancy payment) is likewise £7,800; the maximum compensatory award is £53,500; and so on. However, there *is* no upper limit on the amount of compensation that may be awarded by the tribunals in unlawful discrimination, health and safety, and 'protected disclosure' cases.

1.14
Although an employment tribunal is empowered to order an employer to reinstate or re-engage an unfairly dismissed employee, very few such orders are made – given that the relations between a dismissed employee and his former employers will invariably have broken down. The tribunals are nonetheless duty-bound to consider the practicability of making such an order; and, if such an order is made, may direct the employer in question to pay an additional award of compensation of between 26 and 52 weeks' pay if he refuses or fails (or fails to comply fully) with the terms of that order. It is as well to add that the tribunals and courts have no authority to oblige an employer to reinstate or re-engage a dismissed employee if the employer is unwilling to do so (*Source*: ERA 1996, ss 113 to 117).

Common law jurisdiction

1.15

On 12 July 1994, the jurisdiction of the employment tribunals was extended to include certain common law claims for damages at the suit of employees (eg wrongful dismissal, and other breach of contract claims) provided they are outstanding or arose on the termination of the claimant's employment. However, the tribunals are not empowered to 'entertain' claims for damages for personal injuries; breach of contract claims relating to restrictive covenants, confidentiality clauses, terms relating to intellectual property (copyright, trade-marks etc), or claims concerning living accommodation. Nor can they award damages in a breach of employment contract claim for an amount exceeding £25,000. Such claims will continue to be the province of the civil courts. (*Source*: Employment Tribunals Extension of Jurisdiction (England & Wales) Order 1994 and the Employment Tribunals Extension of Jurisdiction (Scotland) Order 1994.)

1.16

Claims for damages arising out of a breach of contract (including 'wrongful dismissal' claims) must be 'presented' to the Secretary to the Tribunals within three months of the effective date of termination of the complainant's contract of employment (see Chapter 3, paras 3.15 to 3.26), or within three months of the date of an employer's failure to comply with a relevant statutory duty (eg the right of an employee to a 'guarantee payment in respect of a workless day'). Where that is not reasonably practicable, the complaint must be presented within such further period as the tribunal considers reasonable in the circumstances (see Chapter 3, paras 3.66 to 3.71) – although acceptance of complaints presented 'out of time' are nowadays rare. An employer must submit his or her claim (or counter-claim) within 21 days of receiving Form IT3 from the Secretary to the Tribunals, accompanied by a copy of the employee's Originating Application (Form IT1).

Representation

1.17

When the tribunals were first given jurisdiction to deal with complaints arising out of an employee's statutory employment rights, the intention was that they should 'provide a quick and cheap remedy for what it had decided were injustices in the employment sphere. The procedure was to be such that both employers and employees could present their cases without having to go to lawyers for help' (per Lawton LJ in *Clay Cross Ltd v Fletcher* [1979] ICR 1, CA). There is a duty on both sides to ensure that a case is dealt with swiftly. An employee who 'lets sleeping dogs lie' for too long, risks having his (or her) claim dismissed on the grounds of want of prosecution (*Credit Aid Ltd v Russell-Taylor*, 28 February 1983, EAT).

Constitution and rules of procedure

1.18
The rules of procedure for tribunal hearings in England and Wales are as laid down in the Employment Tribunals (Constitution & Rules of Procedure) Regulations 2001, which came into force on 18 April 2001, and in the eponymous (Scotland) Regulations 2001, which also came into force on that date.

Although these pages do not permit of an exhaustive review of proceedings before the employment tribunals, interested readers are commended to the following booklets:

How to apply to an employment tribunal. England & Wales (Ref. 02/1243)
How to apply to an employment tribunal. Scotland (Ref. 02/1246)
What to do if taken to an employment tribunal. England & Wales (Ref. 02/1244)
What to do if taken to an employment tribunal. Scotland (Ref. 02/1247)
Hearings at employment tribunals. England & Wales (Ref. 02/1245)
Hearings at employment tribunals. Scotland (Ref. 02/1248)

which may be obtained free of charge by telephoning the Department of Trade & Industry's (DTI) Publications Orderline on 0870 1502 500 (e-mail: publications@dti.gsi.gov.uk). They may also be downloaded from the DTI Web site: www.dti.gov.uk/publications.

Employment Appeal Tribunal and beyond

1.19
Appeals from decisions of the employment tribunals lie (on points of law) to the Employment Appeal Tribunal (EAT) (except those relating to Health and Safety at Work); and from thence to the Court of Appeal, the House of Lords and, in appropriate cases, the European Court of Justice.

European Court of Justice

1.20
The European Court of Justice (ECJ) was established under the Treaty of Rome and sits in Luxembourg. It has power to deal with all employment law laid down in the Treaty, and with Regulations and directives made under that Treaty. The ECJ can give a decision in favour either of an individual who has petitioned it, or of the European Commission set up under the Treaty. The Commission may take proceedings before the ECJ against any Member State (of its own initiative or at the suit of another Member State) which has failed to implement Community law by importing it into its domestic legislation. In recent times, the Commission had occasion to warn the UK of proceedings unless the latter acted

swiftly to import the 'Working Time Directive' (93/104/EEC) into domestic legislation. This, of course, has now been attended to.

1.21
The UK courts are responsible for giving effect to decisions of the European Court. The latter tries to ensure that there is uniform interpretation of the Treaty and that there is no divergence between the case laws of the Community and those of the national courts (*Dzodzi v Belgium, The Times,* 7 January 1991, ECJ).

European Court of Human Rights

1.22
The European Court of Human Rights sits at Strasbourg. The Court can only pronounce judgment against the United Kingdom (or against any other signatory country) on a complaint by another country signatory to the Treaty, or on the petition of a person who alleges that the country in question is in breach of the European Convention on Human Rights. There is no machinery for enforcing a decision of the Court, although in practice a signatory to the Convention will usually comply with any such decision. The UK has, of course, since imported the Convention into UK legislation with the coming into force on 2 October 2000 of the Human Rights Act 1998 (as to which, see Chapter 24).

ACAS AND THE CENTRAL ARBITRATION COMMITTEE

Advisory, Conciliation and Arbitration Service (ACAS)

1.23
ACAS is a statutory body created in 1975 whose general duty is 'to promote the improvement of industrial relations (*Source*: TULRA 1992, ss 209 & 210). Where there is a dispute, or one is apprehended, ACAS may offer its services to try to effect a settlement (if approached by a party or by an interested person) (*Source*: ETA, ss 18 & 19). One of the Service's tasks is to seek to settle any dispute between an employee and his (or her) employer (or former employer). Any advice given by ACAS is confidential and cannot be disclosed in any subsequent proceedings (see also Chapter 2, paras 2.41 & 2.43).

1.24
ACAS may issue codes of practice containing such practical guidance as it thinks fit for the purpose of promoting the improvement of industrial relations. To date, ACAS has produced three such codes, titled:

- *Disciplinary & Grievance Procedures* (COP1);

- *Disclosure of Information to Trade Unions for Collective Bargaining Purposes* (COP2);

- *Time Off for Trade Union Duties & Activities* (COP3).

For further particulars, please turn to Chapter 3, paras 3.98 and 3.99 (*Source*: TULRA 1992, ss 199 to 202).

1.25

ACAS may, on request or otherwise, give employers, employers' associations, workers and trade unions such advice as it thinks appropriate on matters concerned with, or affecting or likely to affect, industrial relations. It may also publish general advice on matters concerned with (or affecting, or likely to affect), industrial relations (*Source*: TULRA 1992, s.213).

ACAS arbitration scheme

1.26

Under the so-called 'ACAS Arbitration Scheme' (which came into being on 21 May 2001) independent arbitrators (appointed by ACAS) are empowered to adjudicate on disputes between employers and employees about the fairness or otherwise of an employee's dismissal. The aim of the Scheme is to promote the settlement of unfair dismissal disputes in a confidential, informal, relatively fast and cost-efficient way. Unlike the handling of such complaints before the employment tribunals, the arbitration scheme avoids the use of formal pleadings, witnesses and documentary procedures. The usual rules of evidence do not apply nor is strict law or legal precedent a determining factor. Instead, in reaching their decisions, the arbitrators will take into account the general principles of fairness and good conduct laid down in ACAS Code of Practice 1 on *Disciplinary & Grievance Procedures* and in related ACAS publications, notably its *Discipline at Work* Handbook. Arbitral decisions (or awards) under the Scheme are final, with very limited opportunities for the parties to appeal or otherwise challenge the outcome.

Note: Information and guidance on the ACAS Arbitration Scheme can be obtained, free of charge, from ACAS Publications on 0870 242 9090 or may be accessed and downloaded from Web site www.acas.org.uk/arbitration.htm.

Central Arbitration Committee (CAC)

1.27

The CAC was also created in 1975 and inherited the duties formerly exercised by arbitration boards and other similar bodies. The CAC arbitrates on disputes referred to it by ACAS. For example, a trade union may complain to the CAC that an employer has refused to disclose information which the trade union needs for the purposes of collective bargaining with that employer (*Source*: TULRA, ss 183 & 259 to 265). Since 6 June 2000, the CAC has also been actively involved in 'trade union recognition' disputes (*ibid* s 70A and Schedule A1).

CERTIFICATION OFFICER

1.28
The Certification Officer is appointed by the Secretary of State for Work & Pensions and is responsible for 'overseeing' the activities of trade unions, including their:

- observance of statutory procedures governing the setting up and operation of political funds and dealing with members' complaints concerning breaches of fund rules (TULRA 1992, ss 71 to 73, 82 & 135);

- compliance with statutory procedures for mergers and transfers of engagements, and complaints about the conduct of merger ballots (TULRA 1992, ss. 21, 44, 46, 59 & 61).

The Certification Officer also:

- maintains a list of unions and employers' associations ensuring that they keep proper accounts and that superannuation schemes conform to requirements for actuarial examination (TULRA 1992, ss 2 to 4, 9, and 123 to 126);

- reimburses unions for certain expenditures incurred in the conduct of secret postal ballots (TULRA 1992, ss 115 & 254); and

- scrutinises and approves the balloting rules of any union wishing to continue spending money on political objectives, and deals with complaints that unions have not held secret ballots for elections to certain offices (*Source*: TULRA 1992, ss 46, 59, 61, 74, 84 & 94, and 254 to 258).

1.29
The Certification Officer must exercise some discretion when asked to reimburse a trade union for expenditure incurred in the conduct of postal ballots. In one case, a trade union had adhered strictly to its own rules when it reasonably disallowed a candidate who had won the highest votes, because the area in question was over-represented. It was held that the union was nevertheless entitled to recover the costs of the ballot. Only weighted voting, block voting or voting through an elected college would entitle the Certification Officer to lawfully withhold such a payment (*R v Certification Officer, ex parte Electrical Power Engineers' Association* [1990] ICR 682, HL).

1.30

A trade union, whose name is on a list maintained by the Certification Officer, may apply for a certificate that it is independent. The Certification Officer will issue a certificate of independence if satisfied that the union is not under the domination or control of an employer, and is not liable to interference by that employer (*Government Communications Staff Federation v Certification Officer & Another, The Times*, 16 December 1992, EAT) (*Source*: TULRA 1992, s.6).

1.31

If the Certification Officer refuses to issue a certificate of independence to a particular trade union, the latter may appeal against that refusal to the EAT. If satisfied that a certificate should have been issued, the EAT will make a declaration to that effect and will give the appropriate directions (*Source*: TULRA 1992, s.9(2) & (3)).

Matters of mutual concern to common law and statute law

EMPLOYEE OR SELF-EMPLOYED?

2.1
In the context of an employee's common law and statutory employment rights, it is important to understand the distinction between an *employee* and a *self-employed person*. While an employer owes a great many duties and responsibilities to his employees (and is vicariously liable for any wrong-doing committed by employees in the course of their employment), his relationship with self-employed persons is different.

2.2
A self-employed person is a person engaged under a *contract for services*. Such a person is in business on his (or her) own account and (unlike the employee engaged under a *contract of service* or under a *contract of employment* as it is more commonly styled) is directly accountable to the Inland Revenue for the payment of tax and national insurance contributions. The self-employed person will submit an invoice for services rendered; must, where appropriate, be VAT-registered with HM Customs & Excise; must prepare and submit annual accounts for scrutiny by the Inland Revenue; and so on. The duties owed by an employer to his employees under both the common law and contemporary employment law do not extend to independent contractors and other self-employed persons working on an employer's premises. But, as the occupier of business premises, an employer must comply with the requirements of the Occupiers' Liability Acts 1957 & 1984, and with his duties under health and safety legislation.

2.3
Some Acts of Parliament (and their subordinate legislation) provide a definition of the word 'employee'. Except for those cases where the word is specifically stated to include a restricted class of independent contractor, as in the Race Relations Act 1976, the ordinary common law tests apply.

2.4
In deciding whether a person is an *employee*, the courts will look at a number of factors, notably the following:

- Is there some measure of control indicative of an employer/employee relationship?

- Is the person carrying out the work for and on behalf of the employer or in business on his (or her) own account?

- Is the person free to accept or refuse work at will?

- Is the person supplied with a uniform and equipment?

- Is the person subject to disciplinary or grievance procedures?

- Must the person take holidays when and as directed?

- Is the person paid regularly either weekly or monthly? And are wages or salary paid gross or net of tax?

- What has been agreed with the Inland Revenue?

(*O'Kelly v Trusthouse Forte plc* [1983] ICR 708, CA.)

2.5
No one test is decisive but the 'most important'... criterion for determining the relationship... is the extent to which the person... is under the direction and control of the other party... with regard to the manner in which he does his work...' (*Narich Pty Ltd v Commission of Payroll Tax* [1984] ICR 286, PC).

2.6
Lack of mutuality may not be fatal. Where a person has worked as an outworker on a full-time basis for several years, there comes a stage when the relationship is likely to be translated into that of employer/employee (*Nethermere (St Neots) Ltd v Gardiner & Another* [1984] ICR 612, CA).

2.7
So too a person working in the construction industry was held to be an employee where he did not provide his own equipment, did not hire helpers, carried no financial risk, and was paid piece work according to the employer's tariff (*Lee Ting Sang v Chung Chi-Keung & Others* [1990] ICR 409, PC). An impression of a person's work activity has to be gained from an accumulation of detail, each of which will be of varying importance. In coming to a decision, the 'traditional contrast between a servant and an independent contractor' is the test that should be applied (*Hall (HM Inspector of Taxes) v Lorimer* [1994] ICR 218, CA).

2.8
If the relationship between the parties 'is in doubt or... is ambiguous, so that it can be brought under the one relationship or the other, it is open to the parties by agreement to stipulate what the legal situation between them shall be' (per Lord Denning MR in *Massey v Crown Insurance Co Ltd* [1978] ITR 5, CA).

2.9

It is not possible for the parties to change the true relationship between them by putting the wrong label on it. A girl had an agreement with an employment agency under which she was employed under a 'contract of service' but worked as a 'temp' for various client firms. It was held that she was not an 'employee'. There was a minimum of control over her, there were no mutual obligations to provide or accept work, there was no continuity, and the arrangement did not resemble any contract of service. So too were 'casual' waiters in a restaurant who could refuse or accept work when they wished (*Wicken v Champion Employment* [1984] ICR 365, EAT and *O'Kelly v Trusthouse Forte plc* [1983] ICR 708, CA).

2.10

Problems can sometimes arise over the true status of agency-supplied workers. Are they employed by the agency, the client firm for whom they are working, or are they self-employed? If they are unable to bring their status under one of these headings, they will be classified as being on a contract *sui generis* (a contract 'of its own kind') (*Ironmonger v Movefield Ltd t/a Deering Appointments* [1988] IRLR 461, EAT and *Construction Industry Training Board v Labour Force Ltd* [1970] 3 AER 220, DC).

2.11

A working director of a company is normally an employee, provided he (or she) is paid a salary as distinct from fees, and satisfies the other tests, eg holidays are fixed, he works only for that company, and is not free to work for others. In some cases it has been held that it does not matter that the person is the sole director and employee of the company. Even if for tax reasons he (or she) draws no salary for a period, but carries on working normally, he does not lose his status of being an 'employee' (*Albert J Parsons & Son Ltd v Parsons* [1979] IRLR 117, CA and *Europanel Processing Co Ltd v Nimmo* 24 April 1992, EAT).

2.12

An employee who has deliberately put a false label on his relationship to obtain fiscal advantages may find himself debarred from obtaining other statutory advantages. 'He gets the benefits of it by avoiding tax deductions and getting his pension contributions returned. I do not see that he can come along afterwards and say it is something else... Having made his bed as being 'self-employed', he must lie on it' (per Lord Denning MR in *Massey v Crown Insurance Co Ltd* [1978] ITR 5, CA).

BURDEN OF PROOF

2.13

Different Acts of Parliament often refer to one party or the other having to 'prove' some fact or to 'satisfy' the tribunal on a particular matter. Irrespective of the actual wording used, the standard of the burden of proof is always the same, namely, that of 'a balance of probabilities'. This means that a tribunal will decide a point based on which allegation is more probable in the circumstances. The members of the tribunal must consider the evidence put before them, assess the reliability of witnesses, and apply their experience in life and common sense. This has some practical importance, because sometimes the burden is on one party at one point and then switches to the other for the next. A failure somewhere along the line might result in an otherwise sound case failing (*The Financial Times Ltd v Byrne & Others*, 7 January 1992, EAT).

2.14
Thus, if an employee proves that he (or she) has been discriminated against (or victimised) by a fellow employee, the employer will normally be held to be vicariously liable. To escape liability, the employer will need to show that he (or she) took all reasonably practicable steps to prevent any such discrimination occurring (see Chapter 11, para. 11.74 and Chapter 12, para. 12.24) (*Sources*: Sex Discrimination Act 1975 (s.41), Race Relations Act 1976 (s.32), and Disability Discrimination Act 1995 (s.58)).

Note: Under the Sex Discrimination (Indirect Discrimination & Burden of Proof) Regulations 2002 (SI 2001/2660), once a complainant employee has established facts from which it may be presumed that she has been the victim of unlawful sex discrimination, the burden of proof shifts to the respondent employer (who must then satisfy the employment tribunal that no such discrimination occurred).

2.15
In (direct) discrimination cases, the burden does not pass to the employer to prove that he (or she) has not discriminated, except where the 'circumstances [are] consistent with the treatment being based on grounds of sex or race [when] the employment tribunal should be prepared to draw the inference that the discrimination was on such grounds unless the alleged discriminator can satisfy the tribunal that there was some other innocent explanation' (per Neill, LJ, *London Borough of Barking & Dagenham v Camara* [1988] ICR 865, EAT and *Baker v Cornwall County Council* [1990] ICR 432, CA). But see again the *Note* at the end of the previous paragraph.

2.16
Where a party relies on inferences to be made from primary facts to prove discrimination, there generally must be some hint of prejudice on racial or sexual grounds before a tribunal can hold that a person has been treated less favourably on either ground in comparison to others. If the explanation given for the treatment is unsatisfactory then a tribunal may infer discrimination (*Quereshi v London Borough of Newham* [1991] IRLR 264, CA and *King v Great Britain China Centre* [1992] ICR 516, CA).

2.17

Where an allegation of failure to mitigate damages is raised, the tribunal has to assess whether there has been adequate mitigation by an employee. The onus still remains on the employer to prove it (see para. 2.58 below) (*Bessenden Properties Ltd v Corness* [1974] IRLR 338, CA).

OBLIGATION TO PROVIDE WORK

2.18

It is now settled law that it is an implied term in every contract of employment that an employee has the right not only to be paid the agreed wage or salary but also to be given the opportunity to do his (or her) work when it is available (*Langston v Amalgamated Union of Engineering Workers* [1974] IRLR 15, CA). Unless a contract of employment *specifically* allows an employer to lay off an employee without pay, any attempt to do so would amount to a fundamental breach of contract. That would entitle the employee to leave (with or without notice) and to claim compensation on the grounds that he or she had been unfairly (constructively) dismissed (see Chapter 3, paras 3.45 to 3.58). Alternatively, the employee could remain in employment but claim damages equivalent to wages lost as a result of the breach (*R H & D T Edwards Ltd v Evans & Walters* 16 July 1985, EAT and *Miller v Hamworthy Engineering Ltd* [1986] ICR 846, CA).

2.19

Even if a contract of employment does allow an employer to lay off without pay, he (or she) may do so for a reasonable time only. If the lay-off or period of supension without pay goes beyond what is 'reasonable', the employee may leave and pursue a claim for compensation. But if the contract provides that the employee may be laid off indefinitely, the length of the lay-off period would be irrelevant (*A Dakri & Co Ltd v Tiffen* [1981] ICR 256, EAT and *Kenneth MacRae & Co Ltd v Dawson* [1984] IRLR 5, EAT).

2.20

Where an employee's income is (mainly) dependent on the employer providing work, eg he or she is paid at an hourly rate without there being a minimum number of hours, or, on a nominal basic salary plus commission, there would be an implied term that the employer would supply that employee with a reasonable amount of work (*Devonald v Rosser & Sons* [1906] 2 KB 726, CA). Sales plummeted when a sales director employed on a commission basis fell ill. This led to a substantial drop in his earnings. It was held that the man's employers had breached their implied contractual duty to take steps to maintain sales during his absence – thereby depriving him of a major portion of his income. He was entitled to resign and present a complaint of unfair 'constructive dismissal' (see para. 2.18 above) (*McClelland Fergusson & Partners v Fergusson*, 1 January1985 EAT).

ILLEGAL CONTRACTS

2.21
If both parties enter into a contract which is wholly or partly illegal, the employee is not generally entitled to invoke the benefits of employment legislation. This applies even if, for instance, his dismissal was manifestly unfair. It matters not whether the point has been raised by one or other of the parties to the contract (*Napier v National Business Agency Ltd* [1951] 2 AER 264, CA and *Tomlinson v Dick Evans U Drive Ltd* [1978] IRLR 77, EAT). Once a tribunal or court (including an appeal court) learns of an illegal contract (or suspects such a contract), it has a duty to investigate. Before giving a ruling, each party must be given the opportunity to call any evidence and/or make submissions to support or refute the point (*Cohen v Sandhu*, 7 May 1981, EAT).

2.22
Illegal contracts generally fall into two groups:

- those which are illegal from the start; and

- those which are *prima facie* legal, but become illegal because of the mode of carrying them out.

The latter generally involve defrauding a third party, usually the Inland Revenue. It does not extend to dishonest conduct by an employee against his employer (*Broaders v Kallare Property Maintenance Ltd* [1990] IRLR 421, EAT).

2.23
A contract of employment which is illegal at inception can never be enforced, whether or not the employee in question is aware of the illegal nature of the contract. The law treats the contract as though it had never been made. They are not restricted to pure criminal acts (*Miller v Karlinski* [1945] 62 TLR 85, CA). Browne-Wilkinson, J (as he then was) said that contracts would not be enforced where they are 'entered into for purposes which are... (although not forbidden by the general law)... immoral... The word 'immoral' connotes only sexual immorality... Illegal contracts... include not only contracts to do criminal acts but also contracts to achieve an immoral purpose' (*Coral Leisure Group v Barnett* [1981] ICR 503, EAT). The fact that a person has, during his employment, committed an unlawful or immoral act will not necessarily, of itself, prevent him from enforcing his rights, unless the contract was entered into for one of those purposes. So the lorry driver who knowingly and frequently uses an overweight vehicle, or the doorman of a hotel who procures prostitutes for guests, can pursue a claim. Whether such a claim will succeed on its merits may be a different matter.

2.24

An agreement that part of an employee's pay should not go 'through the books', and would be paid free of tax, would be illegal. The employee would not be able to enforce his common law or statutory rights. But the employee would not be debarred from making a claim if he (or she) was unaware that his employer had been acting illegally, eg by deducting the equivalent of PAYE tax from the employee's wages but not passing on the tax to the Inland Revenue. The test to be applied is not: *ought* the employee have known, but *did* he know, of the illegality? (*Corby v Morrison t/a the Card Shop* [1980] ICR 564, EAT and *Newland v Simon & Willer (Hairdressers) Ltd* [1981] ICR 521, EAT).

2.25

After an illegality ceases, an employee can pursue his (or her) statutory rights (eg the right to a guarantee payment, statutory maternity pay, or not to be unfairly dismissed) if he has the necessary qualifying period of employment; but that period would only start to run from the date on which the illegal practice ended (*Hyland v J H Barker (North West) Ltd* [1985] ICR 861, EAT). If an employee helps an employer to defraud a third party from which the employee derives no benefit, public policy may not preclude him from bringing a claim. This is especially so where the contract of employment was not illegal at inception (*Hewcastle Catering Ltd v Ahmed & Elkamark* [1991] IRLR 473, CA).

2.26

This has been held to be so where:

- an employee derived no benefit from a fraud;

- had been instructed to participate in it;

- had subsequently co-operated with the authorities in bringing the fraud to an end; and where

- the employer's conduct had been 'so reprehensible in comparison with that of the [employee] that it would be wrong to allow the [employer] to rely on it [to resist the claim]'.

(*Euro-Diam Ltd v Bathurst* [1988] 2 WLR 517, CA.)

2.27

Two waiters were instructed to provide cash customers with separate bills to enable their employers to avoid having to account for VAT to HM Customs & Excise. It was held that the waiters were not precluded from bringing a claim. Their dismissals, which resulted from their helping the authorities to prosecute, were declared unfair. Public policy decreed that employees should be encouraged to disclose frauds on Customs & Excise (*Hewcastle Catering Ltd v Ahmed & Elkamark* [1991] IRLR 473, CA).

Note: Under the Public Interest Disclosure Act 1998 (known as *the Whistleblower's Act*) an employee who makes a so-called 'protected disclosure' (see Index) cannot lawfully be dismissed or subjected to any other detriment for doing so. There is no upper limit on the amount of compensation tnat can be awarded in such cases.

FRUSTRATION OF CONTRACT

2.28
Frustration occurs where the main provisions of a contract cannot be performed because of unforeseen circumstances beyond the control of either party which were not provided for in the contract. Thus, where there is an agreement to rent a chalet, but it is burnt down beforehand, that event effectively brings the contract to an end without any action by either party (*Davis Contractors Ltd v Fareham UDC* [1956] AC 696, HL).

2.29
The doctrine of frustration, which is usually to be found in commercial contracts, does not depend on an opinion, or intention, or even knowledge of any of the parties, but on the occurrence of an event that renders the performance of the contract radically different from that which was agreed. In the absence of any terms to the contrary, the liabilities of each party under the contract cease.

2.30
It has now been settled in the House of Lords that all contracts (including contracts of employment) are subject to the doctrine of frustration. In the employment field, it usually applies in sickness and imprisonment cases. However, not all reported cases can be reconciled (*National Carriers Ltd v Penelpina (Northern) Ltd* [1981] I AER 161, QB).

2.31
The significance of the doctrine of frustration in employment cases is that an employee whose contract has been frustrated will not have been 'dismissed' within the accepted meaning of the word and would, accordingly, forfeit many of his (or her) statutory rights. Some 'common law' rights would also be forfeited. The general rule is that self-induced frustration does not bring the doctrine into operation. So if a singer, for instance, were to lose her voice intentionally by walking coatless and hatless in the winter rain, she would not be able to respond to a civil action for damages by claiming that her contract to sing at a concert had been frustrated by laryngitis. In imprisonment cases, although the view is by no means unanimous, the weight of judicial pronouncements is that an employment contract is frustrated by the employee's being unavailable for work, *not* by his having been sent to prison. The employee could obviously have avoided committing the offence which he must have known would very likely result in his being deprived of his

liberty (*Chakki v The United Yeast Co Ltd* [1982] ICR 140, EAT). It follows that a relatively short term in prison (eg three weeks for non-payment of maintenance) would not be long enough to constitute a frustrating event, bearing in mind that employees are routinely absent from work for similar periods – annual holidays, sick leave, approved leave of absence without pay, etc – without running the risk of losing their jobs. A sentence of 12 months' imprisonment *would*, on the other hand, be a frustrating event. A minimum absence of some months (assuming the earliest release) would make the carrying out of the contract radically different from that contemplated when it was made (*Harrington v Kent CC* [1980] IRLR 353, EAT).

2.32
Even where there was a special procedure for dismissing apprentices for absences (for any reason), it has been held that the concept of frustration still applies. There was no dismissal when a youth was sent to Borstal training, because the contract had been frustrated (*F C Shepherd & Co Ltd v Jerrom* [1986] ICR 802, CA).

2.33
Sickness or serious injury can also be a frustrating event. If a tyre fitter is knocked down by a car and confined to a wheel chair for the rest of his life (unable to do any work), the contract would be frustrated. The same would be true of the contract of a violin player who loses a hand. For less serious matters, it can be difficult to determine the point when frustration occurs and when it does not (*Egg Stores (Stamford Hill) Ltd v Leibovici* [1977] ICR 260, EAT). The general considerations applied are:

- the length of the previous employment and (if relevant) how long it would have been expected to continue;

- the type of work, and the employer's need for the work to be done and/or find a replacement;

- the nature of the illness or disabling event, and the prospects for recovery;

- whether a reasonable employer could be expected to wait any longer;

- any contractual terms relating to sickness and sick pay.

(*Williams v Watsons Luxury Coaches Ltd* [1990] ICR 536, EAT.)

2.34
Where the circumstances are appropriate, the doctrine of frustration also applies to contracts which can be ended at short notice. An employee with 26 years' service suffered a coronary. This prevented him from working again. It was held that the illness had automatically frustrated the contract. The employer did not need to take any further action (*Notcutt v Universal*

Equipment Co (London) Ltd [1986] ICR 414, CA). The margin between whether there has been frustration or not is necessarily blurred. An employer should be wary of assuming that a contract of employment has ended. If he (or she) takes any action inconsistent with the continuance of a contract, he runs the risk of being held to have dismissed the employee. It may turn out to have been unfair on procedural grounds (see Chapter 5, paras 5.93 to 5.99). In a doubtful case, the best advice to an employer would perhaps be to treat the situation as a dismissal on grounds of ill-health (see Chapter 5, paras 5.127 to 5.133) (*Lawton v Bowden International Ltd*, 13 December 1990, EAT).

2.35
If a sick employee is absent from work for an extended period (perhaps on a nominal rate of pay), the subsequent termination of his or her contract (because the employee is incapable of work) will be deemed to be a 'dismissal' in law. In short, it would be unwise of an employer in a similar situation to assume that the employee's contract had become frustrated. The law allows that continuity of employment is preserved if an employee dismissed on grounds of ill-health or injury is re-engaged by the same or an associated employer within the next 26 weeks. But if not re-engaged until after 26 weeks have elapsed, continuity is automatically broken and the employee will have forfeited all statutory rights earned up to the time of his (or her) dismissal (see Chapter 3, para. 3.30). This does not apply, of course, to statutory rights which do not depend on a qualifying period of continuous employment (*Glenboig Union Fireclay Co Ltd v Stewart* [1971] ITR 14, CS) (*Source*: ERA 1996, s.212).

REPUDIATORY OR FUNDAMENTAL BREACH

2.36
Where an employer (or employee) does, or omits to do, something, which amounts to a repudiatory breach of the employment contract, it is open to the other party either to accept the repudiation and consider the contract to be at an end, or to 'affirm' the contract by continuing to work or by allowing the other party to do so (see Chapter 3, para. 3.48). An employee who took an extended holiday to the West Indies, in defiance of his employer's instructions, was held to have repudiated his contract of employment by deliberately making himself unavailable for work. When his employer accepted the repudiation, the contract of employment ended (*London Transport Executive v Clarke* [1980] ICR 532, CA). It is not necessary for an act of repudiation to amount to industrial misconduct. The test is an objective one. During an employee's absence on sick leave his employer closed down the premises where the employee worked. The EAT held that '... the closing of the works [constituted] a dismissal by way of repudiation, even though the employee at that particular time [was] unfit for work. [The] repudiation was accepted by [the employee] when he asked for redundancy payments' (per Browne-Wilkinson J, *Northgate Laundries Ltd v Jenner*, 5 February 1982, EAT).

2.37

A fundamental breach generally occurs when one of the parties to a contract of employment commits a breach so serious that it goes to the very root of the contract. An example of a fundamental breach of contract is that of the employer who unilaterally halves the salary of one of his employees. In some situations, a sequence of less serious breaches might well add up to a fundamental breach (but see Chapter 3, para. 3.48). When there has been a fundamental breach, either party can withdraw from the contract. An employee may resign and seek redress by complaining to a tribunal that he (or she) had been 'constructively dismissed' (see Chapter 3, para. 3.45). But speed is of the essence. An employee might well be deemed to have waived his rights by 'affirming' the contract. Furthermore there must be some overt acceptance of the repudiation communicated to the employer. The contract does not automatically end by a wish of a party that it should do so (*Western Excavating (EEC) Ltd v Sharp* [1978] ITR 132, CA and *Rigby v Ferodo* Ltd [1988] ICR 29, HL).

2.38

If an employer informs an employee that he (the employer) intends to take some unlawful action in the future (an 'anticipatory breach'), the employee need not wait for that breach to occur. If, on the other hand, the employer retracts and notifies the employee accordingly, *before* the employee resigns, the right to act on the anticipated breach is lost (*Norwest Holst Group Administration Ltd v Harrison* [1985] ICR 668, CA).

2.39

An employer's behaviour can be taken into account, along with other breaches, to determine whether, cumulatively, it and they amount to repudiatory conduct. If, on the other hand, there is a continuing series of the same breaches (eg repeated non-payment of commission), each of which would entitle an employee to resign, the employee would not forfeit his (or her) right to rely on any subsequent breach simply because he had failed to react when the first breach occurred (*Lewis v Motorworld Garages Ltd* [1986] ICR 157, CA; and *Reid v Camphill Engravers* [1990] ICR 435, EAT).

2.40

Many constructive dismissal cases arise where it is alleged that there has been a breach of the implied term of mutual trust and confidence (as to which, see Chapter 5, paras 5.84 to 5.90).

'OUT OF COURT' SETTLEMENTS

2.41

Many parties to proceedings will do their best to settle their dispute 'out of court'; that is to say, without going to the expense of a court or tribunal hearing. In tribunal cases, the Advisory, Conciliation & Arbitration Service (ACAS) is duty-bound to attempt to resolve disputes between employers and employees (see Chapter 1, paras 1.23 to 1.25) (*Source*: ETA 1996, ss 18 & 19).

2.42
Any contract of employment which purports to override an employee's statutory rights, including his (or her) right to bring proceedings before an employment tribunal, is *prima facie* void and unenforceable. But that right can be overriden if a dispute or difference of opinion between an employer and one of his employees is settled by means of a 'COT 3' agreement (following the intervention of an ACAS conciliation officer). The same is true of a 'compromise agreement', and of an arbitral agreement concluded with the intervention of an ACAS-appointed independent arbitrator under the ACAS arbitration scheme which came into being on 21 May 2001 (see para. 2.46 below). An employee who signs such an agreement thereby waives his (or her) right to pursue his complaint before an employment tribunal. In other words, he cannot then change his mind. The *quid pro quo* will be an agreed amount of compensation or the employer's agreement to make restitution by other means, including reinstatement or re-engagement.

'COT 3' agreements

2.43
When an originating application (Form IT1) is sent to the Secretary to the Tribunals, an ACAS Conciliation Officer may be invited to intervene to bring about a settlement. If a settlement is reached and terms agreed, both parties to the dispute or disagreement will be invited to put their signatures to Form COT 3. Once this is done, the agreement is legally binding on both parties (*Source*: ERA 1996, s.203(2)(e); ETA 1996, s.18).

Compromise agreements

2.44
A 'compromise agreement' (properly concluded) is also legally binding on both parties. An employee who believes that his (or her) employer has breached one or other of his statutory rights under:

- the Sex Discrimination Act 1975;

- the Race Relations Act 1976;

- the Trade Union & Labour Relations (Consolidation) Act 1992;

- the Disability Discrimination Act 1995;

- the Employment Rights Act 1996;

- the Working Time Regulations 1998; or

- the National Minimum Wage Act 1998;

may agree to 'sign away' his right to bring (or continue with) proceedings in return for a mutually acceptable 'out of court' payment or other form of settlement. To be valid and legally binding:

- a compromise agreement must be in writing and must relate to the particular dispute (liable to give rise to tribunal proceedings) between the conflicting parties;

- the employee must have received legal advice from a 'relevant independent adviser' (see next paragraph) – named in the agreement – as to the terms and effect of the proposed agreement and, in particular, its effect on his (or her) ability to pursue his rights before an employment tribunal;

- there must be in force, when the *relevant independent adviser* gives his (or her) advice, a contract of insurance (or an indemnity provided for members of a profession or professional body) covering the risk of a claim by the employee in respect of any loss arising in consequence of his having acted on that advice; and

- must state that the agreement satisfies the conditions regulating compromise agreements under one or other of the Sex Discrimination Act 1975 (s.77(4A)), the Race Relations Act 1976 (s.72(4A)), the Trade Union & Labour Relations (Consolidation) Act 1992 (s.288(2B)); the Disability Discrimination Act 1995 (s.9(2)(b)); the Employment Rights Act 1996 (s.203(2)(f) & (3)); the Working Time Regulations 1998 (reg. 35); and the National Minimum Wage Act 1998 (s.49).

2.45
A person is a *relevant independent adviser* if he (or she) is:

- a qualified lawyer – that is to say, a barrister, advocate, a solicitor who holds a practising certificate, or (as respects England and Wales) a person other than a barrister or solicitor who is an authorised advocate or authorised litigator (within the meaning of the Courts & Legal Services Act 1990).

Since 1 August 1998, when s.9(1) of the Employment Rights (Dispute Resolution) Act 1998 came into force, a person is also a *relevant independent adviser* if he (or she):

- is an officer, official, employee or member of an independent trade union who has been certified in writing by the trade union as competent to give advice and as authorised to do so on behalf of the trade union; or

- works at an advice centre (whether as an employee or a volunteer) and has been certified in writing by the centre as competent to give advice and as authorised to do so on behalf of the centre; or

- is a person of a description specified in an order made by the Secretary of State.

A person is *not* a *relevant independent adviser* to one of the parties to a dispute if he (or she) is in any way connected with (or employed by) the other party; or if (in the case of advice given by a person working for an advice centre) there is any fee charged for such advice (*Sources*: SDA 1975 (s.77(4A)(d); RRA 1976 (s.72(4A)(c)); TULRA 1992 (s.288(2B)(c)); DDA 1995 (s.9(3)(a)); ERA 1996 (s.203(3)(c)), WTR 1998 (reg. 35(5)), and NMWA 1998 (s.49(6)).

ACAS arbitration agreements

2.46
Under the so-called 'ACAS Arbitration Scheme', established under the Employment Right (Dispute Resolution) Act 1998, ACAS-appointed independent arbitrators are empowered to adjudicate (with the agreement of both parties) on unfair dismissal and flexible working disputes. The purpose of the Scheme is to side-step the employment tribunals by promoting the settlement of such disputes in a confidential, informal, relatively fast and cost-efficient way. Unlike the handling of such complaints before the tribunals, arbitral hearings avoid the use of formal pleadings, witnesses and documentary procedures. The usual rules of evidence do not apply nor is strict law or legal precedent a determining factor. Instead, in reaching their decisions, the arbitrators will take into account the general principles of fairness and good conduct laid down in ACAS Code of Practice 1 on *Disciplinary & Grievance Procedures* and in related ACAS publications, notably its *Discipline at Work* Handbook. Arbitral decisions (or awards) are final, with very limited opportunities for the parties to appeal or otherwise challenge the outcome.

Note: Information and guidance on the ACAS Arbitration Scheme can be obtained, free of charge, from ACAS Publications on 0870 242 9090 or may be accessed and downloaded from Web site www.acas.org.uk/arbitration.htm.

'WITHOUT PREJUDICE'

2.47
Frequently, a party feels that there is justice in his (or her) claim or defence. No amount of persuasion will make him change his mind, even if it comes from an independent and objective source. Any negotiations that take place through ACAS are privileged. Nothing can be revealed as to what has been

said or as to the outcome or that would indicate a view taken by ACAS (*Source*: ETA 1996, s.18(7); TULRA 1992, s.290).

2.48

So-called 'without prejudice' correspondence – which usually arises when one party to a dispute writes (on one or more occasions) to the other party offering to compromise or to settle 'out of court' – is not admissible in evidence before a court or tribunal unless both parties agree. Verbal discussions can also be conducted 'without prejudice'. But if there is a dispute over whether such discussions *were* 'without prejudice', some or all of what was said during those discussions may have to be revealed to the court or tribunal to enable the question to be resolved. By that time, the damage will already have been done. If letters or memoranda are marked 'without prejudice', the question brooks of no argument. But no privilege will be accorded to a 'without prejudice' letter if there was no dispute between the parties (or if no negotiations had begun or taken place) at the time the letter was written (Re *Daintrey, ex parte Holt* [1893] 2 QB 116, QBD).

2.49

When a party to a dispute makes an offer to settle (or reach a compromise), it tends to suggest an admission of some liability – leaving only the question of the amount to be decided. The actions of an employer (or other respondent) in attempting to reach a settlement might be viewed as trying either to rid himself of a troublesome dispute, or to save money. For that reason, it is usually felt better that the adjudicating body does *not* know what has gone on before the case is heard. Indeed in the High Court, and County Court, the judge is not allowed to know about an offer to settle or about any 'payment into court' until the case is concluded and liability has been established. Once correspondence is marked 'without prejudice', it is said to be 'privileged'. It can only be produced in proceedings if both sides agree (*Walker v Wiltshire* [1889] 23 QBD 355, QB). A consequence of this is that a party cannot rely on a 'without prejudice' letter purporting to 'accept' repudiatory conduct (see paras 2.36 to 2.40 above), and so bring the contract to an end, because the letter is ineffective. In any event, it cannot be shown to the court (except by agreement) (*Norwest Holst Group Administration Ltd v Harrison* [1985] ICR 668, CA).

2.50

Where there is a claim for something other than a monetary one, for instance, for a declaration about some matter, and one party put forward proposals 'without prejudice' to settle the action, the letter containing those proposals can be produced after liability has been determined. The court can then decide what order for costs is appropriate. Notice of an intention to take this course of action should be given to the other side (*Cutts v Head & Another* [1984] 1 AER 597, CA). A similar procedure can be adopted in the tribunals where there is no procedure for making a 'payment into court'. An employer might offer a former employee the sum of £500 'without prejudice' in settlement of his claim. If the applicant employee fails to obtain an award above that figure, then the tribunal can be shown the letter and asked to make an order for costs against the employee – on the basis that the proceedings have been carried on unreasonably (*Source*: Employment Tribunals (Constitution & Rules of Procedure) Regulation 2001).

'IN HONOUR ONLY'

2.51

Usually, a union which has concluded a collective agreement with an employer (or association of employers), will not wish to be exposed to a claim for damages in the event of a breach of contract. The union is protected under TULRA 1992, which provides that a collective agreement 'shall be conclusively presumed not to have been intended by the parties to be a legally enforceable contract – unless the agreement is in writing and contains a provision which (however expressed) states that the parties intend that the agreement *shall* be a legally enforceable contract'. The same applies if the parties to the agreement intend that certain clauses in the agreement are intended to be legally enforceable, and the remainder, not (*Source*: TULRA 1992, ss 179 & 180).

2.52

If some of the terms in a collective agreement between an employer and a union are incorporated into a contract of employment, and include the words: 'This agreement is binding in honour only...', it has been held that this clause did not prevent an employee from relying on the terms that formed part of his own contract. The exclusion clause had not been incorporated into the employee's contract of employment (*Marley v Forward Trust Group* [1986] ICR 891, CA and *Robertson v British Gas Corporation* [1983] ICR 351, CA). Only those terms that were apt to be enforced were included, eg those fixing terms of pay, hours of work, disciplinary proceedings etc. Those relating to procedures designed to resolve disputes between employers' and employees' representatives were excluded (*National Coal Board v NUM & Others* [1986] ICR 736, ChD).

2.53

If there is a redundancy clause in a collective agreement, an employee seeking to rely on that clause can do so in two ways. Either he (or she) can show that the clause has been expressly incorporated into his contract of employment or, if unable to do so, may be able to establish an implied incorporation by showing an intent that is apparent within the contract. The wording must be sufficiently clear to show that it was intended to be contractually binding (*Alexander & Others v Standard Telephones & Cables plc* [1990] ICR 291, ChD).

'EX GRATIA' PAYMENTS

2.54

The essence of an award of damages or compensation is that the injured party should be placed in the same position he (or she) would have been in but for the breach of contract (or breach of a statutory duty, or any other wrong-doing). In short, the employee should be compensated, so far as is possible, for the loss and damage he has suffered.

2.55

An employer will make an *ex gratia* payment to a former employee for a variety of reasons. He (or she) may want to 'buy off' a prospective tribunal hearing or court case. He may be uncertain about the extent of his own liability, or he may merely want to be generous. An *ex gratia* payment, paid to an employee in purported settlement of a possible future claim, can be offset against an award of compensation ordered by an employment tribunal. In short, the loss to the employee will have been mitigated to the extent of that *ex gratia* payment (*Chelsea Football Club v Heath* [1981] ICR 323, EAT and *Rushton v Harcros Timber & Building Supplies Ltd*, *The Times*, 17 December 1992, EAT). Difficulties sometimes arise when an *ex gratia* payment has been made, but the employee is held to have been partly responsible for his or her own dismissal (as to which, see also Chapter 5, paras 5.146 to 5.152).

2.56

At the time of his dismissal, an employee received an *ex gratia* payment of £2,000 from his former employer. At the subsequent tribunal hearing, the employee is awarded a total of £5,000 as compensation for unfair dismissal. But the tribunal decides that the employee was 25 per cent to blame for his dismissal. The question is this: Should the tribunal deduct the 25 per cent from the full award of £5,000, or should they deduct that 25 per cent from the net amount now due to the employee (that is to say, £5,000 less the £2,000 already paid)? There is a difference of judicial views; however, on general principles it would seem that the latter approach is the right one (*Parker & Farr v Shelvey* [1979] ICR 896, EAT and *Clement-Clarke International Ltd v Manley* [1979] ICR 74, EAT). The *ex gratia* payment will have to be taken off the gross amount of the loss and not from the statutory limit placed on an award. Thus an employee who has suffered an actual loss of £20,000, and who has received an *ex gratia* payment of £6,000, will still be entitled to £11,500, that is to say, the (then) current maximum 'compensatory' award (*McCarthy v British Insulated Cables plc* [1985] IRLR 94, EAT). For further information about awards of compensation, please turn to Chapter 5 (or the Index to this book).

'MITIGATION OF LOSS'

2.57

It is a cardinal principle of law, and a statutory requirement in unfair dismissal claims, that a person who suffers damage as a result of the wrongful act of another must attempt to 'mitigate' his (or her) loss by making all reasonable efforts to reduce the extent of the damage (*Gallear v J F Watson & Son Ltd* [1979] IRLR 306, EAT and *A G Bracey Ltd v Iles* [1973] IRLR 210, NIRC). That duty will usually be discharged where it can be said that he has acted 'as a reasonable person would do if he had no hope of seeking compensation from his previous employer' (*Archbold Freightage Ltd v Wilson* [1974] IRLR 10, NIRC) (*Source*: ERA 1996, s.123(4)).

2.58

The onus of proving failure to mitigate, both under the common law and statute law, lies on the employer. The test applied is whether the employee has acted reasonably. All the surrounding circumstances including any relating to his (or her) personal situation have to be considered. This does not mean that any whim or fancy will justify a refusal to take a suitable job (*Bessenden Properties Ltd v Corness* [1974] IRLR 338, CA and *Johnson v Hobart Manufacturing Co Ltd*, 20 July 1990, EAT).

A 55-year-old employee with a bad back, who was nonetheless able to perform his work satisfactorily, was held to have been unfairly dismissed. He was rejected for other jobs on health grounds, and so 'signed on sick' with the DSS to get additional benefits. This had the effect of taking him off the work register. After a while, he reverted to his unemployed status. It was held that he had acted reasonably and was entitled to compensation based on his age and likelihood of obtaining other work. It was not limited to the time up to when he signed on sick (*Wilson v Glenrose (Fish Merchants) Ltd & Another*, 21 July 1992, EAT).

2.59

The local economic climate is also important. In difficult times, an employee will generally be expected to accept lower-paid or lower-level employment, or travel further afield. Furthermore, he (or she) must take energetic steps to secure another job. Becoming self-employed, or seeking retraining, may amount to mitigation in appropriate circumstances (*Daley v Dorsett (Alma Dolls) Ltd* [1981] IRLR 385, EAT and *Gardiner-Hill v Roland Berger Technics Ltd* [1982] IRLR 498, EAT).

2.60

Under the common law, when a dismissal is wrongful (Chapter 8, paras 8.21 to 8.25), a contract of employment can subsist in special circumstances. As an employee is only entitled to be paid for work that he actually performs, he is bound to seek alternative employment and thus 'mitigate' his loss (*Gunton v Richmond-upon-Thames BC* [1980] ICR 755, CA).

2.61

Under statute law, a repudiatory act by an employer immediately brings the contract of employment to an end. Consequently, the employee should look for alternative work, unless he (or she) intends to seek reinstatement or re-engagement. In such a case, he must pursue his claim before an employment tribunal as soon as possible (*Robert Cort & Sons Ltd v Charman* [1981] ICR 816, EAT). A dismissed employee's unreasonable refusal to accept an offer of reinstatement or re-engagement by his former employer will ordinarily be treated as having failed to mitigate his loss. However, if the employee had been treated in a humiliating manner while in employment, or if the terms of an offer to re-engage would result in a substantial drop in earnings (and/or a loss of benefits), the employee will usually be entitled to decline that offer (*Fyfe v Scientific Furnishings Ltd* [1989] ICR 648, EAT) (*Source*: ERA 1996 , s.117(8)).

2.62

The rules relating to mitigation do not apply to a redundancy payment (see Chapter 4). Such payments are treated as payments for past service. Nor do they usually apply to the notice period (see Chapter 3, para. 3.9). Any earnings during that time must normally be disregarded when computing the employee's loss (see Chapter 5, para. 5.170) (*TBA Industrial Products Ltd v Locke* [1984] ICR 228, EAT, *Addison v Babcock Fata Ltd* [1987] ICR 805, CA, and *Isleworth Studios Ltd v Richard* [1988] ICR 432, EAT).

2.63

There is conflicting authority over whether a failure to use an internal appeal procedure can amount to a breach of duty to mitigate. The better view is that it might do so in appropriate circumstances. However, where an employee does pursue an appeal, his (or her) failure to seek alternative employment before the hearing does not amount to a failure to mitigate loss (*Hoover v Forde* [1980] ICR 239, EAT, *W Muir Ltd v Lamb* [1985] IRLR 95, EAT, and *Williams v Loyds Retailers Ltd* [1973] IRLR 262, IT).

2.64

Neither do the rules apply to the sum payable to an employee for the period between dismissal and an order for reinstatement or re-engagement (see Chapter 5, paras 5.157 & 5.176) even though the employee delayed instituting proceedings. But if an employer fails to comply with such an order, then the tribunal will bear in mind any failure by the employee to mitigate when it decides at what point within the relevant period (see Chapter 5, paras 5.176 to 5.178) to assess any *additional* award of compensation (*City & Hackney Health Authority v Crisp* [1990] ICR 95, EAT).

3

Statutory employment rights (general)

RIGHTS OF EMPLOYEES NOT TO BE OVERRIDDEN

3.1
As we have seen, employees nowadays have a great many statutory rights. Employers, for their part, have a parallel duty to respect those rights and an implied responsibility to ensure that employees are not kept in ignorance of those rights. The penalties for infringement of an employee's statutory right can be very harsh indeed. Any term in a contract of employment (or other agreement), which purports to exclude or limit the operation of the relevant provisions of the Employment Rights Act 1996, the Trade Union & Labour Relations (Consolidation) Act 1992, or of any related employment legislation (Equal Pay Act 1970, Sex Discrimination Act 1975, etc), is void and unenforceable.

3.2
Any agreement which purports to override an employee's statutory rights, notably the right of an employee to bring proceedings before an employment tribunal, will *not* be legally binding – *unless* it comprises:

- a so-called 'COT 3' agreement (concluded with the intervention of an ACAS conciliation officer);

- a 'compromise' agreement (which satisfies the conditions regulating compromise agreements); or

- a legally-binding arbitral agreement or award (eg concerning the fairness or otherwise of an employee's dismissal) made by an independent arbitrator under the ACAS Arbitration Scheme (as to which latter, see Chapter 2, paras 2.44 & 2.45).

(*Sources*: SDA 1975, s.77(4)(aa); RRA 1976, s.72(4)(aa); DDA 1995, s.9(2)(b); TULRA 1992, s.288(2A); ETA 1996, s.18; ERA 1996, s.203(2)(f);ER(DR)A 1998, ss 7 & 8.)

'COT 3' agreements

3.3

The Employment Tribunals Act 1996 (at s.18) requires an ACAS conciliation officer to attempt to promote the reinstatement or re-engagement of a dismissed employee on equitable terms. If the employee has no wish to be re-employed or such a solution would be impracticable from the point of view of either or both the employer and the employee, the role of a conciliation officer would be confined to promoting an 'out of court' settlement and recording the agreed terms on Form COT 3. However, it is not a conciliation officer's role to express a view about the rights and wrongs of a particular dispute or to propose an appropriate settlement figure. Indeed, anything said by a conciliation officer to the parties in dispute is inadmissible in any subsequent tribunal hearing. Before the parties put their signatures to a 'COT 3 agreement', the conciliation officer will explain the legally binding nature of such an agreement Once the terms are genuinely agreed, they are binding on both parties(*Gilbert v Kembridge Pictures Ltd* [1984] ICR 188, EAT and *Slack v Greenham (Plant Hire) Ltd* [1983] IRLR 271, EAT).

3.4

It should be pointed out that an employee who claims that his (or her) employer has infringed one or other of his statutory rights (eg the right of a pregnant employee to paid time off work for ante-natal care) has no need to resign in order to refer his complaint to an employment tribunal. Indeed, if the employee is dismissed for doing so (or for threatening to do so) the employer will be liable to pay a substantial award of compensation. Once an employee's originating application (Form IT1) has been received by the Secretary to the Tribunals, copies will be sent both to the employer and to ACAS. In such cases, a conciliation officer will intervene only if *both* parties agree. But, if the employee has not yet initiated proceedings, a conciliation officer may intervene at the request of *either* party to the dispute. An employee's agreement not to press ahead with proceedings before a tribunal will be valid so long as a conciliation officer has intervened in the manner described in the previous paragraph.

3.5

In *Trafford Carpets Ltd v Barker (Case A)*, 13 November 1990, EAT, the EAT held that the terms set out in what purported to be a COT 3 agreement were merely a device to enable an employee to gain a benefit under a Government Enterprise Scheme. In *Livingstone v Hepworth Refractories plc* [1992] ICR 287, EAT, an ACAS conciliation officer intervened to promote a settlement in a dispute about an employee's dismissal. The resultant COT 3 agreement stated that the terms agreed were 'in full and final settlement of *all* claims which the [employee] may have against the [employer] arising out of his employment'. The EAT held that the agreement was not all-embracing and did not debar the employee from instituting further proceedings against his employer alleging unlawful discrimination.

'Compromise' agreements

3.6
A so-called 'compromise agreement' (concluded without the intervention of ACAS) is a form of 'out of court' settlement which is binding on the parties if it:

- is in writing;

- relates to the particular complaint and no other;

- was concluded after the employee has received independent advice from a *relevant independent adviser*;

- identifies the adviser;

- states that conditions regulating compromise agreements have been satisfied.

(For further particulars, please turn to Chapter 2, paras 2.44 and 2.45.)

3.7
Even if a tribunal has held a dismissal to have been unfair and has sent the parties away to agree (and they do agree) an acceptable amount of compensation, an employee can still contest that agreed amount before a tribunal. Only if the agreement is a 'COT 3' or 'compromise' agreement will a party be prevented from bringing further proceedings (*Courage Take Home Trade Ltd v Keys* [1986] ICR 874, EAT).

'Arbitration' agreements

3.8
With the establishment on 21 May 2001 of the ACAS 'arbitration scheme', disputes concerning the fairness or otherwise of an employee's dismissal may be referred (with the agreement of both parties) to arbitration by an ACAS-appointed independent arbitrator. The result decision of (and any award made by) the arbitrator is legally-binding on the parties, will very little opportunity to appeal against that decision (see Chapter 2, para. 2.46).

STATUTORY NOTICE PERIODS

3.9
Under the Employment Rights Act 1996, an employee who has worked for his (or her) employer for one month or more is entitled to:

- a minimum of one week's notice to terminate his or her contract of employment; rising to

- two weeks' notice, on completion of two years' service; plus

- an additional week's notice for each further year of service up to a maximum of 12 weeks' notice for 12 and more years' service.

(*Source*: ERA 1996, ss 86 to 91.)

Section 86(2) of the 1996 Act states that an employee who has been continuously employed for one month or more is not required to give more than one week's notice to terminate his (or her) contract of employment – unless the contract requires the employee to give more than that statutory minimum amount.

Note: In computing when the notice period begins and ends, the day on which notice was actually given must be disregarded (*West v Kneels Ltd* [1987] ICR 146, EAT; and *Misset v Council of the European Communities, The Times*, 23 March 1987, ECJ.

3.10
At 'common law' (see Chapter 8) the notice period is either that specified in the contract of employment, or if nothing is said, then that which is implied by law. The length of an implied period is that which is reasonable in the circumstances. This will depend on the nature of the employment, the seniority of the employee, the general custom in that type of occupation, and perhaps also on the period over which pay is calculated. An employee's 'common law' right to notice can vary considerably – with a senior manager being entitled to more than six months' notice in the appropriate circum-stances. In one case, the director of a small company was held to be entitled to three months' notice. In another, the Court of Appeal held that the correct period of notice for a person in charge of several cinemas was six months (*Hill v C A Parsons & Co Ltd* [1971] 3 AER 1345, CA; and *Brindle v H W Smith (Cabinets) Ltd* [1973] ITR 69, CA).

Employee's rights during notice

3.11
An employee must be paid his (or her) normal wages or salary during the notice period (net of any payment of sick pay, statutory sick pay, maternity pay, statutory maternity pay, holiday pay, or otherwise, in respect of that same period of notice). That same rule applies (subject to the *Qualification* below) whether or not it was the employer or the employee who gave notice, if, during the notice period:

- the employee is ready and willing to work but no work is provided for him (or her) to do; or

- the employee is incapable of work because of sickness or injury; or

- the employee is absent from work wholly or partly because of pregnancy or childbirth, adoption, parental or paternity leave; or

- the employee is absent from work in accordance with the terms of his (or her) employment relating to holidays.

Qualification: However, that right arises *if, but only if,* the period of notice required to be given *by the employer* is the same or not more than one week more generous than the notice required to be given in accordance with s.86(1) of the 1996 Act. For example, an employee with two years' service has the statutory right to be given two weeks' notice to terminate his (or her) contract of employment. But his contract states that he is entitled to one month's notice. As his contractual right to one month's notice is more than one week more generous than his statutory right to be given two weeks' notice, he has no right to be paid during the notice period (unless, of course, his contract states otherwise).

Information about notice to be included in the written statement of employment particulars

3.12
The written statement of terms of employment, which an employer is required to give to each of his employees (within two months of the date on which employment began), *must* specify 'the length of notice which an employee is obliged to give and entitled to receive to terminate his (or her) contract of employment'. An employer's refusal or failure to include this information in the written statement will very likely lead to a reference to an employment tribunal and the imposition of legally binding provisions relating to notice with which the employer will have no choice but to comply (*Source*: ERA 1996, ss 1(4)(e), 11 & 12).

Notice and the 'effective date of termination'

3.13
The Employment Rights Act 1996 points out that, unless dismissed for an inadmissible or unlawful reason, an employee does not qualify to present a complaint of unfair dismissal if he (or she) had not been continuously employed for at least two years ending with the 'effective date of termination' of his contract of employment.

3.14
Furthermore, a tribunal will not normally consider a complaint of unfair dismissal unless it is presented before the end of the period of three months

beginning with that 'effective date of termination' (see below). See also paras 3.66 to 3.73 (*Time limits for complaints*).

'EFFECTIVE DATE OF TERMINATION'

3.15

The expression 'effective date of termination' referred to in paras 3.13 and 3.14 above (and elsewhere in this book) has two different meanings. It means one thing when calculating an employee's length of continuous service on the termination of his (or her) employment, and quite another when reckoning the 'time limits' for presenting a complaint to an industrial tribunal.

Definition 1: Had the employee been continuously employed for the requisite period?

3.16

To determine whether an employee had been continuously employed for the prescribed minimum period of one year ending with the 'effective date of termination' of his (or her) employment, that effective date is the date on which the statutory period of notice (if longer than the actual or contractual period of notice) *would have expired* had it been duly given on the date on which notice of termination was given by the employer. Otherwise, it is the date on which the notice actually given by the employer expired. If no notice was given, it is the date on which the statutory minimum period of notice would have expired had it duly been given by the employer on the date on which the employment was terminated. The same 'deeming' rules apply even when an employee has agreed to be paid money in lieu of notice or to accept a shorter period of notice (*Secretary of State for Employment v Staffordshire CC* [1989] IRLR 360, CA). (*Source*: ERA 1996, s.97(2).)

3.17

If it was the employee who gave notice (in circumstances in which he or she was entitled to do so, with or without notice, by virtue of the employer's conduct, ie in a 'constructive dismissal' situation), the 'effective date of termination' is the date on which the *employer's* notice (as required by s.86 of the 1996 Act) would have expired had it been the employer who gave notice to terminate and not the employee. If the employee resigned without notice (in the same 'constructive dismissal' situation), it is the date on which the employer's s.86 notice would have expired had it been given on the date on which the employee left (*ibid* s.97(4)).

3.18

For instance, a man who has been continuously employed by his employer for eleven months and twenty-five days has the statutory right to be given one week's notice by his employer to terminate his contract of employment. If he is dismissed without notice, his employment will nonetheless be deemed to have continued for a further week – which means that on the 'effective date of termination' of his employment he will have completed the prescribed minimum one year's continuous service – sufficient to qualify him to pursue a complaint of unfair dismissal before an employment tribunal.

Note: A dismissal without notice or with less notice than is prescribed either by statute or, if longer, or by an employee's contract of employment, is *prima facie* a 'wrongful dismissal' (not to be confused with the expression 'unfair dismissal'. An employee who has been 'wrongfully dismissed' can apply to a tribunal or court thereby entitling the employee to apply to an employment tribunal or court for damages arising out of his employer's failure to pay wages in respect of the 'missing' notice period. Although an employee forfeits his (or her) entitlement to notice when summarily dismissed for gross misconduct, the 'effective date of termination' (for the purposes of determining whether he or she had been continuously employed for the requisite one year) will be the date on which the statutory period of notice would have expired had it been duly given on the date the dismissal took place.

3.19
The 'effective date of termination' (as defined in paras 3.16 and 3.17 above) will also be used to determine an employee's entitlement or otherwise to a statutory redundancy payment (and the amount of any such payment). Furthermore, that same method of calculation (with minor modifications) is used by an employment tribunal to calculate the basic award of compensation for unfair dismissal.

Definition 2: Complaint to be presented within three months of the 'effective date of termination'

3.20
For the purposes of para. 3.14 above – time limits for presenting a complaint of unfair dismissal – the 'effective date of termination' of an employee's contract of employment is the date on which the employment actually ended (in common parlance, the date on which the employee 'cleared out his [or her] locker or desk' and left, or was escorted from, the premises). If the employee was dismissed with notice, it is the date on which that period of notice expired (regardless of whether the correct amount of notice was given). If the employee was dismissed without notice, it is the date on which the dismissal took place.

3.21
If it was the employee who resigned *with notice*, it is the date on which that notice expired. If the employee resigned *without notice*, it is the date on which the employee actually quit his (or her) job. It follows that an employee minded to present a complaint of unfair or wrongful dismissal to an employment tribunal must do so within three months beginning with the date on which his (or her) employment actually came to an end (*Source*: ERA 1996, s.97(1)).

Summary dismissal – dismissal without notice

3.22

An employee guilty of conduct, which is tantamount to a repudiation of the contract of employment, thereby forfeits his (or her) right to notice and may be dismissed summarily (that is to say, 'on the spot'). In practice, an employer should not dismiss summarily without first investigating the circumstances and giving the employee an opportunity to present his (or her) 'side of the story'. While the facts are being investigated, the employee should be suspended on full pay (*Source*: ERA, s.86(6)).

3.23

To establish whether an employee who has been summarily dismissed has the right to present a complaint of unfair dismissal (in other words: Had he (or she) been continuously employed for one or more years ending with the 'effective date of termination?') the formula described in para. 3.16 above must be applied. To determine the time limits within which such a complaint should be presented, the formula to be used is that described in para. 3.20.

3.24

A newspaper's chief sports writer was annoyed at restrictions placed on his activities. He gave vent to his feelings at a press conference. His summary dismissal on the grounds that his damaging public attack had undermined the trust and confidence that must exist between a journalist and his employers was held to have been fair. What had to be considered was whether his conduct was 'insulting and insubordinate to such a degree as to be incompatible with the continuance of the relation of master and servant' (per Edmund Davies LJ in *Sanderson v Mirror Group of Newspapers Ltd*, 22 May 1986, EAT). See also *Wilson v Racher* [1974] ICR 428, CA.

3.25

Disobeying a lawful order will often be so serious a breach of an employee's contractual obligations as to warrant summary dismissal. However, it has to be established that the repudiation was intentional. An employee was given contradictory instructions by two senior line managers. Uncertain as to which to follow, she chose to comply with those given by her immediate superior. She was then sacked by the more senior of the two managers. It was held that her summary dismissal was unlawful (*Laws v London Chronicle (Indicator Newspapers) Ltd* [1959] 1 WLR 698, CA).

3.26

An employee, who was a shop steward, deliberately made use of an unautho-rised password to gain access to sensitive information stored in his employer's computer. The EAT held that the employee's conduct *prima facie* warranted summary dismissal. The only 'escape' open to the employee would be to show that there were exceptional circumstances which justified his conduct (*Denco Ltd v Joinson* [1991] ICR 172, EAT).

'CONTINUITY OF EMPLOYMENT'

3.27

The concept of 'continuous employment' – first introduced by the (long since repealed) Contracts of Employment Act 1963 – is now to be found in Part XIV, Chapter I of the Employment Rights Act 1996. Many of an employee's statutory rights in employment depend on him (or her) having been 'continuously employed' for a prescribed period. For instance, to qualify for *paid* maternity leave, a pregnant employee must have average weekly earnings of £77 or more (2003/2004) and must have been continuously employed for 26 weeks or more at the beginning of the 14th week before the expected week of childbirth. Likewise, an employee's right to a guarantee payment in respect of a 'workless day' does not arise unless he (or she) had been continuously employed for a period of not less than one month ending with the date immediately preceding the relevant 'workless day'; and so on.

3.28

At a tribunal hearing, a person's employment during any period will be presumed to have been continuous, unless the employer presents clear evidence to the contrary. But where there has been a change of employer, it will be for the employee to prove that continuity has not been broken. This can be shown by establishing that there was no real change in the employment apart from the name of the employer (*Secretary of State for Employment v Cohen & Another* [1987] ICR 570, EAT; and *Cannell v Council of the City of Newcastle upon Tyne*, 8 October 1993, EAT) (*Source*: ERA 1996, s.210(5)).

3.29

An employee's period of employment begins on the day he (or she) started work under the relevant contract of employment – even if not actually at work on that day – and ends on the effective date of termination of that contract of employment (which, as was demonstrated earlier – see paras 3.15 to 3.26) may fall on a date later than that on which termination actually occurred (*General of the Salvation Army v Dewsbury* [1984] ICR 498, EAT). But the continuity of a period of employment will be broken by any week which does not count in computing a period of continuous employment.

3.30

So long as there is a contract of employment, an employee's period of employment under that contract will be deemed to be 'continuous' (unless the employer provides evidence to the contrary). This rule applies to every employee, part-time as well as full-time. Indeed, there are situations in which the interval between an employee's resignation or dismissal and his (or her) subsequent re-employment by the same or an associated employer will nonetheless count as part of an employer's total period of continuous employment. Thus:

(a) Continuity of employment is preserved if an employee resigns or is dismissed on grounds of ill-health or injury and is re-employed by the same or an 'associated' employer within 26 weeks of the effective date of termination of his (or her) previous contract of employment. In other words, the intervening period counts as part of the employee's total period of continuous employment.

Case Law: An employee resigned because the work he was doing became too onerous. He obtained employment elsewhere but, after five weeks, was fit enough to return to his old job. His former employers took him back. It was held that the change to lighter work for health reasons was to bridge the gap in his employment; consequently continuity was preserved (*Donnelly v Kelvin International Services* [1992] IRLR 496, EAT).

(b) Continuity of employment is also preserved if an employee is dismissed because of a temporary cessation of work (as often happens with seasonal workers) and is subsequently re-employed by the same or an associated employer when work once again becomes available. Once again, the intervening period counts as part of the employee's total period of continuous employment (regardless of how long that interval is).

Case Law: A teacher was employed over an eight-year period under a series of fixed-term contracts. It was held that it was necessary to find out the reason for the non-renewal of her contracts on each occasion. Continuity was preserved, as each 'temporary cessation of work' was of a 'transient' nature. The court applied a mathematical approach, because the pattern was regular, eg time at work compared to being away (*Ford v Warwickshire CC* [1983] ICR 273, HL; and *Sillars v Charrington Fuels Ltd* [1989] ICR 475, CA).

Where the pattern of work is irregular, a broad approach should be adopted, reviewing the entire previous period of employment. It is necessary to consider, not whether a temporary absence of work was caused by a cessation of work, but whether the absence from work was caused by a temporary cessation of work (*Fitzgerald v Hall, Russell & Co Ltd* [1970] AC 984, HL; and *Flack & Others v Kodak Ltd* [1986] ICR 775, CA).

If a person is employed by two associated employers (see paras 3.95 to 3.97 below), it is necessary to look at the history with each separately.

If there is continuity in both, then the effect of the change from one company to the other has to be considered. If the break was short and the employee carried on with the same type of work, continuity for the whole period is likely to be preserved (*Corkhill v North Sea Ferries*, 10 November 1992, EAT).

Continuity is lost where there is a break, caused not by a general diminution of work, but because the employer spreads the work amongst others in the same pool of casual labour as the employee (*Byrne v Birmingham DC* [1987] ICR 519, CA).

A break was caused by lack of funds, during which an employee was not paid. It was held that the employee's enforced absence did not break the continuity of his employment (*University of Aston in Birmingham v Malik* [1984] ICR 492, EAT).

(c) Continuity is preserved if an employee is absent from work (for whatever length of time) in circumstances in which, by arrangement or custom, he (or she) is regarded as continuing in his employer's employment for any purpose.

Case Law: A trawler skipper had worked on and off for the same employer for more than 35 years, signing-off at the end of one voyage and signing-on again at the beginning of another voyage. Whenever work was short, the employer would inform the skipper that he would be re-hired as soon as another vessel became available. On one occasion, the skipper had heard nothing for several months and decided to bring proceedings. The EAT held that custom and practice in the relationship between the skipper and the employer over the years resulted in continuity of employment being preserved, even though the final break had lasted nine months (*Boyd Line Ltd v Pitts*, 11 November 1985, EAT; and *Murphy v A Birrell & Son Ltd* [1978] IRLR 458, EAT).

In another case, continuity was *not* preserved when an employee was told, before he left to start up his own business, that he could return to his old job if his venture was not successful. The business failed and he returned to work with his former employer after an interval of five months. An agreement was made that continuity would be preserved during that five-month period of absence. It was held that, because the agreement was retrospective, it was not enforceable under the statute (*Secretary of State for Employment v Davis*, 19 July 1985, EAT).

An employer cannot confer statutory rights simply by agreeing that an employee's service with one employer will be treated as 'continuous' with his (or her) service with a second employer – the more so if the second employer is not an associated employer of (or a successor employer to) the first employer. An employer who breaks such an agreement can be sued for breach of contract under the common law but not under the (now) Employment Rights Act 1996 (*MSA (Britain) Ltd v Docherty*, 18 August 1982).

The same applies:

(d) If the employee is on strike, whether official or unofficial, but returns to work once the strike is over. Although a strike does not break the continuity of a period of continuous employment, the period of absence on strike (measured in days) does not count in computing an employee's total period of continuous employment. In practice, the date on which the employee's period of continuous employment began will be treated as having been postponed by the number of days (during the period of employment) when the employee was on strike (*Source*: ERA 1996, ss 211 & 216).

It matters not whether a worker is sacked during the dispute provided the employer does not replace him (or her) permanently or the employee does not take another permanent job (*Bloomfield & Others v Springfield Honey Finishing Co Ltd* [1972] ICR 91, NIRC).

(e) If the employee was absent from work as a result of a 'lock-out' by the employer (although the number of days lost because of the lock-out will not count in computing the employee's total period of continuous employment (as to which, see (f) below).

The test to be applied is whether the employers had instituted a 'lock-out' with a view to compelling employees to comply with the old or accept new terms of employment – which may or may not have involved a breach of contract (*Express & Star Ltd v Bundy & Others* [1987] ICR 379, CA).

(f) If the employee was engaged wholly or mainly in work outside Great Britain and was *not*, during that period, an employed earner for the purposes of the Social Security Contributions & Benefits Act 1992 in respect of whom secondary Class I National Insurance contributions were payable under that Act (Source: ERA 1996, s.215).

Note: Although continuity of employment is not broken in the circumstances described above, any week during the whole or part of which an employee works outside Great Britain does *not* count in computing his (or her) total period of continuous employment with his employer.

(g) If an employee is reinstated or re-engaged with the same or an associated employer, or by a successor to that employer, in consequence of a successful complaint of unfair or unlawful dismissal or where there is the potential for such a complaint (whether or not an originating application had been forwarded to the Secretary to the Tribunals) but ACAS has successfully intervened and/or a relevant 'compromise' or 'arbitration' agreement (or contract) has been entered into (*Source*: ERA 1996, s.219).

3.31
Changing a lawful contract into an illegal contract at any stage – eg by agreeing that part of an employee's income would not be declared to the Inland Revenue – will result in a break in continuity. The qualifying period of continuous employment would not begin to run again until the illegality has been rectified.

Continuity and the transfer of a business or undertaking

3.32
If a trade, business or undertaking is transferred from one person to another, the transferee 'inherits' the contracts of employment of the persons employed in that trade or business at the time of the transfer and continuity of employment is preserved (*Source*: ERA 1996, s.218). Related provisions are to be found in the Transfer of Undertakings (Protection of Employment) Regulations 1981 (usually referred to as the TUPE Regulations), implementing European Council Directive 77/187/EEC. The two provisions overlap in some respects and this can cause complications. As the EAT remarked in *Green-Wheeler v Onyst (UK) Ltd*, 30 July 1993, it may be necessary to proceed down each route separately, rather than switch from one to the other to try to enhance an employee's statutory rights. Most actions are now brought under the TUPE Regulations, as they are generally more favourable to the employee. For further particulars, please turn to Chapter 22.

3.33
Under s.218 of the Employment Rights Act 1996, continuity is preserved if an employee is employed in a 'trade, or a business or an undertaking' or in an identifiable part of it that is sold. The business must have been purchased as a 'going concern' and this will usually include the goodwill, know-how, benefits of existing contracts, etc (*Melon v Hector Power Ltd* [1981] ICR 43, HL). Use of the term 'part of a business' does not mean that the part in question was previously carried on as a separate or self-contained entity. Suffice that it is capable of being run as a business by the new owner, whether or not he (or she) chooses to do so (*Kenmir Ltd v Frizzell* [1968] ITR 159, DC). It is wrong to look at the transactions from the point of view of the employee. The correct test is whether the purchaser had become the owner of the business in succession to the vendor. If it is a different business after the transfer, continuity is broken (*Woodhouse v Peter Brotherhood Ltd* [1972] ICR 186, CA; and *Crook & Others v H Faiman Ltd*, 10 October 1989, CA).

Case Law: After his employer's business was sold, an employee stayed on with the transferor company for two weeks to deal with normal problems associated with business transfers. He then joined the transferee company. It was held that he was protected by the 1996 Act (*A & G Tuck Ltd v Bartlett & Another* [1994] IRLR 162, EAT).

3.34
Continuity is not lost:

(a) when an employee transfers from one firm to another, where that other is an 'associated employer' (see paras 3.95 to 3.97 below); or

(b) where there is a change of partners. There is some doubt whether this applies where there is a transfer from one person (a 'sole partner') to several partners, or from several partners to a single person. Usually the employee's position is protected by section 218(5) of the Employment Rights Act 1996 (*Wynne v Hair Control* [1978] ITR 401, EAT; *Jeetle v Elster* [1985] ICR 389, EAT; and *Allen & Son v Coventry* [1980] ICR 870, EAT).

3.35
As was indicated earlier, Council Directive 77/187/EEC (the 'Acquired Rights' directive) was imported into UK legislation by the TUPE Regulations 1981. They make provision for the continuance of an employee's employment by the purchaser of the business (the transferee) upon the acquisition of a business. The Regulations have been dubbed a 'Pandora's box of ambiguities'.

3.36
Continuity of employment is maintained where there is a 'relevant transfer' of 'any trade or business' and the employee was employed in that trade or business 'immediately before the transfer'. It does not matter that no property had been transferred (*Dr Sophie Redmond Stichting v Bartol & Others* [1992] IRLR 366). An earlier provision in the Regulations that the relevant trade or business had to be a 'commercial venture' has since been revoked. There never was any such requirement in the 'Acquired Rights' directive. Regulation 5(1) states that '... a relevant transfer shall not operate so as to terminate the contract of employment of any person employed by the transferor in the undertaking or part transferred; but any such contract which would otherwise have been terminated by the transfer shall have effect after the transfer as if originally made between the person so employed and the transferee'. Regulation 5(2) adds that 'on completion of a... transfer... all the transferor's rights, powers, duties and liabilities under or in connection with any such contract shall be transferred... to the transferee; and anything done before the transfer is completed by or in relation to the transferor in respect of that contract or a person employed in that undertaking or part shall be deemed to have been done by the transferee'.

3.37

The phrase 'immediately before the transfer' is given a wide interpretation. It covers any person in the employ of the vendor who is dismissed in anticipation of a proposed sale, whether or not negotiations for the sale had yet been completed or a buyer identified (see Chapter 5, para. 5.18). It could apply where a liquidator trims his workforce to make his business more attractive to would-be purchasers, but will not apply if the order book is empty and there is a genuine redundancy situation (*P Bork International A/S v Foreningen af Arbejdsledere i Danmark* [1989] IRLR 41, ECJ; *Litster v Forth Estuary Engineering Ltd* [1989] ICR 341, HL; and *Wendleboe v L J Music Aps* [1985] ECR 457, ECJ).

For a further examination of the TUPE Regulations 1981, please turn to Chapter 22.

DISMISSAL

3.38

To claim a redundancy payment or compensation for unfair dismissal, an employee must, of course, have been dismissed. Section 95 of the Employment Rights Act 1996 states that an employee will be treated as having been dismissed by his (or her) employer if:

- the contract under which that person is employed is terminated by the employer (with or without notice);

- the person is employed under a limited-term contract and that contract terminates by virtue of the limiting event without being renewed under the same contract (a 'limiting event' being, in the case of a contract for a fixed-term, the expiry of that term; in the case of a contract made in contemplation of the performance of a specific task, the performance of that task; and, in the case of a contract which provides for its termination on the occurrence of an event (or the failure of an event to occur), the occurrence of that event (or the failure of the event to occur);

- the employee terminates the contract of employment (with or without notice) in circumstances in which he (or she) is entitled to do so – without notice – by reason of the employer's conduct (commonly referred to as a 'constructive dismissal') (*Western Excavating (EEC) Ltd v Sharp* [1978] ITR 132, CA); or

- the employer gives notice to the employee to terminate his (or her) contract of employment, to which the employee responds by resigning with notice which expires on a date earlier than the date on which the employer's notice to terminate is due to expire – in which event, the reason for the dismissal will be taken to be the reason for which the employer gave notice.

(*Source*: ERA 1996, s.95, as amended by the Fixed-term Employees (Prevention of Less Favourable Treatment) Regulations 2002 [SI 2002/2034].)

Employer's dismissal

3.39
There will be occasions when an overwrought and angry employee will tell his (or her) employer that he 'wants his cards'. If the employee and the employer both know that the employee has no intention of leaving but is merely giving vent to his anger, the employer's acceptance of the employee's words 'at face value' would constitute a dismissal, not a resignation. In one case, an employee resigned when he was told that 'You might as well put your jacket on' after having been twice reassured that he was not about to be dismissed for failing to carry out his duties. The circumstances surrounding the incident suggested that the employee had not been dismissed, even though the employer's true intentions were unclear (*Tanner v D T Kean* [1978] IRLR 110, EAT; and *Norrie v Munro's Transport (Aberdeen) Ltd*, 7 December 1988, EAT).

3.40
But, if (as happened in *Sothern v Franks Charlesly & Co* [1981] IRLR 278, CA) an employee states in unambiguous terms and perfectly normally that she is resigning, her resignation must stand. It does not matter that she did not intend her employer to accept her words at face value. The criterion is: What is the legal effect of what she said? See also *Walmsley v C & R Ferguson Ltd* [1989] IRLR 112, CS. The position may be different where the circumstances should have led the reasonable employer to doubt the employee's intentions, especially if the situation is somewhat unusual. By failing to seek clarification, the employer runs the risk of being informed by a tribunal that he had wrongly interpreted the facts (*Goodwill Inc (Glasgow) Ltd v Ferrier*, 8 August 1989, EAT; and *Kwik-Fit (GB) Ltd v Lineham* [1992] ICR 183, EAT).

3.41
Following a heated meeting with her manager, a woman tendered her resignation which was accepted. When she later sought to retract it, the employer responded by giving her one month's notice. It was held to be an *employer's dismissal*. Although a resignation, once submitted, cannot unilaterally be withdrawn, it was implicit in the manager's reaction that he had accepted that withdrawal. But he then chose to give her a month's notice of dismissal (*Senews Ltd v Baker*, 11 February 1988, EAT).

3.42
Even if an employee has agreed that his (or her) contract of employment will end if he fails to report for work on a pre-agreed date (eg following an extended and reluctantly-approved holiday abroad) his failure to turn in for work on the due date would not bring about an automatic termination without a proper

investigation. The 'reasonableness' test would still apply. Any agreement purporting 'to exclude or limit' the operation of the 1996 Act is void and unenforceable (see paras 3.1 & 3.2 above) (*Igbo v Johnson Matthey Chemicals Ltd* [1986] ICR 505, CA).

3.43
The fact that a particular manager had no contractual right to dismiss an employee does not necessarily mean that his (or her) dismissal of an employee was invalid – so long as neither party was aware that the manager had exceeded the limits of his authority and that the termination could have been ignored. However, there is nothing to prevent an employee who is aware of the true position from applying to the civil court to have the dismissal nullified. If successful, his employment would continue (*Warnes & Another v Trustees of Cheriton Oddfellows Social Club* [1993] IRLR 58, EAT).

Expiry and non-renewal of fixed-term contracts

3.44
With the coming into force on 25 October 1999 of section 18 of the Employment Relations Act 1999 and, on 1 October 2002, of the Fixed-term Employees (Prevention of Less Favourable Treatment) Regulations 2002 – and the concomitant repeal of section 197 of the Employment Rights Act 1996 – waiver clauses in fixed-term contracts that purport to override an employee's right to pursue a complaint of unfair dismissal, or to lay claim to a statutory redundancy payment, on the expiry and non-renewal of that contract) are void and unenforceable.

Constructive dismissal

3.45
An employee has the right to resign and present a complaint of unfair 'constructive dismissal' if the employer's breach of a fundamental term of the employment contract is so serious as to destroy the very basis of the contractual relationship. There must be a contractual breach, not merely a failure on the employer's part to act 'reasonably' (*Wadham Stringer Commercials (London) Ltd & Another v Brown* [1983] IRLR 46, EAT).

3.46
The test to be applied to an alleged 'constructive dismissal' is objective. The fact that an employee erroneously felt that his employers were in breach of the implied term of mutual trust and confidence was held not to be good enough. But an employee was held to have been 'constructively' dismissed when his employer stopped paying him in the genuine but mistaken belief that he had resigned (*Pressurefast Ltd v Turner*, 20 January 1994, EAT; and *Brown v JBD Engineering Ltd* [1993] IRLR 568, EAT).

3.47

A mobility clause in his contract of employment operated harshly against a particular employee who felt that he had been left with no choice but to resign. The EAT held that it was of no consequence that the employer had acted unreasonably in enforcing the mobility clause. The test was: Had there been a fundamental breach of contract? (*Rank Xerox Ltd v Churchill & Others* [1988] IRLR 280, EAT.) In a not dissimilar case, a junior bank employee with a sick wife and two children was given just six days in which to settle his affairs and move from Leeds to another branch of the bank in Birmingham. He resigned when his pleas for more time went unheard. Although there was a clearly stated mobility clause in the employee's contract of employment, the EAT, which upheld his complaint of unfair constructive dismissal, remarked that 'in our view, [a mobility clause in a contract] includes, as a necessary implication, first, the requirement to give reasonable notice and, secondly, the requirement so to exercise the discretion to give relocation or other expenses, in such a way as not to make performance of the employee's duties impossible' (*United Bank Limited v Akhtar* [1989] IRLR 507).

3.48

Further, an employee who resigns in response to one of several breaches of contract by his (or her) employer (having waived his rights under the others) will normally lose his entitlement to claim constructive dismissal if that one breach does not amount to a fundamental breach of the employment contract (but see Chapter 2, paras 2.36 to 2.40) (*Watson v Bedford Bakery Ltd*, 20 January 1988, EAT). An employer does not have to have acted maliciously. A serious breach of contract can occur quite unintentionally. This happened when an employee lost his job when a partnership comprising two solicitors was dissolved. At the time, the employee was working under a fixed- term contract which had not run its full term. The dissolution of the partnership meant that the employee's contract had been repudiated. Once the employee accepted that repudiation, the contract was brought to an end. Furthermore, the repudiation meant that the employee was no longer bound to comply with the restrictive covenants in that contract (see Chapter 10) (*Briggs v Oates* [1990] ICR 473, ChD).

3.49

A manager's contract of employment contained a clause to the effect that he could be demoted if he did not attain a satisfactory level of performance. Following a series of warnings relating to administrative errors, including a failure to keep up with his paperwork, the manager was indeed demoted. He resigned and claimed unfair constructive dismissal. The EAT held that the employers had acted correctly within the terms of the contract (*Halstead v Marshall of Wisbech Ltd*, 5 October 1989, EAT).

3.50

When pursuing a complaint of unfair constructive dismissal, an employee must show that he (or she) resigned because of his employer's breach of contract. If he would have left anyway, his complaint would not be upheld (*Walker v Josiah Wedgwood & Sons Ltd* [1978] ICR 744, EAT). Furthermore, an employee minded to resign, because of his employer's breach of contract, must act reasonably promptly. If he delays making a decision, he could be deemed to have 'affirmed' the contract and would lose his right to resign and pursue a complaint of unfair 'constructive' dismissal (*W E Cox Toner (International) Ltd v Crook* [1981] ICR 823, EAT). Once an employee has tendered his (or her) resignation, it cannot be withdrawn without the employer's express agreement. The same applies if an employer has served unconditional notice of dismissal on an employee. If the employee is happy to have his job back, well and good. If not, the dismissal stands (*Tanner v D T Kean* [1978] IRLR 110, EAT).

3.51

If an employee tenders his (or her) resignation (with notice), and his employer responds by dismissing him within the notice period, the general rule is that the employee will be treated as having been dismissed. But if the employer exercises a contractual right to waive the notice period and pay money in lieu of notice, the employee will be treated as having resigned (*British Midlands Airways Ltd v Lewis* [1978] ICR 782, EAT; and *Marshall (Cambridge) Ltd v Hamblin* [1994] IRLR 260, EAT).

3.52

An employee threatened with dismissal unless he (or she) resigns will be treated in law as having been dismissed by the employer, even if the employee resigns in consequence of such a threat. This is because the employer's behaviour is tantamount to a breach of the duty of 'mutual trust and confidence' implicit in every contract of employment (*Allders International Ltd v Parkins* [1981] IRLR 68, EAT). The same rule applies if an employee is given false information by his employer and is effectively tricked into resigning (*Caledonian Mining Co Ltd v Bassett & Steel* [1987] ICR 425, EAT).

3.53

Advance notification that a factory is likely to close at some unspecified time in the future does not give an employee the right to resign and claim that he (or she) had been (constructively) dismissed. If the closure date is fixed, and the employee quits before that date, having forewarned his employer that he would do so, his resignation would (generally) be held to be a 'dismissal' (*Haseltine Lake & Co v Dowler* [1981] ICR 222, EAT; *Ready Case Ltd v Jackson* [1981] IRLR 312, EAT). Whether or not such a dismissal would be characterised as 'unfair' is quite another matter.

3.54

There would, on the other hand, be no dismissal in law if an employee resigns with a mutually-agreed severance package after being told that his (or her) employer would prefer that he left. The same would apply if an employee faced with disciplinary proceedings is given the *option* to quit and does so – when the outcome of the proceedings is by no means certain (*Sheffield v Oxford Controls Co Ltd* [1979] ICR 396, EAT; *Birch & Humber v University of Liverpool* [1985] ICR 470, CA; and *Martin v MBS Fastening* [1983] IRLR 198, CA). The test usually applied when an employee alleges unfair dismissal, on the grounds that he was given no choice but to resign, is: 'Who really terminated the employment?' or 'Who was it made the final decision for a particular employee?'. A subjective approach is generally appropriate in such circumstances (*Bickerton v Inver House Distillers Ltd*, 20 April 1992, EAT).

3.55

If a contract of employment is terminated by mutual agreement, there is no 'dismissal'. But mere acquiescence by two directors in their own redundancies, forced upon them by their company's deteriorating financial position, does not mean that they have not been dismissed, regardless of the fact that they had voted for their own dismissals. When they took that decision, they were 'wearing their directors' hats' (*Birch & Humber v University of Liverpool* [1985] ICR 470, CA; and *Morley v C T Morley Ltd* [1985] ICR 499, EAT).

3.56

A 'dismissal' can also occur if an employee is guilty of gross misconduct which amounts to a repudiation of his (or her) contract of employment (see Chapter 2, paras 2.36 to 2.40). The dismissal takes place when the employer 'accepts' that repudiation. There is conflicting authority as to when such a dismissal becomes effective. The better view is that it occurs when the employee is notified of that fact, either expressly or impliedly (*London Transport Executive v Clarke* [1980] ICR 532, CA; and *Hindle Gears Ltd v McGinty* [1985] ICR 111, EAT). The acceptance of repudiatory conduct (either by the employer or the employee) must be clear and unambiguous before it becomes effective. Continued acceptance by an employee of a reduced rate of pay, in clear breach of his (or her) contractual right to a higher rate of pay, could be construed as an 'affirmation' of contract – unless the acceptance is accompanied by protests or is on a 'without prejudice' basis (see Chapter 2, paras 2.47 to 2.50) (*Vose v South Sefton Health Authority*, 15 October 1985, EAT; and *Bliss v SE Thames Regional Health Authority* [1987] ICR 700, CA).

3.57

An employee's obligations under his (or her) contract of employment may also be discharged by performance, eg when a person engaged to carry out a specific task completes that task. In such a case there *is* no 'dismissal' – so long as the employee has been given to understand that his employment would end when he had done what he had been employed to do (*Wiltshire CC v Natfhe* [1980] ICR 455, CA).

3.58

But there *is* a 'dismissal' when a compulsory winding-up order of a company is made. The contracts of all staff are automatically ended, except for those kept on by the liquidator.

Frustration of contract

3.59

Contracts of employment can end in many ways without there being a 'dismissal'. There could be a termination if the employer dies, or a termination brought about by frustration of contract if an employee is sent to prison for a lengthy period or is permanently disabled and unable to carry on working in any capacity (see Chapter 2, paras 2.28 to 2.35) (*Notcutt v Universal Equipment Co (London) Ltd* [1986] ICR 414, CA).

Failure to permit return to work after childbirth – treated as a dismissal in law

3.60

Denying a woman her statutory right to return to work after childbirth (in the job in which she was employed at the beginning of her ordinary maternity leave period) is a dismissal in law and automatically unfair – unless justifiable on grounds which have nothing whatsoever to do with her having been pregnant, or given birth, or having availed herself of her statutory maternity rights.

3.61

With the coming into force on 11 November 2002 of the Maternity & Parental Leave (Amendment) Regulations 2002, the maternity rights of pregnant employees whose expected weeks of childbirth (EWCs) begin on or after 6 April 2003 have been enhanced. However, the statutory rights of employees whose EWCs begin or began before that date remained unchanged. For further particulars, please turn to Chapter 14.

Other considerations

3.62

When (as often happens) an employee is not required to work out his (or her) notice period, it is not clear whether the employment ended on the day the employee stopped work or whether termination occurred on the day on which the period of notice expired. In *Stapp v Shaftesbury Society* [1982] IRLR 326, CA, it was held that employment ends on the date on which the employee stops work – unless there are indications to the contrary, eg tax deducted from the money given in lieu of notice, retention of a company car during the notice period, or some prior indication by the employer that the employee would be treated as remaining 'on the books' until the period of notice expired.

3.63

If no notice of dismissal was given, the general rule is that the employment ended on the day on which the employment ended. This rule applies even though the dismissal itself is in breach of contract. It may also apply where the employee appeals against the dismissal and is suspended pending the hearing, provided the decision to dismiss is subsequently upheld on appeal. If an employee's appeal against dismissal is successful, the notice of dismissal would be cancelled with retrospective effect (*Batchelor v British Railways Board* [1987] IRLR 136, CA; *J Sainsbury Ltd v Savage* [1981] ICR 1, CA).

Time of dismissal

3.64

A summary dismissal (that is to say, a dismissal without notice), arising out of gross misconduct by an employee, generally brings the employment to an end immediately. It is of no consequence that the employee had been paid until the end of the relevant working day or had been paid for the time spent travelling to and from the final disciplinary hearing (*Octavius Atkinson & Sons Ltd v Morris* [1989] IRLR 158, CA).

3.65

Where an employer sends a notice of dismissal by post, it is only effective from the date when it is received, or is deemed to have been received, and *not* when it is posted (*Brown v Southall & Knight* [1980] ICR 617, EAT). But where an employee wishes to 'accept' his (or her) employer's repudiatory conduct and terminate the employment (see Chapter 2, paras 2.36 to 2.40), the contract only ends when he has adequately communicated his intention to his employer. This may be done indirectly. For instance, if the employer has been informed by the Department of Employment that the employee had applied for a Jobseeker's Allowance or equivalent benefits, this would be effective notice. The Department is obliged to obtain confirmation that the person is no longer in the employer's employ (*Norwest Holst Group Administration Ltd v Harrison* [1985] ICR 668, EAT; and *Wight v Blackstone Franks Smith & Co*, 2 April 1988, EAT).

TIME LIMITS FOR COMPLAINTS

3.66

Employment legislation lays down that a complaint to an employment tribunal must be presented within three months (or, in some situations, within six months) of the 'effective date of termination' of an employee's contract of employment. Unless the originating application – consisting either of Form IT1 or a simple letter which includes the appropriate information – is 'presented' to the Secretary to the Tribunals before midnight on the last day, it will be 'out of time'. As the Court of Appeal pointed out in *Hetton Victory Club Ltd v Swainston* [1983] ICR 341, there is a letter box outside most regional tribunal offices. If the last day for presenting a complaint to a tribunal falls on a bank holiday, that day does not count. Technically, a bank or public holiday is a *dies non* (a non day), and time limit is extended by one day (*Ford v Stakis Hotels & Inns Ltd* [1987] ICR 943, EAT).

3.67
In considering time limits, the precise words used are important. In tribunal rules, the phrase 'before the date of the hearing' will be found. This means that where notices have to be given or where documents have to be served within a fixed number of days those days must be clear days in order for service to be valid. The words 'beginning with' mean that the day in question is included in the period (*Derrybaa Ltd v Castro-Blanco* [1986] ICR 546, EAT). If there is no corresponding date in a future month, eg in February of a leap year, the last date of that month will be the last date for presenting a complaint to a tribunal (*University of Cambridge v Murray* [1993] ICR 460, EAT).

3.68
A complaint presented 'out of time' will not normally be heard unless a tribunal is satisfied that it was 'not reasonably practicable' for the complaint to have been presented within the prescribed time limits, but only if the tribunal considers it 'just and equitable' to do so. The various Acts of Parliament lay down which test has to be applied (dealt with elsewhere in this handbook under the appropriate heads of claim) (*Source*: ERA 1996, ss 111 & 164).

3.69
The expression 'not reasonably practicable' means that there must have been some physical or other cogent reason to explain a complainant's failure to present his (or her) complaint on time (eg illness or injury, absence overseas, inability to attend to one's affairs, etc). Perhaps the relevant documents were sent off in good time but were inexplicably held up in the post (*Palmer & Saunders v Southend-on-Sea BC* [1984] IRLR 119, CA).

3.70
The onus lies on the employee (the putative complainant) to show that it was not 'reasonably practicable' for him (or her) to have presented his complaint on time (see Chapter 2, paras 2.13 to 2.17) and that could be difficult. In one instance, the burden was discharged when dismissed employees were able to prove that their former employers had misled them into believing that they would be re-employed after a short break. They delayed submitting their

claims until the firm went into liquidation (*James W Cook & Co (Wivenhoe) Ltd v Tipper & Others* [1990] ICR 716, CA).

3.71
Where a person suspects that he (or she) has been discriminated against but only acquires proof of that discrimination after the time limit for presenting a complaint has expired, then provided the period of elapsed time is not excessive and he acts promptly, leave to proceed will normally be granted (*Clarke v Hampshire Electro-Plating Co Ltd* [1992] ICR 312, EAT).

Amending an Originating Application to include other claims

3.72
Where an amendment is sought 'out of time' to add or substitute a new claim to an Originating Application, the test to be applied is different. A tribunal would have to consider the relative hardship and injustice that both parties would suffer if the amendment was permitted. If reference in the facts was impliedly made to such a claim, it would normally be allowed. But the ordinary tests would apply where there was a change in the identity of the respondent (*British Newspapers Printing Corporation (North) Ltd v Kelly & Others* [1989] IRLR 222, CA; and *Ketteman & Others v Hansel Properties Ltd* [1987] 2 WLR 312, HL).

3.73
In some instances a chairman sitting alone is empowered to extend the time limits, merely by using his (or her) discretion. For instance, the chairman may validate a Notice of Appearance filed 'out of time'. Although discretion is normally exercised because of the importance of trying to arrive at the truth in a case, nevertheless time limits should not be taken too lightly. An adverse decision by a chairman may be difficult to overturn on appeal. However, before an order is made on an employee's application, the employer must be sent a written notice giving him the opportunity to show cause why an extension should not be granted before a decision is made on the application (*147 Snooker Club v Shirley*, 28 April 1988, EAT; and *Aspris & Sons Ltd v Demetriou* [1989] ICR 246, EAT).

WHO 'ORDINARILY WORKS' IN GREAT BRITAIN?

3.74
Before 25 October 1999 (when section 32 of the Employment Relations Act 1999 came into force) employees who ordinarily worked outside Great Britain were, for the most part, excluded from the rights and benefits afforded by the UK's domestic employment legislation. For example, before 25 October 1999, an employee would not qualify for a statutory redundancy payment if he (or she) ordinarily worked outside Great Britain – unless, on the relevant date, he

was in Great Britain in accordance with instructions given to him by his employer. Such exclusions no longer apply. Related provisions in the Trade Union & Labour Relations (Consolidation) Act 1992 have also been repealed, as have those in the Sex Discrimination Act 1975, the Race Relations Act 1976, and the Disability Discrimination Act 1995 (per the Equal Opportunities (Employment Legislation) (Territorial Limits) Regulations 1999, which latter came into force on 16 December 1999).

Note: Mariners who are ordinarily resident in the UK will continue to qualify for certain rights under the Employment Rights Act 1996 if, but only if, the ship on which they are employed is registered as belonging to a port in the UK and the work they are employed to do under their contracts of employment is not wholly outside the UK (per s.199(7), ERA 1996, as inserted by s.32(4), ERA 1999).

3.75
These repeals facilitate the implementation in the UK of Council Directive 96/71/EC of 16 December 1996 'concerning the posting of workers in the framework of the provision of services'. In future, UK workers sent by their employers to carry out temporary work in another EU Member State must receive no less favourable treatment (in terms of minimum rates of pay, holidays, rest breaks, etc) than the workers who ordinarily live and work in that other Member State. The same rules apply to workers from another EU Member State who are sent to work temporarily in the UK – hence the removal of the restrictive provisions referred to in the previous paragraph.

MEANING OF THE EXPRESSION 'A WEEK'S PAY'?

3.76
The amount of a 'week's pay' is relevant when a tribunal is assessing the amount of compensation to be awarded to an employee who has been unfairly dismissed. It is also needed to establish an employee's entitlement to a statutory redundancy payment. This does not present too great a difficulty when an employee is/was paid a fixed wage or salary under his (or her) contract of employment.

3.77
If the evidence shows that an employee's gross earnings varied from week to week, or that he (or she) was paid at piece rates or on a 'commission only' basis, the amount of a week's pay will be the average of the employee's gross earnings over the period of 12 weeks ending with the last complete week before the relevant calculation date (or, if the calculation date is the last day of a week, the period of 12 weeks ending with that week). If an employee was duty-bound, under the terms of his contract, to work a certain amount of overtime or to work at hours in respect of which a higher rate of pay applies, the calculation of a week's pay must include those additional amounts. But if

the employee worked overtime on a voluntary basis only or did so at his employer's sole discretion, that must not be included, even though its exclusion has the effect of diluting the employee's average hourly rate of pay (*Tarmac Roadstone Holding Ltd v Peacock* [1973] ICR 273, CA; and *British Coal Corporation v Cheesborough & Another* [1990] ICR 317, HL) (*Source*: ERA 1996, ss 220 to 229).

3.78
A bonus or merit payment or other amount which is regularly made, forms part of the 'week's pay'. Tips are not included unless they emanated from an obligatory service charge paid to the employer who then distributed it in fixed proportions to staff. So too if voluntary payments representing tips were added to a cheque or credit card voucher in settlement of a bill. It becomes the property of the employer and when distributed to staff becomes part of their 'pay' (*Palmanor Ltd v Cedron* [1978] IRLR 303, EAT; and *Nerva & Another v RLOG Ltd*, 9 June 1994, QBD).

Upper limit to the amount of a week's pay

3.79
For the purposes of assessing the amount of a statutory redundancy payment (see Chapter 4, paras 4.33 to 4.37) or the basic or additional award of compensation for unfair dismissal (see Chapter 5, paras 5.167 to 5.169 and 5.176 to 5.178), a 'week's pay' is the employee's average gross weekly pay or £260, whichever is the lesser of those two amounts. £260 is the current (2003/04) upper limit on the amount of a week's pay for these purposes. For the purposes of calculating the amount of the compensatory award in an unfair dismissal case (see Chapter 5, paras 5.170 to 5.175), the net figure is used, subject to a limit of £53,500 (*Source*: ERA 1996, s.227).

'NORMAL RETIRING AGE'

No redundancy pay for employees aged 65 or over

3.80
Section 156 of the Employment Rights Act 1996 states that an employee does *not* have a right to a redundancy payment if before his (or her) employment ended, he had attained the age of 65 *or*, if there was a 'normal retiring age' of less than 65 for an employee holding the position which that employee held (which lower retiring age must be the same whether the employee holding that position was a man or a woman), that 'normal retiring age'. The age limits described here do not, repeat do not, apply if an employee believes that he (or she) was selected for redundancy for an inadmissible or unlawful reason (as to which, please turn to Chapter 5, paras 5.20 *et seq*).

3.81

An employee aged 65 or over at 'the effective date of termination' of his (or her) contract of employment is likewise debarred from presenting a complaint of unfair dismissal *unless* the 'normal retiring age' for a person occupying the same or an equivalent position was higher (or lower) than 65 and that normal retiring age was the same regardless of the sex of the person occupying that position (*Source*: ERA 1996, s.109(1)). Again this rule does not apply to an employee who is dismissed (or alleges that he or she has been dismissed) for an inadmissible or unlawful reason (see again Chapter 5, paras 5.20 *et seq*). There is a presumption that the 'normal retiring age' is the retiring age specified in the contract of employment. This presumption is open to rebuttal if the evidence shows that, in practice, employees in the same position tend to (and can reasonably expect to) retire at a specific age, in which case that other age applies. If they retire at different ages then the fall-back age of 65 applies (*Waite v Government Communications Headquarters* [1983] ICR 653, HL).

3.82

If an employer, as a matter of administrative policy, changes the age at which a group of staff is required to retire, that new age will be the normal retiring age for persons in that group. But where the change was from a retiring age of 65 years to a new retiring age of between 62 and 63 years, the latter band was held to be too imprecise – and so the fall-back position applied (*Swain v Health and Safety Executive* [1986] ICR 498, EAT). Where it is shown that there were abnormal or particular circumstances (of a temporary nature) which necessitated people remaining at work beyond the contractual retiring age, the 'normal retiring age' would nonetheless be the age specified in their contracts of employment. Further it is not permissible to look only at the reasonable expectations of those approaching retirement age: the expectations of everyone in the group have to be taken into account (*Whittle v Manpower Services Commission* [1987] IRLR 441, EAT; and *Brooks & Others v British Telecommunications plc* [1992] ICR 414, CA).

Note: Although discrimination on grounds of age is not yet illegal in the UK, the UK Government (along with other EU Member States) has until 2 December 2003 to implement Council Directive 2000/78/EC ('establishing a general framework for equal treatment in employment and occupation') which outlaws discrimination in employment on grounds of age, religion or belief, disability or *sexual orientation*. However, Article 18 of the Directive allows that , in order to take account of particular conditions, Member States may, if necessary, delay implementation of the Directive's provision relation to age discrimination. It is not yet clear whether the UK Government intends to take advantage of that permitted derogation.

DISCIPLINARY RULES AND PROCEDURES

3.83

Most employers have well-documented procedures for dealing with allegations of misconduct (or whatever) at the workplace. Indeed, the written statement of terms of employment which employers are duty-bound to issue to every employee (in compliance with ss 1 to 7 of the Employment Rights Act 1996) must include a note specifying any disciplinary rules applicable to the employee or referring the employee to a document specifying such rules which is reasonably accessible to the employee. The note must also specify (by description or otherwise) a person (such as a supervisor or manager) to whom the employee can apply if dissatisfied with any disciplinary decision relating to him (or her). If there are further steps consequent on any such application, the note must also explain those steps or refer the employee to a document explaining them which is reasonably accessible to the employee.

However, these requirements do not apply to businesses or organisations in which the total number of people employed – *including* people employed in other branches or offices of the same organisation or by any associated employer – is fewer than 20.

Note: Once the 'dispute resolution' provisions in Part 3 of the Employment Act 2002 come into force (no date has yet been set), all employers (large as well as small) will be duty-bound to adopt statutory minimum two or three-stage procedures (DDPs) for dealing with disciplinary and associated issues within the workplace. There is to be a standard procedure (for larger organisations) and a modified (two-stage) procedure for use within the smaller business or undertaking. An employer's failure to comply with those statutory minimum procedures before taking the decision to dismiss an employee will lead to an increase of up to 50 per cent in the amount of unfair dismissal compensation otherwise awarded to that employee by an employment tribunal.

3.84

The approach of tribunals and courts to an employer's internal disciplinary hearings was succinctly put by Lord Denning, MR, thus: 'We must not force these disciplinary bodies to become entrammelled in the nets of legal procedure. So long as they act fairly and justly, their decisions should be supported' (*Ward v Bradfield Corporation* [1971] LGR 27, CA). Domestic disciplinary hearings should not be conducted like a court of law. All an employer has to do is follow certain basic rules, which may need to be adapted to deal with particular problems. It is possible to identify certain areas where employers have been held to be in default.

3.85

The *first* requirement is that there must be openness. An employee accused of misconduct or incompetence must know what he (or she) is alleged to have done or failed to do. Furthermore, the employee must be given the opportunity to state his own case and to repudiate (or challenge) the allegations or complaints made against him (*Khanum v Mid-Glamorgan Health Authority* [1979] ICR 40, EAT). So where an employee was accused by his employers of having started a fight, natural justice required that he not only be given a chance to put his side of the story but that he should also be told in sufficient detail about what was being said against him (*Bentley Engineering Co Ltd v Mistry* [1979] ICR 47, EAT). This can be done either by allowing the employee to listen to what witnesses have to say or by providing him with copies of witness statements. If he is not given a detailed account of the case against him, his dismissal is likely to be adjudged unfair. In the appropriate circumstances, he should be afforded an opportunity to cross-examine his accusers (*Louies v Coventry Hood & Seating Co Ltd* [1990] ICR 54, EAT; and *Shakespeare & Another v British Coal Corporation*, 30 March 1988, CA). A chief constable had received a report from a delegated officer containing assessments on a probationary police officer. The report recommended that the probationer be dismissed. The probationer was not shown a copy of the report. His dismissal, in reliance on the delegated officer's report, which he had not seen, was held to have been a breach of natural justice (*R v Chief Constable of Thames Valley Police, ex parte Stevenson, The Times*, 22 April 1987, QBD).

3.86

The *second* matter that should be borne in mind is that an employee attending a disciplinary hearing should be given an opportunity to be represented (or accompanied) either by his (or her) union representative or by a fellow employee of his own choosing. An employee might become inarticulate or confused, or be 'reduced to jelly', when confronted by senior members of management. He might fail to put over his case effectively, which could lead to a dismissal on the basis of erroneous information. Such a dismissal might well be held to have been unfair, even wrongful, the more so if the employee is young, naive or a bit 'simple'. In the absence of an express contractual right (or agreement) to the contrary, an employee has no right (but see the *Note* below) to insist on being legally represented at an employer's disciplinary hearing. 'The ordinary realities of everyday industrial relations do not permit of quasi-legal trials on every disciplinary occasion' (per Browne-Wilkinson J in *Sharma v British Gas Corporation*, 27 July 1983, EAT).

Note: Section 10 of the Employment Relations Act 1999 which came into force on 4 September 2000 allows that a worker who is required by his (or her) employer to attend a disciplinary or grievance hearing has the legal right (on request) to be accompanied at that hearing either by a workmate of his own choosing, by a shop steward or works convenor, or by a full-time trade union official. An employer who refuses or fails to allow a worker to be so accompanied will be ordered by an employment tribunal to pay compensation to the worker of an amount not exceeding two weeks' pay.

3.87

Thirdly, it may be advisable to allow an employee to meet his (or her) accusers face to face, or at least permit her representative to interview them or call them to a hearing. This is especially so where acts of violence are concerned, or where the issues are complex and there is likely to be some difficulty in arriving at the truth (*British Railways Board v Kugler*, 16 May 1989, EAT; and *Ulsterbus Ltd v Henderson* [1989] IRLR 251, CA (Northern Ireland)). The same principle applies when complaints are made by others against an employee. But where written complaints from several patients about a nurse were produced at the disciplinary hearing, and objection was limited to the panel reading them, but there was no request for the patients to be called, it was held that the dismissal was fair (*Khanum v Mid-Glamorgan Health Authority* [1979] ICR 40, EAT). Problems sometimes arise when an employee gives damaging information about a fellow employee but refuses to be identified for fear of reprisals. Likewise, supplying employees with a copy of an anonymous letter naming them as having engaged in industrial misconduct could unwittingly reveal the identity of the author. What should an employer do in such a case? Every case must depend on its own facts. Provided there has been a full and reasonable investigation of the circumstances, and there is sufficient independent evidence to support the allegations, a disciplinary hearing (and any appeal) may act on the evidence before it without disclosing the source of that information. However, an employer would have to be satisfied that there would be a real risk of danger should the identity of the informants be disclosed or ascertainable (*Barr & Others v Kay Metzeler Ltd*, 5 March 1991, EAT).

3.88
That very same issue was raised (more recently) in *Asda Stores Ltd v Thompson & Others* [2002] IRLR 245, EAT. There, at an interlocutory hearing, the EAT held that an employment tribunal dealing with a complaint of unfair dismissal (brought by employees dismissed for allegedly using and supplying drugs at a company-organised function) had been wrong to order the disclosure of the relevant witness statements 'in their totality'. In short, said the EAT, the tribunal had failed properly to exercise its long-established discretionary power to direct disclosure of documents in an anonymised or edited form. That is what the tribunal should have done in this case in order to conceal the identity of the witnesses and to maintain the employer's promise of confidentiality. If statements have not only to be anonymised but also edited to achieve this objective, that is what the tribunal should direct. In investigating complaints where hard drugs are allegedly involved, it is entirely proper for an employer to give a promise of confidentiality, and one which the tribunal should respect. Nothing should be disclosed that in any way identifies the makers of any of the statements, unless they specifically agree to be identified. If this means that some statements have to be excluded in their entirety because it is not possible to conceal the identities of the people who made them, that is what will have to occur and the question of the fairness of the dismissal will have to be judged in due course by the employment tribunal on that basis.

3.89
Fourth, there must be good faith and fairness by the adjudicators in the conduct of disciplinary hearings. They must do all that they reasonably can to get at the truth (*Calvin v Carr* [1980] AC 573, PC). Persons conducting a disciplinary

hearing must exercise a degree of discretion on what matters it may or may not consider. The decision must be one that a reasonable employer could reach, ie one that is not 'so absurd that no sensible person could have dreamt that it lay within the powers of the authority. [For] example... the red-haired teacher dismissed because she had red hair. It is so unreasonable that it might also be described as being done in bad faith' (per Lord Greene MR in *R v Hertfordshire CC ex parte NUPE & Others* [1985] IRLR 258, CA). See also *Associated Provincial Pictures Ltd v Wednesday Corporation* [1948] 1 KB 223, CA).

3.90
Fifth, justice must not only be done in a particular case, it 'must be manifestly seen to be done'. This principle is subject to a degree of flexibility according to the particular circumstances. It is not possible to define precisely where the borderline between a breach and a non-breach lies; but it can usually be recognised (*Peter Simper & Co Ltd v Cooke* [1986] IRLR 19, EAT; and *Wiseman v Borneman* [1971] AC 279, HL). It is generally advisable to place the investigative and disciplinary functions in different hands to avoid any accusation of bias. A failure to do so may be a breach of procedure (for which there may be a remedy in either of the civil courts or the tribunals), but it would not necessarily make a dismissal unfair. It would be one of the factors to be taken into account when determining the reasonableness or otherwise of a dismissal (*Slater v Leicestershire Health Authority* [1989] IRLR 16, CA).

3.91
Sixth, no person should be a judge in his (or her) own cause. What really matters is that the disciplinary body should act fairly and justly (*Haddow & Others v ILEA* [1979] ICR 202, EAT). A person who has presided at a tribunal which heard and rejected an application by an aggrieved employee will not normally be debarred from adjudicating at a later hearing by the same individual concerning other applications (*R v Oxford Regional Mental Health Review Tribunal, ex parte Mackman, The Times*, 2 June 1986, DC). When there are several tiers of appeal, those who make decisions or carry out investigations at a lower level should not sit in judgement at a higher level appeal hearing. A person cannot be expected to be impartial when considering an appeal from his (or her) own decision or views formed during investigations. It does not mean that there must not be any contact between people at different levels, but they must all act fairly and justly (*Rowe v Radio Rentals Ltd* [1982] IRLR 177, EAT; and *Byrne v BOC Ltd* [1992] IRLR 505, EAT).

3.92
Lastly, even if an employee has been acquitted of the same offence in a magistrates' court or the Crown Court, that does not undermine an employer's right to take disciplinary action against the same employee always provided that he (or she) has reasonable grounds for believing that the employee committed the offence in question. It could be that the employer had lost

confidence in the employee's ability to perform his duties effectively (*Saeed v Greater London Council (ILEA)* [1986] IRLR 23, QBD).

Consequence of a breach

3.93

A breach of the rules of natural justice will not automatically make a dismissal unfair. It depends largely on whether a decision is being reviewed by the ordinary courts or by the tribunals. A tribunal may find that an employer has not acted entirely fairly. But if the facts show that the employer has an over-whelming case against the employee, and that the employee would have been dismissed regardless of the breach in procedure, the dismissal will not normally be unfair (*Polkey v A E Dayton Services Ltd* [1988] ICR 142, HL). If it is alleged that a breach of natural justice occurred when an employee was denied an opportunity to state his case, the courts apply the following test: 'Would there be any 'real,... sensible,... substantial chance of any further observations on the applicant's part [which would] in any way alter... the final decision?' (*R v Chief Constable of Thames Valley Police, ex parte Cotton* [1990] IRLR 344, CA).

Internal appeals

3.94

If an internal appeal consists of a complete rehearing as opposed to a review of the decision reached at an earlier disciplinary hearing, then any defect at the earlier hearing may be cured provided that '... at the end of the day, there has been a fair result reached by fair methods... ' (*Shearlaw v British Aerospace plc*, 17 December 1987, EAT; and *Calvin v Carr* [1980] AC 573, PC).

'ASSOCIATED EMPLOYER'

3.95

The term 'associated employer' appears regularly in the statutes. Section 231 of the Employment Rights Act 1996 states that 'any two employers shall be treated as associated if:

- one is a company of which the other (directly or indirectly) has control; or
- both are companies of which a third person (directly or indirectly) has control

and 'associated employer' shall be construed accordingly'. The 'associated employers' provision applies in several situations. As access to a number of statutory rights is dependent on an employee having been 'continuously employer' for a prescribed minimum period, s.231 of the 1996 Act must be strictly construed. This has led to some curious results. The word 'company' means a company limited under the Companies Act 1985, or, if it is a foreign firm, then it must, in its essentials, be similar to a British limited company. The US term 'Inc' was held to be similar to 'Ltd' under the Companies Act 1985 (*Merton London Borough Council v Gardiner* [1981] ICR 186, CA; and *Hancill v Marcon Engineering Ltd* [1990] ICR 103, EAT) (*Source*: Companies Act 1985, s.735).

3.96

'Control" is restricted to cases where a person is a major shareholder in a company with voting rights attached. That a person operates with *de facto* control is not enough. Nor is it enough if a person has a 50 per cent share-holding and the 'control' consists of an ability to block any resolution (*Wynne v Hair Control* [1978] ITR 401, EAT; *Zarb & Samuels v British & Brazilian Produce Co* [1978] IRLR 78, EAT; and *Hair Consultants Ltd v Mena* [1984] IRLR 386, EAT). It is now established that the 'third person' must have voting control in each of two relevant companies which together are 'associated employers'. Generally, the 'third person' may not consist of two persons who normally act in concert. But when the third party does consist of two or more persons, it must be the same combination of persons in each company. Where a husband has sole control over company A, and joint control with his wife over company B, those two companies are not 'associated employers' (*Strudwick v Iszatt Brothers Ltd* [1988] ICR 796, EAT; *South West Laundrettes v Laidlow* [1986] ICR 455, CA; and *Cardiff Galvanizers (1969) Ltd v Parsons*, 20 October 1989, EAT).

3.97

Where justice demands it, the rules can be stretched on occasion. A person employed by a builder was temporarily transferred to a limited company to carry out a particular job of work. The limited company was owned in equal parts by the builder and his wife. The wife's position was merely nominal in order to comply with relevant requirements of the Companies Acts. It was held that the builder and the limited company were one and the same employer (*Payne v Secretary of State for Employment* [1989] IRLR 352, CA). A girl worked in a hairdressing business for a sole proprietor. She then moved to another salon which was jointly owned by that same proprietor and a partner. It was held that the two salons were not 'associated employers'. Neither was a limited company. But continuity of employment may be preserved under s.218 of the 1996 Act (see paras 3.27 to 3.31 above) (*Wynne v Hair Control* [1978] ITR 401, EAT). In a similar case, an employee had worked for four local authorities for more than 12 years doing similar work for each of them. The Court of Appeal held that the authorities in question were not 'associated employers'. None of them was a limited company and no third person had control over them. Nor did one control the other (*Gardiner v London Borough of Merton* [1981] ICR 186, CA).

CODES OF PRACTICE

3.98

In the employment arena, codes of practice may be (and have been) issued by:

- the Advisory, Conciliation & Arbitration Service (ACAS);
- the Secretary of State for Trade & Industry (DTI);
- the Equal Opportunities Commission (EOC);
- the Commission for Racial Equality (CRE);
- the Health & Safety Commission (HSC); and
- the Disability Discrimination Commission (DDC);
- the Information Commissioner (formerly the Data Protection Commissioner);

and, as might be expected, provide guidance on areas and activities which include disciplinary and grievance procedures, disclosure of information to trade unions for collective bargaining, time off for trade union duties and activities, picketing, industrial action ballots, equal pay, sex, racial and disability discrimination, and a great many issues relating to health and safety at the workplace.

3.99

A failure on the part of any person (employer, trade union official or employee) to observe any provision of an approved code of practice does not of itself render that person liable to proceedings before a court or tribunal. But in proceedings brought, for example, under the Sex Discrimination Act 1975, the failure to observe any relevant provision of an accompanying code of practice is admissible in evidence and will be taken into account in relation to any question which arises during such proceedings.

THE PARTIES TO A DISPUTE

3.100

Generally, it is the employer who is the 'respondent' at a tribunal hearing (the employee being the 'applicant' or 'complainant'). It is the 'respondent' who is liable to pay any award of compensation ordered by the tribunal.

3.101

An employer, who alleges that a trade union or other person (eg a shop steward) used the threat of industrial action to put pressure on him (or her) to dismiss a particular employee (perhaps because he or she had refused to be or remain a member of the trade union in question), may apply to an employment tribunal for an order directing that the union or person who exercised that pressure be joined (or, in Scotland, sisted) as a party to the subsequent tribunal proceedings. Such a request will be granted if made before the hearing begins, but may be refused if submitted after that time. If the tribunal upholds the dismissed employee's complaint and agrees that the union or other person was wholly or partly responsible for the employee's dismissal, it will order the union or person in question to pay the whole or part of any award of compensation ordered to be paid to the employee (*Source*: TULRA 1992, ss 152 & 160).

3.102
The same applies if an employer takes 'action short of dismissal' against an employee for being or seeking to become a member of an independent trade union, or for refusing to be or remain a member of a particular trade union (or of any trade union), or for taking part in the activities of an independent trade union. If the employer's actions were wholly or partly attributable to pressure brought to bear on him by a trade union or other person, the union may yet again be joined or sisted as a party to any subsequent tribunal proceedings and may be ordered to pay the whole or part of any compensation awarded to the employee (*Source*: TULRA 1992, ss 146 & 150).

VEXATIOUS LITIGANTS

3.103
There are some (essentially litigious) people who are prone to complain to an employment tribunal for any minor or imagined slight, knowing full well that their complaints have little chance of being upheld. There is very little that a tribunal can do to prevent a case going ahead. The prospect of the applicant being ordered to pay a deposit of up £500 under Regulation 11(1) and Schedule 1 of the Employment Tribunals (Constitution & Rules of Procedure) Regulations 2001 – to be forfeited if his or her complaint is not upheld – is unlikely to faze an applicant or complainant who is living on State benefits. Para. 7 of Schedule 1 (*ibid*) states that 'no order shall be made under this rule unless the tribunal has taken reasonable steps to ascertain the ability of the party... to comply with such an order, and has taken account of any information so ascertained in determining the amount of the deposit'.

Restriction of vexatious proceedings

3.104
The Attorney General or Lord Advocate may make an application to the EAT seeking 'a restriction of proceedings order' against an individual. Such an order would prevent that person from bringing, continuing or making an

application in any proceedings before the tribunal or the EAT without obtaining leave from EAT. Before an order is made EAT has to be satisfied that the litigant has habitually, persistently and without any reasonable grounds either instituted vexatious proceedings or made vexatious applications in such proceedings, whether before the tribunal or EAT. There is no right of appeal from that decision (*Source*: ETA 1996, s.33).

Redundancies

GENERAL INFORMATION

4.1
Since 1965, employers have been duty-bound to pay redundancy payments to those of their employees who have been dismissed on grounds of redundancy. Part-time employees nowadays enjoy the same statutory rights as their full-time colleagues, including the right to redundancy payments. The amount payable in each case is determined by the employee's age, length of service and income when their employment ends. But there are conditions.

4.2
To qualify for a statutory redundancy payment, an employee must have been continuously employed for two or more years ending with the 'effective date of termination' of his (or her) contract of employment (excluding any period of employment which began before the employee's 18th birthday). Furthermore, on that effective date, the employee must have been below the 'normal retiring age' for a person occupying the position he held or below 65 (whichever occurs sooner). The 'normal retiring age' for a woman must be the same as that for a man occupying the same position; otherwise the normal retiring age will be deemed to be 65. See also para. 4.11 below (*Excluded Classes of employment*)(*Source*: ERA 1996, ss 155 & 156).

Meaning of 'effective date of termination'

4.3
The 'effective date of termination' (or 'relevant date') referred to in the previous paragraph is the date on which the notice given to a redundant employee expires. But if no notice was given or the notice actually given was less than that required by section 86 of the Employment Rights Act 1996, the effective date of termination will be the date on which that section 86 notice would have expired had it been duly given on the day that notice *was* given. The same 'deeming' rules apply even when an employee has agreed to be paid money in lieu of notice or to accept a shorter period of notice (*Secretary of State for Employment v Staffordshire CC* [1989] IRLR 360, CA). (*Source*: ERA 1996, s.97(2)). See also Chapter 3, paras 3.15 to 3.26).

4.4

For example: John Smith, a 35-year-old warehouseman, had worked for the same firm for some nine years and 11 months when he was told by his boss at the beginning of the week that he was to be made redundant on the following Friday. John's contract stated (wrongly) that he was entitled to just one month's notice to terminate his contract of employment. Under section 86 of the Employment Rights Act 1996, John is legally entitled to a minimum of nine weeks' notice (one week for each complete year of service). Although John actually finished work on the Friday, his employment is nonetheless 'deemed' to have continued for a period of nine weeks starting with the day following the day on which his boss told him that he had been made redundant. This means also that, by the time John's contract had ended in law, he had completed 10 years' service and was, therefore, entitled to 10 weeks' statutory redundancy pay. The same 'deeming' provisions would apply even if John had been dismissed without notice on the Monday.

4.5

For redundancy payment purposes, there has always been a statutory upper limit on the amount of a week's pay. For 2003/2004 (the figure is reviewed annually), that upper limit is £260. It follows that when calculating an employee's entitlement to a statutory redundancy payment, earnings in excess of £260 must be disregarded. Service in excess of 20 years (reckoned backwards from the 'effective date of termination') must likewise be disregarded. Redundancy payments are payable for complete years of service only; which means that odd months must also be discounted. See *'Calculation of Redundancy Pay'* (paras 4.33 to 4.37) below.

4.6

There is nothing in law to prevent an employer 'topping-up' a statutory redundancy payment with a so-called severance payment. The latter might be paid on an 'ex gratia' basis or in accordance with severance terms written into an employee's contract of employment. Redundancy and severance payments are tax-free, so long as the total paid to a redundant employee does not exceed £30,000. An accompanying payment of money in lieu of notice is also tax free unless the employee has a contractual right to such a payment as an alternative to serving out the notice period.

4.7

It should be borne in mind that the purpose of the redundancy payments scheme is to compensate an employee for the loss of his (or her) job. It is *not* intended to provide a redundant employee with sufficient funds to survive a period of unemployment (*Wynes v Southrepps Hall Broiler Farm Ltd* [1968] ITR 407). For that reason, a redundancy payment will not be taken into account by the authorities when assessing an employee's entitlement to a Jobseeker's Allowance and associated social security benefits. A redundancy payment does not have to be repaid, even if the recipient starts work with a new employer within a matter of days. The same applies if he is re-employed by his former employer within a week of his dismissal – as might very well happen if his employer's business expectations are suddenly revived (eg following the receipt of a sizeable order from an unexpected quarter).

4.8
The tribunals are now dealing with a great many cases brought by employees alleging either that there was no genuine redundancy situation at the time of their dismissal, or that they had been unfairly selected contrary to an agreed redundancy procedure, or that their selection had been for an inadmissible or unlawful reason (eg on grounds of sex, race, disability, trade union membership, etc).

4.9
An employee who believes that he (or she) has been unfairly or unlawfully selected for redundancy (or that there was not a genuine redundancy situation) may present a complaint of unfair dismissal before an employment tribunal. If the tribunal upholds his complaint, the employer will be directed to pay compensation comprising a *basic award* (calculated in much the same way as the statutory redundancy payment), a *compensatory award* (current upper limit: £53,500) and, very possibly, an *additional award* (of between 26 and 52 weeks' pay) based on the reasons for the dismissal and the employer's refusal or failure to comply fully with an order for reinstatement or re-engagement. Unlawful selection for redundancy is discussed in Chapter 5 (paras 5.20 to 5.52).

WHO IS ENTITLED TO REDUNDANCY PAY?

4.10
As a general rule (and subject to the provisions explained earlier) every 'employee' (part-time as well as full-time), with two or more years service, is entitled to a redundancy payment if legitimately dismissed on the grounds of redundancy.

Excluded classes of employment

4.11
However, the following are not entitled to redundancy payments:

- persons employed in a public office within the meaning of section 39 of the Superannuation Act 1965;

- persons employed in employment which is (for the purpose of pensions and other superannuation benefits) treated as service in the civil service of the State;

- persons employed in any capacity under the Government of an overseas territory;

- persons employed in domestic service in a private household where the employer is the parent (or step-parent), grandparent, child (or step-child), grandchild or brother or sister (or half-brother or half-sister) of the employee;

- serving members of the naval, military or air forces;

- persons employed as the master, or as a member of the crew, of a fishing vessel where employees are remunerated only by a share in the profits or gross earnings of the vessel (unless the redundancy dismissal consists of a failure to permit an employee to return to work after childbirth).

(*Source*: ERA 1996, ss 159, 160(1), 161, 191(6) & 199(2).)

Employment outside the United Kingdom

4.12
With the coming into force on 25 October 1999 of section 32(1) of the Employment Relations Act 1999 (and the concomitant repeal of section 196 of the Employment Rights Act 1996), employees engaged in work wholly or mainly outside the UK are no longer excluded from the right to be paid redundancy payments on the termination of their employment. This change was introduced in compliance with Council Directive 96/71/EC of 16 December 1996 (the 'Posted Workers' Directive)(not otherwise reviewed in this book).

Fixed-term contracts

4.13
With the coming into force on 1 October 2002 of the Fixed-term Employees (Prevention of Less Favourable Treatment) Regulations 2002, and the concomitant repeal of section 197(3) of the Employment Rights Act 1996, so-called 'waiver clauses' in fixed-term contracts (or in connected agreements) purportedly waiving the right of employees with two or more years' service from claiming statutory redundancy payments when their contracts expire (without being renewed under the same contracts) are void and unenforceable.

Offer of suitable alternative employment

4.14
An employee under notice of redundancy is *not* entitled to a redundancy payment if, before the end of his (or her) employment, his employer (including any associated employer):

- offers him suitable alternative employment (on the same or very similar terms) to begin *either* on the first working day following the end of his employment in his present job *or* within the next four weeks;

- but the employee unreasonably refuses that offer (*Source*: ERA 1996, s.141).

(*Benton v Sanderson Kayser Ltd* [1989] ICR 136, CA; and *McHugh v Hempsall Bulk Transport Ltd*, 1 June 1992, EAT.)

In determining whether the new job offered is suitable and whether the employee had good reason to reject it, the tribunal must consider the personal circumstances of the employee. In appropriate cases, his (or her) standards and aspirations should be taken into account provided they are 'reasonable in the round' (*National Carrier Control Services v Urey*, 14 September 1990, EAT).

Trial period in new job (if terms different)

4.15
If an employer (or an associated employer) offers an otherwise redundant employee a job which is less favourable to the employee in terms of pay, location, skills, etc, and which is intended to start either on the first working day after his (or her) present job finishes or within the next four weeks, the employee has the legal right to try out the new job for a period of up to four weeks (or longer, if both parties are agreed and further training is needed). If, at the end of the trial period, the employee decides that the job is unsuitable, he will be treated in law as having been made redundant on the date on which his original job ended (*Source*: ERA 1996, s.138(2), (3) & (4)).

4.16
Two redundant school cleaners declined to accept a new contract on reduced working hours to carry out essentially the same cleaning duties. Even though their employers were prepared to accept lower standards, the cleaners were held not to have acted unreasonably. They were entitled to redundancy pay (*Gloucester CC v Spencer & Another* [1985] ICR 401, CA). The offer of a new job on different terms should specify what the new terms of employment are (pay, working hours, duties, etc), but only to the extent that those terms differ from those otherwise included in the written statement of employment particulars issued in accordance with sections 1 to 7 of the Employment Rights Act 1996 (as to which, see Chapter 9, paras 9.3 *et seq*). To ensure that continuity of employment is preserved, the new job must commence within four weeks of the cessation of the old job (*McKindley v William Hill (Scotland) Ltd* [1985] IRLR 492, EAT and *McHugh v Hempsall Bulk Transport Ltd*, 1 June 1992, EAT).

4.17
An employee who volunteers for redundancy is usually entitled to a redundancy payment (subject to the usual qualifying conditions relating to age and length of

service) but only if the employer has appealed for volunteers as part of the pre-redundancy consultation process. However, where an 'early retirement' scheme was put forward and two employees decided to apply for it, it was held that the agreement to retire early did not amount to a 'dismissal'. The employees were debarred from recovering any redundancy pay. The critical question is: What brought the employment to an end? (*Burton, Allton & Johnson Ltd v Peek* [1975] IRLR 87, EAT and *Birch & Humber v University of Liverpool* [1985] ICR 470, CA.)

Are 'bumped' employees genuinely redundant?

4.18

The question arises as to whether an employee is truly redundant (and therefore entitled to a redundancy payment) if he (or she) is 'bumped' out of his job in order to make way for a more senior or longer-serving employee whose own job has been made redundant. In *Gimber v Spurrett* (1967) 2 ITR 308 (followed by the EAT in *Elliott Turbomachinery Ltd v Bates* [1981] ICR 218), it was held that an employee dismissed in such circumstances had indeed been dismissed by reason of redundancy.

4.19

But, in a more recent case, that of *Church v West Lancashire NHS Trust* [1998] ICR 423, the EAT ruled otherwise, declaring that although 'bumping' was one way of managing a redundancy situation, the 'bumped' employee's dismissal was not of itself attributable to a diminution in the requirement for employees to do work of the kind done by that employee.

4.20

Although the *Church* decision has been appealed to the Court of Appeal, the 'bumping' issue appears to have been resolved by the decision of the House of Lords in *Murray & Another v Foyle Meats Limited* (8 July 1999). There, the Law Lords held that an employee's dismissal could be due to redundancy even if the work on which he (or she) was engaged was unaffected by a fall in demand or a business set-back elsewhere within the employing organisation. There was no reason, they said, why the dismissal of such an employee should not be attributable to a diminution in the employer's need for employees to do work of a particular kind, although an employer in such a case would nonetheless need to explain the causal connection.

WHEN DOES A REDUNDANCY SITUATION ARISE?

Meaning of 'redundancy'

4.21

Section 139 of the 1996 Act explains that an employee who is dismissed shall be taken to be dismissed by reason of redundancy if the dismissal is wholly or mainly attributable to the fact:

- that the employee's employer has ceased or intends to cease

  (a) to carry on the business for the purposes of which the employee was employed by him; or

  (b) to carry on the business *in the place* where the employee was so employed; or

- that the requirements of that business

  (c) for employees to carry out work of a particular kind; or

  (d) for employees to carry out work of a particular kind *in the place* where the employee was employed by the employer;

- have ceased or diminished or are expected to cease or diminish.

Sub-paragraphs (a) and (b) envisage a situation in which a business or a major portion of an employer's business either shuts down completely or moves to another part of the country, or to another part of the same city or town. If a business shuts down completely, everyone working in that business will be redundant. The same applies if the business is relocated – unless, of course, some or all of the workforce is prepared to move to the new site on mutually acceptable terms. If an identifiable part of a business shuts down, most but not necessarily all of the employees will be redundant. Some of them might well be absorbed within the remaining part of the business or be prepared to relocate elsewhere.

Sub-paragraph (c) envisages a situation in which the introduction of new technology, or a major change in working practices, or a near-empty order book, will prompt an employer to streamline the workforce in order to remain competitive or simply 'to stay afloat'. Sub-paragraph (d) envisages a situation in which an employer with several branch offices or outlets may decide to close several of those offices or outlets, or to transfer some of the activities carried on in those outlets to a central location.

4.22
The presumption of redundancy might well be countered by an employer who produces evidence to the effect that a particular employee was dismissed wholly or mainly for a reason other than redundancy, eg incompetence or misconduct. An employee's selection for redundancy might likewise be challenged on the grounds that there was no genuine redundancy situation or that his (or her) dismissal had little to do with redundancy but was wholly or mainly for an inadmissible or unlawful reason (eg on grounds of sex, race, trade union membership or non-membership, disability and so on).

4.23

The fact that the amount of work within a firm remains the same, but increased efficiency or reorganisation, mechanisation or automation, results in an employee being dismissed, will generally not debar that person from claiming a redundancy payment. The Act preserves the employee's rights where there has been a diminution in the requirements of the business for the employee to do the work in the place where he was engaged (*Halfords v Roche*, 30 January 1989, EAT).

4.24

Furthermore, an employee is not precluded from recovering a redundancy payment:

• where his (or her) employer's business is sold or transferred to another employer and he is dismissed for an 'economic, technical or organisa-tional' (ETO) reason' involving changes in the workforce (see Chapter 22) before or after the sale (*Gorictree v Jenkinson* [1985] ICR 51, EAT); or

• where there is a reallocation of duties following a reorganisation or mech-anisation in the business and the employee is dismissed as a result of there being a cessation or diminution of the work previously carried out by him (or her). It matters not that there has been no general reduction in the employers' business (*Sutton v Revlon Overseas Corporation Ltd* [1973] IRLR 173, NIRC and *Murphy v Epsom College* [1985] ICR 80, CA).

The test that must be applied is this: What caused the employer to dismiss the employee? When that question is answered, it then has to be shown that the reason for dismissal matches the statutory definition of redundancy (*Limb Group of Companies v Baxter & Others*, 30 July 1993, EAT).

4.25

To be eligible for a redundancy payment, an employee must bring his (or her) case strictly within the statutory definition. A part-time teacher was displaced by a full-time master who had been transferred from another school that was overstaffed. As there was no diminution of work, the Court of Appeal held that the part-timer was not entitled to redundancy pay upon her dismissal (*Fay v North Yorkshire CC* [1986] ICR 133, CA).

4.26

The contractual position of the parties is important to determine whether there is an entitlement to a redundancy payment. So if an employee can be required, under the terms of a 'mobility clause' in his (or her) contract, to transfer to other work and he unreasonably refuses to do so, he will lose any such entitlement (*Cowen v Haden Ltd* [1983] ICR 1, CA). Mobility clauses can sometimes cause problems. An employer who owned several premises had

mobility clauses in the contracts of employment of all his staff. He also specified where they were to work. He closed down an office and offered an
employee a position at another location far away from her home. She refused
it. It was held that the mobility clause could not defeat her claim to a redundancy payment. Her contract specified her place of work, and the premises
had closed down (*Bass Leisure Ltd v Thomas* [1994] IRLR 104, EAT).

4.27

The phrase 'work of a particular kind' may include, in appropriate circumstances, a change from night work to day work. So where employees were not
contractually bound to change, but were dismissed for refusing to do so, they
could still claim redundancy pay. But a minor adjustment to working hours
may not amount to a change in the kind of work that the relevant employees
were employed to do (*Macfisheries v Findlay* [1985] ICR 160, EAT; *Johnson v
Nottingham Combined Police Authority* [1974] ICR 170, CA; and *Ransomes Sims
& Jefferies Ltd v Tatterton*, 14 April 1992, EAT). Difficulties sometimes arise
when an employer, who is running out of work for a particular employee to
do, tells that employee to either accept other work, on less favourable terms,
or leave, and the worker reluctantly accepts that other work for a short time,
and then leaves (*Marriott v Oxford & District Co-Operative Society Ltd* [1969]
ITR 377, CA). If there was not a true agreement by the employee to the variation in the contract, the effect in law will be that this amounts to a dismissal
by the employer. The employee will be entitled to a redundancy payment; but
if there is too long a delay, he 'will be regarded as having elected to affirm the
contract' (*Western Excavating (EEC) Ltd v Sharp* [1978] ITR 132, CA [as
explained in *W E Cox Toner (International) Ltd v Crook* [1981] ICR 823, EAT].

4.28

An HGV driver who was disqualified from driving was given temporary
alternative work at a nearby depot while a permanent job was sought for him.
When that other site closed and no other position could be found, he was
dismissed. It was held that the termination of his contract was mainly
attributable to the loss of his driving licence. Accordingly, he was not entitled
to a redundancy payment (*Tipper v Roofdec Ltd (No. 2)*, 11 March 1991, EAT).

LAY-OFFS AND SHORT-TIME WORKING

4.29

In the absence of any contractual agreement to the contrary, an employer has
no legal right to lay off his workers or put them on short-time, even if the
business is running into difficulties. However, if there is such an agreement or
arrangement (understood and accepted by the employees), any employee
who is laid off or kept on short time will in time be entitled to resign and claim
a statutory redundancy payment. The procedure is explained in Chapter III,

Part XI of the Employment Rights Act 1996. A person is 'laid-off' for a week if he (or she) is available for work but receives no wages or salary at all in respect of that week . A person is on 'short-time' for a week if he (or she) receives less than half his contractual entitlement to wages for that week. Employees laid off or kept on short time nonetheless have the qualified right to be paid guarantee payments (maximum £17.30 a day) by their employers for each of up to five 'workless days' in any period of three consecutive months (as to which, see Chapter 15, paras 15.43 to 15.48).

An employee, otherwise available for work, who is laid off by his (or her) employer or kept on short time for four or more consecutive weeks, or for six or more weeks in the aggregate (of which not more than three were consecutive) during a period of 13 consecutive weeks, or a combination of both, is entitled to terminate his (or her) employment and apply for a statutory redundancy payment (*Source*: ERA 1996, ss 147 & 148).

4.30
Within four weeks of the end of either of the periods referred to in the preceding paragraph, the employee must serve written notice on the employer that he (or she) intends to claim a redundancy payment (which notice is referred to in the 1996 Act as a 'notice of intention to claim'). The employer can contest his liability to pay a redundancy payment by serving a written counter-notice on the employee within the next seven days reassuring the employee that normal working will resume for a period of at least 13 consecutive weeks, starting within the next four weeks.

If no counter- notice is served, the employee must (within the next four weeks) give at least one week's written notice to terminate his (or her) contract of employment. If the employee's contract stipulates a longer period of notice, he must comply with that stipulation. If the employer serves a counter-notice but subsequently withdraws it, the employee must tender his resignation within three weeks of that withdrawal. If an employment tribunal confirms that the employee is entitled to a redundancy payment, the resignation must be tendered within three weeks of the tribunal's decision.

STRIKES AND OTHER INDUSTRIAL ACTION

4.31
Employees who withdraw their labour by going on strike are *prima facie* in breach of contract and (under the common law) have effectively dismissed themselves. All an employer needs to do in such circumstances is accept the repudiation and the termination is automatic. Any employee given notice of dismissal on grounds of redundancy, who responds by going on strike and is 'dismissed' for doing so, thereby forfeits any and all entitlement to a

redundancy payment which might otherwise have been paid had the employee continued to work normally. The employer may, on the other hand, write to the employee offering to pay any redundancy payment due so long as the employee agrees to make up for the number of working days lost because of the strike action. In short, the employee would have to return to work after the strike ends and must remain at work until he (or she) has made up for the number of working days lost because of the strike. The employer must explain his reasons for making that offer, and must also make it clear that non-acceptance will result in the forfeiture of any redundancy payment otherwise payable (*Source*: ERA 1996, ss 140(2) and 143).

4.32
A strike does not break the continuity of a period of employment so long as the employee in question returns to work (or is permitted to do so by his [or her] employer) after the strike has ended. But days spent on strike do not count as part of a period of continuous employment. This means that when determining an employee's total period of continuous employment, any days spent on strike must be deducted (by effectively postponing the date on which employment began by the number of days spent on strike) – which may impact on the amount of any redundancy payment subsequently payable to the employee on the termination of his (or her) employment (*Source*: ERA 1996, s.216).

CALCULATION OF REDUNDANCY PAY

4.33
An employee's entitlement to a statutory redundancy payment is calculated by:

(a) determining the period, ending with the effective date of termination (or 'relevant date'), during which the employee has been continuously employed;

(b) reckoning backwards, from the end of that period, the number of years of employment – not exceeding 20 – falling within that period;

(c) allowing the 'appropriate amount' for each of those years of employment.

Redundancy payments are payable in respect of up to 20 complete years of service, reckoned backwards from the effective date of termination, but ignoring any period of employment which began before the employee's 18th birthday. As is illustrated in the next paragraph, an employee's age at the time of his (or her) dismissal is also an important factor.

4.34
A redundant employee under 'normal retiring age' or under the age of 65 (whichever occurs sooner) at the time of his (or her) dismissal, who has been

continuously employed for two or more years, is entitled to a statutory redundancy payment calculated as follows:

- one-and-a-half weeks' pay for each complete year of service in which the employee was not below the age of 41;

- one week's pay for each complete year of service in which the employee was below the age of 41 but not below the age of 22; and

- a half week's pay for each complete year of service in which the employee was below the age of 22 but not below the age of 18.

It follows that the maximum redundancy payment payable to any redundant employee (given the present 2003/04 upper limit of £260 on the amount of a week's pay) is £7,800 – payable to a employee aged 61 and over, with 20 years' service 'under his (or her) belt' and average weekly earnings in excess of £260 (but see next paragraph) (*Source*: ERA 1996, s.162).

Redundancy pay reduced if employee over the age of 64

4.35
In a situation in which a redundant employee had already reached the age of 64 before the 'effective date of termination' of his (or her) contract of employment, the employer may lawfully reduce the amount of any redundancy payment due to that employee on the termination of that employment by *one-twelfth for each whole month of service beyond that 64th birthday*. Accordingly, a redundant employee aged 64 years and eight months at the effective date of termination of his (or her) contract of employment can expect to have his redundancy pay reduced by eight-twelfths (or two-thirds) when the employment ends. However, it should be pointed out that there is nothing in law to prevent an employer ignoring this provision or, indeed, any provision imposing a limit on the amount of redundancy pay payable, always provided that the amount that the employer *does* pay (by way of a severance payment, or whatever) is not less than that to which the employee is lawfully entitled under the 1996 Act (*Source*: ERA 1996, s.162(4) & (5)).

Offsetting pension payments

4.36
In certain circumstances, an employer may choose to offset pensions and any lump sum payable to an employee under an occupational pension scheme against any statutory redundancy payment otherwise due to be paid to that employee. The amount to be offset in such circumstances will depend on the employee's total period of continuous employment, including service with previous employers – except where the pension (or a lump sum) was being

(or had been) paid before the dismissal took effect (*Royal Ordinance plc v Pilkington* [1989] ICR 437, CA). Full details of the statutory provisions relating to reductions on account of pension, and examples showing the method of calculation, are to be found in leaflet RPL 1 available on request from any redundancy payments office of the Department of Trade & Industry (DTI) (*Source*: Redundancy Payments Pension Regulations 1965).

Meaning of a 'week's pay'

4.37
A week's pay in the case of an employee paid monthly (whose salary is invariably expressed as an annual amount) is his annual salary divided by 52. When an employee's pay varies with the amount of work done, as when pay is partly made up of bonuses or commission, the amount of a week's pay will be the *average of that employee's gross weekly earnings over the 12-week period ending with the last complete week in which he (or she) actually worked*. The same rule-of-thumb applies in the case of hourly-paid employees or people paid on piece-work rates. Overtime payments should not feature in calculations unless the employee's contract requires the employer to provide a specified number of overtime hours each week and requires the employee to work those extra hours. If overtime working is in any way voluntary or discretionary, the premium payments it generates must be disregarded, even if overtime has been a regular feature of the employee's working arrangements for a number of years.

AN EMPLOYER'S REFUSAL OR FAILURE TO PAY

4.38
An employee may complain to an employment tribunal if his (or her) employer has refused (or failed) to pay a redundancy payment to which the employee is lawfully entitled. If the tribunal upholds the employee's complaint, it will make a declaration to that effect and will order the employer to pay the amount due (with interest). However, before presenting such a complaint, the employee must have taken all reasonable steps (short of legal action) to persuade the employer to pay the money owed.

4.39
If the employer is insolvent or in serious financial difficulties, and therefore unable to pay, the employee may apply to the Secretary of State (effectively, the Department of Trade & Industry (the DTI)) for a payment out of the National Insurance Fund. If the DTI is satisfied that the employee has little chance of recovering the money from his (or her) former employer, the money due will be paid directly to the employee. The Department will then take whatever steps are necessary to recover the money from the defaulting employer (or, as appropriate, from the relevant liquidator or trustee in bankruptcy) (*Source*: ERA 1996, ss 166 to 169).

4.40

A complaint to an employment tribunal in the circumstances described above must be presented within six months of the employer's refusal or failure to pay. A complaint presented 'out of time' will not normally be heard unless the tribunal is satisfied that was not reasonably practicable for the complaint to have been presented sooner.

PRE-REDUNDANCY CONSULTATIONS

Collective redundancies

4.41

An employer contemplating making 20 or more employees redundant within a period of 90 days or less is duty-bound to consult with persons who are *appropriate representatives* of any of the employees who may be affected by the proposed dismissals or may be affected by measures taken in connection with those dismissals (*Source*: TULRA 1992, s.188). The expression *appropriate representatives* means either *trade union representatives* (shop stewards, and the like) appointed by one or more independent trade unions who are recognised by the employer as having bargaining or negotiating rights in respect of some or all of the employees (or description of employees) who are likely candidates for redundancy or, in the absence of trade union-appointed representatives (or trade union involvement), *employee representatives* (either specifically elected by fellow-workers to consult about their employer's redundancy proposals or previously elected by their colleagues to represent their interests in other matters). In a workplace in which there are both employee-elected and trade union-appointed representatives, the employer must defer to the former (if the would-be redundant employees are of a description in respect of which the union in question is a recognised independent trade union). Otherwise, he should consult with both (*Source*: TULRA 1992, s.188(1B)).

4.42

If the employees in a particular workplace have not yet elected one or more of their colleagues to represent their interests in redundancy consultations, the employer must allow then sufficient time to do so – *before* the consultation process is due to begin (see next paragraph) (*Source*: TULRA 1992, s.188(7A)).

When must redundancy consultations begin?

4.43

Consultations with the *appropriate employee representatives* must begin at the earliest opportunity, and must in any event begin:

- at least 90 days before the first of the dismissals is due to take place – if 100 or more employees at the same establishment are to be dismissed as redundant within a period of 90 days or less; or

- at least 30 days before the first dismissal takes effect – if 20 or more, but fewer than 100, employees at the same establishment are to be dismissed as redundant within 90 days or less.

An employer is *not* relieved of his (or her) duty to consult if he plans to make fewer than 20 people redundant. Case law suggests that he must consult with *every* such employee on a one-to-one basis to consider any counter-proposals and ensure that the employee is treated reasonably and fairly. See '*Individual consultations*', paras 4.50 & 4.51 below.

4.44

The consultation period is calculated from the time the redundancies are notified until the date when it is *proposed* that the first of the dismissals will take place. It is not when they actually take place. So, if one or more employees leave earlier as a result of negotiation or for other reasons, then there is no breach of the (now) 1992 Act (*TGWU v R A Lister & Co*, 21 May 1986, EAT). It is unlawful and unacceptable for an employer to refuse to enter into consultations with the *appropriate representatives*, or to fail to provide the written particulars listed in paragraph 4.45 below, on the grounds that the decision to make 20 or more employees redundant was taken by a parent company located elsewhere in the UK, or overseas, and that he does not have the authority to explore ways and means of avoiding the redundancies or reducing the number of employees to be dismissed (*Source*: TULRA 1992, s.188(7)).

Scope of consultations

4.45

For consultation purposes, an employer contemplating 20 or more redundancies must write to the appropriate representative/s:

(a) explaining the reasons for the dismissals;

(b) listing the numbers and descriptions of employees likely to be made redundant;

(c) specifying the total number of employees of any such description who are currently employed at the establishment in which the redundancies are to take place;

(d) outlining the criteria to be used for selecting the employees who may be made redundant;

(e) explaining how and when the dismissals are to take place and over what period; and

(f) explaining what severance payments (if any) are to be make to the redundant employees – in addition to their entitlement (if any) to statutory redundancy pay – and how those severance payments are to be calculated.

The letters or documents containing the information described in (a) to (f) above must either be delivered by hand to each representative or be posted to an address nominated by the representatives. Trade union-appointed representatives will usually require the letter (or a copy of it) to be sent by post to the union's head office (*Source:* TULRA 1992 s.188).

4.46
The information referred to in the preceding paragraph must be disclosed before the consultation process begins. Furthermore, the consultations must not be a sham. Their purpose must be to find ways to avoid the redundancy dismissals, reduce the numbers of employees to be dismissed, and mitigate the consequences of the dismissals. In short, they must be undertaken with a view to reaching an agreement with the representatives concerned (*Source:* TULRA 1992, s.188(2)).

4.47
If there are special circumstances that render it not reasonably practicable for the employer to comply with any of the requirements listed above, he (or she) must nonetheless take all such steps towards compliance as are reasonably practicable in the circumstances. Where, for example, a sudden disaster strikes a company, making it necessary to close the whole or part of the business, then plainly that would be a matter capable of amounting to a 'special circumstance'. And that would be so whether the disaster was physical or financial. 'If, on the other hand, an employer's insolvency was due merely to a gradual rundown of the company, then those are facts on which the [employment] tribunal can come to the conclusion that the circumstances were *not* special. In other words, to be 'special" the event must be something out of the ordinary, something uncommon...' (per Lane LJ, *Clarks of Hove Ltd v The Baker's Union* [1978] IRLR 366, DC). A compulsory winding-up order was made against an insolvent company pursuant to directions given by a judge. This had the effect of terminating the employment of all staff, which was deemed to be on the grounds of redundancy. It was held that this was not a 'special circumstance'. The application for leave to proceed to claim a protective award (see below) was refused because the administrator was not proposing to dismiss for redundancy. There was no duty to consult (In *re Hartlebury Printers Ltd & Others (in liquidation)* [1992] ICR 559, ChD).

Duty to notify Secretary of State

4.48

When contemplating or proposing 20 or more redundancies at the one establishment, an employer must not only enter into consultations with the *appropriate representatives*, but must also inform the Secretary of State (in practice the nearest Redundancy Payments Office of the Department of Trade & Industry [DTI]) about his (or her) plans *before* he puts those plans into effect (*Source*: TULRA 1992, s.193). The notification must be given in writing (on Form HR1, supplied by the DTI):

- at least 90 days before the first of the dismissals is intended to take place – if 100 or more employees are to be dismissed as redundant within a period of 90 days or less; or

- at least 30 days before the first dismissal is due to take place – if 20 or more (but fewer than 100) employees are to be dismissed as redundant within a period of 90 days or less.

A copy of the completed Form HR1 must also be sent to each of the appointed representatives involved in the consultation process (*Source*: TULRA 1992, s.193).

4.49

Once the DTI has received formal notification of proposed redundancies, it may approach the employer for further information. Any employer who refuses or neglects to forewarn the DTI about those proposals, or who fails to respond to a request for further information, is guilty of an offence and liable, on summary conviction, to a fine of up to £5,000 (*Source*: TULRA 1996, s.194).

Individual consultations

4.50

'Redundancy' is one of a number of so-called 'permitted' reasons for dismissal listed in section 98 of the Employment Rights Act 1996 (see Chapter 5, para. 5.14). As such, it must be approached in much the same way as a dismissal for any other permitted reason. In short, an employer must not dismiss any employee on grounds of redundancy (or for any other reason) without first discussing the matter with the employee in question and allowing that employee to advance his (or her) own views and (where appropriate) to put forward counter-proposals. Otherwise, the fairness of the dismissal might be successfully challenged before an employment tribunal. In a redundancy context, the employer should at least consider the possibility of finding suitable alternative employment for the employee elsewhere within the business or organisation.

4.51

The importance of consultation at an individual level was emphasised in *Langston v Cranfield University* [1998] IRLR 172. There, a research assistant was made redundant when the last of a series of fixed-term contracts expired without being renewed. He complained to an employment tribunal that he had been unfairly selected for redundancy. The tribunal dismissed his complaint. However, on appeal, the EAT held that by failing to consult the employee about the non-renewal of his contract and by failing to take reasonable steps to find alternative employment for him, the employers had acted unreasonably. In doing so, the EAT referred, *inter alia*, to the House of Lords decision in *Polkey v A E Dayton Services Ltd* [1987] IRLR 503. There Lord Bridges had remarked that 'in the case of redundancy, the employer will normally not act reasonably unless he warns and consults any employees affected..., adopts a fair basis on which to select for redundancy and takes such steps as are reasonable to avoid or minimise redundancy by redeployment within his own organisation'.

PROTECTIVE AWARDS

4.52

A complaint may be presented to an employment tribunal that an employer has refused or failed to comply with his (or her) duty to consult the *appropriate representatives* about his redundancy proposals. The complaint may be brought by an employee-elected representative, the relevant trade union or (if there were no representatives) by any of the employees who have been (or may be) dismissed as redundant. Such a complaint must be presented either before the date on which the *last* of the intended dismissals takes effect or within three months beginning with that date, or within such further period as the tribunal considers reasonable in the circumstances (*Source*: TULRA 1992, s.189). If an employment tribunal upholds such a complaint, it will make a declaration to that effect and may order the employer to pay a protective award to the employees who were (or are about to be) made redundant. A protective award is equivalent in effect to an employee's normal earnings, to be paid by the employer for a 'protected period' of up to 90 days. The rate of remuneration under a protective award is a week's pay for each week of the protected period; and remuneration in respect of a period of less than one week shall be calculated by reducing proportionately the amount of a week's pay (*Source*: TULRA 1992, ss 190 to 192).

4.53

As was indicated earlier, an employer may argue in his (or her) defence that there were special circumstances which rendered it not reasonably practicable for him to comply with his statutory duties, or that he took all such steps as were reasonably practicable in the circumstances (*Source*: TULRA 1992, s.189(6)).

4.54

A protective award made by a tribunal covers all employees of the description specified in the award, whatever their length of service. It requires the employer to pay remuneration for such part of the 'protected' period as the tribunal deems fair and equitable in all the circumstances. The effect of a protective award is to preserve the employment for such period as is stipulated by the tribunal (*Transport & General Workers Union v Ledbury Preserves (1928) Ltd* [1986] ICR 855, EAT).

4.55

An employer, who sold his business, made all of his staff redundant without first consulting the [appropriate trade union representatives]. It was held that liability for a protective award remained with him and was not transferred across to the purchaser (*Angus Jowett & Co v NUTGW* [1985] ICR 646, EAT). Only an employee can complain to a tribunal if he or she receives no payment under the terms of a protective award. The complaint must be presented within three months of the last date on which payment should have been made or, if that was not reasonably practicable, within such further period as the tribunal considers reasonable (*Source*: TULRA 1992, s.192(2)).

Unfair dismissal

GENERAL INFORMATION

5.1

Nowadays, most people employed under contracts of employment (or service) have the right not to be dismissed unfairly. Furthermore, that general (if qualified) right extends to part-time employees as well as to their full-time counterparts. The distinction is no longer relevant. The exceptions to this rule and the conditions which apply before an employee can present a complaint of unfair dismissal to an employment tribunal are explained below (*Source*: ERA 1996, Part X).

Qualifying conditions

5.2

Except when dismissed (or allegedly dismissed or selected for redundancy) for an inadmissible or unlawful reason (see paras 5.20 to 5.52 below), an employee does not qualify to present a complaint of unfair dismissal to an employment tribunal unless:

- continuously employed for a period of at least one year at the effective date of termination of his (or her) contract of employment; and

- under 'normal retiring age' at that time.

For the meaning of the expression 'effective date of termination', please turn to Chapter 3, paras 3.15 to 3.21.

The 'normal retiring age' for a person holding down the same or an equivalent job must be the same, regardless of the sex of the person concerned. If there is no 'normal retiring age' for the employment in question or if the retiring age is different for men and women doing the same or equivalent jobs, that normal retiring age will be deemed to be 65 (*Source*: ERA 1996, s.109(1)).

5.3

However, as was indicated earlier, the qualifying conditions summarised above (based on age and length of service) do *not* apply if the employee in question was (or claims to have been) dismissed (or selected for redundancy) for a so-called inadmissible or unlawful reason (sex, pregnancy, race, disability, trade union membership, etc) – as to which, please see '*Inadmissible & Unlawful Reasons for Dismissal*' (at paras 5.20 to 5.52 below).

Complaints of unfair or unlawful dismissal

5.4
A complaint of unfair or unlawful dismissal must be presented to an employment tribunal within three months of the 'effective date of termination' of the employee's contract of employment (as defined in Chapter 3, paras 3.15 to 3.21). A complaint presented 'out of time' will not normally be entertained unless there is an especially good reason for the delay. (*Note*: That period extends to six months in the circumstances described in paras 5.9, 5.11 & 5.13 below)(*Source*: ERA 1996, ss 108(1) & 111).

If any such complaint is upheld, the tribunal will order the employer either to reinstate or re-engage the dismissed employee (although this is not always a practicable proposition) or to pay that employee an award of compensation (discussed later in this Chapter).

EXCLUDED CLASSES

5.5
The right to present a complaint of unfair or unlawful dismissal is available only to 'employees' (see Chapter 2, paras 2.1 to 2.12). That right is not available to self-employed persons (ie, to people engaged under contracts *for* services). However, a self-employed person, whose contract is abruptly terminated by the other party to that contract (or who is not paid for services rendered) may pursue a claim for damages before the civil courts.

5.6
The 'unfair dismissal' provisions of the Employment Rights Act 1996 do not apply to the following classes of employment:

- employment as master, or as a member of the crew, of a fishing vessel where the employee is remunerated only by a share in the profits or gross earnings of the vessel – unless dismissed during her maternity leave period or denied the right to return to work after childbirth (*ibid* s.199(2) & (3));

- employment under a contract of employment in police service (that is to say, service as a member of a constabulary maintained by virtue of an enactment) (*ibid* s.200).

Any dismissed employee who has reached an 'out of court' settlement with his (or her) employer – by putting his signature to a 'COT 3' agreement, a 'compromise' agreement – or whose complaint has been resolved by an independent arbitrator under the ACAS Arbitration Scheme, is thereby precluded from initiating unfair dismissal proceedings before an employment tribunal. For further information about 'out of court' settlements, please turn to Chapter 2, paras 2.41 to 2.46.

Employees dismissed for taking unofficial industrial action

5.7

Under the common law, an employee who withdraws his (or her) labour by going on strike has effectively terminated his contract of employment and has not been 'dismissed' in the strict legal sense of the word. In practice, the employer accepts the repudiation by informing the employee that his employment has ended (usually on the date on which the strike began). That common law position is reinforced by s.237(1) of the Trade Union & Labour Relations (Consolidation) Act 1992, which cautions employees that they forfeit their right to complain of unfair dismissal if, at the time of their dismissals, they were taking part in an *unofficial* strike or other form of *unofficial* industrial action' (but see the next paragraph).

5.8

Note the use of the word 'unofficial' in the preceding paragraph. An unofficial strike or other form of unofficial industrial action (eg an overtime ban or a call-out ban) is one that does not have the support of a ballot in favour of such action and has not been authorised or endorsed by the trade union of which the employee is a member. Trade union officials must repudiate unofficial industrial action as soon as it comes to their notice. The procedure is explained in Chapter 7, paras 7.21 to 7.36. Once the repudiation has been relayed to the striking workers (or to those taking some other form of unofficial action), those workers *must* resume normal working at the beginning of the working day or shift next following the date on which the notice of repudiation was received. If they do *not* do so, they automatically forfeit their right to complain of unfair dismissal and (as indicated above) have effectively dismissed themselves. This same rule applies to workers who are not members of the trade union in question (or of any trade union), but who have nonetheless elected to take part in the strike or other form of industrial action mounted by those of their colleagues who are members of that trade union (*ibid*).

Employees dismissed for taking official industrial action

5.9

Employees taking part in an *official* strike or other form of *official* industrial action are no less liable to dismissal. However, they enjoy a greater measure of protection than is available to those taking part in unofficial action.

To avoid the prospect of having to respond to one or more complaints of unfair dismissal, an employer who dismisses employees taking part in *official* industrial action must dismiss each and every one of those employees. Furthermore, he (or she) must *not* make any positive offer to re-engage any one or more of those employees for at least three months beginning with the date on which the last of their number was dismissed (*Highland Fabricators v McLaughlin* [1985] ICR 183, EAT) (*Source*: TULRA 1992, s.238) – but see next paragraph.

5.10

An employee dismissed for taking part in *official* industrial action (other than in the circumstances described in para. 5.11 below) retains the right to complain of unfair dismissal if, but only if, it is apparent that one or more of his (or her) striking colleagues had not been dismissed, or that one or more of his colleagues had been offered their jobs back within three months of the date of his own dismissal (but that no such offer had been made to him). Such a complaint must be presented to an employment tribunal within the period of *six* months beginning with the effective date of termination of the employee's contract of employment (or, if that is not reasonably practicable, within such further period as the tribunal considers reasonable in the circumstances) (*Source*: TULRA 1992, s.239).

Dismissal during 'protected industrial action'

5.11

However, there is an exception to the rule relating to the selective dismissal or re-employment of employees who took part in official industrial action.

Sections 238(2B) and 238A of the Trade Union & Labour Relations (Consolidation Act 1992, which came into force on 24 April 2000) caution employers that, notwithstanding section 238(2) of the 1992 Act, dismissing an employee for taking part in an *official* strike (or other form of *official* industrial action) will be treated as unfair if:

(a) the dismissal occurred within the period of eight weeks beginning with the day on which the employee started to take official industrial action; or

(b) the dismissal occurred more than eight weeks after the day on which the employee first took official industrial action, in circumstances in which the employee had returned to work within those first eight weeks; or

(c) the dismissal occurred more than eight weeks after the employee first went on strike (or took some other form of official industrial action), in circumstances in which the employee had not returned to work and his employer had failed to take all reasonable steps to resolving the dispute to which the official industrial action related.

Contrary to the usual qualifying conditions (see para. 5.2 above), an employee dismissed in the circumstances described in sub-paragraphs (a), (b) or (c) above (ie, while taking protected industrial action) may complain to an employment tribunal *regardless* of his or her age or length of service at the material time (*ibid* s.239(1)).

Note: Whether or not the employer in (c) above had taken reasonable procedural steps to resolve the industrial dispute will depend in large part on the extent to which either party had complied with (or had been willing to comply with) any previously-agreed 'dispute resolution procedure' (eg, as laid down in a collective agreement), or on the willingness of either of the parties to commence or resume negotiations with a view to bringing the industrial action to an end, or whether an offer of conciliation by ACAS had been made and rejected (and by whom), or whether either or both of the parties had unreasonably refused a request that mediation services be used in relation to procedures to be adopted with a view to ending the dispute.

Case law

5.12
The words 'other industrial action' do not necessarily indicate a breach of contract. It is generally sufficient that the action is concerned with pressure being applied by two or more employees to obtain an advantage in relation to a 'trade dispute' (see Chapter 7, paras 7.17 to 7.19). Anything said before and at the time of dismissal will be relevant (*Glenrose (Fish Merchants) Ltd v Chapman & Others*, 11 December 1990, EAT).

Thus a refusal by several employees to work essential overtime, which they were not contractually required to do, was held to be 'industrial action'. Their motives in applying pressure on the employer over pay had to be considered (*Power Packing Casemakers Ltd v Faust* [1983] ICR 292, CA). A concerted refusal to work obligatory overtime, in order to force a concession from the employer, is classified as a strike. The fact that the industrial action lasted just a short time is of no consequence (*Anderson & Others v British Coal Corporation* 28 January 1993, QBD).

A strike generally starts from the moment the workers express their intention to withdraw their labour – not from the time that they are normally expected to be at work. An employer is not bound to wait until the workers are contractually bound to be at work before acting (*Winnett v Scamaska Bros Ltd* [1978] ICR 1240, EAT).

An employer who fails to dismiss every worker taking part in *official* industrial action, or who offers to re-employ one or more but not every such worker, will need to contest any subsequent complaint of unfair dismissal on its merits. Was the complainant dismissed for a reason unconnected with the strike, eg sickness-related absenteeism? The motive is irrelevant. However, if an employee resigns or retires at that time, then he is no longer an 'employee' and consequently his existence may be disregarded (*Manifold Industries Ltd v Sims & Others* [1991] ICR 504, EAT, *Coates & Another v Modern Methods Materials Ltd* [1982] IRLR 318, CA, and *Jenkins v P & O European Ferries (Dover) Ltd* [1991] ICR 652, EAT).

There must have been a positive offer to re-engage an employee dismissed for taking part in official industrial action (see paras 5.9 & 5.10 above). Reliance on an advertisement inviting former employees to apply for their previous jobs is not sufficient (*Crossville Wales Ltd v Tracey & Others* [1993] IRLR 60, EAT).

Time can be crucial. A dismissal notice sent by post will not take effect until the letter is delivered (see Chapter 3, para. 3.65). Striking workers, who return to work before receiving letters notifying them of their dismissals, are not debarred from bringing proceedings. If workers notify their employers that the strike has been called off, then any dismissals later on the same day may be subject to proceedings (*Heath & Another v J F Longman (Meat Salesmen) Ltd* [1973] ICR 407, NIRC).

An employer can escape liability for unfair dismissal if a former employee uses subterfuge to obtain reinstatement, eg by giving a false name and address. But a tribunal *can* adjudicate on the issue if the employee's true identity should have been known (*Bigham & Keoch v GKN Kwikform Ltd* [1992] ICR 113, EAT).

It is not necessary for an employee to be offered his (or her) old job back, but only one that is reasonably suitable. The employer is entitled to impose terms, eg by notifying the employee that he is on a final warning and will be dismissed if he again takes industrial action (*Williams & Others v National Theatre Board Ltd* [1982] ICR 715, CA).

Dismissal during a 'lock-out'

5.13
An employee dismissed during an employer's 'lock-out' may complain of unfair dismissal if one or more 'relevant employees' had not been dismissed or if his (or her) (former) employer had made a positive offer to re-engage one or other of those same employees within three months of the effective date of termination of his own contract of employment – but had made no such offer to him. The time limit for presenting a complaint of unfair dismissal to an employment tribunal, in the circumstances described here, is *six* months (or

within such further period as the tribunal considers reasonable) (*Source*: TULRA 1992, ss 238 & 239).

In a 'lock-out' situation, the 'relevant employees' are those who were directly affected or interested in the dispute at the date of the institution of the lock-out (*H Campey & Sons Ltd v Bellwood* [1987] ICR 311, EAT).

PERMITTED OR LEGITIMATE REASONS FOR DISMISSAL

5.14
Section 98 of the Employment Rights Act 1996 lists seven (7) permitted or legitimate reasons for dismissal. These are dismissal on grounds of:

* incompetence (an employee's inherent inability to carry out the duties of his [or her] job);

* illness or injury (accompanied by unacceptable levels of absenteeism);

* lack of qualifications;

* misconduct;

* redundancy;

* illegality of continued employment (eg forfeiture of driver's licence; no legal right to seek and obtain work in the UK; and so on); or

* 'some other substantial reason' of a kind such as to justify the dismissal of an employee holding the position which that employee held.

Although these may be legitimate reasons for dismissal, it will be for an employment tribunal to deal with the question of 'fairness' (as to which, see paras 5.57 *et seq* below).

TUPE-related dismissals

5.15
Where an undertaking or part of an undertaking is transferred from one person to another the contracts of employment of the persons employed by the transferor (the vendor) are automatically 'inherited' by the transferee (the purchaser) (see Chapter 22). If any such employee is dismissed in consequence of the sale or transfer (other than for an 'economic, technical or organisation [or 'ETO'] reason involving changes in the workforce), that dismissal will be treated in law as having been automatically unfair (*Source*: TUPE Regs 1981, Reg. 8). If an ETO dismissal is held to have been fair, it will be treated as having been for 'some other substantial reason', that is to say, for one of the 'permitted' reasons described in the previous paragraph.

Comment: Although the 1981 Regulations clearly state that a dismissal in such circumstances is automatically unfair, a somewhat contradictory amendment introduced, with effect from 26 October 1995, by the Collective Redundancies & Transfer of Undertakings (Protection of Employment) (Amendment) Regulations 1995, means that such an employee would not qualify to present a complaint of unfair dismissal to an employment tribunal unless continuously employed for a minimum period of one year ending with the effective date of termination of the employee's contract of employment. The 'upper age limit' rule referred to in para. 5.2 above would also apply.

Case law

5.16
Without any instructions, the liquidator of an insolvent company dismissed the employees one hour before he sold the business to another firm. It was held that the dismissals were unfair as they were for a reason connected with the transfer. The liability of the liquidator to pay the compensation (which he was unable to do) was automatically passed to the purchaser (*Litster & Others v Forth Estuary Engineering Ltd* [1989] ICR 341, HL).

5.17
In another case, the liquidator's liability for redundancy payments was not passed on to the purchaser. The employees had been dismissed by the time of the completion of the sale and there were genuine grounds for their dismissal. Furthermore, where receivers hoped to keep on all staff and sell a business as a going concern, but it became necessary to rationalise costs and minimise trading losses by dismissing some of those staff, it was held that the dismissals were for a reason unconnected with the transfer (*Secretary of State for Employment v Gilbraith & Others*, 10 July 1987, EAT and *Longden & Another v Ferrari Ltd & Another* [1994] IRLR 157, EAT).

5.18
Where administrators of a company unfairly dismissed staff before the possibility of a transfer was little more than a possibility, their liability to those staff was not passed on to the firm which subsequently purchased the company (*Ibex Trading Co. Ltd v Walton & Others*, *The Times*, 29 July 1994, EAT).

5.19
A purchaser of a business dismissed a number of staff when it became clear that its modest turnover was unable to support the number of staff previously employed. The EAT agreed that the dismissals had been for an 'economic, technical or organisational reason' involving changes in the workforce. However, they were unfair because the purchaser had failed in his duty to forewarn the employees and to carry out proper consultations with their representatives (*Trafford v Sharpe & Fisher (Building Supplies) Ltd* [1994] IRLR 325, EAT).

INADMISSIBLE AND UNLAWFUL REASONS FOR DISMISSAL

5.20
The Employment Rights Act 1996 and the Trade Union & Labour Relations (Consolidation) Act 1992 point out that the dismissal (or selection for redundancy) of any employee in the circumstances described in the following paragraphs is either 'inadmissible' or automatically unfair. What this means is that a complaint may be presented to an employment tribunal by any affected employee regardless of that employee's length of service or age at the time the dismissal took place. Furthermore, the penalties on a finding of unfair dismissal are likely to be considerably higher than those awarded in routine unfair dismissal cases.

Similar provisions are to be found in the Sex Discrimination Act 1975 (see Chapter 11), the Race Relations Act 1976 (see Chapter 12), and in the Disability Discrimination Act 1995 (see Chapter 13). Indeed, allegations of unlawful discrimination on grounds of sex, marital status, gender reassignment, race or disability might more profitably be pursued under one or other of those three enactments – given that there is no upper limit on the amount of compensation that may be awarded in such cases.

Dismissal on grounds of pregnancy or maternity, etc

5.21
An employee will be treated in law as having been unfairly dismissed, if the reason (or, if more than one, the principal reason) for her (or his) dismissal (or selection for redundancy) was a reason relating to:

- pregnancy, childbirth or maternity (including suspension from work on maternity grounds);

- ordinary, compulsory or additional maternity leave;

- ordinary or additional adoption leave;

- parental leave or time off for dependants; or

- paternity leave.

Complaints of unfair dismissal (or unfair selection for redundancy) on any such grounds may be presented to an employment tribunal regardless of the complainant's age or length of service at the material time. Such a complaint must nonetheless be presented within three months of the effective date of termination of the employee's contract of employment, or within such further period as the tribunal considers reasonable in a case where it is satisfied that it was not reasonably practicable for the complaint to be presented before the end of that period of three months (*Source*: ERA 1996, ss 99 & 111).

5.22
An employee who is made redundant during her ordinary or additional maternity leave period (or during his or her ordinary or additional adoption leave period) has the right to be offered 'suitable alternative employment' by her employer to take effect immediately on the termination of her employment under her original contract (*Note:* Adoption leave is available to either of a child's adoptive parents, if eligible, male or female, but not both). It will be for the employer to satisfy an employment tribunal that no such employment was available or that he had made an offer of suitable alternative employment which the employee had accepted or unreasonably refused (*Source*: Regulations 10 & 20 of the Maternity & Parental Leave, etc Regulations 1999,(SI 1999/3312, as amended) and regulations 24 & 29 of the Paternity & Adoption Leave Regulations 2002(SI 2002/2788)).

5.23
An employee denied her right to return to work at the end of her additional maternity leave period, or her (or his) additional adoption leave period (or, if that period ends by dismissal, immediately before the dismissal), will not be treated as having been unfairly dismissed if, immediately before the end of that period of leave, the number of employees employed by the employer, added to the number employed by any associated employer, did not exceed five, and it was not reasonably practicable for the employer (who may be the same or a successor employer) to permit her to return to a job that is both suitable for her and appropriate for her (or him) to do in the cirumstances or for an associated employer to offer her a job of that kind (*ibid*).

Note: An employee's right to maternity, adoption, parental and paternity leave (under the Employment Rights Act 1996) are discussed in more detail in Chapter 14.

5.24
A pregnant woman was given notice of the termination of her existing job to take effect when she would have been on maternity leave. At that time, she could have been re-engaged in an alternative post. It was held that her dismissal was for a reason connected with her pregnancy, and was therefore unfair (*Stockton-on-Tees BC v Brown* [1988] ICR 410, HL; and *Intelligent Applications Ltd v Wilson*, 6 October 1992, EAT). It is no defence for an employer to show that special circumstances obliged him to dismiss an employee who was absent on maternity leave.

5.25
A dentist was held to have fallen foul of the law when he dismissed his dental nurse within a few days of the birth of her child. He had argued that he had

found it impossible to recruit a temporary replacement and that he had no choice but to recruit somebody on a permanent basis. At the time of her dismissal the nurse had not yet served notice of her intention to return to work (*Clayton v Vigers* [1989] ICR 713, EAT).

Dismissal on grounds of trade union membership or activities

5.26
An employee's rights in relation to trade-union membership and activities are to be found in Part III of the Trade Union & Labour Relations (Consolidation) Act 1992.

An employee will be treated as having been unfairly dismissed if the reason (or, if more than one, the principal reason) for his (or her) dismissal (or selection for redundancy) was that the employee:

- was, or proposed to become, a member of an independent trade union; or

- had taken part, or proposed to take part, in the activities of an independent trade union – either at a time outside his (or her) contractual working hours, or at a time within those working hours at which, in accordance with arrangements agreed with (or consent given by) his employer, it is permissible for him to take part in such activities; or

- was not a member of any trade union, or of a particular trade union, or of one of a number of particular trade unions, or had refused, or proposed to refuse, to become or remain a member; or

- had refused, or proposed to refuse, to make a payment to his (or her) employer, or to agree to have money deducted from his wages or salary as an alternative to trade union membership – regardless of any term to the contrary in his contract of employment.

An employee dismissed in the circumstances described above may complain of unfair dismissal regardless of his (or her) age or length of service at the material time. Such a complaint must nonetheless be presented within three months of the effective date of termination of the employee's contract of employment, or within such further period as the tribunal considers reasonable in a case where it is satisfied that it was not reasonably practicable for the complaint to be presented before the end of that three-month period (*Source*: TULRA 1992, ss 152, 153 & 154; ERA 1996, s.111). See also paras 5.53 to 5.56 below (*Interim relief*).

Collective bargaining: recognition

5.27
Since 6 June 2000, when section 70A and Schedule A1 to the Trade Union & Labour Relations (Consolidation) Act 1992 came into force, it has been

inadmissible and automatically unfair for an employer to dismiss an employee (or to select such an employee for redundancy) for:

- acting with a view to obtaining or preventing recognition of a union;

- indicating support for, or opposition to, trade union recognition;

- acting with a view to securing or preventing the ending of bargaining arrangements;

- indicating support or opposition to the ending of bargaining arrangements;

- influencing or seeking to influence the way in which other workers cast their votes in a ballot for trade union recognition;

- influencing or seeking to influence other workers to vote or to abstain from voting in a ballot for trade union recognition;

- voting in a ballot for trade union recognition;

or for proposing to do, failing to do, or proposing to decline to do, any of the things referred to in the list above. See also paras 5.53 to 5.56 below (*Interim relief*).

Note: Under section 70A and Schedule A1 to TULRA 1992, employers with 21 or more workers 'on the payroll' (including workers employed by any associated employer) must respond positively to a valid request for recognition by one or more independent trade unions. If an employer refuses or fails to respond to a request for recognition, or rejects such a request out of hand, the union or unions in question may apply to the Central Arbitration Committee (CAC) for a determination. If all else fails, recognition will be accorded if a majority of workers (comprising 40 per cent or more of those entitled to vote), vote in favour of recognition. Full details of the statutory procedures (not otherwise covered in this book) may be downloaded from Web site: www.cac.gov.uk/publications/pubstore/recog2.htm#GUIDANCE%20 BOOKLETS.

Dismissal in health and safety cases

5.28
Under regulation 7 of the Management of Health & Safety at Work Regulations 1999 (SI 1999/3242), every employer is obliged to appoint one or more 'competent persons' to advise and assist him, and to help him understand and comply with his duties under health and safety legislation. The Health & Safety at Work etc Act 1974 likewise requires an employer to provide facilities and paid time off work for trade union-appointed safety representatives or (where there is no recognised trade union) *representatives of employee safety* (elected by the workforce). There is also provision for the establishment of safety committees.

5.29

It is inadmissible and automatically unfair to dismiss a 'competent person', safety representative, representative of employee safety, member of a safety committee, or any other person designated by the employer to carry out activities in connection with preventing or reducing risks to health and safety (or to select such a person for redundancy), if the reason (or, if more than one, the principal reason) for the dismissal (or selection) was that the employee carried out (or proposed to carry out) his or her safety-related functions. See also paras 5.53 to 5.56 below (*Interim relief*).

5.30

The same rule applies if an employee is dismissed or selected for redundancy for using reasonable means to draw his (or her) employer's attention to circumstances connected with his work which he reasonably believed to be harmful or potentially harmful to health and safety – although this rule only applies if there were no safety representatives and no safety committee at the employee's place of work, or if it was not reasonably practicable for the employee to raise his concerns by those means.

5.31

It is also *prima facie* unfair to dismiss an employee or select him (or her) for redundancy:

(a) for leaving (or proposing to leave) his place of work in circumstances of danger – which the employee reasonably believed to be serious and imminent and which he could not reasonably have been expected to avert; or

(b) for refusing to return to his place of work (or any dangerous part of his place of work) so long as the danger in (a) persisted; or

(c) for taking (or proposing to take) appropriate steps to protect himself or other persons from that danger.

Whether or not the steps the employee in (c) above took (or proposed to take) were appropriate must be judged by reference to all the circumstances including, in particular, his (or her) knowledge and the facilities and advice available to him at the time. Indeed, the employee will not be treated as having been unfairly dismissed if the employer can satisfy an employment tribunal that it was (or would have been) so negligent for the employee to have taken the steps he took (or proposed to take) that any reasonable employer might have dismissed him for taking (or proposing to take) such steps.

5.32

An employee dismissed in the circumstances described in paras 5.28 to 5.31 above may complain of unfair dismissal regardless of his (or her) age or length of service at the material time. Such a complaint must nonetheless be presented within three months of the effective date of termination of the employee's contract of employment, or within such further period as the tribunal considers reasonable in a case where it is satisfied that it was not reasonably practicable for the complaint to be presented before the end of that three-month period (*Source*: ERA 1996, ss 100, 105, 108, 109 & 111).

Dismissal for refusing Sunday work

5.33
It is inadmissible and automatically unfair to dismiss a *protected* or *opted-out* shop worker or betting worker (or to select such a person for redundancy) if the reason (or, if more than one, the principal reason) for the dismissal was that the worker in question had refused (or proposed to refuse) to do shop or betting work on Sundays or on a particular Sunday (*Source*: ERA 1996, s.101).

5.34
It is similarly unfair to dismiss an *opted-out* shop or betting worker, or to select such a person for redundancy, if the reason (or, if more than one, the principal reason) for the dismissal was that the worker gave (or proposed to give) an opting-out notice to his (or her) employer.

5.35
An employee dismissed in the circumstances described in paras 5.33 and 5.34 above may complain of unfair dismissal regardless of his (or her) age or length of service at the material time. Such a complaint must nonetheless be presented within three months of the effective date of termination of the employee's contract of employment, or within such further period as the tribunal considers reasonable in a case where it is satisfied that it was not reasonably practicable for the complaint to be presented before the end of that three-month period (*Source*: ERA 1996, ss 101, 105, 108, 109 & 111).

5.36
Workers employed (or recruited to work) in shops or betting shops must be informed in writing of their statutory rights in relation to Sunday work. A shop worker or betting worker who is happy to work on Sundays will be asked to sign an *opting-in* notice stating that he or she wishes to work on Sundays or does not object to doing so. Both parties (the employer and the employee) will then enter into an express agreement setting out what shop work the employee will undertake, and/or on what Sunday[s]. The consent may be withdrawn so long as the employee gives three months' advance written notice, during which time he or she must continue to work on Sundays in accordance with the agreement. If the employer had failed to explain the employee's rights, that notice period is reduced to one month.

Working time cases

5.37
Under the Working Time Regulations 1998, which came into force on 1 October 1998, every worker (save for a worker in an excepted occupation) has the legal right to refuse to work more than an average 48-hour week calculated over a reference period of 17 consecutive weeks (or such longer reference period, up to 52 weeks, as may have been agreed under the terms of a collective or workforce agreement). The Regulations also impose minimum standards in relation to night work, in-work rest breaks, and daily and weekly rest periods, and give workers the legal right to four weeks' paid holiday in every 'holiday year'. There are more stringent rules on the working hours of young workers under the age of 18. For further particulars, please turn to Chapter 18.

5.38
Any employee or worker who is dismissed (or selected for redundancy) will be treated, for the purposes of Part X of the Employment Rights Act 1996 (*Unfair Dismissal*) as having been unfairly dismissed if the reason or (if more than one, the principal reason) for the dismissal (or selection) was that he (or she) had:

- refused (or proposed to refuse) to comply with a requirement which the employer imposed (or proposed to impose) in contravention of the employer's obligations under the Working Time Regulations 1998;

- refused (or proposed to refuse) to forego a right conferred by those Regulations;

- failed to sign a workforce agreement for the purposes of those Regulations, or to enter into, or agree to vary or extend, any other agreement with the employer as provided for in those Regulations; or

- being (i) a representative of members of the workforce for the purposes of Schedule I to those Regulations (*Workforce Agreements*), or a candidate in an election which any person elected will, on being elected, be such a representative, performed (or proposed to perform) any functions or activities as such a representative or candidate.

(*Source*: Employment Rights Act 1996, ss 101A & 104, as inserted or amended by Reg. 30(1) & (2) of the 1998 Regulations.)

5.39
Any worker or *workforce representative* (or candidate for election as such a representative) who is dismissed (or selected for redundancy) for pursuing his (or her) rights under the 1998 Regulations or for carrying out or presuming to carry out his functions as such a representative (or candidate)

may present a complaint to an employment tribunal regardless of his (or her) age or length of service at the material time. The complaint must be presented within three months of the effective date of dismissal or within such further period as the tribunal considers reasonable in the circumstances. If such a complaint is upheld, the worker or representative will be awarded compensation for unfair dismissal (including a minimum basic award [2003/04] of £3,500). See also paras 5.53 to 5.56 below (*Interim relief*).

Dismissal of a pension scheme trustee

5.40
An employee who is a trustee of a relevant occupational pension scheme has the legal right to perform his (or her) duties as such a trustee without interference and without fear of being dismissed for doing so. Indeed a pension scheme trustee (duly nominated and elected in accordance with the provisions of the Pensions Act 1995) is entitled to a reasonable amount of paid time off work (during normal working hours) to enable him (or her) to carry out such duties.

5.41
A pension scheme trustee who is dismissed (or selected for redundancy) for carrying out his (or her) duties may present a complaint to an employment tribunal regardless of his age or length of service at the material time. In short, his dismissal will be treated as inadmissible and automatically unfair. If the employee's complaint is upheld, he will be awarded compensation for unfair dismissal (including a minimum basic award of £3,500 – which latter is the figure for 2003/04). The complaint must be presented within three months of the effective date of termination of the employee's contract of employment. A complaint presented 'out of time' will not be heard unless there are exceptional reasons for the delay (*Source*: PA 1995, s.16; ERA 1996, s.102). See also paras 5.53 to 5.56 below (*Interim relief*).

Dismissal of an 'employee representative'

5.42
An employee who is dismissed will be treated in law as having been unfairly dismissed if the reason (or, if more than one, the principal reason) for his (or her) dismissal (or selection for redundancy) is that the employee, being:

- an *employee representative* for the purposes of Chapter II of Part IV of the Trade Union & Labour Relations (Consolidation) Act 1992 (employer's duty to consult with 'appropriate representatives' concerning proposed collective redundancies) or Regulations 10 & 11 of the Transfer of Undertakings (Protection of Employment) Regulations 1981 (duty to consult with 'appropriate representatives concerning the proposed sale or transfer of an undertaking);

- a candidate in an election for the role of *employee representative* had performed (or proposed to perform) any functions or activities as such a candidate.

An employee dismissed in the circumstances described may complain to an employment tribunal regardless of his (or her) age or length of service at the effective date of termination of his contract of employment. The complaint must be presented within three months of the effective date of termination or within such further period as the tribunal considers reasonable in the circumstances (*Source*: ERA 1996, s.103). See also paras 5.53 to 5.56 below (*Interim relief*).

Dismissal for making a 'protected disclosure'

5.43
It is inadmissible and automatically unfair to dismiss an employee (or to select such an employee for redundancy) if the reason (or, if more than one, the principal reason) for the dismissal (or selection) is that the employee had made a protected disclosure. For these purposes, a 'protected disclosure' is any disclosure of information (to an employer or other responsible person which, in the reasonable belief of the person making the disclosure tends to show:

- that a criminal offence has been committed, is being committed or is likely to be committed;

- that a person has failed, is failing or is likely to fail to comply with any legal obligation to which he (or she) is subject;

- that a miscarriage of justice has occurred, is occurring or is likely to occur;

- that the health or safety of any individual has been, is being or is likely to be damaged;

- that the environment has been, is being or is likely to be damaged; or

- that information or evidence concerning any of the above matters has been, or is likely to be, deliberately concealed.

There is no upper limit on the amount of compensation that may be awarded to an employee held to have been unfairly dismissed or selected for redundancy for having made a 'protected disclosure'. See also paras 5.53 to 5.56 below (*Interim relief*).

(*Source*: s.103A, Employment Rights Act 1996, inserted by the Public Interest Disclosure Act 1998, s.1.) See also Chapter 20.

Dismissal for asserting a statutory right

5.44
It is inadmissible and automatically unfair for an employer to dismiss an employee (or to select such an employee for redundancy) for complaining to a tribunal about an infringement of a 'relevant statutory right' in employment *or* for alleging that his (or her) employer had infringed one or other of those rights. It is of no consequence that the employee's claim to that right (and that it had been infringed) was incorrect – so long as it was made in good faith (*Source*: ERA 1996, s.104).

5.45
For these purposes, a 'relevant statutory right' is:

- any right conferred by the Employment Rights Act 1996 for which the remedy for its infringement is by way of a complaint (or reference) to an employment tribunal;

- the right of an employee under s. 86 of the 1996 Act to minimum notice to terminate his (or her) contract of employment;

- any right conferred by ss 68, 86, 146, 168, 169 and 170 of the Trade Union & Labour Relations (Consolidation) Act 1992, namely:

    (a) the right of an employee not to have trade union dues deducted from his (or her) pay without prior authorisation;

    (b) the right of an employee to opt-out of paying contributions to a trade union's political fund;

    (c) the right of an employee not to have 'action short of dismissal' taken against him (or her) because of his membership or non-membership of a trade union, or for taking part at an 'appropriate time' in the activities of an independent trade union;

    (d) the right of a trade union official (eg shop steward or works convenor) to take paid time off work for the purposes of carrying out his (or her) duties as such an official; and

    (e) the right of an employee, who is a member of a recognised independent trade union, to take unpaid time off during working hours for the purposes of taking part in any activities of that union (either as a member or as a representative of that union), excluding any activities which themselves consist of industrial action.

National minimum wage cases

5.46
It is inadmissible and automatically unfair to dismiss an employee (or to select such an employee for redundancy) for enforcing or proposing to

enforce his (or her) entitlement to be paid the national minimum wage; or for having been instrumental in prosecuting his employer for an offence under the National Minimum Wage Act 1998; or because the employee qualified (or would or might have qualified) for the national minimum wage (*Source:* Employment Rights Act 1996, ss 104A & 105(7A)).

5.47
Under the National Minimum Wage Regulations 1999 (SI 1999/584), which came into force on 1 April 1999, every worker (employee or otherwise) aged 18 to 21, inclusive, must be paid no less than £3.60 an hour. For workers aged 22 and over (save for those receiving 'accredited training' during their first six months of employment), the appropriate national minimum wage (NMW) is £4.20 an hour. The 1999 Regulations do not prescribe a NMW for workers aged 16 and 17. For more information on the NMW, please turn to Chapter 19. The figures quoted above are those for 2003/04. NMW rates are reviewed and, if need be, adjusted on 1 October each year.

Tax credit cases

5.48
An employee will be treated in law as having been unfairly dismissed if the reason (or, if more than one, the principal reason) for his (or her) dismissal or selection for redundancy was that he had taken or proposed to take action to enforce (or otherwise secure the benefit of) a right conferred by regulations made under the Tax Credits Act 2002 or that the employer had been penalised for refusing or failing to comply with his obligations under that Act (*ibid* ss 104B & 105(7B)).

Note: Under the 2002 Act, which repealed and replaced the Tax Credits Act 1999, employers are responsible for paying working tax credits through the payroll to eligible employees. They must also include related information in the itemised pay statements necessarily issued to those employees. An employer who refuses or fails to comply with his obligations under the 2002 Act is guilty of an offence and liable to a penalty of up to £3,000.

European Works Councils cases

5.49
With the coming into force on 15 January 2000 of the Transnational Information & Consultation of Employees Regulations 1999 (SI 1999/3323) (the 'TICE Regulations') (not otherwise reviewed in this handbook), any large company or organisation employing 1,000 or more employees within the European Economic Area (EEA) (of whom 150 or more work in each of at least two EEA Member States) must respond positively to a valid request from employees for the establishment of a European Works Council (EWC).

Note: The TICE Regulations (sometimes referred to as 'TICER') implement Council Directive 97/74/EC of 15 December 1997 'on the establishment of a European Works Council or a procedure in Community-scale undertakings and Community-scale groups of undertakings for the purposes of informing and consulting employees'. The EEA comprising the 15 EU Member States and the three remaining Contracting Parties of the EEA (Norway, Liechtenstein and Iceland).

5.50
Any employee who is dismissed (or selected for redundancy) for being instrumental in promoting, supporting or enforcing the establishment of an EWC, or for standing as a candidate for election as a member of a 'special negotiating body'(SNB), or for voting in a ballot for the election of employees to an SNB, or for performing (or proposing to perform) his (or her) functions as an elected or appointed member of an SNB or EWC, or as an information and consultation representative, etc., will be treated in law as having been unfairly dismissed – regardless of his or her age or length of service at the material time. (*Source*: Regulations 28 & 29 of the TICE Regulations 1999 and s.105(7D), Employment Rights Act 1996).

Part-time workers

5.51
Since 7 April 2000, part-time workers have had the legal right not to be treated less favourably than comparable full-time workers working in the same establishment and engaged under the same types of contracts as those part-time workers. The relevant legislation is to be found in the Part-time Workers (Prevention of Less Favourable Treatment) Regulations 2000 (SI 2000/1551). Any part-time worker (employee or otherwise) who is dismissed or selected for redundancy for exercising his or her rights under those Regulations, or for refusing to forego a right conferred by those Regulations, or for questioning or challenging any alleged infringement of those rights (whether before an employment tribunal or otherwise) may complain (or complain yet again) to an employment tribunal, regardless of his or her age or length of service at the material time, and will be awarded substantial compensation if that complaint is upheld (*ibid* Reg. 5 and s.105(7E), Employment Rights Act 1996). For further information on the rights of part-time workers, please turn to Chapter 17.

Fixed-term employees

5.52
Under the Fixed Term Employees (Prevention of Less Favourable Treatment) Regulations 2002, which came into force on 1 October 2002, employees working under fixed-term or task-related contracts (for however long or short a period) must not be treated less favourably (in terms of pay and other

terms and conditions of employment) than comparable permanent employees working at the same establishment as those employees, and must be afforded equal access to opportunities for promotion, transfer and training. Any fixed-term employee who is dismissed or selected for redundancy for asserting his or her rights under the 2002 Regulations, or for questioning or challenging any alleged infringement of those rights, may complain to an employment tribunal (regardless of his or her age or length of service at the material time) and will be awarded substantial compensation if that complaint is upheld. For futher particulars, please turn to Chapter 16.

INTERIM RELIEF PENDING DETERMINATION OF COMPLAINT

5.53
An employee who has presented a complaint to an employment tribunal that he (or she) has been unfairly dismissed (or unfairly selected for redundancy) for one or other of the following reasons, that is to say:

- for being or not being (or for refusing to become or remain) a member of an independent trade union (or for taking part in the activities of an independent trade union) (see para. 5.26);

- in the circumstances described in para. 5.27 above (*Collective bargaining: Recognition*);

- for carrying out (or attempting to carry out) his (or her) functions as a safety representative or representative of employee safety, or as a 'competent person' or other person designated by his employer to carry out safety-related functions (see para. 5.29);

- for carrying out his (or her) functions as a workforce representative elected to represent the interests of fellow workers when negotiating a workforce agreement (or as a candidate for election as such a representative) for the purposes of Schedule 1 to the Working Time Regulations 1998 (see para. 5.39 above);

- for carrying out (or proposing to carry out) his or her functions either as a *trustee of a relevant occupational pension scheme* or as an *employee representative* when collective redundancies or a TUPE transfer are, or is, mooted (see paras 5.40 to 5.42 above;

- for having made a *protected disclosure* within the meaning given to that expression by section 43A of the Employment Rights Act 1996 (see Chapter 20)

may apply for interim relief, that is to say, an order for reinstatement or re-engagement pending a full hearing of the employee's complaint (*Source*: ERA 1996, s.128; TULRA 1992, ss 152 & 161 to 167).

5.54

An application for 'interim relief' must be submitted to the Secretary to the Tribunals within seven days of the *effective date of termination* of the employee's contract of employment (see Chapter 3, paras 3.15 to 3.21). In the case of a dismissal on grounds of trade union membership or activities, the employee's application must be accompanied by a certificate signed by an authorised official of the relevant trade union confirming that there appears to be reasonable grounds for supposing that the employee had indeed been dismissed for one or other (or both) of those reasons. The hearing of an application for interim relief must take place as quickly as possible – but not before the employer has been sent a copy of the employee's application and has been given at least seven days' advance notification of the date, time and place fixed for the hearing. If the application relates to a dismissal on alleged trade union grounds, the employer will also receive a copy of the trade union certificate referred to in the previous paragraph.

5.55

If an employment tribunal, in considering whether to grant 'interim relief', is satisfied that the claim is 'likely' to succeed at a full hearing, it will make a declaration to that effect. What this means in practice is that a tribunal will grant an application for interim relief if (using the non-legal vernacular) they decide that the complaint has 'a pretty good chance of success' (*Taplin v C Shipham Ltd* [1978] ICR 1068, EAT).

5.56

The employer will be invited to reinstate or re-engage the employee on terms which are acceptable to the employee, until such time as the full tribunal hearing takes place. If the employer does not consent or fails to attend the interim hearing, the tribunal will order the continuation of the employee's contract of employment until the proceedings are completed. An employer who refuses to reinstate the employee until the date set for the full tribunal hearing must, nonetheless, continue to pay that employee his (or her) full wages or salary from the date of dismissal until the tribunal hearing *does* take place. The total sum paid by way of wages or salary will not be recoverable even if the employee loses his case at the main hearing. Although there is a duty on the tribunal to ensure a speedy trial, the employer too must take energetic steps to arrange for an early hearing, if only to keep his (or her) losses to a minimum (*Initial Textile Services v Rendell*, 23 July 1991, EAT).

DISMISSAL – FAIR OR UNFAIR?

5.57

At a tribunal hearing on a complaint of unfair dismissal (or unfair selection for redundancy), the onus is on the employer (the respondent) to show:

- the reason (or, if more than one, the principal reason) for dismissing the employee; and

- that the reason fell within one of the permitted reasons for dismissal listed in para. 5.14 above.

In short the employer will need to satisfy the tribunal that the employee had been dismissed because he (or she) was:

- incompetent;

- incapable of work due to illness or injury;

- unqualified;

- guilty of misconduct;

- redundant; or

- illegally employed.

If none of those reasons apply, the employer will need to demonstrate that the employee was dismissed for 'some other substantial reason' of a kind such as to justify the dismissal of a person holding the position which that employee held.

5.58
Once the (respondent) employer has shown what the reason (or principal reason) for the dismissal was, and has demonstrated that it was for a permitted reason, the determination of the question whether the dismissal was fair or unfair (having regard to the reason shown by the employer) depends on whether, in all the circumstances (including the size and administrative resources of the employer's undertaking), the employer had acted reasonably or unreasonably in treating it as a sufficient reason for dismissing the employee, and the answer to that question shall be determined in accordance with equity and the substantial merits of the case (*Source*: ERA 1996, s.98).

Dismissal on grounds of incompetence or lack of capability

5.59
These grounds may be relied upon where the employee's 'skill, aptitude, health or any other physical or mental quality' falls below that which is required for the job. The duties on which the worker is engaged must relate to 'work of a kind which he (or she) was employed... to do'.

This will usually include incompetence where it relates to an inherent fault and not just to laziness or negligence (*Sutton & Gates (Luton) Ltd v Boxall* [1979] ICR 67, EAT).

Dismissal on grounds of misconduct

5.60

An employee who is insubordinate, abusive, lazy, aggressive, violent, dishonest, habitually late for work, disdainful of safety rules, etc, is arguably guilty of misconduct. Unless he (or she) responds quickly to advice, counselling and warnings, dismissal is inevitable. In serious cases, such an employee is guilty of gross misconduct and can be dismissed 'on the spot'. However, in every case, the employer must be able to demonstrate that he had acted reasonably and fairly before taking the decision to dismiss. An employee might have an answer to the complaints and allegations made against him. He might assert that he was the victim of violence (not the aggressor); or that he misunderstood the rules about claiming expenses, or that he did not intend to be rude when confronted by an angry or violent customer; and so on.

5.61

There is at times a thin dividing line between capability and conduct. For instance, an employee may keep on making mistakes despite being warned of the serious consequences. If he (or she) is dismissed, it may be difficult to determine whether he is wilfully in default or is inherently incapable of doing his work properly. If an employee's competence is at issue, the employer will need to satisfy a tribunal that he made every effort (through guidance, counselling and training) to improve the employee's performance in his job.

Dismissal on grounds of redundancy

5.62

Although redundancy is a permitted reason for dismissal, an employer will still need to satisfy the test of 'reasonableness'. If an employee was selected for redundancy for an inadmissible or unlawful reason (see paras 5.20 *et seq*), or contrary to any agreed selection procedure, the dismissal will be held to have been unfair (or automatically unfair).

Illegally employed?

5.63

There will be occasions when it would be unlawful for an employer to continue employing a particular employee. Such a situation would arise if a HGV driver is banned from driving for a year or if a foreign national's work permit has expired and there is no prospect of its being renewed, or if an employee is an illegal immigrant. Pregnant women and women 'of reproductive capacity' must not be employed in work which exposes them to lead or to ionising radiation; and so on. In every such case, the employer will nonetheless need to demonstrate that he had done all that he reasonably could to resolve the particular problem before taking the decision to dismiss. In the case of a new or expectant mother, the employer would be expected either to offer 'suitable alternative employment' or to suspend the woman on full pay until such time as it was lawful for her to resume her normal duties (as to which, please turn to Chapter 14, para. 14.117).

5.64

Under the Asylum & Immigration Act 1996 (which came into force on 27 January 1997) an employer is liable to a fine of up to £5,000 if he employs a person subject to immigration control if the person in question has not been granted leave to enter or remain in the UK; if the person's leave to enter or remain is no longer valid and subsisting; or if the leave to enter or remain is subject to a condition precluding him (or her) from taking up employment.

Dismissal for 'some other substantial reason'

5.65

This is a very wide provision. It gives the employer protection where, for instance, he carries out a genuine reorganisation to improve the efficiency and profitability of his business, eg by introducing new working methods or a different pattern of shifts [to accommodate a full order book] or by simply coming to terms with advances in technology. If, when doing so, he has to dismiss one or more employees, they would usually be entitled to a redundancy payment. Lord Denning, MR put it this way: 'It is important that nothing should be done to impair the ability of employers to reorganise their workforce and their terms and conditions of work so as to improve efficiency'. But the terms offered must be reasonable in the circumstances. The issue is not of weighing the advantages to the employer against the disadvantages to the employee, but the interests of each party have to be considered (*Lesney Products Ltd v Nolan & Others* [1977] ICR 235, CA)*Robinson v British Island Airways* [1978] ITR 111, EAT; *Elliott Turbomachinery Ltd v Bates* [1981] ICR 218, EAT).

5.66

There must be real negotiations with the employee, or his representatives, or an attempt made to come to an agreement if the employee is being especially difficult. The position must be fully explained to him. This extends to non-contractual matters and the employer's plans to abolish 'institutionalised' overtime (*Ford v Milthorn Toleman Ltd* [1980] IRLR 30, CA; and *Trebor Bassett Ltd v Saxby & Another*, 3 November 1993, EAT). What has to be examined is the employer's motives. If the changes he has in mind are arbitrary and of little advantage to the business, they will fail the test of 'reasonableness'. But if they are accepted by the union and many employees, then they will probably be held to be reasonable (*Catamaran Cruisers Ltd v Williams & Others* [1994] IRLR 386, EAT).

5.67

An employee who has been hired *specifically* to replace another employee who is absent on maternity leave, or who has been suspended from work on medical or maternity grounds, can lawfully be dismissed when that other employee returns to work – if, but only if, the replacement employee had been informed in writing (before accepting the offer of employment) that his (or her) employment would be terminated as soon as the permanent employee returns to work (see also paras 5.155 & 5.156 below). A dismissal on such grounds will be treated as having been for 'some other substantial reason' and will be held to be fair. However, the outcome might well be different if the replacement employee had been given to understand, rightly or wrongly, that he (or she) would be transferred to another job when the permanent employee returned to work (*Webb v EMO Air Cargo (UK) Ltd (No. 2)* [1995] IRLR 645) (*Source*: ERA 1996, s.106).

5.68

When a trade union, a shop-steward or some other person brings pressure to bear on an employer to dismiss another employee, the employer's yielding to such pressure would not amount to 'some other substantial reason' for dismissing the employee in question. An employer's fear of industrial action is no defence to a complaint of unfair dismissal (*James Ferries & Co. Ltd v Johnstone*, 30 October 1984, EAT) (*Source*: ERA 1996, s.107).

5.69

The fact that a man could not get on with his fellow workers would be relevant in considering whether it was 'fair and equitable' to dismiss. But that position would have to be ignored if the threat of industrial action over the person's presence was the real reason for dismissal (*Yusuf v Aberplace Ltd* [1984] ICR 851, EAT).

5.70

Third party pressure to dismiss can, in certain circumstances, entitle an employer to plead 'some other substantial reason'. In order for the plea to be successful, efforts must have been made to find suitable alternative employment for the employee in question. A local authority had a contractual right to approve security staff provided by a contractor at an airport. Friction developed between one of the contractor's employees and an authority manager. The contractor was instructed to remove the man from the site. As there was no alternative work for the man to do, he was dismissed. The dismissal was held to be fair on the grounds of 'some other substantial reason' (*Dobie v Burns International Security Services (UK) Ltd* [1984] ICR 812, CA).

5.71

The 'some other substantial reason' provision is a sweeping-up provision designed to deal with situations which are not covered by one of the other permitted grounds for dismissal. If a husband and wife run a public house together, with accommodation 'thrown in', and one is dismissed, the sacking of the spouse may be justified on that ground. So too where a fixed-term contract comes to an end with no other work being available for the employee. Or where a new recruit is dismissed for misrepresenting his (or her) qualifications at the employment interview and it is found that he could not perform his job properly.

Actual reason for dismissal

5.72

Under normal circumstances, it devolves on the employer to prove the reason (or, if more than one, the principal reason) for dismissing an employee and that that reason fell within one of the *permitted* reasons for dismissal discussed earlier. The fact that the employer had put the 'wrong label' on the dismissal is irrelevant – so long as the real (or correct) reason for the dismissal was a *permitted* reason.

5.73

An exception to the 'some other substantial reason' rule arises in *constructive dismissal* cases (see Chapter 2, paras 2.36 to 2.40). If an employee in such a situation states that he (or she) is going to resign, and the employer responds by taking steps to recruit and train a replacement, the subsequent dismissal of the employee who had changed his mind would be labelled as having been for 'some other substantial reason'. The fact that the employee had subsequently sought to retract his declared course of action, or that the employer had misinterpreted the employee's true intentions, did not render the dismissal unfair (*Ely v YKK Fasteners (UK) Ltd* [1993] IRLR 500, CA).

The test of 'reasonableness'

5.74

Bristow, J summarised the principle as follows: '[it] is concerned only with the reasonableness of what you do, not how you do it... Very often... the way in which you do something affects, or may affect, the question: Was it reasonable for you to do it at all? If... you dismiss a senior employee of long standing at a moment's notice with no consultation whatever, you are not simply treating him with discourtesy... you are depriving yourself of the opportunity to explore with him the possibility of finding another slot in which to place him; and, on this basis, it would be open... to find your action in dismissing him in the circumstances to be unreasonable' (*Abbotts & Standley v Wessex-Glyndwood Steels Ltd* [1982] IRLR 51, EAT).

5.75

The issue of 'reasonableness' has generated a welter of reported cases. It is important to remember that each case is decided on its own peculiar facts. No two cases are exactly alike. The outcome of one case with near identical facts to another could nonetheless lead to a different outcome (*Rentokil Ltd v Mackin & Another* [1989] IRLR 286, EAT).

5.76

In a consolidated appeals hearing, that of *The Post Office v Foley; HSBC Bank plc* (formerly the Midland Bank) *v Madden* (31 July 2000),the Court of Appeal effectively reinstated the mantra that a tribunal should not substitute its own views for that of an employer and the 'band of reasonable responses' test enunciated by the Court of Appeal in *British Leyland UK Ltd v Smith* [1981] IRLR 91 and reinforced by the EAT (with guidance, subsequently approved by the Court of Appeal) in *British Home Stores v Burchell* [1978] IRLR 379 and *Iceland Frozen Food Ltd v Jones* [1983] ICR 17. In 1999, in *Haddon v Van den Bergh Foods Limited* [1999] IRLR 91, the EAT had characterised the 'band of reasonable responses' test and the mantra as being 'singularly unhelpful. It conjured up, said the EAT, the possibility of extreme views at either end of the band or range, and posed a danger to tribunals testing the fairness of a dismissal by reference to the extreme. We disagree, said the EAT in *Midland Bank plc v Madden* [2000] IRLR 288. Under the doctrine of precedent, it is not for the EAT to outlaw the 'band of reasonable responses' test, thereby presuming to invalidate a decision of the Court of Appeal. Quite so, said the Court of Appeal. The EAT in *Haddon* had been wrong to encourage tribunals to act upon their own subjective views of what they would have done had they been 'in the employer's shoes'. It is sufficient that the employer had a reasonable belief in the employee's guilt and had carried out a reasonable investigation before taking the decision to dismiss. So long as that decision was within the 'band of reasonable responses', it is not open to a tribunal to say: 'We would have done otherwise'.

The employer's duty to consult

5.77

Except in very rare cases, an employee should never dismiss an employee without first consulting that employee about his intention and listening to what the employee has to say. Lord Bridge put it thus: 'An employer having *prima facie* grounds to dismiss... will in the great majority of cases not act reasonably... unless and until he has taken steps, conveniently classified... as 'procedural', which are necessary in the circumstances to justify that course of action. Thus, in the case of incapacity, the employer will not normally act reasonably unless he gives the employee fair warning and an opportunity to mend his ways and show that he can do the job; in the case of misconduct, the employer will normally not act reasonably unless he investigates the complaint of misconduct fully and fairly and hears whatever the employee wishes to say in his defence or in explanation or mitigation; in the case of redundancy, the employer will normally not act reasonably unless he warns and consults any employees affected or their representative, adopts a fair basis on which to select for redundancy and takes such steps as may be reasonable to avoid or minimise redundancy by redeployment within his own organisation'(*Polkey v A E Dayton Services Ltd* [1988] ICR 142, HL).

5.78

An employee was informed in no uncertain terms that he (and any other employee) would be dismissed if he brought drugs onto the employer's premises or reported for work in a drugged or intoxicated state. The employers were also entitled to carry out drug-screening tests. The employee in question provided a sample which proved positive on a fail-safe test. It was held that his summary dismissal without a formal hearing was fair. Prior consultation would have served no useful purpose (*Sutherland v Sonat Offshore (UK) Inc.*, 1 July 1993, EAT). An employer does not have to prove that he had made a conscious decision not to consult; only that, on the facts known to him at the time, a reasonable employer would have concluded that consultation would have been useless (*Duffy v Yeomans & Partners Ltd*, *The Times*, 26 July 1994, CA). An employer's decision to dismiss does not need to have been perverse before an employment tribunal will intervene. Suffice that it is outside the 'band of reasonable responses'. That is to say no reasonable employer could have taken that course (*Cullion v Scottish Midland Co-Operative Society Ltd*, 27 September 1989, EAT).

5.79

In some extreme cases where the facts are basically agreed, the answer is obvious. If an employee is sent to prison for five years for setting fire to his (or her) employer's premises, a dismissal on grounds of misconduct would be patently fair. In any event, the employee's contract would almost certainly be frustrated by the length of the prison sentence (as to which, see Chapter 2, paras 2.28 to 2.35).

5.80

On the other hand, it would probably be unfair to dismiss an employee who has been sent to prison for six weeks for non-payment of his wife's mainte-nance. What would need to be taken into account in such a situation is whether the employer could reasonably hold the man's job open until his release. But, if this was the tenth time in two years that the employee had lost his liberty, there would come a stage when his employer could lawfully say: 'Enough is enough!'

5.81

It is what happens up to the date of dismissal (or an appeal) that has to be considered and not what occurred afterwards. So, if an employer's failure to dismiss an employee with the notice he was entitled to be given under his contract resulted in the employer not offering the employee a job which had become unexpectedly vacant after the employee had actually left, that was irrelevant (*BSC Sports & Social Club v Morgan* [1987] IRLR 391, EAT; and *Treganowan v Robert Knee & Co* Ltd [1975] ITR 121, QB). Likewise, if an employer discovers after making an employee redundant that the employee had been stealing, then if no true redundancy existed, the dismissal would be held to have been unfair. But compensation would be reduced to nil on the basis that the employee would only be entitled to an award that is 'just and equitable' in the circumstances (*W Devis & Son Ltd v Atkins* [1977] ICR 662, HL; and *Trico Folberth Ltd v Devonshire* [1989] IRLR 396, CA).

Express and implied terms in the contract

5.82
In deciding whether a dismissal is fair or unfair, a tribunal may have to look to the employee's contract to find out the contractual position of the employee (see Chapter 8, paras 8.3 to 8.7). For instance, was there an express or implied term in the employee's contract which required him to spend nights away from home? There may be an express clause to that effect. Or such a term may be implied by the very nature of the employee's job. This would be so in the case of a long-distance lorry driver.

In ascertaining whether there is an 'implied term' in a contract, the underlying principle is:

* whether such a term is necessary in order to give the contract 'business efficacy'; that is to say, to make it work in practice; *and*

* whether it would probably have been agreed to by the parties, had they applied their minds to it at the time the employment began, that such a term was not only reasonable but sensible.

(*Jones v Associated Tunnelling Co Ltd* [1981] IRLR 477, EAT; and *Courtaulds Northern Spinning Ltd v Sibson & Another* [1988] ICR 451, CA.)

5.83
If a long-distance lorry driver were to refuse to undertake any long-distance trips which involved spending nights away from home, a dismissal for that reason would probably be fair – so long as there is nothing in the employee's contract to justify the refusal. The test to be applied when an employee has refused to obey a lawful instruction is whether the employer had acted reasonably in the circumstances (*UCATT v Brain* [1981] ICR 542, CA; and *Davies v Jack Troth t/a Richards Transport*, 16 December 1987, EAT).

Mutual trust and confidence

5.84

Some terms are implicit in every contract of employment. There must be mutual trust and confidence (*BBC v Hearn* [1977] IRLR 273, CA). The test is: '[Y]ou have to look at the conduct of the party whose behaviour is being challenged and determine whether it is such that its effect, judged reasonably and sensibly, is to disable the other party from properly carrying out his or her obligations' (per Talbot J in *Post Office v Roberts* [1980] IRLR 347, EAT).

5.85

A female employee complained to her manager that two supervisors had sexually assaulted her. The manager's refusal to act on the complaint undermined not only her own confidence, but that of the other female staff. It was held that the complainant had every right to quit her job and present a complaint to an employment tribunal that she had been constructively dismissed (*Bracebridge Engineering Ltd v Darby* [1990] IRLR 3, EAT).

5.86

A bank sought to exercise its contractual right to transfer a lowly-paid employee from Leeds to Newcastle with just one week's notice and no relocation allowances. With a sick wife and two small children, it was virtually impossible for the employee to comply with his employer's instructions. He resigned in protest, claiming that he had been constructively dismissed and that his dismissal had been unfair. It was held that the employer had been in breach of an overriding implied duty not to behave in a way likely to destroy or seriously damage the relationship of confidence and trust between himself and his employees. There *was* a constructive dismissal and it *was* unfair (*United Bank Ltd v Akhtar* [1989] IRLR 507, EAT).

5.87

On the other hand, where an employer, in the exercise of an unfettered right, transferred an employee to another department and this resulted in a loss of income, it was held that there was no fundamental breach. The employee was not entitled to leave. The 'reasonableness' test could not be imported through the back door (*White v Reflective Roadstuds Ltd* [1991] ICR 733, EAT).

5.88

An employee only gained a very small sum of money from a deliberate fraud. It was held that, whatever the sum, it struck at the fundamental relationship of mutual trust and confidence, entitling the employer to dismiss (*Conlin v United Distillers* [1994] IRLR 169, CS). When a section leader with 20 years' service in a retail store was dismissed for shoplifting in another shop, his dismissal was held to be fair. The trust necessary in the job had been undermined (*Moore v C & A Modes* [1981] IRLR 71, EAT).

5.89
There is a fundamental obligation on an employer not to treat an employee arbitrarily, capriciously and inequitably in matters of pay. To do so would entitle the employee to leave and claim constructive dismissal. This would be on the basis of a breach of the implied term of mutual trust and confidence (*GEC Avionics Ltd v Sparham*, 12 October 1993, EAT).

5.90
An employee must serve his (or her) employer faithfully. If he secretly sets up a competitive business or passes his employer's secrets to another firm, he may be dismissed without notice. Except on procedural grounds it would be most unlikely that any such dismissal would ever be unfair (see Chapter 10).

Breach of disciplinary rules

5.91
Most employers lay down specific rules of conduct and behaviour. Indeed, in organisations employing 20 or more employees (including persons employed by any associated employer) the 'written statement of terms of employment' issued to every employee must include a note specifying any disciplinary rules applicable to the employee or referring the employee to some other document which specifies such rules. Depending on the nature of the employer's business, some of those rules will be held to be more important than others. Drunkenness by an employee in charge of a high-speed cutting machine or when working in a hospital operating theatre would be infinitely more serious than that by a farm labourer hoeing onions in a distant field. If an employer specifies that breach of a particular rule will lead to summary dismissal, he may need to justify the fairness of the rule itself as well as show that it had been reasonable for him (or her) to rely on it (*Ladbroke Racing Ltd v Arnott & Another* [1983] IRLR 154, CS; and *Leonard v Fergus & Haynes Civil Engineering Ltd* [1979] IRLR 235, CS).

Introduction of new rules

5.92
As his business grows and expands, so will an employer introduce new rules and working practices. For example, the acquisition of new machinery will lead to the imposition of more stringent health and safety rules. Some rules may affect or clash with the views of members of staff. Provided those rules are appropriate and within the scope of the contract of employment, an employee who leaves in consequence of them cannot later claim constructive dismissal. An employee, who was a heavy smoker, worked in a hospital theatre. The local Health Board, after extensive consultations with staff and other interested parties, introduced a total smoking ban throughout their

premises. The applicant found it impossible to comply with the ban and resigned. It was held that where a rule is introduced for a legitimate purpose, the fact it bears harshly on a particular employee does not in itself justify an inference that the employer has acted in such a way as to repudiate the employee's contract of employment (*Dryden v Greater Glasgow Health Board* [1992] IRLR 469, EAT).

Procedural defect

5.93

An employer who ignores or fails to follow the grievance or disciplinary procedures set out in his employees' contracts of employment may find that a dismissal in breach of those procedures is castigated as unfair. The way in which procedural breaches can occur is considered in Chapter 3, at paras 3.83 to 3.94 (*Polkey v A E Dayton Services Ltd* [1988] ICR 142, HL). It is of no consequence that, on a balance of probabilities, it would have made no difference to the outcome had the correct procedure been followed or had there been no breach of natural justice. However, if there were facts known to the employer at the time, which justified the dismissal, and the breach was technical, the dismissal is likely to be fair.

Note: Once the 'dispute resolution' provisions in Part 3 and Schedule 2 of the Employment Act 2002 come into force (late 2003/early 2004), all employers (large as well as small) will be duty-bound to follow minimum statutory dismissal and disciplinary procedures (DDPs) before taking a decision to dismiss an employee. At the same time, the 'no difference' rule, reversed by the House of Lords in *Polkey* (qv) is to be largely reinstated. A new section 98A is to be inserted into the Employment Rights Act 1996 obliging the tribunals to disregard failures by employers to take procedural steps outside the framework of the relevant DDP, provided that following such additional procedural actions would have had no effect on the decision to dismiss. Employers who dismiss an employee without meeting their obligations under the relevant DDP will be ordered by the tribunals to pay that employee a minimum of four weeks' pay on top of any basic or compensatory award of compensation for unfair dismissal payable to that employee.

5.94

There can be a subtle difference between a 'procedural' and 'substantive' default. If a redundancy programme is carried out without any consultation ('procedural') but the basis of the selection is flawed ('substantive'), there would be a substantive unfair dismissal and compensation would be at large (*Stell Stockholders (Birmingham) Ltd v Kirkwood*, 10 August 1993, EAT).

5.95

Minor breaches, provided they are not of fundamental importance when considered 'in the round', will not usually turn a fair dismissal into an unfair one. This applies even where there has been a breach of natural justice. In a marginal case it may be safer to start the disciplinary procedures again. This would be especially so where there has been a flaw which could only be cured on an appeal, but that would be dependent on the employee appealing (see Chapter 3, para. 3.94) (*Sartor v P & O European Ferries (Felixstowe) Ltd*, 13 February 1992, CA; *Fuller v Lloyds Bank plc* [1991] IRLR 336, EAT; and *Spink v Express Foods Group Ltd* [1990] IRLR 320, EAT). But where a dismissal is technically unfair, the compensation may be reduced to 'Nil' if the employee would certainly have been dismissed had the proper procedure been followed. If he (or she) might have been dismissed, some compensation should be awarded – the amount being governed by the degree of doubt (*Moore v Sumner Products plc*, 14 June 1988, EAT).

5.96

Where an employer relies on an employee's plea of 'guilty' to a criminal offence to justify a dismissal, he should know the basis upon which the plea was made. Except in rare circumstances, the employee should normally be afforded an opportunity to state his (or her) side of the story. He may have pleaded guilty to avoid publicity or have been badly advised by a lawyer, but still have a cast iron defence to the charge (*McLaren v National Coal Board* [1988] ICR 370, CA). An employee unambiguously admitted that he used a fraudulent parking voucher, and then advanced a variety of explanations for his conduct. It was held that the employer did not need to make an independent investigation to satisfy himself that the employee had forged the document. The dismissal for the forgery was fair (*Rumbelows Ltd v Ellis*, 15 June 1988, EAT).

5.97

The words of Sir Robert Megarry, Vice-Chancellor, should be borne in mind: 'When something is obvious' they may say, 'why force everybody to go through the tiresome waste of time involved in framing charges and giving an opportunity to be heard? The result is obvious from the start'. Those who take this view do not, I think, do themselves justice. As everyone who has anything to do with the law knows, the path of law is strewn with examples of 'open and shut' cases, which somehow were not; of unanswerable charges which, in the event, were completely answered; of inexplicable conduct which was fully explained; of fixed and unalterable determination that, by discussion, suffered a change. Nor are those with any knowledge of human nature who pause to think for a moment likely to underestimate the feelings of resentment of those who find that a decision against him has been made without their being afforded any opportunity to influence the course of events' (*John v Rees & Others* [1969] 2 AER 274, CD).

5.98

This does not always prove to be the case. An employer called in the police when he discovered that a substantial quantity of high grade metal had gone missing from his factory. The police asked him not to disclose their presence while they covertly observed the activities of several employees. After making suitable enquiries, the employer was satisfied that two of his staff had manipulated samples so as to increase their bonuses. He dismissed them without giving them an opportunity to state their cases. The dismissals were held to be fair in view of the need for secrecy. At the tribunal hearing, the employees were unable to give any satisfactory answer to the allegations made against them (*Pritchett & Dyjasek v J McIntyre Ltd* [1987] ICR 359, CA).

5.99
As a general rule of thumb, an employee who has been dismissed should be given an opportunity to appeal against his (or her) dismissal. But the fact that no such opportunity was given does not, of itself, make a dismissal unfair. In a small business, the decision to dismiss may necessarily be taken by the directors. There may not be anyone more senior with whom to lodge an appeal. Even so, where there is no contractual right of appeal, it may be appropriate or even prudent to hold one (*Sanderson v H K Clarkson & Sons Ltd*, 25 January 1988, EAT; and *Whitbread & Co plc v Mills* [1988] ICR 776, EAT).

Gross misconduct

5.100
The term 'gross misconduct' is imported from the common law. It means conduct of sufficient seriousness to warrant dismissal without notice (see Chapter 3, paras 3.22 to 3.26). The term is often used by employers in their disciplinary rules, which usually include examples of conduct regarded as constituting 'gross misconduct'. In *Hamilton v Argyll & Clyde Health Board*, 18 August 1992, EAT, an employee was dismissed for gross misconduct when she failed to follow instructions given to her by a doctor. However, her employer told her that he would be prepared to re-employ her in another area. She refused the offer and complained to an employment tribunal that her employer's offer to re-engage her in another job was inconsistent with his decision to dismiss her for gross misconduct. It was held that although the employee's insubordination *did* amount to gross misconduct, that did not mean that she was unsuitable for any other job.

Dismissal after final warning

5.101
Ordinarily, an employee has no redress when dismissed for committing the same or a similar offence while subject to a final written warning for an earlier offence. It would be inappropriate to review the sequence of events which prompted the employers to issue a final warning unless the final warning itself was manifestly inappropriate. If it had been issued for an oblique

motive, eg to lay the ground work for a dismissal on a minor matter, that sequence of events might be considered. It is of no consequence that the employee had chosen not to appeal against the final warning (*Stein v Associated Dairies Ltd* [1982] IRLR 447, EAT; and *Co-Operative Retail Services Ltd v Lucas*, 15 November 1993, EAT).

Mitigation

5.102
Care should be taken not to confuse 'mitigation' with 'fairness' in a dismissal for dishonesty case. Length of good service, the amount of money or value of goods involved, the loss of pension or other rights, and the circumstances of the appropriation are all relevant. But where the theft destroys the trust that must exist between employee and employer, a dismissal will not be unfair. Although another employer might well have responded differently in the light of any mitigating circumstances, the dismissal does not thereby become unfair (*ECC International Ltd v McKenna & Another*, 14 July 1987, EAT).

'Blanket' dismissals

5.103
Sometimes, an employer will suspect that two or more employees in a group are involved in theft or some other dishonest activity. It might be impossible for him to 'pin down' which of the group is responsible or to establish how many employees are involved. If the matter is serious, and provided the employer has carried out reasonable investigations, his decision to dismiss every employee in the group will not be unfair even if one or more innocent employees are included amongst the dismissals. The suspects must be given the opportunity to state their cases. If any of their number advances an explanation consistent with innocence, he (or she) should not be dismissed. Otherwise, the dismissal is likely to be unfair (*Monie v Coral Racing Ltd* [1981] ICR 109, CA; and *Molloy & Mundell v Kemps Contact Lenses Ltd*, 30 July 1986, EAT).

5.104
Where the reason for dismissal relates to capability (eg stock losses caused by negligence or stupidity), the employer should not carry out a 'blanket' dismissal unless:

- satisfied on solid and sensible grounds that the action, if committed by an individual, would warrant dismissal; and

- a full investigation and proper procedures have been carried out; and he believes on reasonable evidence that more than one person could have been responsible; and

- the act was capable of being done by the applicant as well as by those within the identified group.

If those checks have been carried out, the possible innocence of one of the suspect group would not render that employee's dismissal unfair (*Whitbread & Co plc v Thomas & Others* [1988] ICR 135, EAT; and *Parr v Whitbread plc t/a Threshers Wine Merchants* [1990] ICR 427, EAT).

5.105
An employer may have strong and cogent reasons for believing that one member of a suspect group is incapable of negligence or dishonesty. If he retains that employee, but dismisses his (or her) colleagues, the dismissal of the latter would not necessarily be unfair. The case of each employee has to be considered separately (*Frames Snooker Centre v Boyce* [1992] IRLR 472, EAT).

Employee facing criminal charges

5.106
Difficulties often arise in cases where the trial of an employee, charged with a criminal offence relating to his employment, is unlikely to take place for several months. Interviews with witnesses might be construed as interference with the course of natural justice thereby limiting an employer's powers of investigation. It may be possible to suspend an employee pending the outcome of his trial. But the suspension would have to be on full pay, unless the employee's contract specifies otherwise. If, however, the case against the employee is very strong, and the employer has been able to make a reasonable investigation, the dismissal may be fair. The employee must first be given an opportunity to answer the allegations. If the evidence against the employee is very strong and the matter serious, the dismissal is unlikely to be held unfair. However, the employer will need to satisfy an employment tribunal that he had carried out a reasonable investigation of the circumstances before taking the decision to dismiss. A suspension ought nonetheless be considered. There is a large 'grey' area in this field.

5.107
In determining whether a dismissal is fair, an employment tribunal will not be influenced by the fact that the employee had been prosecuted for an offence connected with his work and had subsequently been acquitted (*Saeed v Greater London Council (ILEA)* [1986] IRLR 23, QBD). It is not the function of an employment tribunal to determine whether the employee was guilty or innocent of the alleged crime, but to consider the behaviour of the employer. In short, had the employer shown that he had acted reasonably in treating the employee's involvement in the alleged offences as a sufficient reason for dismissing him (per Phillips J, *Harris (Ipswich) Ltd v Harrison* [1978] IRLR 382, EAT)

Criminal convictions

5.108

If, on the other hand, an employee has pleaded guilty in court to theft from his (or her) employer, that fact, coupled with conduct known to the employer that is consistent with dishonesty, will be sufficient grounds for dismissal. It does not matter if the employee later protests his innocence, alleging that he pleaded guilty to avoid a possible sentence of imprisonment (*British Gas plc v McCarrick* [1991] IRLR 305, CA). If an employee pleaded 'Not Guilty' to the charges laid against him, but was nonetheless convicted, an employer would be entitled to rely on the conviction as legitimate grounds for dismissal – even if the employee later claims that he had been the victim of a miscarriage of justice. But it would be wise for an employer to have supporting evidence to confirm that there was a solid basis upon which the court returned a verdict of 'Guilty'.

5.109

So where money which was in the possession of a prison officer went missing, and no credible explanation was given for its disappearance, a dismissal was held to be fair. If the offence is trivial or not relevant to the employment, a dismissal may not be reasonable (*Secretary of State for Scotland v Campbell* [1992] IRLR 263, EAT).

Dishonesty

5.110

Allegations of dishonesty will not necessarily involve the police or criminal prosecution. An employee found stealing from the till may often simply be summarily dismissed. Before taking the decision to dismiss, an employer must investigate the circumstances, listen to what the employee has to say and have *reasonable grounds* for believing that the employee is guilty (*British Home Stores Ltd v Burchell* [1980] ICR 303, EAT).

Incompetent representatives

5.111

If an employee entrusts his (or her) case to a representative, who fails to put the case adequately at a disciplinary hearing, or at the subsequent appeal hearing, a tribunal cannot reverse the decision unless the spokesperson was so incompetent that no reasonable employer would have relied on his assertions (*Al-Mehdaw v Secretary of State for the Home Department* [1990] AC 876, HL). Where the representative is a trade union-nominated official, the employer's ability to intervene may be more limited. In procedural matters, any failures by the representative will usually be deemed to be those of the employee.

Criminal offences outside employment

5.112

Where an employee is convicted of an offence committed outside his (or her) employment but the offence is relevant to the type of work he is employed to do, an employer should generally consider the possibility of an alternative post before dismissing that employee. A groundsman at a girls' school pleaded guilty to indecently assaulting his daughter and admitted to committing similar offences with two elder daughters. It was held that it was incumbent on the school to see whether there was work where there would be little risk to other girls (*P v Nottingham County Council* [1992] ICR 706, CA). When a branch manager of a firm of estate agents was charged with gross indecency, he made it known that he intended to plead guilty to the offence in court. He was dismissed. It was held that the tribunal could not intervene. The employer was entitled to consider the effect on his work colleagues and the adverse publicity. There was no alternative work for him to do (*Royal Life Estates (South) Ltd t/a Fox & Sons v Campbell*, 1 October 1993, EAT).

Selection for redundancy

5.113

One of the greatest sources of dispute lies in cases involving selection for redundancy, especially where there is no laid-down selection procedure. If someone has to be made redundant, the employer has the invidious task of deciding who that person should be. How to proceed? The most important thing to do is to reflect, weigh up the options and give everyone, so far as is possible (through their elected representatives, if there are any), an opportunity to air their views. If an employee is dismissed without any form of consultation, a tribunal will very likely find that the dismissal was unfair – even though it is shown that consultation would very likely have made no difference to the outcome. It has to be proved, based on facts known to the employer at the time, that any consultation would have been 'utterly useless' or 'futile' (*Polkey v A E Dayton Services Ltd* [1988] ICR 142, HL); but see para. 5.93 above (and its accompanying *Note*).

5.114

An instance of this defence being successful occurred when employers restructured their organisation in secrecy and within strict time limits as a result of pressure from those who provided their sole source of revenue. The job performed by a director was lost and he was selected for redundancy without any consultation. The evidence established that there was no alternative position available for him. It was held that, in the exceptional circumstances, the dismissal was fair (*Leese v Food From Britain*, 4 March 1991, EAT).

5.115

An employer running a small business is not absolved from the duty to consult. But the consultation process may be very informal or indeed perfunctory. The important thing is that the would-be redundant employee is given an opportunity to put forward his views (*De Grasse v Stockwell Tools Ltd* [1992] IRLR 269, EAT). Where an employer is contemplating making an employee redundant, he is duty-bound to provide a trade union, which he recognises for bargaining purposes, with written reasons for making the person redundant. But breach of this requirement does not, of itself, make a dismissal unfair.

5.116

The best starting-off point is to ask for voluntary redundancies. But, if this does not produce sufficient candidates, there must be compliance with any agreed formula for redundancy selection. If there is no formula, the employer must decide who is to be made redundant, weighing up the 'pros' and 'cons' in each case. Many employees will find reasons why someone else should have been selected for redundancy in preference to themselves. The criterion applied by the tribunals is whether the person selected is one of a number of candidates for redundancy whom the employer, in his discretion, might reasonably have selected. Whether the tribunal would have selected someone else is immaterial. When an employer uses vague and subjective selection criteria, such as an employee's attitude to his (or her) work, consultation is most important. The fact that, on an earlier occasion, the workforce expressed the view that they would prefer not to be consulted about proposed redundancies, does not absolve the employer from having to consult employees who have not waived their right to put forward their own views (*Graham v ABF Ltd* [1986] IRLR 90, EAT).

5.117

Every employee who is a candidate for redundancy should normally be spoken to individually, and be given an opportunity to suggest ways in which he (or she) might be kept in employment. This 'rule of thumb' applies even though the employer is adhering to a formula agreed with the employee's trade union – unless the numbers involved are so large that it would be impractical to carry out individual consultations (*Walls Meat Co Ltd v Selby* [1989] ICR 601, CA; and *Duncan v Marconi Command & Control Systems Ltd (Case B]*, 14 October 1988, EAT).

5.118

Where a redundancy selection is made on the basis of a poor attendance record, an employer does not have to consider whether an employee's absences were due to an industrial injury sustained at work or mere malingering. Often it would not be practical to try to find out the reason. But the criteria for selection must be fair (*Dooley v Leyland Vehicles Ltd*, 17 June 1986, CS).

5.119

Difficulties are likely to arise when questions of sex, marital status, race or disability are taken into consideration. For instance, a married Asian girl is selected for redundancy ahead of a single white widower with three children and a heavy mortgage. If the decision is taken on personal circumstances, or for humanitarian reasons, and not based on competence, experience, reliability and so forth, the dismissal is not only likely to be unfair but will also be in breach of the Sex Discrimination and Race Relations Acts 1975 & 1976, or of the Disability Discrimination Act 1995 (see Chapters 11, 12 & 13, respectively).

Suitable alternative employment

5.120

There is always a need to try to re-locate an otherwise redundant worker. Failure to do so could result in a finding of unfair dismissal. It must be shown that the point had been considered at the time and there was no suitable alternative work available. The employer should not assume that the employee would not accept work at a more junior level. The employee might be prepared to 'lower his (or her) sights'. This duty usually extends to making enquiries of any 'associated employer' (see Chapter 3, paras 3.95 to 3.97), but a failure to do so may not be fatal (*Thomas & Betts Manufacturing Ltd v Harding* [1980] IRLR 255, CA; *MDH Ltd v Sussex* [1986] IRLR 123, EAT; and *Dick v Boots The Chemist Ltd*, 25 June 1991, EAT).

Breach of the duty of fidelity

5.121

There is an implied duty of fidelity in every contract of employment. That is to say, an employee may not act in a way which is contrary to his employer's legitimate interests (see Chapter 8, paras 8.16 to 8.19). An intention to set up in competition in the future will not in itself amount to a breach, unless the person has abused his position as an employee, eg by making lists of his employer's customers (*Golden Cross Hire Co Ltd v Lovell* [1979] IRLR 267, EAT; and *Laughton & Hawley v Bapp Industrial Supplies Ltd* [1986] ICR 634, EAT). Where there is a serious breach of the duty of fidelity, a dismissal will usually be fair always provided that there has been a full investigation of the circumstances and proper procedures have been followed. An employee who leaks important confidential information and trade secrets to a third party will be without any redress for his dismissal (*Berts Brewery Co Ltd & Others v Hogan* [1945] 2 AER 570, HC). A managing director colluded with a senior manager in attempting to persuade a colleague to join him in another company with a view to depriving their employers of their best client. He was dismissed. It was held to be fair (*Marshall v Industrial Systems & Control Ltd* [1992] IRLR 294, EAT).

Divided loyalties

5.122
Sometimes a husband and wife are employed in the same business and one leaves to join a competitor. If the one who remains has access to confidential information which would damage the employer's business interests if disclosed to a rival, and provided the risk of disclosure is unacceptably high, it would be not unfair to dismiss (*Dyer v Inverclyde Ltd*, 25 November 1987, EAT). If, on the other hand, a woman is dismissed because she has married a man employed by a rival firm – on the grounds that she might relay confidential information to her husband – her employer's reasons were held to be no defence to a claim of sex discrimination (see Chapter 11). The dismissal was based on the assumption that a man was more likely to be the primary supporter of his wife and children (*Coleman v Skyrail Oceanic Ltd t/a Goodman Tours* [1981] ICR 864, CA).

Internal appeals

5.123
It is not intended that a disciplinary panel within an employing organisation should follow the procedures of ordinary courts of law. All that is required is that the members of the panel should act fairly, and should give the appearance of doing so. This is particularly important when considering the final stages of an appeal process, where there is often the risk of error through a breach of natural justice (see paras 5.134 to 5.138 below). For an appeal to be able to cure procedural defects, the appellate process must 'be able to stand on its merits as conferring upon the employee all the rights which the contract of employment is intended to protect, notably proper notice of the complaint, and a full opportunity of stating the employee's case' (*Byrne v BOC Ltd* [1992] IRLR 505, EAT).

5.124
A distribution manager dismissed an employee following an admission of forgery, for which various explanations were given. But as the distribution manager was present at the appeal hearing conducted by a line manager and remained behind while the line manager deliberated, the dismissal was held to have been unfair. His presence gave the impression of bias and undue influence (*Rumbelows Ltd v Ellis*, 15 June 1988, EAT).

5.125
Often, a procedural defect in the disciplinary process will result in a dismissal being ruled unfair. But, if an employee appeals against the dismissal and there is a proper investigation of the facts and a full hearing at which the employee is allowed to state his case, that appeal can 'cure' the procedural

defect. It can turn what might otherwise have been an unfair dismissal into a fair one. A mere review of the original decision to dismiss would not be sufficient (*Whitbread & Co plc v Mills* [1988] ICR 766, EAT; and *Clark v Civil Aviation Authority* [1991] IRLR 412, EAT).

5.126

An employer's disciplinary procedure contained detailed provisions for an appeal at each stage in the procedure. Breach of one of those stages turned an otherwise fair dismissal into one which was unfair. The employee had been denied his contractual rights. However, compensation was dealt with on the merits of the case (*Stoker v Lancashire County Council* [1992] IRLR 75, CA).

Illness and injury as grounds for dismissal

5.127

Dismissals for sickness are fraught with difficulties. Although employers cannot guarantee the continued good health of their employees, they have a common law and statutory duty to do all that they reasonably can to protect and preserve the health and safety at work of their employees, eg by taking steps to ensure that employees do not come into contact with injurious substances.

5.128

The dismissal of a genuinely sick or injured employee is generally characterised as a 'capability' dismissal. Where it is for malingering or similar reasons (such as abuse of an employer's sick pay scheme), it is a 'conduct' dismissal. In rare circumstances, the dismissal can be for 'some other substantial reason', eg where the employee occupies a key position and is persistently absent for a series of unrelated illnesses (*Wharfedale Loudspeakers Ltd v Poynton*, 18 May 1993, EAT).

5.129

The distinction between lack of capability and conduct is narrow and blurred. But it may affect the procedures to be used. In the latter case, the ordinary disciplinary procedure should be followed. This also applies where the dismissal is based on a mixture of both grounds. But before dismissing an employee with a poor attendance record occasioned by genuine ill-health, the employer should:

- consult the employee about his concerns, and the effect such absences are having on the employee's work and – although not essential – should forewarn him (or her) of the likely consequences if those absences continue (*A Links & Co Ltd v Rose* [1991] IRLR 353, CS);

- review the employee's situation, obtaining independent medical advice where necessary; and

- discuss the position with the employee, especially concerning any medical opinion obtained, to see whether there is any chance of improvement (*Scott v Secretary of State for Scotland*, 14 July 1988, EAT).

If the employer's need for the work to be done outweighs the employee's need to have still more time off work to recover, the dismissal will generally be held to be fair.

5.130
In exceptional circumstances there may be no need to consult. An employer, who urgently needed to replace a long-term sick employee, learnt from the woman's doctor that her condition was more serious than she appeared to realise. If the employer visited her and told her the truth about her condition, it might cause great harm. Her dismissal was held to have been fair (*Eclipse Blinds Ltd v Wright* [1992] IRLR 133, CS).

5.131
An employer suspended an employee who had returned to work late, after the midday break, heavily intoxicated. The employer learnt that the employee had an underlying medical problem and made some perfunctory enquiries of the employee's doctor. He dismissed him for gross misconduct. The dismissal was held to have been unfair. It was unreasonable of the employer to have reached a conclusion without obtaining proper medical reports (*Forth Ports Authority v Lorimer*, 8 March 1991, EAT).

5.132
If an employee is frequently absent from work for a series of minor and unrelated illnesses – some supported by medical certificates – his (or her) employer does not generally need an independent medical opinion before taking the decision to dismiss. But he must warn the employee of the likely consequences should those absences persist (*International Sports Co Ltd v Thomson* [1980] IRLR 340, EAT). Under normal circumstances, an employer should not dismiss a sick employee without first seeking up-to-date medical advice. The employee should also be given an opportunity to discuss his situation with his employer. If, despite everything, there is little prospect of an improvement in the employee's health, the employer should consider his obligations under the Disability Discrimination Act 1995 (is the employee covered?) before taking the decision to dismiss. The employer should also consider the possibility (or practicability) of transferring the employee to less onerous duties within the organisation.

5.133
Employers should remember that they may not approach an employee's doctor without first obtaining the employee's written consent. The employee must also be informed of his (or her) legal rights under the Access to Medical

Reports Act 1988. The employee's consent is not required if he (or she) is to be examined by a company doctor or other specialist nominated by his employer.

Natural justice

5.134
In nearly every case, there are two sides to a story. Except in the most hopeless of cases, the employee should be allowed to state his (or her) case before any decision is taken to dismiss (*Clarke v Trimoco Group Ltd & Another* [1993] ICR 237, EAT). Further, an employer must carry out a reasonable investigation to try to find out the truth before he reaches his final decision. If he was misled over the position because the employee failed to inform him of an important fact, that would not be fatal. The 'reasonableness' test will continue to apply from the moment the employee is notified of his dismissal until the time he actually leaves (*Morton v City of Glasgow District Council*, 20 March 1989, EAT; and *Stacey v Babcock Power Ltd* [1986] ICR 221, EAT).

5.135
If an employee has been summarily dismissed (that is to say, 'on the spot'), the decision to dismiss will be adjudged on the facts known to the employer at that time, unless further information is presented on appeal (*Monie v Coral Racing Ltd* [1981] ICR 109, CA).

5.136
If a decision to dismiss was patently correct on the information available when the employee was dismissed, but fresh evidence produced on appeal suggested that the decision to dismiss was wrong, the employer would be liable because 'the right of appeal... is a necessary element in the overall process of terminating the employment' (per Lord Bridge in *West Midlands Co-operative Society v Tipton* [1986] ICR 192, HL).

5.137
The same principle applies where an employee has been denied his (or her) contractual right to appeal or if the agreed procedure for hearing appeals has not been adhered to (*National Coal Board v Nash*, *The Times*, 7 May 1986, EAT). The fact that the worker is appealing against one or more previous warnings, on which the employer partly relies in deciding to dismiss for a subsequent offence, does not make a dismissal unfair. What is relevant is that the employee had been warned and was under that warning when he (or she) committed the subsequent offence. The fact that his appeal had not yet been heard would also have to be taken into consideration. If the appeal was due to be heard shortly after the disciplinary hearing, the latter should be delayed (*Tower Hamlets Health Authority v Anthony* [1989] IRLR 394, CA). In the case of a dismissal for redundancy, there is an exception to the rule that there should

normally be a right of appeal. The absence of an appeals procedure in such a situation does not make the dismissal unfair (*Robinson & Others v Ulster Carpet Mills Ltd* [1991] IRLR 348, CA, Northern Ireland). If an employer decides to switch to outside contractors for economic or cost reasons, he does not have to justify those grounds or even show that they were beneficial (*Hodgkins v CJB Developments Ltd*, 30 July 1984, EAT).

5.138
A person was dismissed for a valid reason but the dismissal was held to be unfair because of a breach of procedure. The compensation was reduced to 'Nil' for contributory fault. It was the employee who had caused the dismissal. An employer's irregularities, although unfortunate, did not bring about the dismissal (*Smith v Lodge Bros (Funerals) Ltd*, 19 October 1989, EAT).

Parity of treatment and penalties

5.139
There is an implied term in every contract of employment that an employer will *not* treat his employees arbitrarily, capriciously or inequitably. Failing to give an employee an annual pay rise to which she had become accustomed and which was given to other staff, did not amount to a fundamental breach of contract. It mattered not that the employer had behaved heartlessly: he had dealt with her case on its merits (*Murco Petroleum Ltd v Forge* [1987] ICR 282, EAT).

5.140
In deciding the appropriate remedy for misconduct, the punishment awarded to other employees for similar offences in the same circumstances is a relevant factor. It is always necessary to consider each case separately. If there are important distinguishing features, then failure to take them into account could be fatal (*Post Office v Fennel* [1981] IRLR 221, CA; and *Cowton v British Railways Board*, 28 November 1989, EAT). A disparity in treatment may be justified on the grounds that one person was young and led astray by a more senior employee, or one person had received several warnings whereas another had not. Where there had been a considerable increase in some particular type of trouble and employees had been warned to expect more severe punishment, then only those cases that occurred after that caution should be compared (*Whitbread & Co plc v Allen & Bishop*, 17 January 1989, EAT; and *Procter v British Gypsum Ltd* [1991] IRLR 7, EAT).

5.141
But, after making reasonable enquiries, an employer is entitled to come to a decision based on facts known to him at the time. This includes any findings and conclusions made by an appeal panel. If the dismissal was within the band

of reasonable responses, it would not be unfair (*Securicor Ltd v Smith* [1989] IRLR 356, CA; and *Heald & Others v National Coal Board*, 27 January 1988, CA).

The duty of the tribunal

5.142

A tribunal does not apply a critical, or take a meticulous, approach to decisions taken by employers (*Iredale v Huddersfield Health Authority*, 20 April 1993, EAT). Nor does it apply its own views on what course it would have taken. It generally hears the evidence that was previously before the employer and asks itself: 'Have the employers made adequate enquiries into the incident and was there credible evidence on which they might reasonably have come to the view that they took? Was it within the band of reasonable responses for the employee to have been dismissed?' (*Scottish Midland Co-operative Society Ltd v Cullion* [1991] IRLR 261, Ct S). The validity of the 'band of reasonable responses' test, enunciated by the Court of Appeal in *British Leyland UK Ltd v Smith* [1981] IRLR 91, and since reinstated by the Court of Appeal in *HSBC Bank plc v Madden* (see para. 5.76 above) was called into question by the EAT in *Haddon v Van den Burgh Foods Limited* [1999] IRLR 672 (see next paragraph), giving renewed credence to the decision of the Court of Appeal in *Gilham & Others v Kent County Council (No. 2)* [1985] IRLR 18. There, the Court emphasised that the question as to whether a dismissal was fair was a pure question of fact for the industrial tribunal. 'The wording of section 98(4)', said Griffiths LJ, 'is straightforward and easy to understand, and I do not myself think that it helps to try and analyse it further, save only this, that a tribunal in applying the section must not ask themselves what they would have done, but must ask themselves how a reasonable employer would have acted'.

5.143

In *Haddon (qv)* the retiring President of the EAT, Mr Justice Morison, characterised the mantra: 'the tribunal must not substitute their own decision for that of the employer' as simply another way of saying that the tribunal must apply the reasonableness test by going somewhat further than simply asking what they themselves would have done. 'It is likely, however, that what the tribunal would themselves have done will often coincide with their judgment as to what a reasonable employer would have done'. And again, 'providing [the tribunal] apply the test of reasonableness, it is their duty both to determine their own judgment and to substitute it where appropriate'. That is a point of view, said the EAT in *Midland Bank plc v Madden* [2000] IRLR 288. But it is not for the EAT to outlaw the 'band of reasonable responses' test, thereby presuming to invalidate a decision of the Court of Appeal. While the members of an employment tribunal cannot help but apply their own judgements, it is not open to them to substitute their own views for those of the reasonable employer.

5.144

A tribunal must not substitute its own views on the credibility of witnesses for those of the employer. At a disciplinary hearing, the employer preferred the story given by one employee in preference to that advanced by another. The tribunal, having heard the witnesses, took the opposite view. The Court of Appeal held that the tribunal's views were irrelevant unless no reasonable employer could have taken the same view as the employer (*Linfood Cash & Carry Ltd v Thomson* [1989] ICR 518, EAT; and *Morgan v Electrolux Ltd* [1991] ICR 369, CA).

5.145

Although a tribunal will make a finding as to the *actual* reason for a dismissal, it is important that it should identify the precise basis upon which the decision was made, eg drunkenness in a hospital operating theatre. The 'reasonableness' test has to be applied to that ground (if within one of the seven 'permitted' reasons for dismissal) (see para. 5.14 above) (*British Railway Board v Jackson* [1984] IRLR 235, CA). A tribunal does not apply the criteria of what they would have done in all the circumstances (*Moon & Others v Homeworthy Furniture (Northern) Ltd* [1977] ICR 117, EAT). A tribunal cannot tell an employer how to run his business and it is not its function to take into account policy decisions even if they had brought about a redundancy situation. Lord McDonald put it in this way: 'It may be, as the tribunal suggests, that the [employer] entered into the contract unreasonably, if not recklessly. Many employees have to be dismissed as a result of incompetent business management, but that does not make the dismissals unfair' (*Meikle v McPhail (Charleston Arms)* [1983] IRLR 351, EAT).

CONTRIBUTORY FAULT

5.146

The Acts provide that each of the basic and compensatory awards of compensation for unfair dismissal (see later) may be reduced by such amount as is 'just and equitable' if, in the opinion of the tribunal, the employee contributed to or was wholly or partly to blame for his (or her) dismissal.

The basic and special awards of compensation may also be cut if the evidence shows that the employee had unreasonably refused an offer by his (or her) employer which (if accepted) would have had the effect of reinstating him in his employment in all respects as if he had not been dismissed (*Courtaulds Northern Spinning Ltd v Moosa* [1984] ICR 218, EAT; *Nelson v British Broadcasting Corporation (No. 2)* [1980] ICR 110, CA; and *TNT Express (UK) Ltd v Rigby & Others* [1994] ICR 1, EAT).

5.147

In assessing the amount of the reduction when an employee was dismissed while on strike, it is necessary to consider (a) the reason for the dismissal,

(b) whether any conduct of the employee was blameworthy and (c) whether that conduct contributed to his (or her) dismissal. The merits of the strike or other industrial action on the part of a trade union considered in isolation has no bearing on the tribunal's decision (*Crossville Wales Ltd v Tracey & Another*, 14 March 1994, EAT). If a striking worker had incited others to take unconstitutional action, that might be one reason for reducing the award (*Gosling v Ford Motor Co Ltd*, 29 June 1992, EAT).

5.148

If a worker is habitually late for work, and his (or her) manager 'sees red' one day and sacks him without warning, the dismissal would probably be unfair. The employee might be two-thirds to blame for his dismissal; in which event, he would recover only one-third of the total compensation awarded. In some circumstances, a tribunal will find that an employee was 100 per cent to blame for his dismissal, and the employee will recover nothing (*Sulemanji v Toughened Glass Ltd* [1979] ICR 499, EAT).

5.149

An employee's failure to make use of his (or her) employer's grievance or disciplinary procedures (including his right of appeal) does not amount to contributory fault; but it could be characterised as a breach of his duty to mitigate his loss, which would have the same effect (*W Muir Ltd v Lamb* [1985] IRLR 95, EAT). In appropriate circumstances, the performance of an employee caused by a lack of competence or his mental approach can be taken into account in determining contributory fault. A reduction in compensation would be warranted, for instance, if an employee is lazy or makes no attempt to improve (*Finnie v Top Hat Frozen Food* [1985] ICR 433, EAT).

Note: Under section 127A of the 1996 Act, an employment tribunal is empowered to reduce the amount of the compensatory award for unfair dismissal (see para. 5.170 below) by the equivalent of up to two weeks' pay – if the evidence shows that the employee had failed to exercise his (or her) contractual right to appeal against his dismissal. If, on the other hand, it is clear that the employer had denied the employee his right of appeal, the amount of the compensatory award would be *increased* by up to two weeks' pay.

5.150

If a person is dismissed for one reason that turns out to be misconceived, but there were valid other grounds for doing so, the dismissal would be unfair. The compensation could be reduced to 'Nil' where this would be just, based on contributory fault relating to those other grounds. Where the employer took the view that it would not be right to dismiss for those other grounds, there could be no reduction in the compensation (*Trico Folberth Ltd v Devonshire* [1989] IRLR 396, CA).

Constructive dismissal cases

5.151
Even in constructive dismissal cases, an employment tribunal may reduce an award where no reason for the dismissal has been advanced. There does not have to be a direct causal link between the dismissal and contributory fault – only whether the action or record of the employee to any extent contributed to the dismissal. Further, there do not have to be exceptional circumstances (*Morrison v Amalgamated Transport & General Workers Union* [1989] IRLR 361, CA; *Holroyd v Gravure Cylinder Ltd* [1984] IRLR 259, EAT; and *Polentarutti v Autocraft Ltd* [1991] ICR 757, EAT).

5.152
In deciding on the degree of fault, the tribunals employ a 'broad brush' approach to the whole employment record, avoiding legalism as much as possible. They consider whether there was any blameworthy, including 'bloody-minded', conduct by the employee that was causative of his (or her) dismissal (*Brown v Rolls Royce* (1971) Ltd [1977] ITR 382, EAT; *Warrilow v Robert Walker Ltd* [1984] IRLR 304, EAT; and *Cullen v Austin Rover Group Ltd*, 24 April 1986, EAT).

'Just and equitable'

5.153
Compensation may also be reduced under the 'just and equitable' provisions where, for example, the employer relies on conduct that was not known to him at the time of dismissal. This could occur where he dismisses an employee (unfairly) for incompetence, but discovers during the notice period that the employee had also been stealing from him (*Tele-Trading Ltd v Jenkins* [1990] IRLR 430, CA; and *Polkey v A E Dayton Services Ltd* [1988] ICR 142, HL).

5.154
If an employer has not followed his own procedural rules, including a failure to give an employee an opportunity to explain his (or her) conduct, and is accordingly adjudged to have dismissed the employee unfairly, the compensation may similarly be reduced in appropriate cases under the 'just and equitable' provisions. This would apply where all the information on misconduct was known to the employer at the time. The compensation can be reduced to 'Nil' or to a nominal amount (*Chaplin v H J Rawlinson Ltd* [1991] ICR 553, EAT). Compensation might also be reduced when a tribunal, in a 'breach of procedure' case, decides the degree of likelihood that the employee might still have been dismissed even if the proper procedure had been followed (*Rao v Civil Aviation Authority* [1994] IRLR 240, CA). However, in *King v Eaton (No. 2)* [1998] IRLR 686, the Court of Session allowed that an employment tribunal

could refuse to allow an employer to advance additional evidence, that an employee would have been dismissed even if fair procedures had been followed, if admitting such evidence would be unrealistic or impracticable, or would place the tribunal in the invidious position of having to speculate on what might or might not have happened.

DISMISSAL OF REPLACEMENT EMPLOYEES

5.155
Section 106 of the Employment Rights Act 1996 allows that employees who have been specifically recruited to replace permanent employees who are absent from work on maternity or adoption leave (or for any other reason connected with pregnancy, childbirth or adoption) may be dismissed with (relative) impunity once those employees have returned to work and taken up their normal duties. Their dismissals will be treated in law as having been 'for a substantial reason of a kind such as to justify the dismissal of an employee holding the position which the employee held'. Provided the employer has acted 'reasonably' in such cases, the dismissals will be characterised as 'fair'.

5.156
That same rule applies to people hired on a purely temporary basis to provide cover for employees who have been suspended from work, either on medical or maternity grounds, in accordance with ss 64 and 66 of the 1996 Act. However, every such temporary employee must be given to understand, in writing, before accepting an offer of employment on such terms, that his (or her) employment *will* be terminated when the person he is replacing returns to work (*ibid* s.106(2) & (3)).

REMEDIES FOR UNFAIR DISMISSAL

5.157
There are two options open to a dismissed employee:

    (a) to seek reinstatement or re-engagement; or

    (b) to claim compensation for unfair dismissal.

(*Source*: ERA 1996, s.113.)

5.158
An employment tribunal's power to order the reinstatement or re-engagement of a dismissed employee is entirely discretionary. Indeed, it is rarely used – if only because the relationship between an employee and his (or her) former

employer may well have become soured, given the circumstances which prompted the dismissal in the first place. Nonetheless, it is a tribunal's first duty to look to the practicability of making an order for reinstatement or re-engagement; and, in doing so, to consider the views of both parties (*Source*: ERA 1996, s.116).

5.159
An order for reinstatement means that the dismissed employee should be returned to his (or her) old job on the same terms as before and with the same seniority etc, whereas re-engagement means being taken back on slightly different terms. An order for re-engagement must specify the identity of the employer, the remuneration, arrears of pay and benefits, rights and privileges (including seniority and pension rights) and the date for compliance. The employer must be allowed a reasonable time to rearrange his affairs (*Stena Houlder Ltd v Keenan*, 13 December 1993, EAT).

5.160
If an employer has established and genuinely believes that the relationship of trust and confidence has been irretrievably lost, that of itself would be enough to give a tribunal pause for thought. What a tribunal cannot do is substitute its own commercial judgement for that of the employer. Nor (generally) can a tribunal make an order which would have the effect of disrupting the employer's workforce, or which would result in another employee being made redundant in order to avoid overstaffing (*Mabirizi v National Hospital for Nervous Diseases* [1990] IRLR 133, EAT; *Port of London Authority v Payne & Others* [1993] ICR 447, CA; and *Cold Drawn Tubes Ltd v Middleton* [1992] ICR 318, EAT).

5.161
There must be strict compliance with the basic terms of an order for reinstatement. Where an employer, who purported to do so, but in fact gave two employees less favourable terms, it was held that that constituted a failure to reinstate in accordance with the law. It resulted in his having to pay the employees compensation that amounted in all to £38,147 (*Artisan Press v Srawley & Parker* [1986] ICR 328, EAT).

5.162
When minded to make an order for reinstatement or re-engagement, a tribunal must not be swayed or influenced by the employer's plea that he had already recruited someone to take the place of the dismissed employee – unless he can demonstrate either:

- that it was not reasonably practicable for the employee's work to have been done by anyone other than a permanent replacement; or

- that a reasonable time had elapsed before the employee indicated his wish to have his (or her) job back, and that he had no option but to take on a permanent replacement (*Source*: ERA 1996, s.116(6)).

An employer who recruited a permanent replacement before a tribunal order for reinstatement was made, can escape liability by proving that he had made genuine efforts to find alternative employment but none was available. There is no duty to dismiss another employee to create a vacancy (*Freeman plc v Flynn* [1984] ICR 874, EAT).

5.163

An order directing an employer to reinstate or re-engage an unfairly dismissed employee will specify any benefit, including loss of earnings, which must be reimbursed to the employee when the employee returns to work. As there is no upper limit on the amount to be reimbursed in such circumstances, it is advantageous for a highly-paid employee to seek such an order, especially so if there has been a long delay between dismissal and the tribunal hearing and he (or she) has been unable to find employment elsewhere (*Source*: ERA 1996, ss 117(2) and 124(3)). In making an award concerning back-pay following an order of re-engagement, the tribunal may take into account any contributory fault, but not a failure to mitigate (*City & Hackney HA v Crisp* [1990] ICR 95, EAT).

5.164

An employer cannot be compelled to comply with an order for reinstatement or re-engagement. But if he refuses to comply, or fails to comply fully with the terms of any such order, the tribunal will order him to pay an *additional* award of compensation over and above any basic or compensatory award of compensation for unfair dismissal.

WHO PAYS THE COMPENSATION?

5.165

As a rule, it is up to the employer to pay the full amount of any award of compensation for unfair dismissal. But, if the proceedings were brought not only against the employer but also against a trade union or other person which/who used the threat of industrial action to pressurise the employer into dismissing the employee, the union or person concerned may (at the request of either the employer or the employee) be joined or sisted as a party to the proceedings. Indeed, that other party might well be ordered to pay the whole or part of any such award of compensation. It should be borne in mind that an order for compensation can only be made against a party who appears or is represented before a tribunal. An employer may claim that he dismissed an employee (the complainant) because of pressure brought to bear by a trade union or some other person, but unless the union or other person had been joined or sisted as a party to the proceedings, the employer will have 'to carry the can' himself (*Source*: TULRA 1992, s.160).

HOW COMPENSATION IS CALCULATED

5.166
There are three heads of compensation for unfair dismissal. These are:

- the basic award;
- the compensatory award;
- the additional award.

Basic award

5.167
The basic award is calculated in very much the same way as the statutory redundancy payment (as to which, see Chapter 4, paras 4.33 to 4.37 – except that service before the age of 18 is *included* in calculations. The award is subject to the same pro-rata reduction as occurs in redundancy payments if the employee was over the age of 64 at the effective date of termination of his (or her) contract of employment. Contributory fault is taken into account except (a) in redundancy cases, and (b) where the employee had unreasonably refused an offer of full reinstatement, which latter is deemed to be a failure to mitigate (as to which, see Chapter 2, paras 2.57 to 2.64) (*Source*: ERA 1996, ss 119 & 122).

From 1 February 2003, the maximum basic award of compensation for unfair dismissal is £7,800.

Minimum basic award in certain circumstances

5.168
But the basic award of compensation will be a minimum £3,500 if the employee in question was dismissed (or selected for redundancy) for an inadmissible reason, that is to say:

- for carrying out (or proposing to carry out) his (or her) duties as a *trade union-appointed safety representative*, or as an elected *representative of employee safety*, or as a member of a safety committee, or as a person designated by the employer to carry out health and safety-related activities; or

- for performing (or proposing to perform) any functions or activities as a *workforce representative* for the purposes of Schedule 1 to the Working

Time Regulations 1998 (SI 1998/1833), or as a candidate for election as such a representative; or

- for performing (or proposing to perform) his (or her) functions as a *trustee of a relevant occupational pension scheme*; or

- for performing (or proposing to perform) any functions or activities connected with his (or her) role as (or as a candidate for election as) an *employee representative*, that is to say, as a person elected to represent the interests of fellow-employees in a situation involving collective redundancies or a transfer under the Transfer of Undertakings (Protection of Employment) Regulations 1981.

But that minimum award of £3,500 (2003/04) may also be reduced if the employee contributed to an extent to his (or her) own dismissal. But not so if the employee was unlawfully selected for redundancy on grounds related to his (or her) trade union membership or activities. In such a case, the reduction can only be made to the difference (if any) between the normal basic award and that £3,500 (*Source*: TULRA 1992, s.156; ERA 1996, s.120).

Basic award of two weeks' pay in certain cases

5.169
A redundant employee held to have been unfairly dismissed for having unreasonably refused an offer of suitable alternative employment (and who does not otherwise qualify for a redundancy payment) will nonetheless receive a basic award of compensation equivalent to two weeks' pay (ERA 1996, ss 121, 138 & 141).

Compensatory award

5.170
The compensatory award for unfair dismissal is such amount as an employment tribunal considers to be 'just and equitable' having regard to the loss sustained by the complainant', subject to a 2003/04 upper limit of £53,500. However, that upper limit may be exceeded to the extent necessary to enable the award fully to reflect the losses (including arrears of pay) sustained by the employee for the period between the date on which his (or her) employment ended and the date on which he was reinstated or re-engaged. If an employee has not been reinstated or re-engaged in compliance with a tribunal order to that effect, the upper limit on the amount of the compensatory award may likewise be exceeded to the extent necessary to enable the aggregate of the compensatory and additional awards fully to reflect those same losses (*Source*: ERA 1996, ss 117(1) & (2) and 124(3)).

Note: There is no upper limit on the amount of compensation (or the amount of the compensatory award) that may be awarded by an employment tribunal when an employee is found to have been unfairly dismissed or unfairly selected for redundancy for having taken action in a health and safety case (either as a designated 'competent person', safety representative, representative of employee safety, member of a safety committee, or as an employee) or if dismissed or unfairly selected for redundancy for having made a 'protected disclosure' (as defined by section 43A of the Employment Rights Act 1996).

5.171

The compensatory award includes:

- The estimated loss of wages (net of tax and other deductions) up to the time the employee secured employment elsewhere; or, if the employee's new job pays less than he (or she) was earning in his previous job, up to the date of the tribunal hearing. As a rule, the employee will not be given credit for income received during the notice period, but any money paid in lieu of notice will be taken into account (*Fentiman v Fluid Engineering Products Ltd* [1991] ICR 570, EAT) (*Source*: ERA 1996, ss 134 & 124).

- The estimated future loss of earnings, based on the employee's age, personal circumstances, qualifications and skills, state of health, likelihood of obtaining work elsewhere within a 'reasonable' time and so on. But the award will not be assessed by reference either to the degree of unfairness of the dismissal itself or to the mental distress occasioned by the dismissal (*Fougere v Phoenix Motor Co Ltd* [1976] IRLR 259, EAT; *Ging v Ellward Lancs Ltd* [1991] ICR 222, EAT; and *Morris v Accro Co Ltd* [1985] ICR 306, EAT; *Addis v Gramophone Co* [1909] AC 488, HL; and *Re BCCI SA* [1994] IRLR 282, ChD).

- The loss of any benefits, including pension rights, and expenses. Pensions can form a big item, raising the total award to well above the maximum. It is extremely complicated and, where necessary, actuarial advice should be sought.

- The loss of statutory rights (of usually about £100 – £200) (*S H Muffett Ltd v Head* [1987] ICR 1, EAT).

- Any expenses reasonably incurred in consequence of the dismissal, eg costs incurred in seeking a new job, but not legal expenses.

All of the above are subject to a pro-rata reduction for contributory fault together with a reduction for any failure on the part of the employee to mitigate his or her loss. This would include a person removing himself from the labour market by taking a training course for 12 months (see Chapter 2, paras 2.57 to 2.64), although if for a short period with little prospect of getting a job during that period, it may not apply (*Holroyd v Gravure Cylinder Ltd* [1984] IRLR 259, EAT).

5.172

The amount of the compensatory award may be reduced or increased by the equivalent of up to two weeks' pay if the employee declined his (or her) employer's invitation to appeal against his dismissal (in accordance with his employer's internal appeal procedures) or if his employer refused to allow such an appeal (*ibid* section 127A).

5.173

If, following an employee's dismissal, the firm for which he (or she) worked closed down, the compensatory award cannot run beyond the date of closure. It is of no consequence that it would have been economically viable for the business to have continued (*James W Cook & Co (Wivenhoe) Ltd v Tipper & Others* [1990] ICR 716, CA).

5.174

If an employee was initially dismissed on the basis of incorrect information, but his (or her) employer subsequently uncovered evidence of misconduct on which the employee could validly have been dismissed, then although the dismissal itself might have been technically unfair, the compensation can be reduced to 'Nil' on the basis of that new information – on the basis of the 'just and equitable' provision (*W Devis Sons Ltd v Atkins* [1977] ICR 662, HL).

5.175

In arriving at the net amount, account will (generally) be taken of money paid in lieu of notice and/or of any *ex-gratia* payments (see Chapter 2, paras 2.54 to 2.56) and of any earnings after the expiry of the notice period (see Chapter 3, paras 3.9 & 3.10) (*TBA Industrial Products Ltd v Locke* [1984] ICR 228, EAT).

Additional award

5.176

If an employer refuses or fails to comply *fully* with an order for reinstatement or re-engagement, the tribunal in question will order him to pay such amount of compensation as it thinks fit, having regard to the loss sustained by the employee in consequence of his (or her) employer's failure to comply fully with the terms of the order.

5.177

But if the employee is not reinstated or re-engaged in compliance with the order, the tribunal will not only order the payment of basic and compensatory awards for unfair dismissal (as described above), but will also order the employer to pay an *additional award* of not less than 26 nor more than 52 weeks' pay – unless the employer satisfies the tribunal that it was not practicable to comply with that order. However, it is no defence for an employer to argue that he (or she) had already engaged a permanent replacement for the dismissed employee, unless he can demonstrate that it was not practicable for him to arrange for the dismissed employee's work to be done without engaging a permanent replacement (*Source*: ERA 1996, s.117).

Note: For these purposes, the current (2003/04) upper limit on the amount of a week's pay is £260.

5.178

In deciding the amount of the additional award, the tribunal has to consider (i) the employer's conduct and (ii) the employee's loss. A deliberate refusal to take an employee back without any justification would warrant a figure at the top of the range. If, on the other hand, there is evidence that the employee would have been away sick for much of the period or was not prepared to consider any offer of alternative employment, it would be appropriate for a tribunal to adopt an amount at the lower end of the scale (*Morganite Electrical Carbon Ltd v Donne* [1987] IRLR 363, EAT).

RECOUPMENT OF SOCIAL SECURITY BENEFITS

5.179

An employer ordered by an employment tribunal to pay an award of compensation for unfair dismissal will be served with a *recoupment notice* by the Department of Social Security if the employee in question had received a jobseeker's allowance or income support pending the hearing of his (or her) complaint. The recoupment notice (which must be served within 21 days of the tribunal's decision) effectively requires the employer to deduct from the award an amount equal to the amount of any jobseeker's allowance or income support received by the employee between the date of his (or her) dismissal and the date on which the tribunal hearing took place (*Source*: Employment Protection (Recoupment of Jobseeker's Allowance & Income Support) Regulations 1996 (SI 1996/2349)).

5.180

In short, an award of compensation for unfair dismissal (or rather the prescribed element of that award) must not be paid to the employee in question until the employer has received a recoupment notice from the DSS. The 'prescribed element' is that portion of the award that relates to loss of income between the date on which the employee was dismissed and the date on which the tribunal reached its decision. When making an award of compensation, a tribunal will (where appropriate) remind the employer of his (or her) obligations under the 1996 Regulations.

If the parties to a dispute agree upon the figure for compensation, the recoupment regulations do not apply – which works to the advantage of the employee. The regulations do not apply to Social Security invalidity benefits, as these are classed as insurance benefits (*Hilton International Hotels (UK) Ltd v Faraji* [1994] ICR 259, EAT).

TIME LIMITS FOR 'PRESENTING' A COMPLAINT

5.181

A complaint of unfair dismissal must be 'presented' to the Secretary to the Tribunals (in practice, to the nearest Regional Office of the Employment Tribunals Service) within three months of the 'effective date of termination' of the employee's contract of employment (see Chapter 3, paras 3.15 to 3.21), or within six months if the employee was dismissed in the circumstances described in paras 5.9 to 5.11 & 5.13 above. An employment tribunal will not consider a complaint presented 'out of time' unless satisfied that it was not reasonably practicable for the complaint to have been presented sooner (*Source*: TULRA 1992, s.239; ERA 1996, ss 111).

Action short of dismissal and victimisation

GENERAL INFORMATION

6.1
Nowadays, employees have the statutory right:

- not to have 'action short of dismissal' taken against them on trade union grounds (eg because they are, or are not, members of a trade union, or because of their involvement in trade union activities);

- not to be discriminated against (or subjected to any detriment) on grounds of sex, marital status, gender reassignment, race or disability;

- not to be victimised, harassed or subjected to any detriment for exercising (or proposing to exercise) certain of their statutory rights in employment.

These provisions are to be found, respectively, in:

- the Sex Discrimination Act 1975 (s.4);

- the Race Relations Act 1976 (s.2);

- the Trade Union & Labour Relations (Consolidation) Act 1992 (s.146);

- the Disability Discrimination Act 1995 (s.55);

- the Employment Rights Act 1996 (ss 44 to 47);

- the National Minimum Wage Act 1998 (s.23);

- the Tax Credits Act 2002 (s.27 & Schedule 1);

- the Working Time Regulations 1999 (see Chapter 18);

- the Part-time Workers (Prevention of Less Favourable Treatment) Regulations 2000 (Reg. 7) (See Chapter 17); and

- the Fixed-term Employees (Prevention of Less Favourable Treatment) Regulations 2002 (Reg. 6) (see Chapter 16).

Employees (and, in some instances, workers who are not employees) have the legal right not to be subjected to any detriment, by any act or deliberate failure to act, by their employers, for exercising or presuming to exercise their statutory rights under the legislation listed above, or for questioning or challenging any alleged infringement of those rights. Employees and other workers who have been victimised, disiplined or subjected to any other detriment for asserting their statutory rights may complain to the employment tribunals (without having to resign in order to do so) and will be awarded appropriate compensation if their complaints are upheld.

An employee who is dismissed (or selected for redundancy) for bringing proceedings against his (or her) employer to enforce a relevant statutory right, or for simply alleging that such a right has been infringed, may complain to a tribunal regardless of his age or length of service at the material time. If such a complaint is upheld, the employer is liable to pay a substantial amount of compensation (as to which, see Chapter 5, paras 5.157 to 5.178)(*Source*: ERA 1996, ss 104 & 105).

Trade Union & Labour Relations (Consolidation) Act 1992

6.2
An employee has the legal right not to have 'action short of dismissal' taken against him (or her) as an individual by an employer for the purpose of:

* preventing or deterring him from, or penalising him for, becoming a member of an independent trade union or taking part in its activities at 'an appropriate time'; or

* compelling him to be or become a member of any trade union, or of a particular trade union, or of a number of particular trade unions.

Nor may an employee be penalised for refusing either to have money deducted from his (or her) pay or to make a payment to charity (or whatever) as an alternative to paying trade union dues (*Source*: TULRA 1992 ss 146 & 151).

Note: The expression 'at an appropriate time' means a time, within the employee's normal working hours, at which, in accordance with arrangements previously agreed with, or consent given by his (or her) employer, it is permissible for him to take part in the activities of a trade union.

Complaint to an employment tribunal

6.3
An employee may complain to an employment tribunal that he (or she) has been subjected to 'action short of dismissal' contrary to section 146 of the 1992 Act. The complaint must be presented within three months of the date on which the action complained of relates; or, if that action was part of a series of similar actions, within three month of the last of those actions. A complaint presented 'out of time' will not normally be heard unless the

tribunal is satisfied that it was not reasonably practicable for it to have been presented sooner.

6.4

If the complaint is upheld, the tribunal will make a declaration to that effect and will order the employer to pay compensation to the employee of such amount as the tribunal considers 'just and equitable' – having regard to the infringement complained of and to any loss sustained by the employee (loss of benefit, expenses reasonably incurred, etc) as a result of the employer's unlawful actions. A trade union or other person which pressurised the employer into acting in the way he did may be joined or sisted to the tribunal proceedings and may be ordered to pay the whole or part of any award of compensation payable to the employee. There may be a reduction in the amount of compensation awarded if the evidence shows that the employee caused or contributed to a greater or lesser extent to his (or her) employer's unlawful conduct (*Source*: TULRA 1992, ss 147 to 150).

What is 'action short of dismissal'?

6.5

'Action short of dismissal' (in the context of an employee's statutory right to be, or not to be, a member of a trade union) means any 'penalty' imposed by an employer (often characterised by the not-so-subtle bullying tactics of managers, supervisors, foremen, shop stewards and the like) which falls short of dismissal but is designed to force an employee either to quit his (or her) job (which resignation might well amount to a 'constructive dismissal) or to resign from or join a particular trade union. Using spurious reasons to deny a person promotion or opportunities for training, withholding an expected pay rise, submitting dishonest or ambiguous reports about the employee's capabilities, refusing to allow overtime working, over-loading the employee with work and threatening disciplinary action if he (or she) is unable to meet impossibly-high targets, or simply sending him 'to Coventry' – all are examples of the tactics sometimes employed by unscrupulous employers to 'persuade' a reluctant employee to do, or not to do, something that he (or she) has every legal right not to do or to do. It should be pointed out that if an employer's actions are in any way attributable to pressure tactics (such as the threat of industrial action) brought to bear by a trade union or other person (eg a shop steward), the latter may be joined (or sisted) as a party to proceedings before an employment tribunal; and may, in the event, be ordered to pay the whole or part of any award of compensation payable to the employee.

6.6

It is the object that the employer desires or seeks to achieve that has to be considered. The fact that his actions offended against the 1992 Act is irrelevant. An employee, who performed full-time union duties, had been frustrated in his attempts to gain promotion. However, he could not show that his managerial abilities were adequate. It was held that although the effect of the requirement was to prevent advancement, there was never any intention to hinder his union activities. His claim failed (*Gallagher v Department of Transport* [1994] IRLR 231, CA).

6.7

The statutory provisions also cover job applicants who are refused employment on the grounds of their trade union membership or activities. In one case, a man was denied employment because he was considered to be a political activist. The employer was concerned that the man might prove to be a disruptive influence because of his alleged predilection for trade union activities. The Court of Appeal held that a job applicant should not be turned away simply because of his reputation (*Fitzpatrick v British Railways Board* [1982] ICR 221, CA) (*Source*: TULRA 1992, s.137).

6.8

Where a tribunal finds that the employer had two or more purposes, one of which was to further a change in the relationship with all or any class of his employees, and another one fell within para. 6.2 above, then it must disregard the latter unless they consider that no reasonable employer would have taken that action (*Source*: TULRA 1992, s.148). The action must be directed at deterring a person individually from being a member, or not being a member, of a union. It would seem that where a union is de-recognised and it has the effect of altering an employee's conditions of service, it does not offend against the Act even where the effect is to reduce the power of the union, or it deters employees from being members of it. If the detriment were extreme it might be caught by the 1992 Act (*Source*: ERA 1996, s.104).

6.9

The provisions in para. 6.2 above may enable a person to rely on the Act where there is an inter-union dispute and the employer treats one group of workers differently from another. The trade union, of which the employee bringing the complaint is a member, must, however, be independent.

6.10

Members of the United Democratic Mineworkers' Union (UDM) were paid more than the National Union of Mineworkers (NUM), who alleged a breach of section 146 of the 1992 Act. It was held that as the employer's intention was to penalise the NUM, his action breached that section. The Act was designed to prevent an employee from being victimised for being a member of a particular (independent) union. Furthermore, the employer's actions were directed against the employees as 'individuals' even though primarily directed against the union (*National Coal Board v Ridgway & Another* [1987] ICR 641, CA).

6.11
Certain recognised unions had the right to distribute parking tickets to those of their members who worked in the employers' telephone exchange. An employee was refused a parking permit because he was not a member of one or other of the unions in question. The EAT held that the action complained of was capable of being 'action short of dismissal', so long as the action had been taken against him as an individual and he had accordingly been subjected to a detriment for not being a member of a recognised independent trade union (*Carlson v The Post Office* [1981] IRLR 479, EAT).

6.12
A lecturer, who was also a trade union official, was passed over for promotion. The job was offered to a less-qualified candidate. The lecturer complained that she had been passed-over because of her trade union activities and her strong views about one of the training courses run by her employers. The tribunal held that the lecturer's failure to be promoted was due to her deeply-held views which were inconsistent with a wholehearted commitment towards the course in question (*McCarthy v Somerset CC*, 29 February 1981, EAT).

Sex Discrimination Act 1975

6.13
An employer will be held to have unlawfully victimised an employee (or job applicant) on grounds of sex, marital status or gender reassignment if he (or she) treated the employee in question less favourably than he treated (or would have treated) other persons (ie, single persons or persons of the opposite sex) in similar circumstances, and did so because the employee in question:

- brought proceedings before an employment tribunal; or

- gave (supporting) evidence or information to a tribunal in connection with any such complaint; or

- alleged that the employer (or would-be employer) had committed an unlawful act

contrary to the provisions of the Sex Discrimination Act 1975, the Equal Pay Act 1970, or ss 62 to 65 (implied 'equal treatment rule' in occupational pension schemes) of the Pensions Act 1995 (*Source*: SDA 1975, s.4) (see also Chapter 11).

Complaint to an employment tribunal

6.14
A complaint of unlawful victimisation under the enactments referred to in the preceding paragraph must be presented to an employment tribunal within

three months of the alleged discriminatory act, or within such further period as the tribunal considers reasonable in the circumstances. If the tribunal finds that the employee's complaint is well-founded, it will make an order declaring the rights of the complainant and respondent employer in relation to the act complained of and / or will order the employer to pay the employee compensation of an amount corresponding to any damages the employer might have been ordered to pay by a county court or by a sheriff court – which damages may include an element of compensation for injury to feelings. The tribunal might also recommend that the offending employer 'puts his (or her) house in order' by changing his policies and practices to ensure that there is no recurrence of the type of victimisation which prompted the employee's complaint in the first place. If the employer chooses to ignore any such recommendation (compliance with which may be 'policed' by the Equal Opportunities Commission), the tribunal may increase the award of compensation by such amount as it considers to be 'just and equitable' in the circumstances, in the light of the employer's justification for doing so (*Source*: SDA 1975, ss 63 to 65).

Race Relations Act 1976

6.15
Similar provisions are to be found in the Race Relations Act 1976, section 2 of which reminds employers that an employee will be treated as having been unlawfully victimised if he or she is treated less favourably (eg by being denied access to promotion, training, benefits, pay rises, transfers, etc) than other persons within the employing organisation on grounds of colour, race, nationality or ethnic or national origins (*Source*: RRA 1976, s.2) (see also Chapter 12).

6.16
Complaints to, and the penalties imposed by, an employment tribunal for a breach of the 'non-victimisation' provisions of the Race Relations Act 1976, are the same as described in para. 6.14 above).

Disability Discrimination Act 1995

6.17
The Disability Discrimination Act 1995 came into force on 2 December 1996 and repealed the largely ineffective (and, to an extent, outdated) Disabled Persons (Employment) Acts 1994 & 1958 (see also Chapter 13).

Under the 1995 Act, it is unlawful for an employer to discriminate against disabled persons in his employ by paying them lower wages or salaries (or associated benefits) solely because they are disabled, or by offering other less favourable terms and conditions of employment. To refuse to promote or transfer a disabled person or to deny that person opportunities to improve his (or her) skills, is likewise unlawful.

6.18
An employee who is discriminated against in this way has every right to challenge the employer's actions before an employment tribunal and is under no obligation to terminate his (or her) employment in order to do so. If the employer responds to any such challenge (or to an allegation of unlawful discrimination) by victimising or dismissing the employee, that too is unlawful and will inevitably lead to a further complaint to a tribunal and an award of compensation.

Complaint to an employment tribunal

6.19
A complaint of unlawful discrimination under the 1995 Act must be presented to an employment tribunal within three months of the act complained of (or within such further period as the tribunal considers reasonable in the circumstances). Should the complaint be upheld, the powers of the tribunal are as described in para. 6.14 above (*Source*: DDA 1995, ss 8 & 55, and Schedule 3, Part I, paras 3 & 4).

Employment Rights Act 1996

6.20
Sections 44 to 47C of the Employment Rights Act 1996 state that an employee (and, in some situations, a worker who is not an 'employee') has the right not to be subjected to any detriment by any act (or deliberate failure to act) by his (or her) employer done on the ground that:

- the employee – in his (or her) capacity as a 'competent person', safety representative, representative of employee safety, member of a safety committee, or as a person designated by the employer to carry out activities in connection with preventing or reducing risks to health and safety – brought to his employer's attention, by reasonable means, circumstances connected with his work which he reasonably believed were harmful or potentially harmful to health or safety (*ibid* s.44);

- the employee – as a protected or opted-out shop worker or betting worker – had refused (or proposed to refuse) to do shop work or betting work on Sunday or on a particular Sunday (*ibid* s.45);

- the worker (as an employee or otherwise) had refused to comply with a requirement which his (or her) employer imposed (or proposed to impose) in contravention of the employer's duties under the Working Time Regulations 1998; or had refused either to sign a 'workforce agreement' or to forego his (or her) rights under those Regulations; or, being a representative of the workforce, or as a candidate for election as such a representative, had performed (or proposed to perform) his (or her) functions as such a representative or candidate (*ibid* s.45A);

- the employee – being a trustee of a relevant occupational pension scheme – performed (or proposed to perform) any of his (or her) functions as such a trustee (*ibid* s.46);

- the employee – being an employee representative for the purposes of Chapter II of Part IV of the Trade Union & Labour Relations (Consolidation) Act 1992 (consultations over collective redundancies) or Regulations 10 & 11 of the Transfer of Undertakings (Protection of Employment) Regulations 1981 (consultations over a proposed TUPE sale or transfer), or a candidate seeking election as an employee representative – had performed (or proposed to perform) any of his (or her) functions or activities as such a representative or candidate (*ibid* s.47).

- the employee (as a young person aged 16, 17 or 18) had exercised (or proposed to exercise) his (or her) statutory right, under sections 63A and 63B of the 1996 Act, to take time off during his normal working hours in order to undertake study or training leading to a relevant qualification (*ibid* s. 47A);

- the employee (or worker) had made a 'protected disclosure' (as defined in *ibid* section 43A) (*ibid* s.47B) (as to which, see Chapter 20);

- the employee had exercised her (or his) right to maternity leave, adoption leave, parental leave, paternity leave and time off for dependants, payment on suspension on maternity grounds, ante-natal care, and the like, or the right to apply for flexible working arrangements (as to which, see Chapter 14).

Complaint to an employment tribunal

6.21

An employee may present a complaint to an employment tribunal that he (or she) has been subjected to a detriment in contravention of sections 44, 45, 45A, 46, 47, 47A, 47B or 47C of the 1996 Act. The complaint must be presented within three months beginning with the date of the act or failure to act or, where the act or failure to act was part of a series of similar acts or failures, the last of them. A complaint presented 'out of time' will not be heard unless the tribunal is satisfied that it was not reasonably practicable for it to have been presented sooner.

6.22
If the employee's complaint is upheld, the tribunal will make a declaration to that effect and may make an award of compensation (payable by the employer to the complainant) of such amount as it considers 'just and equitable' having regard to the infringement to which the complaint related and any loss attributable to the employer's actions. The award would include compensation for any expenses reasonably incurred by the complainant and any loss of benefit which the employee might reasonably be expected to have had but for his (or her) employer's act or failure to act. The compensation may be reduced by an appropriate amount if the evidence showed that the employee had been partly responsible for the employer's infringement of his statutory rights (*Source*: ERA 1996, ss 48 & 49).

National Minimum Wage Act 1998

6.23
Section 23 of the National Minimum Wage Act 1998, cautions that workers have the right not to be punished, victimised or subjected to any detriment (by any act, or by any deliberate failure to act) by their employers, for enforcing (or attempting to enforce) their statutory right to be paid no less than the appropriate national minimum wage (NMW).

6.24
In short, workers cannot legally be punished (or dismissed) for qualifying (or for being about to qualify) for the NMW, for challenging or questioning their employer's refusal or failure to pay the appropriate NMW rate, for demanding sight of their payroll records, for reporting their employer's conduct to an Inland Revenue enforcement officer, or for bringing proceedings before an employment tribunal or court. A worker may pursue his (or her) rights under the 1998 Act regardless of his age or length of service at the material time. Nor need a worker resign in order to do so.

6.25
On a successful complaint to an employment tribunal, the worker's employer will be ordered to pay the worker such compensation as the tribunal considers 'just and equitable' in the circumstances, having regard to the infringement to which the complaint related and to any loss sustained by the worker which was attributable to the employer's actions. A worker who is not an employee, in the sense that he (or she) is not employed under a contract of employment, whose contract has been terminated in the circumstances described above, nonetheless has the right (as has an employee who has been dismissed) to challenge the fairness of that detrimental treatment before an employment tribunal, and will be awarded compensation if his complaint is upheld (as to which, please turn to Chapter 5).

Tax Credits Act 2002

6.26

An employer ordered by the Tax Credits Office (TCO) to pay working tax credits to an employee 'through the payroll' may not legitimately victimise that employee (or subject him or her to any other penalty or detriment) for that reason. An employee in those circumstrances may complain to an employment tribunal (without having to resign in order to do so) and will be awarded appropriate compensation if his or her complaint is upheld (ERA 1996, s.47D).

Other 'no detrimental treatment' provisions

6.27

See also Chapters 16, 17 and 18 for similar provisions under the Fixed-term Employee (Prevention of Less Favourable Treatment) Regulations 2002, the Part-Time Workers (Prevention of Less Favourable Treatment) Regulations 2000; and the Working Time Regulations 1998.

Liability of trade unions and their officials for torts

BACKGROUND

7.1
Over the past twenty or so years, the law has vacillated over the liabilities of unions for the loss and damage caused to others by the civil wrong-doing or unlawful acts of their officials and members. In the field of employment, the problem generally manifests itself in the 'torts' of inducing or procuring a breach of an employment or commercial contract. It will usually occur during the course of industrial action when a trade union unlawfully interferes with a trade or business or uses intimidation to cause loss and damage to an employer.

7.2
If a union or one of its representatives (eg a shop steward) persuades employees in an unrelated company to stop providing services to the company with whom the union is in dispute, it will have committed an actionable wrong. The employees in the first company would have broken their contracts of employment with *their* employer, which would have the 'knock-on' effect of blocking the supply of goods or services to the company in dispute with the union in breach of its (commercial) contract with the latter (*Lumley v Gye* [1853] 118 ER 740, HL). On the other hand an action directed at strangers to the contract, where the effect on the contracting party is indirect, is not actionable unless unlawful means have been used. So the distribution of leaflets to persuade shoppers not to buy mushrooms at a supermarket because of a dispute between the pickers and their employers was not actionable. It was too remote (*Middlebrook Mushroom Ltd v Transport and General Workers Union & Others* [1993] ICR 612, CA).

7.3
Before liability can be established, it has to be shown that the action is unlawful. To bring about a breach of a commercial contract, there must have been some pressure on employees to break their contracts (eg by physically preventing them entering their own place of work or using similar tactics to halt the delivery of goods to the customer's premises. Further, it would need to be shown that the person inducing or procuring the breach knew (whether directly or inferentially) of the existence of such a commercial contract, and

that the breach would be a necessary consequence of his action. Further, it must be shown that loss was sustained as a result (*Stratford & Son Ltd v Lindley* [1966] AC 269, HL; *Cornellia Tankers Ltd v ITWF* [1976] ICR 274, CA; and *Read v FSOS* [1902] 2 KB 732, CA).

7.4

Unlawful interference with a trade or business can occur where there are commercial expectations. Thus even where there is no firm contract to supply services, but they are reasonably expected and the action is intended to frustrate these hopes, the unlawfulness is complete (*Hadmore Productions Ltd v Hamilton* [1982] ICR 114, HL).

7.5

Intimidation could occur where, with a view to causing damage to the employer or a third party, a person threatens violence or a union threatens employees with loss of union membership if they fail to comply with an unlawful union instruction. Usually a person(s) would be caught under the 'procuring or inducing breach of contract' provisions (above) as well as for conspiracy to unlawfully cause loss and damage to the employer or any third party affected by this action.

7.6

The immunity from actions in tort enjoyed by the trade unions before 1971 and, to a lesser extent, between 1971 and 1974, has now been largely eroded. The Trade Union & Labour Relations Act 1974 (long since repealed) restored the protection for economic torts, but not for other types of tort. The current position, incorporated in the Trade Union & Labour Relations (Consolidation) Act 1992, is more in line with that in other major industrialised nations. As the subject has strong political overtones, there is likely to be a further see-sawing in the position – but to what extent is a matter of conjecture.

7.7

Trade union officials and rank-and-file members of unions have never enjoyed the same measure of protection as the unions themselves. But few employers were prepared to take them to court. Doing so could be counter-productive (especially when very heavy losses were being sustained) and would very likely inflame an already over-heated situation. Obtaining an injunction against a union would not have been worthwhile unless an employer had access also to the union's funds.

7.8

If a party (a 'tort-feasor') is liable for damages to another arising out of a 'tort', even though others were responsible for part of the loss, the party would be liable to pay the whole amount to the victim. He could seek a contribution from his fellow 'tort-feasors' to the extent to which they were responsible. The loss and damage recoverable is that which would normally flow from the 'tortious act'. Thus, if a person negligently injures another person thereby preventing that other from performing a lucrative three-month contract to sing in the United States, the singer would be entitled to compensation not only for the injuries he has sustained, but also for his net financial loss.

THE CURRENT POSITION

7.9
The law has been described as a 'legislative maze'. It is extremely complicated. As mentioned earlier, it has since been consolidated into the 1992 Consolidation Act, which makes it easier to find the relevant parts (*Dimbleby & Sons v National Union of Journalists* [1984] ICR 386, HL).

7.10
A union is 'vicariously' liable for the acts of its officials and (in certain circumstances) union members under both the 'common law' and the relevant statutory provisions .

When liability arises

7.11
The position at 'common law' lacks certainty and depends on the law of agency. This in turn requires consideration of the rule book of the union, and of any express or implied authority that a union official or member may have for taking any action. The current position may not be properly recorded (*Heaton's Transport Ltd v TGWU* [1972] ICR 308, HL; and *General Aviation Services (UK) Ltd v TGWU* [1985] ICR 615, HL).

7.12
Under the 1992 Act, it is provided that a tort shall be taken to have been done by a union *if authorised or endorsed by the union*. Furthermore, 'an act shall be taken to have been authorised or endorsed by a trade union if it was done, or was authorised or endorsed:

- by any person empowered...; or

- by the principal executive committee or the president or general secretary; or

- by any other committee of the union or any other official... (whether employed or not) including any other group of persons constituted in accordance with the rules of the union or by a member of that group, the purpose of which included organising or co-ordinating industrial action.

(*Source*: TULRA 1992, s.20.)

7.13
A committee or any other person, such as a shop steward, will be *prima facie*
liable for their actions if they/he/she decide to call a strike without reference
to executive members of the union – whether or not that group or individual
has authority to take such action. An official of a union was authorised by an
'authorised person' to go ahead with a strike after negotiations with an
employer had broken down. The official had acted within that delegated
power. It was held that immunity was not lost because there was a close relationship between the two (*Tanks & Drums Ltd v TGWU* [1992] ICR 1, CA). The
only way for a union to avoid liability for the actions of its officials is to
publicly disavow those actions. The disavowal must be communicated in
writing not only to the victim of the unlawful action but also to each member
of the group or to the official concerned, using the following words:

> Your union has repudiated the call (or calls) for industrial action to
> which this notice relates and will give no support to unofficial indus-
> trial action taken in response to it (or them). If you are dismissed while
> taking unofficial industrial action, you will have no right to complain of
> unfair dismissal.

(*Source*: TULRA 1992, s.21(3).)

7.14
A union which fails to repudiate unofficial industrial action will be vicariously
liable for damages flowing from the 'tort' committed by the group or individual. However, there will be no loss of immunity if the industrial action:

- relates to interferences with contracts of employment;

- is done 'in contemplation or furtherance of a trade dispute';

- does not involve certain types of *primary* or *secondary* action (or unlawful
  picketing);

- has the support of the members under a secret ballot;

- does not induce a breach of statutory duty, and is not designed to bring
  about union membership.

(*Source*: TULRA 1992, ss 220, 222, 224, & 226 to 234.)

Interference with contracts of employment

7.15
The nub of the immunity relates to an indirect attack upon an employer by
means of breaches of the contract of employment. This is usually done by
taking part in strikes, part withdrawal of labour, 'blacking' of goods, and

other forms of industrial action, thereby preventing or hindering the employer from meeting his obligations under business or commercial contracts with his clients. Immense damage can be done on such occasions.

7.16
Employees may take industrial action of their own initiative, or be persuaded by others to do so , and may do so for a variety of purposes. What is lawful now is very limited. There are elaborate formulae for determining which types of industrial action enjoy immunity and which do not.

'In contemplation or furtherance of a trade dispute'

7.17
The expression 'in furtherance of a trade dispute' means a dispute between a worker and his (or her) employer relating wholly or mainly to one or more of the following:

- terms and conditions of employment;

- engagement or non-engagement, termination or suspension of employment;

- allocation of work;

- discipline;

- membership or non-membership of a union;

- facilities for officials of unions;

- machinery for negotiation or consultations, including recognition issues.

(*Mercury Communications Ltd v Scott-Garner* [1984] ICR 74, CA.)

(*Source*: TULRA 1992, s.244.)

7.18
Industrial action in support of a dispute with a company outside the United Kingdom is action 'in contemplation or furtherance of a trade dispute' if its purpose (or intended outcome) is to improve terms and conditions or to secure bargaining rights, etc for the company's employees *within* the United Kingdom. For example, industrial action by UK employees in support of similar action by employees in the United States (eg for a shorter working week) would be lawful if both groups of employees work for the same international company and the success of the strike in the United States would lead to an improvement in the terms and conditions of employment of their colleagues in the UK. Industrial action prompted by fear of job losses can also be characterised as action 'in contemplation or furtherance of a trade dispute' because it relates to 'the termination of employment', but it must be genuinely

based on 'something definite and of real substance' (*General Aviation Services (UK) Ltd v TGWU* [1985] ICR 615, HL; and *Conway v Wade [1909] AC 506, HL*).

7.19
However, the immunity is lost if there is interference with a contract by unlawful means, eg by nuisance, violence, or intimidation (*News Group Newspapers Ltd & Others v SOGAT '82 & Others* [1987] ICR 181, QBD; and *Associated British Ports & Others v TGWU, CA* (but overturned by the House of Lords on another point) [1989] ICR 557).

'Primary' and 'secondary' action

7.20
Primary action occurs when employees take direct industrial action against their employer, eg by going on strike or operating a 'go slow' in support of a claim for higher wages. *Secondary* action occurs when a person induces another to break or interfere with his (or her) contract of employment, or threatens that his (or her) own or another's contract will be broken or interfered with, where the employer in question is not involved in the dispute (*Source*: TULRA 1992, s.224(2)). Except where there is lawful picketing (see paras 7.37 to 7.42 below), *all* forms of secondary actions are unlawful. Striking workers manning a picket line outside their employer's premises may use peaceful means to attempt to persuade drivers working for a supplier not to deliver goods to their employer. But if they succeed in turning drivers away or use violent or intimidatory tactics, they (or their union) may be sued for damages by the supplier whose commercial and employment contracts have been interfered with. Criminal prosecutions might also ensue (*Source*: TULRA 1992, s.224).

'Support under a secret ballot'

7.21
Immunity from actions for tort will also be lost unless the industrial action has the support of a properly-conducted secret ballot. A majority of those voting must vote in favour of the proposed action. Every person entitled to vote in the ballot must be sent a voting paper by post to his (or her) home address and be given a convenient and cost-free opportunity to vote by post. Each voting paper must contain the following unqualified statement:

'If you take part in a strike or other industrial action, you may be in breach of your contract of employment.

However, if you are dismissed for taking part in strike or other industrial action which is called officially and is otherwise lawful, the dismissal will be unfair if it takes place fewer than eight weeks after you started taking part in the action and, depending on the circumstances, may be unfair if it takes place later.'

(*Source: TULRA* 1992, ss 226 & 230, as amended by s.4 and Schedule 3 to the Employment Relations Act 1999.)

7.22
Separate ballots have to be conducted at each place of work unless (a) at least one of the members at each (or some) of those workplaces is affected by the same dispute; or (b) the union in question reasonably believes that it is balloting all its members in a particular occupational category (or categories) who are employed by one or more of the employers with whom the union is in dispute; or (c) the union reasonably believes that it is balloting all its members who are employed by one or more employers with whom the union is in dispute. All members who are entitled to vote must be allowed to participate and there must be a majority in favour of action at that workplace before it is taken (*Source*: TULRA 1992, ss 228 & 228A).

7.23
These requirements apply to industrial action as well as to strikes, and there must be a specific unequivocal question relating to each. The instructions to take the action must be issued within four weeks of the ballot, otherwise it will be unlawful. It does not matter that the action is taken beyond the period provided it relates to those instructions (*Monsanto plc v TGWU* [1987] ICR 269, CA; and *Secretary of State for Scotland v Scottish Prison Officers Association & Others* [1991] IRLR 371, CS). A temporary suspension of action while negotiations take place would not affect the validity of the ballot. But if the industrial action ceases because the union decides to change tactics, say, by mounting a public relations campaign, then a fresh mandate must be obtained before industrial action is resumed (*Post Office v Union of Communications Workers* [1990] ICR 258, CA).

7.24
If during the four-week period a court prohibits the industrial action and the order subsequently either lapses or is discharged, an application can then be made to the same court within eight weeks of the ballot for a direction that the time lost under the order should be disregarded when adding up the four weeks (*Source*: TULRA 1992, s.234).

7.25
A union put four matters to its members and asked whether they were prepared to take strike action. It was held that the ballot was invalid. There was no 'trade dispute' in respect of three of them (see para. 7.17 above). If there had been one concerning all, it would have been lawful (*London Underground Ltd v National Union of Railwaymen* [1989] IRLR 341, QBD).

7.26

Those union members who '... it is reasonable at the time of the ballot for the union to believe will be induced to take part, or... to continue to take part in the industrial action in question ...' must be allowed to vote, and no others. The exclusion extends to those union members who are indirectly interested in the outcome of the dispute (*Presho v DHSS* [1984] ICR 463, HL) (*Source*: TULRA 1992, s.227). Those eligible to vote must be sent a voting paper by post and, so far as is reasonably practicable, be allowed to return their votes by post without interference or constraint, in secret and without direct cost. The results must be fairly and accurately counted and the results made known to those entitled to vote. A complaint by an employer that a union had not given all of its members an opportunity to vote did not invalidate the ballot. The union was able to prove that they had taken all reasonably practicable steps to circulate all of its members. Furthermore, what failure there was would not have affected the result. The ballot would be unlawful if a person called on to strike is denied the right to vote, in the sense of being wrongly disqualified (*British Railways Board v National Union of Railwaymen* [1989] ICR 678, CA) (*Source*: TULRA 1992, s.227).

Reporting the results of a ballot

7.27

Once the votes cast in a ballot have been counted, the trade union must, as soon as is reasonably practicable, inform every relevant employer *and* every person entitled to vote in the ballot of:

(a) the number of votes cast in the ballot;

(b) the number of individuals who answered 'Yes' to the question or, as the case may be, to each of the questions on the voting paper;

(c) the number of individuals who answered 'No' to the question or, as the case may be, to each of the questions in the voting paper; and

(d) the number of spoilt voting papers (if any)(*ibid* sections 231 and 231B).

A failure to notify all relevant employers of the outcome of the ballot (where there have been separate workplace ballots) would make it unlawful for the union to call out those of its members whose employers had not been correctly informed of the outcome of the ballot (*ibid* sections 231 & 231A).

Majority vote in favour of industrial action

7.28

If there has been a majority vote in favour of a strike and/or industrial action short of a strike (such as an overtime ban or a call-out ban), and the union decides to go ahead with that action, it must inform the affected employer (or employers), at least seven days beforehand (but not before it has informed the employer of the outcome of the ballot), of the date on which it intends to call its members out on strike or to take industrial action short of a strike. However, the seven-day notice period made be suspended for an agreed period so as to enable the parties to the dispute to attempt to negotiate a settlement. In other words, it will no longer be necessary for the trade union to issue a fresh seven-day notice if such negotiations prove unsuccessful (ss 231A & 234A, as amended by the Employment Relations Act 1999).

7.29
The notice of strike action (or of industrial action short of a strike) must contain such information in the union's possession as would help the employer to make plans and bring information to the attention of those of his (or her) employees whom the union intends to induce (or has induced) to take part (or continue to take part) in that action. If the union possesses information as to the number, category or workplace of the employees concerned, the notice must contain that information (at least); but the union is under no statutory obligation to name the employees in question (thereby putting paid to the decision of the Court of Appeal in *Blackpool and The Fylde College v NATFHE* [1994] ICR 648, CA) (*Source*: TULRA 1992 s.234A(5A)).

7.30
Furthermore, the notice given to the employer must state whether the industrial action is to be 'continuous' or 'discontinuous' (eg, an uninterrupted strike or a series of one-day strikes). If the industrial action is to be 'discontinuous', the union must specify the dates or days on which that action is to take place. The notice of intended industrial action given by the trade union in the circumstances described in this paragraph must also state that it is given for the purposes of section 234A(7)(*ibid*).

7.31
A trade union's call for industrial action, following a majority vote in favour, must be made by the person or persons specified on the voting paper within four weeks of the date (or the last of the dates) on which the ballot took place. However, that four-week period may be extended by up to a further four weeks if, but only if, both the trade union and the employer in question agree to such an extension (eg, with a view to achieving a settlement of the dispute between them). Where there have been separate workplace ballots, an agreement to extend would apply to those workplaces only in which such an agreement has been reached. If it is not, the proposed industrial action will be 'unprotected' and 'unofficial' and (if proceeded with) will expose the trade union to the risk of civil actions for damages from all affected quarters (*ibid* ss 233(3)(b) & 234).

7.32

The industrial action may also be deferred beyond the four-week period if, for one reason or another, there is a court order prohibiting the union from calling for industrial action during the whole or part of that period or if the union has itself given an undertaking to the court not to proceed with such action. When the injunction or undertaking lapses or is set aside, the union may immediately apply to the court for an order extending that four-week period. The court may refuse to do so if, following submissions by interested parties, it is persuaded that the result of the ballot no longer represents the views of the union members concerned, or something else has happened (or seems about to happen) which would prompt those members to vote against industrial action if offered another chance to vote in a ballot (*ibid*).

7.33

Trade unions must give notice to employers of the various stages involved in calling a strike, including describing the employees likely to be involved, and must provide them with detailed results of the ballot. A further delay is caused while various formalities are complied with relating to the necessity to serve notices of the intended action on the employer. Failure to follow these requirements nullifies the procedure and will result in the union losing its immunity. So where a union told the employers that its 'members employed at a college' would be called out on a one-day strike, it was held that the notice did not comply with the rules. The employers were unable to identify the individual employees involved. It mattered not that as between the union and its members, disclosure of the latters' names might be a breach of their right to privacy.

7.34

A union instructed its members to take industrial action without a prior ballot. This resulted in expense to a ticket holder who was prevented from travelling home by rail. The union was ordered to indemnify the commuter for his loss because they had unlawfully induced a breach of contract between British Rail and the traveller (*Falconer v NUR & ASLEF* [1986] IRLR 331, County Court).

7.35

A person may apply to the High Court (or the Court of Session) for an injunction if a trade union or other person has acted unlawfully, or is likely to do so, with a view to inducing a person to take part in industrial action, the effect (or likely effect) of which will be to prevent or delay the supply of goods or services or to reduce the quality of goods and services supplied to the individual. It would appear that the consequence will be that a person may intervene where he (or she) has suffered no harm. It will be sufficient that the proposed passenger was deprived of the opportunity of travelling (*ibid* s.235A).

7.36
Every voting paper must state the names of the individuals authorised by the union to call industrial action in the event of a majority vote in favour of such action. Immunity will be lost if an unauthorised person, eg a shop steward, instructs members to take industrial action (*ibid* s.229).

LAWFUL PICKETING

7.37
Picketing is lawful if, but only if, it is done by a person in contemplation or furtherance of a trade dispute *at or near his (or her) own place of work* (or, if dismissed, his former place of work). Picketing must be for the purpose of peacefully obtaining or communicating information or peacefully persuading another person to abstain from working. A trade union official may take part in a picket if he (or she) does so in a lawful manner and is representing his members at the time (*ibid* s.220).

7.38
Several employees were made redundant when their employer lost a cleaning contract for a building. They picketed the building. The picket was held to be unlawful because there was no 'trade dispute' between the employer (the owner/occupier of the building) and those picketing. Their picketing was directed at the company which was awarded the new contract, not their former employer (*J & R Kenny Cleaning Services (a firm) v Transport & General Workers Union, The Times*, 15 June 1989, CA).

Harassment on the public highway

7.39
Unreasonable harassment of employees on the public highway as they enter and leave their place of work constitutes a 'tort'. It matters not whether it is done by weight of numbers, intimidatory conduct or even physical obstruction. The union, which had encouraged large numbers to attend, were held vicariously liable for the consequences (*Thomas v NUM (South Wales Area)* [1985] IRLR 136, ChD).

Code of Practice

7.40
A *Code of Practice on Picketing* produced by the Secretary of State recommends that the number of pickets on a picket line should be *limited to six* at each of the entrances to their employer's premises. The police should be consulted before a picket line is mounted, and there must be no interference with essential services. A member of a union may not be disciplined for crossing an unauthorised picket line, or one manned by member(s) not at their place of work.

Inducing a breach of statutory duty

7.41
If an employer is duty-bound to carry out certain statutory duties, any attempt to persuade the employees to stop work can constitute action that is outside the protection of any immunity. But it must be shown that the action actually prevented compliance with those statutory duties and not merely that the action made compliance more difficult (*Meade v Haringey LBC* [1979] ICR 494, CA; and *Barretts & Baird (Wholesale) Ltd v Institute of Professional Civil Servants* [1987] IRLR 3, QBD).

Action designed to bring about union membership

7.42
Immunity is lost if one of the reasons for taking industrial action is that the employer has hired (or intends to employ) non-union labour or persons who are not members of a particular trade union. The result is the same, if the purpose of the industrial action is to pressurise employers into treating non-union members less favourably (*ibid* s.222).

STRICT COMPLIANCE ESSENTIAL

7.43
A union will be liable if there is a failure to comply at any stage with any of the technical requirements of the 1992 Act. It must disassociate itself from unofficial action, especially if taken contrary to the rules or directions. Even if a union does disassociate itself, it may still be caught on occasions by factors outside its knowledge (*Shipping Company Uniform Inc v International Transport Federation & Another* [1985] ICR 245, QB; and *Metropolitan Borough of Solihull v NUT* [1985] IRLR 211, ChD).

Political and sympathy strikes

7.44
Political and sympathy strikes are no longer immune, nor are 'wildcat' strikes or those called by a union official out of spite. Furthermore, any grievance must be communicated to the employer first. Demarcation strikes are also no longer immune because they are not between an employee and his employer (*Conway v Lindley* [1965] AC 269, HL; *Torquay Hotels Co Ltd v Cousins* [1969] 2 Ch 106, ChD; and *Norbrook Laboratories Ltd v King* [1984] IRLR 200, CA). But motive, eg hatred of an employer, does not remove the immunity, provided the purpose of industrial action falls within the statutory provisions. However, the person taking the action must honestly and genuinely believe

that his (or her) objective is likely to be achieved by such action (*Express Newspapers Ltd v McShane* [1980] ICR 42, HL).

7.45
A newspaper group in dispute with its printers switched its work to a non-union printer. The National Union of Journalists, which was itself in dispute with an 'associated employer' of the non-union printer, instructed its members to 'black' all work sent to the non-union printer. The instruction was held to be unlawful (*Dimbleby & Sons v National Union of Journalists* [1984] ICR 386, HL). The union also failed in its attempt to create a *primary* dispute over terms and conditions of employment by demanding the insertion of a clause in the contracts of its members – to the effect that they would not be required to produce work for printing by a non-union printer. It did not come within the strict definition, ie, the dispute was not 'wholly or mainly' related to it (see para. 7.17).

LIMITS ON DAMAGES

7.46
The maximum amount of damages that may be awarded against a union depends on its size. The figures opposite apply in respect of all actions against a union except for personal injury or a breach of duty arising out of a property dispute. The maximum applies to *each* case against a union (*Source*: TULRA 1992, s.22(2)).

Total membership	Maximum damages
less than 5,000	£10,000
5,000 to 24,999	£50,000
25,000 to 99,999	£125,000
100,000 or more	£250,000

TIME LIMITS

7.47
Proceedings must be begun within six years of the breach complained of; otherwise they will be 'statute-barred'.

8

A contract under the 'common law'

GENERAL INFORMATION

8.1
The 'common law' has evolved over the centuries from the decisions of the judiciary in a variety of cases. The great body of 'case law' created in this way remains the cornerstone of contemporary UK law. Up to 1963, the law governing contracts of employment was almost exclusively derived from this source. Nowadays, the employment tribunals have (limited) jurisdictions to entertain claims for breach of contract arising out of (or outstanding) on the termination of employment (see Chapter 1, paras 1.15 and 1.16) (*Source*: Employment Tribunals Extension of Jurisdiction (England & Wales) Order 1994 and the Employment Tribunals Extension of Jurisdiction (Scotland) Order 1994).

8.2
Under contemporary employment legislation, employees and their employers have a great many rights and obligations. However, many common law concepts still apply. The problem that generally arises is the meaning to be attached to various words and phrases, which frequently leads to litigation.

8.3
A contract of employment comes into being when an offer of employment is made and accepted on terms which are either mutually agreed or stipulated by the putative employer when inviting job applicants to come forward. A contract of employment will contain terms which are express (eg job title, rate of pay, working hours; and so on). It will also contain implied terms, such as the employer's implied duty of care, and the implied mutual duty of trust, confidence and fidelity. It would be otiose to suggest that an employee has an implied common law and contractual duty not to divulge his employer's trade secrets, chemical formulations, production processes, marketing strategies, pricing policies, etc to unauthorised persons; although that duty would (sensibly) appear as an express term in the contracts of employment of those who have routine access to such information. Implied terms are necessary to give business efficacy to the contract. The relationship in a particular case is such that it could not really work without them. The 'reasonableness' test is not applied (*Morley v Heritage plc* [1993] IRLR 400, CA).

8.4

So it was held that teachers had a professional and implied common law (or contractual) obligation to co-operate in the running of a school during school hours – in accordance with the timetable and other administrative arrangements. They were also duty-bound to carry out all reasonable instructions given to them from time to time (*Liverpool CC v Irwin* [1977] AC 239, HL; and *Sim & Others v Rotherham Metropolitan BC & Others* [1986] ICR 897, ChD).

8.5

Terms had been negotiated with a representative body, which conferred valuable rights on employees. But before an employee could benefit from them, he (or she) had to follow certain procedures. He knew nothing about them and could not reasonably be expected to be aware of them. It was held that the employer had an implied contractual duty to take reasonable steps to draw such terms to the employee's attention. Failure to do so entitled the employee to compensation for the loss that followed (*Scally & Others v Southern Health & Social Services Board & Another* [1991] ICR 771, HL).

8.6

When a contract of employment is silent on the question of mobility of employment, it has been held that an employer has an implied contractual right to move an employee from one site to another, for any reason, provided that the employee continues to work within reasonable daily reach of his home (*Courtaulds Northern Spinning Ltd v Sibson & Another* [1988] ICR 451, CA).

Conflict between express and implied terms

8.7

Sometimes an express term in an employment contract appears to conflict with an implied term. The general rule is that the express term prevails. But courts have ruled otherwise where justice demands it. An express term gave an employer discretion to order an employee to work overtime. The employee was required to work long hours which were clearly affecting his health. It was held that, notwithstanding the express term, an employer has an implied contractual duty to take reasonable care for the health and safety of his employees (*Johnstone v Bloomsbury Health Authority* [1991] ICR 269, CA).

WRITTEN STATEMENT OF EMPLOYMENT PARTICULARS

8.8

Nowadays, every employee has a legal right to receive written particulars of the terms and conditions of his (or her) employment – including precise information about rates of pay, working hours, holidays, sickness benefits;

and so on (explained in more detail in Chapter 9). This clearly narrows the areas of dispute.

8.9

It should be borne in mind that people's memories are notoriously fickle when recollecting verbally-agreed terms. Although a handshake at the factory gate is just as enforceable as a contract reduced to writing, there is the inevitable risk of a misunderstanding between the parties (as to what was actually said and agreed). A written contract is always preferable.

WHAT IS A BREACH OF CONTRACT?

8.10

There is a 'breach of contract' when one or other of the parties fails to comply with his (or her) contractual obligations. For instance, an employer cannot impose a pay cut without the employee's express permission. If he does so, he is in breach of contract and must either reinstate the employee's rate of pay immediately or face the consequences. A 'breach of contract' gives rise to a 'common law' cause of action that entitles the aggrieved party to claim various rights including recovery of any damage sustained by him. In assessing the amount, payments from an occupational pension scheme must be disregarded (*Hopkins v Norcross plc* [1994] ICE 18, CA). Nowadays, the employment tribunals also have (limited) jurisdiction to entertain 'breach of employment contract' claims (see Chapter 1, paras 1.15 & 1.16).

CONSEQUENCE OF A BREACH

8.11

The precise terms of a contract of employment are important because the nature of the remedy depends on the extent and seriousness of the breach. If the breach is so fundamental as to go to the very root of the contract, the innocent party is entitled to treat the contract as at an end (see Chapter 2, paras 2.36 to 2.40) and sue for any loss suffered. But he (or she) is obliged to do all that he reasonably can to mitigate his losses (see *ibid* paras 2.57 to 2.64). An employee who resigns (with or without notice) in circumstances in which he is entitled to resign without notice – by reason of his or her employer's repudiatory conduct – is treated in law as having been 'constructively' dismissed. Such an employee can seek redress by presenting a complaint of unfair constructive dismissal to an employment tribunal. In some circumstances (notably if he [or she] is claiming damages in excess of £25,000) the employee might prefer to have the issues resolved by a civil court.

8.12

It is not necessary for the conduct of a party to be culpable. For instance, an employer might be under a misapprehension that an employee could be required to spend nights away from home, whereas the employee's contract might stipulate otherwise. An attempt to force that employee to make an overnight trip could amount to a fundamental breach entitling him (or her) to quit his job and sue for breach of contract. In such a situation, neither the circumstances inducing the breach nor the circumstances that led the employee to accept such a repudiation, are relevant (*Wadham Stringer Commercials (London) Ltd. & Another v Brown* [1983] IRLR 46, EAT).

8.13
The disreputable conduct of a manager who, for instance, sexually assaulted his (or her) secretary would be a breach so fundamental as to entitle the secretary to resign and sue for damages. An employee who secretly sets up a competitive business, or who makes use of confidential information to undermine the employer's business, is guilty of gross misconduct and may be summarily dismissed (that is to say, without notice). One act of disobedience or misconduct can justify a summary dismissal where it is of such a nature as to show that the employee is repudiating the contract or one of its essential conditions. The secretary of a club, which was about to be closed down, refused to attend two committee meetings – in the mistaken belief that he was no longer obliged to attend such meetings. It was held that his employer was entitled to dismiss him 'on the spot' because he had deliberately chosen not to carry out an important duty (*Laws v London Chronicle (Indicator Newspapers) Ltd* [1959] 1 WLR 698, CA; and *Blythe v Scottish Liberal Club* [1983] IRLR 245, CS).

8.14
If the breach of contract is not serious, the contract continues and the aggrieved can only sue for damages. In practice, the worker (if he [or she] is the victim) will not begin proceedings against his employer if he wishes to retain his job. It is uncommon also and almost certainly counter-productive for an employer to sue an employee who, for instance, has quit his job without giving the notice of termination required by his contract of employment.

8.15
When an employee refused to perform the full range of his duties, his employers told him that he would not be required to work and would not be paid until he agreed to comply fully with his contractual obligations. The Court of Appeal held that the employers were entitled to withhold the whole of the employee's remuneration, even though he voluntarily attended for work and carried out a substantial part of his work (*Wilusznskiv v Tower Hamlets London Borough Council* [1989] ICR 493, CA). Likewise, an employee in a managerial position would be in breach of his implied obligation to perform his duties faithfully if he participates in a withdrawal of goodwill and/or takes part in half-day strikes. Accordingly, a claim for payment by the manager for a period when she was laid off, because of her refusal to give an

undertaking to work normally, failed. The employer was entitled to refuse to accept part-performance of her contract (*British Telecommunications plc v Ticehurst & Another* [1992] ICR 383, CA).

ACTING IN GOOD FAITH

8.16

An important implied term requires employees to carry out their duties in 'good faith'. But that same implied term does not require an employee to disclose his (or her) own misconduct, whether it occurred before the contract or during it. But there is an obligation 'to inform against other fellow servants [even] if by so doing you inevitably incriminate yourself... [but this] depends on the contract and on the terms of employment of the particular servant. He may be so placed in the hierarchy as to have a duty to report either the misconduct of his superior as in *Swain v West (Butchers) Ltd* [1936] 3 AER 261 or the misconduct of his inferiors, as in this case' (per Stephenson, LJ, *Sybron Corporation v Rochem Ltd* [1983] ICR 801, CA).

8.17

A person who has a 'fiduciary' relationship with his (or her) employers, the nature of whose job requires him to act in the utmost good faith, must disclose any breaches of contract made by himself when negotiating a further agreement. This might apply where he was settling the terms of a 'golden handshake' package (*Horcal Ltd v Gatland* [1984] IRLR 288, CA).

8.18

A betting shop manager, who wished to place a bet at another betting shop, borrowed £15 from the till, replacing it with an IOU. He returned the money to the till before his employers found out about it. It was held that, although the manager had not necessarily acted dishonestly, he knew full well that his employers would not have approved of his actions. What he had done was inconsistent with the implied mutual duty of trust and confidence which is a necessary feature of every such contractual relationship. The employers were entitled to dismiss him summarily. (*Sinclair v Neighbour* [1966] 3 AER 988, CA). There is also an implied duty of fidelity in every contract of employment. An employee may not work for a competitor during the continuance of the contract, or secretly set up a private business which runs in conflict with his (or her) employer's interests (*Provident Financial Group plc & Another v Hayward* [1989] ICR 160, CA).

8.19

An employee is not duty-bound to disclose information to his (or her) employer about his own affairs which affect his employer's business interests – always provided that he had obtained that information outside the course of his employment. So when an employee was summoned to appear before a liquidator and to answer questions, the transcript of the exchange between the two men need not be disclosed, even though the questions were of great interest to the employer (*Macmilland inc v Bishopsgate Investment Trust plc & Others* [1993] ICR 385, ChD).

Implied duty of confidentiality

8.20
As was indicated earlier, there is also an implied duty of confidentiality in every contract of employment. Employees must not reveal their employers' trade secrets or other confidential information to unauthorised third parties. Those in breach may be injuncted from doing so. Employers are similarly bound not to disclose to third parties information given to them in confidence by their employees. This would include names and addresses of employees given solely in the course of the employer/employee relationship (*Dalgleish & Others v Lothian & Borders Police Board* [1991] IRLR 422, CS).

WRONGFUL DISMISSAL

8.21
A wrongful dismissal usually occurs when a person is dismissed with insufficient notice or when the employer has been in breach of certain procedural requirements laid down in the contract of employment (*Jones v Lee & Another* [1980] ICR 310, CA). A local authority dismissed a social worker without a disciplinary hearing on the grounds that an independent panel of enquiry had stated, in a report, that she had been 'grossly negligent' in the supervision of a child under her care. It was held that she had been wrongfully dismissed. Under her contract of employment, she was entitled to a pre-dismissal hearing. By not holding such a hearing, her employers had denied her her contractual right to explain her conduct and to put forward any mitigating factors (*Dietman v Brent LBC* [1988] IRLR 299, CA). So too, when an employer presumed to sack a prison officer without following the statutory procedures relating to dismissal laid down in the Code of Discipline, the court held that the purported dismissal was void (*R v Secretary of State, ex parte Benwell* [1984] ICR 723, DC).

8.22
In considering whether a dismissal is wrongful, an employer is entitled (contrary to the position under the statutory law) to rely on any facts he discovers after the dismissal so as to justify it (*Boston Deep Sea Fishing & Ice Co v Ansell* [1888] 39 ChD 339, CA). It is not necessary that a party should intend to breach the contract of employment. Suffice that he does. So if a contract is silent on what notice (at common law) should be given to an employee, and the latter is dismissed with, say, three months' notice, but a

court finds that a more reasonable period would have been six months, the employer will be liable (*Wadham Stringer Commercials (London) Ltd & Another v Brown* [1983] IRLR 46, EAT).

8.23

Where there has been a wrongful dismissal, the employee can choose whether to accept the repudiation or not. If he (or she) declines to do so, and is able to carry on working, the contract subsists, but he is only entitled to his salary while he works (*Decro-Wall International SA v Practitioners in Marketing Ltd* [1971] 2 AER 216, CA). If the employee is prevented from doing so, he is duty-bound to 'mitigate' his loss (see Chapter 2, paras 2.57 to 2.64). In practice, this means looking for work elsewhere. Once the employee enters other employment, he (or she) puts it out of his power to perform his duties under the original contract, and consequently will be 'taken to have accepted his wrongful dismissal as a repudiatory breach leading to a determination of the contract of service' (per Buckley LJ, *Gunton v Richmond-upon-Thames BC* [1980] ICR 755, CA).

8.24

Damages can be very high on occasions. Under his contract of employment, the Chairman of a company was entitled to 30 months' notice. His summary dismissal was held to be wrongful and he was awarded £84,300 as compensation for loss of salary and other benefits – after the court had taken account of his duty to mitigate his loss (*Shove v Downs Surgical plc* [1984] ICR 32, QB).

8.25

Some contracts come to an end by operation of law, eg by a winding-up order or by an Act of Parliament. On such occasions, employees are not entitled to notice, or money in lieu of notice. So when the Greater Manchester Council was abolished by the Local Government Act 1985, the council employees were debarred from relying on their contractual severance scheme which provided for a payment in lieu of notice (*R v Greater Manchester CC ex parte Greater Manchester Residuary Body*, 14 July 1987, CA).

THE EMPLOYER'S RIGHT TO DISMISS

8.26

Under the common law, an employer can 'hire and fire' whom he (or she) chooses (see para. 8.35 below). He has no need to justify his conduct or give a reason for dismissing an employee. He is (generally) immune from any claim for damages so long as he gives the required length of notice and complies with any express or implied disciplinary or dismissal procedures laid down in the contract of employment. Thus, when a Chief Education Officer (with the approval of the local authority Education Committee) decided to dismiss a number of employees and offer them new contracts, the court held that the decision was void. The Education Officer had no power to dismiss, and the error was not put right by the Committee confirming the decision (*R v Birmingham CC ex parte NUPE & Others, The Times*, 24 April 1984, DC).

8.27
Public sector employers are likely to be in a different position to those in the private sector. When making a decision, they must consider all pertinent matters, omitting all irrelevant collateral considerations. It must be a decision to which a reasonable employer would also come (*R v Hertfordshire CC ex parte NUPE & Others* [1985] IRLR 258, CA).

8.28
An employee guilty of gross misconduct may be dismissed without notice. He (or she) is not entitled to money in lieu. Although there is no statutory definition of 'gross misconduct' it will usually include grave acts of fraud or dishonesty, physical violence, sexual or racial harassment, other forms of assault, drunkenness or drug-taking, working for a competitor, or otherwise seriously damaging the employer's business interests. It also extends to gross incompetence by an allegedly skilled man (or woman), and to instances where an employee's conduct is seriously insulting or insubordinate (*Jilley v Transfleet Services Ltd*, 16 January 1981, EAT; and *Wilson v Racher* [1974] ICR 428, CA).

THE RIGHT TO SUSPEND

8.29
Sometimes a contract expressly or impliedly empowers an employer to suspend an employee in prescribed circumstances. For example, an employee will normally be suspended on full pay pending the outcome of an investigation into allegations of gross misconduct. In less serious circumstances, an employee might be suspended without pay (for a limited period) as an alternative to dismissal. Any period of suspension without pay, which persists for longer than two or three working days, could amount to a repudiation of contract.

8.30
As a general rule, an employee must be paid his normal wages or salary while suspended from work, unless his (or her) contract of employment makes provision to the contrary. An employer must comply with any procedural requirements, unless those requirements are non-contractual. So an Education Authority, which had a statutory power to suspend staff who were deemed medically unfit, were not entitled to suspend a teacher on half pay. The Authority had failed to adhere strictly to the formal requirements laid down in the Conditions of Service for Schoolteachers (*Whitley v Harrow London Borough Council, The Times*, 29 March 1988, QB).

INJUNCTIONS RESTRAINING DISMISSAL

8.31

The High Court has power to make an order of 'specific performance' of contracts or of 'prohibition' in certain employment cases. Such an order would not be made if it would have the effect of requiring an employer to continue to employ someone against his (or her) will. A failure to comply would amount to contempt of court, leading on occasions to dire consequences. If there is still mutual trust and confidence, or the applicant employee can be relied upon to carry out his (or her) duties properly, and there is a 'workable situation', a court may injunct an employer not to terminate an employee's contract of employment pending the full trial. In rare instances, a court may grant an injunction, even where trust and confidence are lost. An employer was in breach of contract when he dismissed a senior employee who was suspended on full pay at the time. A court order restoring the position enabled the employee to pursue rights that he would otherwise have lost (*Robb v London Borough of Hammersmith & Fulham* [1991] ICR 514, QBD).

8.32

An employer reluctantly dismissed an employee with insufficient notice after bowing to trade union pressure. It was held that, as the employer was willing to reinstate the employee and it was practicable for him to do so, a declaration could be made nullifying the effect of the notice. The employee remained in employment until there was a full trial on the issues (*Hill v C A Parsons & Co Ltd* [1971] 3 AER 1345 CA).

8.33

If a contract is underpinned by statutory disciplinary procedures, a court is more likely to intervene in an employee's favour. A dispute arose between an ophthalmologist and a consultant in charge of a health clinic. To resolve the problem, the Health Authority dismissed the ophthalmologist in clear breach of a statutory disputes procedure. Had the injunction not been granted, the doctor would have become unemployable within the National Health Service and would have been unable to use its facilities for his private patients. The court held that a refusal to intervene would have allowed the Authority to 'snap its fingers' at the employee's contractual rights (*Irani v Southampton South Western Health Authority* [1985] IRLR 203, HC).

8.34

An offer of employment 'subject to satisfactory references' usually means references which are adequate in the eyes of the employer in question, not in those of a reasonable employer. The job applicant would never become an employee until accepted by the employer to whom he had applied for work, so no question of an injunction arose (*Wishart v National Association of Citizens' Advice Bureaux Ltd* [1990] IRLR 393, CA).

8.35

A tribunal may order an employer to reinstate or re-engage a particular employee (see Chapter 5, paras 5.157 to 5.164), but has no power to enforce compliance with any such order. A refusal to comply will only lead to additional financial penalties. As Lord Davey famously remarked in the House of Lords in *Allen v Flood* [1898] AC 1, 'An employer may refuse to employ [a workman] for the most mistaken, capricious, malicious or morally reprehensible motives that can be conceived, but the workman has no right of action against him... A man has no right to be employed by any particular employer, and has no right to any particular employment if it depends on the will of another.'

VARIATION IN TERMS OF EMPLOYMENT

8.36

If an employer wishes to vary an employee's terms and conditions of employment, against the employee's wishes, he can do so at common law without exposing himself to an action for damages – provided he acts in a proper manner. If a manager is entitled to six months' notice, his (or her) employer can give him notice of dismissal to come into effect six months later. He might then offer to re-engage the same employee at half his (or her) former salary. Although the dismissal would not be wrongful, it might well be unfair (see Chapter 5).

8.37

Unless an employer has an express or (less likely) an implied contractual right to reduce an employee's rate of pay (or to vary any other condition of employment), his decision to do so would entitle the employee to resign and pursue a complaint of unfair constructive dismissal and/or to seek damages for any loss sustained by him (or her) as a result of the employer's actions (*Miller v Hamworthy Engineering Ltd* [1986] ICR 846, CA). What an employer cannot do is give notice to 'vary' a contract. He can only give the appropriate notice to dismiss the employee and offer new terms to come into effect after the notice period. The employee has the option either to accept the new terms or to terminate the employment (*Rigby v Ferodo Ltd* [1988] ICR 29, HL).

8.38

A local authority tried to substitute essential 'car user allowances' given to two employees under their contracts of employment. Instead of driving their own cars on official business they were told that they had to use pool cars instead. The Court of Appeal declared the move unlawful under the contract. It was of no effect (*Heir & Williams v Hereford & Worcester CC* [1985] IRLR 505, CA).

8.39

If a contract of employment provides scope for contractual variations, the employer who imposes such variations is immune from any subsequent claim for damages. Tax men refused to use computers for collecting PAYE. It was held that, although they needed to acquire new skills in order to operate the machines, the requirement was not beyond the scope of their existing contracts of employment. In short, their consent to the new working methods was not necessary. 'It can hardly be considered that to ask an employee to acquire basic skills... is something the slightest bit esoteric or even nowadays unusual' (per Walton J, *Cresswell v Board of Inland Revenue* [1984] ICR 508, ChD). It was further held that the employers were entitled to suspend without pay those who refused to operate the computers. The legal principle of 'no work, no pay' applied when the tax men refused to carry out a lawful requirement.

8.40

Employers retained the right in the contracts of employment with their staff to amend their rules 'from time to time'. Having introduced a non-contributory life scheme, they subsequently revoked it. It was held that the employers' decision fell within the powers conferred on them under the contracts and so was immune from interference by the courts (*Cadoux v Central Regional Council* [1986] IRLR 131, CS).

8.41

If an employer is in breach of contract by unilaterally varying the terms of a contract, it is for the employee to decide how to respond to that breach. He can leave the employment and claim damages for wrongful dismissal, and/or compensation for unfair 'constructive dismissal'. Or he can seek a declaration (from the courts) that the purported variations were unlawful and unenforceable against him. Alternatively, he can claim damages for any loss sustained because of the employer's breach (*Rigby v Ferodo Ltd* [1988] ICR 29, HL; and *Miller v Hamworthy Engineering Ltd* [1986] ICR 846, CA).

8.42

If an employee's response to a breach of contract is to do nothing and to carry on working as normal, he (or she) will, in time, be deemed to have 'affirmed' the contract, and will be bound by the new terms. The acceptance of a reduction in salary may be evidence of an affirmation. That assumption can be rebutted by evidence that the variation was accepted 'without prejudice' to the employee's other rights (see Chapter 2, paras 2.47 to 2.50) or where he (or she) has indicated that he objects to the variation and takes some action to assert his rights. In all such cases, the employee must act promptly (*Bliss v SE Thames Regional Health Authority* [1987] ICR 700, CA).

COMPENSATION FOR BREACH OF CONTRACT

8.43
As was indicated earlier in this chapter, a wrongful dismissal will ordinarily give rise to a claim for damages (see para. 8.11) before a tribunal or court. Damages are assessed on the basis of the difference between what the employee would have earned had he (or she) not been prematurely deprived of his job and what he earned (or might have expected to earn). The amount of damages is always subject to a duty on the employee to mitigate his loss by seeking alternative employment (see Chapter 2, paras 2.57 to 2.64).

8.44
If money is paid 'in lieu of notice', it may be paid either gross or net of tax and National Insurance contributions – at the whim of the employer. Although it may be expressed as a payment based on what the employee would have earned had he been permitted to work out his notice, it is nevertheless a payment intended to ward off a claim for breach of contract. In other words, it is a settlement figure. It is only where judgement is given for a breach of contract that it has to be net of tax. Perhaps surprisingly, the employer does not have to account to the Revenue for the notional tax deducted (*Gothard v Mirror Group Newspapers Ltd* [1988] ICR 729, CA).

8.45
The measure of damages is not generally affected by the employer's motives, except where there was an intention to avoid making a payment in breach of his statutory obligations. The fact that an employee was dismissed in a harsh and humiliating manner does not entitle him (or her) to compensation for 'injury to feelings'. Nor is it relevant that the manner of the employee's dismissal made finding alternative employment more difficult, although this would be taken into account by the court or tribunal when considering whether he (or she) had taken adequate steps to mitigate the loss (*Addis v Gramophone Co* [1909] AC 488, HL). A person who has been deprived of publicity, which would have enhanced his (or her) reputation, is entitled to damages in respect of that deprivation. Thus, the Court of Appeal held that an actor was entitled to recover damages when he was wrongfully prevented from appearing at a music-hall. But he could recover nothing for his injured feelings (*Withers v General Theatre Corporation* [1933] 2 KB 536, CA).

TIME LIMITS

8.46
Claims for damages arising out of a breach of contract will be heard either by the civil courts or (within limits) by the employment tribunals. Claims before the civil courts will become 'statute-barred' if not brought within six years of

the alleged breach, although an extension can be obtained in limited circumstances. Claims intended to be heard by the employment tribunals must be 'presented' within three months of the effective date of termination of the claimant's contract of employment. A claim presented 'out of time' will not be heard unless a tribunal is persuaded that it was not reasonably practicable for it to have been presented within the prescribed three-month period.

8.47

The employment tribunals have jurisdiction to hear most breach of employment contract disputes which arise or remain unresolved on the termination of employment. However, they have no jurisdiction to deal with claims in respect of personal injury, or relating to intellectual property, tied accommodation, obligations of confidence, or covenants in restraint of trade. Nor can a tribunal order the payment of an amount exceeding £25,000. Claims for damages in excess of that figure must be referred to the civil courts (*Source*: Employment Tribunals Extension of Jurisdiction (England & Wales) Order 1994 and the Employment Tribunals Extension of Jurisdiction (Scotland) Order 1994).

Contracts of employment

MINIMUM NOTICE PERIODS

9.1
On completion of one month's service, every employee (part-time as well as full-time) has the legal right to be given a minimum of one week's notice to terminate his (or her) contract of employment. The notice period increases to two weeks on completion of two years' service, three weeks on completion of three years' service; and so on, at the rate of one week's notice for each complete year of service – subject to a statutory upper limit of 12 weeks' notice on completion of 12 years' service (*Source*: ERA 1996, ss 86 to 91).

Note: In computing when the notice period begins and ends, the day on which notice was actually given must be disregarded (*West v Kneels Ltd* [1987] ICR 146, EAT; and *Misset v Council of the European Communities, The Times*, 23 March 1987, ECJ). In other words, the notice period begins to run from the day following the day on which notice was given.

9.2
For their part, employees must give their employer a minimum of one week's notice to terminate their contracts of employment. These statutory minimum periods of notice may, of course, be overridden by more generous contractual rights and obligations (*Source*: Employment Rights Act 1996, ss 86 to 91). Nowadays, it is commonplace for senior employees and employees with specialist skills, who cannot be readily replaced, to be required/entitled under their contracts to give/receive at least six months' notice.

WRITTEN STATEMENT OF EMPLOYMENT PARTICULARS

9.3
The Employment Rights Act 1996 also requires employers to issue *each* of their employees (part-time, full-time, permanent or temporary) with an accurate and up-to-date *written* statement of employment particulars. Furthermore, the employer must issue that written statement within two months of the date on which the employee's employment began, or – in the case of an employee who is required to work outside the UK within a month of being recruited – before the employee actually leaves the UK to take up his (or her) duties overseas. Any change in the particulars to be included in the

written statement must be notified to the employee (again in writing) within four weeks of the effective date of change (see also para. 9.37 below) (*Source*: ERA 1996, ss 1 to 7).

9.4
The written statement may be issued, either as:

- a single document which contains *all* of the prescribed particulars listed in the next paragraph; or

- a so-called 'principal statement' (containing the particulars listed in para. 9.6 below) supplemented by two or more instalments containing the rest of those prescribed particulars.

Particulars to be included in the written statement

9.5
The written statement (whether presented in instalments or otherwise) must contain the following particulars:

(a) the names of the employer and the employee;

(b) either the place of work or, where the employee is required or permitted to work at various places, an indication of that and of the address of the employer;

(c) the date on which the employment began;

(d) the date on which the employee's period of continuous employment began (which may differ from the date in (c) above) – taking into account any employment with a previous employer which counts towards that period;

(e) the title of the job which the employee is employed to do or a brief description of the work which the employee has been employed to do;

(f) the scale or rate of remuneration (wages, salary, etc) expressed as an hourly, weekly, monthly or annual figure, or the method to be used for calculating remuneration;

(g) the intervals at which wages or salary are to be paid (eg weekly or monthly);

(h) any terms and conditions relating to hours of work (including any terms and conditions relating to normal working hours);

(i) any terms and conditions relating to the employee's entitlement (if any) to holidays, including public holidays and holiday pay (the particulars given being sufficient to enable the employee's entitlement, including any entitlement to accrued holiday pay on the termination of employment, to be *precisely* calculated);

(j) any terms and conditions relating to incapacity for work due to sickness or injury, including any provision for sick pay;

(k) any terms and conditions relating to pensions and pension schemes, plus a note stating whether there is in force a contracting-out certificate (issued in accordance with Chapter 1 of Part III of the Pension Schemes Act 1993) stating that the employment is contracted-out employment (for the purposes of that Part of the 1993 Act);

(l) the length of notice which the employee is required to give and entitled to receive to terminate his (or her) contract of employment;

(m) where the employment is not intended to be permanent, the period for which it is expected to continue or, if it is for a fixed term, the date when it is to end; and

(n) particulars of any collective agreement which directly affect the terms and conditions of the employment, including (where the employer is not a party to such an agreement) the names of the parties by whom the agreement was made;

(o) where the employee is required to work outside the UK for a period of more than one month:

   (i) the period for which he (or she) is to work outside the UK;

   (ii) the currency in which remuneration is to be paid while he (or she) is working outside the UK;

   (iii) any additional remuneration payable to the employee, and any benefits to be provided to or in respect of him (or her) by reason of his being required to work outside the UK; and

   (iv) any terms and conditions relating to the employee's return to the UK.

As was indicated earlier, the written statement of employment particulars (whether given in instalments of otherwise) must contain all of the particulars (a) to (n) summarised above. If there are no particulars to be entered in the statement under any of those heads, the statement *must* say so. A 'Nil' return (or the omission of any reference to any one or other of those particulars) is *not* acceptable. If, for instance, an employer has no occupational sick pay scheme, the statement must say as much ('You will not be paid any part of your wages or salary if you are incapacitated for work because of illness or injury') – although the employer would do well to remind the employee that he (or she) nonetheless has the legal right (subject to the usual qualifying conditions) to be paid statutory sick pay (SSP) in respect of any such period of incapacity for work.

The same applies if an employee has no contractual right to annual holidays, paid or otherwise. That fact *must* be mentioned in the written statement. Again, silence on the subject is unacceptable and may lead to a reference to an employment tribunal.

Note: Under the Working Time Regulations 1998, which came into force on 1 October 1998, every worker (part-time as well as full-time), is entitled to a minimum of four weeks' paid annual holiday in every 'holiday year' and to accrued holiday pay on the termination of his (or her) employment (regardless of his length of service at the material time). Furthermore, those four weeks must be taken in the 'holiday year' in which they fall due. Unused holidays may not be carried forward into the next holiday year; nor is a worker entitled to money in lieu of unused holidays other than when his or her employment ends (*ibid* Regs 12 to 15).

Particulars to be included in the 'principal statement'

9.6
As was mentioned in para. 9.4 above, the written statement of terms of employment may be issued either as a single statement (incorporating *all* of particulars (a) to (n) listed in para. 9.5 above) *or* it can be issued in instalments. However, one of those instalments (the so-called 'principal statement') *must* contain all of the particulars (a) to (i) repeated hereunder, that is to say:

(a) the names of both the employer and the employee;

(b) either the employee's place of work or, where the employee is required or permitted to work at various places, an indication of that and of the address of the employer;

(c) the date on which the employee's employment began;

(d) the date on which the employee's period of continuous employment began (including any period of employment with a previous employer which counts towards that period);

(e) the title of the job which the employee is employed to do or a brief description of the work which the employee has been employed to do;

(f) the scale or rate of remuneration (wages, salary, etc) expressed as an hourly, weekly, monthly or annual figure, or the method to be used for calculating remuneration;

(g) the intervals at which wages or salary are to be paid (eg weekly or monthly);

(h) any terms and conditions relating to hours of work (including any terms and conditions relating to normal working hours);

(i) any terms and conditions relating to the employee's entitlement (if any) to holidays, including public holidays and holiday pay (the particulars given being sufficient to enable the employee's entitlement, including any entitlement to accrued holiday pay on the termination of employment, to be *precisely* calculated).

The 'principal' statement and its accompanying instalments must, nonetheless, be issued to each employee within two months of the date on which his (or her) employment began. It should be pointed out that an employer has nothing to gain by withholding the written statement until the employee in question has completed two months' service (a not uncommon, if pointless, practice). An employee can still rely on the particulars to be included in the statement, whether or not he (or she) has actually received the statement.

Supplementary instalments

9.7
All of the remaining particulars (namely (j) to (n), [and (o), where appropriate] in para. 9.5) may be included in a single document (eg a staff or works handbook) or in two or more separate documents or instalments. However, each of those documents or separate instalments must collectively give all of the information the employee is likely to need in relation to those particulars. Referring the employee to the existence and accessibility of other documents is *not* acceptable – *except* in the case of documents which explain terms and conditions relating to sickness or injury (sub-para. (j)) and terms and conditions relating to pensions and pension schemes (sub-para. (k)).

Disciplinary rules and procedures

9.8
The written statement must also include a note specifying any disciplinary rules applicable to the employee or referring the employee to the provisions of a document which the employee will have a reasonable opportunity to read or which will be readily accessible to the employee in some other way and which explains those rules. The note must also specify (by name or job title) a person to whom the employee can apply if he (or she) is dissatisfied with any disciplinary decision taken against him (and what needs to be done in order to register dissatisfaction). If there are further steps in the procedure, the note must either explain those steps or refer the employee to some other reasonably accessible document which explains them in some detail (*ibid* section 3(1)(a), 3(1)(b)(i) & 3(1)(c)). See also para. 9.33 and the *Note* appended to para. 9.9 below.

The requirement to include a note in the written statement explaining the employer's disciplinary rules and procedures does *not* apply to organisations in which the number of persons employed (including persons employed at other branches of the same organisation or by any associated employer) is less than 20 (*ibid* section 3(3)). However, it is well to point out that once the 'dispute resolution' provisions of the Employment Act 2002 come into force (September 2003), every employer, regardless of the size of his business or undertaking, will be duty-bound to develop and implement statutory minimum dismissal and disciplinary procedures (DDPs) and to make use of those procedures when disciplinary issues arise.

Grievances and procedure

9.9

In addition to information about disciplinary rules and procedures, the written statement must also include a note specifying, by description or otherwise, a person to whom the employee can apply for the purpose of seeking redress of any grievance relating to his (or her) employment, and the manner in which any such application should be made.

Note: Section 10 of the Employment Relations Act 1999 allows that a worker who is required or invited by his (or her) employer to attend a disciplinary or grievance hearing has the right to be accompanied at that hearing by a single companion of his own choosing. That companion may be a fellow-employee, a shop steward or a (suitably qualified and experienced) full-time trade union official. The companion has the right to make representations but not to answer questions on the worker's behalf. Should the chosen companion be unavailable to attend on the date appointed for the hearing, the employer must postpone the hearing for up to five working days. The companion (if a fellow worker) must be allowed paid time off work to attend the hearing. It should be noted that section 10 of the 1999 Act (which came into force on 4 September 2000) does not impose any duty on trade union officials or other workers to accompany a colleague at a disciplinary or grievance hearing. But, any worker who does agree to accompany a colleague at such a hearing may not lawfully be dismissed or disciplined for doing so.

If there are further steps in the grievance procedure (eg appeals to progressively higher levels of management), the note must either explain those steps or refer the employee to some other document which explains them – so long as the employee has reasonable opportunities to read that document in the course of his (or her) employment or it is made reasonably accessible in some other way (*ibid* section 3(1)(b)(ii) & 3(1)(c)). It is as well to point out that once the 'dispute resolution' provisions of the Employment Act 2002 come into force (September 2003?), every employer, regardless of the size of his business or undertaking, will be duty-bound to develop and implement statutory minimum grievance procedures (GPs) for the resolution of workplace grievances. See also para. 9.35 below.

COMMENTARY

9.10

Although the written statement (often, although not entirely accurately, described as the 'contract of employment') is not expected to have the same precision and clarity as a lease or a will, care ought nonetheless be taken when writing it. This is especially true of a contract given under seal (which will ordinarily include the particulars required to be given in the written statement). Quite expensive consequences can follow if an employee's contractual rights are expressed in terms which are imprecise or ambiguous.

For example, before a tribunal or court can determine the rights and wrongs of an alleged 'wrongful dismissal', the obligations of the parties to the contract must be ascertainable. This depends on what was agreed and written into the contract. Was the steel erector's work restricted to a radius of 100 miles of Birmingham, or could he (or she) be sent to work on a job anywhere in the British Isles? If he was sacked for refusing to work on a project in Bodmin, the question of what he could and could not be required to do would be crucial in deciding whether his refusal was in breach of his contract of employment, or whether his resultant dismissal was fair or unfair.

9.11

Not every term or condition of employment is suitable for incorporation in a contract of employment. So a recommended minimum period of notice in a redundancy situation was held to be for guidance only and was not contractually binding. In any event, the recommendation was contained in an Appendix which was directed primarily at procedural matters. It was too imprecise (*Griffiths v Buckinghamshire County Council* [1994] ICR 265, QBD).

9.12

The Employment Rights Act 1996 does not require an employee to sign his (or her) copy of the written statement; but he will nonetheless be bound by its terms. If the employee disputes any of the terms and conditions, he should make his objections known from the very outset (*W E Cox Toner (International) Ltd v Crook* [1981] ICR 823, EAT; and *System Floors (UK) Ltd v Daniel* [1982] ICR 54, EAT). The same principle applies where there is a variation of the terms. But, where the variation has no immediate practical effect, it is less likely that the employee will be taken to have affirmed it (*Jones v Associated Tunnelling Co Ltd* [1981] IRLR 477, EAT).

9.13

The fact that the principal terms of a contract are set out in writing does not necessarily mean that they are conclusive. If there is a dispute about any of those terms, those set down in writing in the document are likely to be very persuasive. In the absence of strong evidence to the contrary, a term will usually be held to be binding (*Gascol Conversions Ltd v Mercer* [1974] IRLR 155, CA).

9.14

Some terms are implied by law. Various regulations were incorporated into the contract of employment of a medical practitioner. Unknown to him, his employers amended his contract following negotiations with his trade union. The new terms conferred valuable rights on him. But, he failed to take the required procedural steps to gain access to those rights. It was held that the man's employer was under an implied duty to inform staff about the new scheme. His failure to do so resulted in damages being award to the practitioner of an amount equal to his loss (*Scally & Others v Southern Health & Social Services Board & Another* [1991] ICR 771, HL).

The names of the employer and employee

9.15

The requirement to include the names of both the employer and the employee in the written statement is not just a formality – a lot can depend on it. It identifies the employer, so that, if the need arises, the proper party can be sued. For instance, if the employer is stated to be H G Jones, then Mr Jones will be personally liable for any claim or debt. If it is stated to be H G Jones Ltd, then only the limited company will be held responsible, not the individual directors. A former employer (to the immediate past one) can also be liable in certain circumstances.

Date on which employment began

9.16

This is a very important insertion in the 'contract of employment' as it might well be critical in determining the employee's statutory employment rights, including his (or her) right not to be unfairly dismissed or his right to be paid a statutory redundancy payment. In giving the date on which the employee's period of continuous employment began, the written statement must state whether any period of employment with a previous employer counts towards that period. This might be the case if the employee worked for an associated employer or for a company (firm or organisation) sold or transferred to his (or her) current employer in circumstances covered by Chapter I, Part XIV of the Employment Rights Act 1996 ('Continuous Employment') or by the Transfer of Undertakings (Protection of Employment) Regulations 1981 (see Chapter 22). Other statutory rights, such as the right to statutory maternity pay (SMP), extended maternity leave, a guarantee payment, and so on, are also dependent on an employee having been continuously employed for a prescribed minimum period.

9.17

If an employee had taken part in strike action on one or more occasions during his (or her) period of employment, the date on which that period of employment began will be held to have been postponed by the number of days lost on account of such action. This approach must be adopted to establish the total period of continuous employment when determining an employee's entitlement to a statutory redundancy payment, the amount of the basic award of compensation for unfair dismissal; and so on (*Source*: ERA 1996, s.216).

The title of the job

9.18

The written statement must state the employee's job title or give a brief description of the work for which he (or she) is employed. If a degree of job flexibility is required, the statement should say as much or be accompanied by some other document, such as a job description, which emphasises the importance of flexible working arrangements. This is especially important in the case of production-line workers (eg in a food factory) where changing production requirements may require workers to transfer from one department to another. The scope of an employee's duties under his (or her) contract of employment will also be important in equal pay, discrimination and redundancy cases. A 'mobility clause' should also be inserted at this point.

9.19

A divisional contract surveyor, whose contract required him to carry out any duties consistent with his qualifications and experience, was made redundant when the job of 'divisional contract surveyor' ceased to exist. It was held that his dismissal was unfair because there were other jobs available which he was 'capable' of doing (*Cowen v Haden Ltd* [1983] ICR 1, CA).

Scale of remuneration and intervals when paid

9.20

An employee clearly has the right to know how much he (or she) is to be paid and at what intervals. The statement should anticipate and provide the answers to the following questions. Is overtime working compulsory? If so, how many hours a week? What are the overtime premium rates? What will I be paid if I work (or agree to work) on bank and public holidays? How is my pay calculated? Am I entitled to a bonus or commission? How are they calculated? Is the bonus discretionary or payable as of right?

Note: Under the National Minimum Wage Regulations 1999 (SI 1999/584), every adult worker aged 22 and over must be paid a minimum of £4.20 an hour for all hours worked (or a minimum of £3.60 an hour if taking part in 'accredited training' for at least 26 days in the first six months of his or her employment). The prescribed national minimum wage (NMW) for workers aged 18 to 21, inclusive, is £3.60 an hour. These are the 2003/04 figures. At present, there is no prescribed NMW for workers aged 16 or 17. The written statement of employment particulars issued to every employee must acknowledge the employee's right to be paid no less than the appropriate NMW. Any term in a contract of employment (or written statement) which purports to override or undermine a worker's right to be paid the NMW is null and void. The 1999 Regulations are 'policed' by Inland Revenue enforcement officers. Paying a worker less than the appropriate NMW is an offence under the National Minimum Wage Act 1998, for which the penalty on summary conviction is a fine of up to £5,000 (for each offence).

If there are to be deductions from pay (or demands for payment) in respect of poor workmanship, spoilt or damaged goods, cash shortages or stock deficiencies, the contract (or written statement) must be very specific as to the exact circumstances in which any such deduction (or payment) will be made (or will be required to be paid) – while at the same time acknowledging the employee's statutory rights under Part II of the Employment Rights Act 1996 ('Protection of Wages'). The employer would also be well-advised to secure the employee's written agreement (by asking the employee to sign the written statement) to the making of any such deduction (or demand for payment).

Working hours

9.21
The hours which an employee is required to work are important, not only from the point of view of the employee's contractual right not to be required to work longer hours than those spelt out in the written statement, but also as a means of calculating his (or her) weekly pay. If overtime is to be compulsory, that fact should be stated. If voluntary, that too should be made clear. The employee should also be left in no doubt as to the possibility of his (or her) being transferred from day work to night work (or to shiftwork) and the circumstances in which such a change might be imposed.

Are meal breaks (and coffee or tea breaks) paid or unpaid? Can an employee be required to work at weekends or on bank and public holidays? If so, is the employee entitled to be paid at premium rates for such work; and is there provision for time off work in lieu of work carried out on such days?

Note: Under the Working Time Regulations 1998 (SI 1998/1833) adult workers (unless empolyed in an excluded category) cannot be required to work more than an average 48 hours a week calculated over a reference period of 17 consecutive weeks. Individual workers may agree to work more than that average 48 hours, so long as they do so individually, voluntarily and in writing, and are reminded of their right to change their minds (without penalty). Workers under the age of 18 cannot be required to work more than 40 hours a week or for more than 8 hours a day. These latter limits are absolute (with no provision for averaging their working hours). Any term in a collective or workforce agreement which purports to override a worker's rights under the 1998 Regulations is null and void. For further information, please turn to Chapter 18.

Holidays and holiday pay

9.22

An employee's entitlement to holidays and holiday pay must be clearly spelt out in the written statement, as must his (or her) entitlement to accrued holiday pay on the termination of employment. Indeed, the information to be included under this head in the written statement must be sufficient to enable the employee to calculate *precisely* his residual entitlement on termination.

Under the Working Time Regulations 1998, every worker (a term encompassing individuals who are not 'employees' in the strict legal sense), has the legal right to a minimum four weeks' paid holidays in every holiday year. Workers have no legal right to carry forward unused holidays into the next holiday year nor to be paid money in lieu of unused holidays (unless their contracts terminate part-way through a holiday year). Any contract of employment (or otherwise), that purports to override a worker's statutory rights under the 1998 Regulations, is void and unenforceable.

9.23

Employers in some industries require their employees (notably those in production) departments to take their annual holidays to coincide with the annual factory shut-down (for essential maintenance). Although custom and practice in this respect over the years will usually be imported into the contract of employment, employers would be well-advised to include this requirement in the written statement or in an accompanying staff or works handbook, so long as the principal particulars appear in the statement itself. The same applies to holidays over the Christmas and New Year periods.

9.24

It remains to be seen whether an employee can be expected to 'nibble away' at his (or her) entitlement to annual holidays when asking for time off for dental visits or to deal with any domestic problems (death of a member of the family; and so on). With the coming into force on 15 December 1999 of the 'time off for dependants' provisions of the Employment Relations Act 1999 (now section 57A of the Employment Rights Act 1996), employees have the legal right to take a reasonable amount of *unpaid* time off work:

- to provide assistance when a dependant falls ill, gives birth, or is injured or assaulted;

- to make arrangements for the care of a dependant who is ill or injured;

- when a dependant dies (eg, to make funeral arrangements and/or to attend at the funeral);

- to make emergency arrangements for the care of a dependant (when current arrangements are unexpectedly disrupted or terminated); or

- to deal with an unexpected incident involving one or other of the employee's children while at school (eg, a playground accident, a disciplinary matter, or whatever).

Note: For these purposes, the term 'dependant' in relation to an employee means the employee's husband or wife, child, parent, or a person (other than a tenant, lodger or boarder) who lives in the same household as the employee, who reasonably relies on the employee either for assistance when injured, assaulted or taken ill or to make arrangements for the provision of care in the event of illness or injury. For further particulars, please turn to Chapter 14, paras 14.100 to 14.110.

Given that an employee has no statutory right to be paid when exercising his or her rights under the 'time off for dependants' provisions of the 1996 Act, the written statement (or accompanying staff or works handbook) issued to that employee may make provision either for a short period of *paid* time off on compassionate grounds or afford employees the opportunity to use some of their annual holiday entitlement for that purpose.

Temporary employment and fixed-term contracts

9.25

If an employee is hired to do a specific job of work, which is expected to be completed within a few weeks or months (or whatever), the written statement must indicate the period for which the employment is expected to continue. If the contract is for a fixed term, the statement must indicate when that term is to end.

Information about pensions and pension schemes

9.26

The full particulars of such a complex subject are not easily incorporated into the written contract. It will usually suffice to deal with it in general terms, referring to other documents which will set out the relevant terms in greater detail. If there are no pension rights, the statement must say as much. It would also be helpful to explain other options available to employees (contracting-out of the State Earnings-Related Pension Scheme, portable pension plans, etc).

Terms relating to incapacity for work due to sickness or injury

9.27

If an employee has no contractual right to be paid the whole or any part of his (or her) wages or salary during absences from work occasioned by illness or injury, the written statement should say as much. Silence on the subject is not acceptable. Indeed, should the employer's silence on this issue be referred to an employment tribunal, the latter might well import terms relating to sickness benefits into the employee's contract (with which the employer will be left with no choice but to comply).

Employers should not lose sight of the fact that employees generally (subject to certain *qualifying conditions*) have the legal right to be paid statutory sick pay (SSP) for a period of up to 28 weeks in any single period (or series of linked periods) of incapacity for work (PIWs). Any term in a contract (or written statement) which purports to override an employee's right to SSP, or to impose more stringent conditions, is void and unenforceable (*Source*: Social Security Contributions & Benefits Act 1992, Part XI).

9.28
If an employer chooses to make *discretionary* payments (in addition to any entitlement to SSP) to employees who are absent from work on grounds of sickness or injury, he (or she) should make it clear – either in the written statement or some other document – that such payments *are* discretionary. Any contractual entitlement to benefits under an occupational sick pay scheme could pose problems if a sick or injured employee is dismissed *before* that entitlement is exhausted. Indeed, in such a situation, the employee could pursue a claim for damages (either in the civil court or before an employment tribunal) arising out of his (or her) employer's breach of his contractual rights.

9.29
Any employee who is unable to attend for work because of illness or injury should be aware of his (or her) employer's rules about the time limits for informing the relevant manager or supervisor (or the Personnel Department) about his non-availability for work. The rules about self-certificates for illness and the eventual production of a doctor's sick note should also be made clear, preferably in the written statement. It should be pointed out here that the notification and evidential rules, in the context of an employee's entitlement (if any) to SSP, are not as stringent as those necessarily laid down by an employer left to deal with the (sudden and unexpected) absence of a key employee.

9.30
Finally, SSP is payable to employees who are 'deemed' to be incapacitated for work in circumstances not ordinarily encompassed by an occupational sick pay scheme. For example, an employee who takes time off work for a breast-enhancement operation or for a vasectomy, or who is injured on a skiing holiday (or while taking part in an exceptionally hazardous sport), will be 'deemed' to be incapacitated for work under the Employer's SSP Scheme, but will not necessarily be entitled to payment under the terms of his (or her) employer's occupational sick pay scheme.

The employer's rules should state whether an employee can expect to be credited with additional days of holiday if he (or she) falls ill or is injured during his (or her) annual holidays (thereby foreshortening or interrupting those holidays).

Notice periods

9.31
The notice which an employee is required to give (or is entitled to receive) to terminate his (or her) contract of employment should not undermine (or presume to undermine) the employee's statutory right to a minimum period of notice (as to which, see Chapter 3 (paras 3.9 to 3.14) and para. 9.1 above). If the minimum period of notice given by an employer is less than that prescribed by statute, the 'effective date of termination' of that employee's contract of employment will (for the purposes of establishing his [or her] right to present a complaint of unfair dismissal, or to claim a redundancy payment) be the date on which the statutory period of notice would have expired had it been duly given by the employer on the date on which the notice to terminate was actually given.

9.32
An employee who is not given the notice to which he (or she) is entitled under the relevant contract of employment, or the notice prescribed by the Employment Rights Act 1996 (at section 86), whichever is the longer, may pursue a claim (or present a complaint) for damages arising out of that breach of contract. The employee is nonetheless under a common law duty to mitigate his (or her) loss, eg by actively looking for work elsewhere (see Chapter 2, paras 2.57 to 2.64) (*Robert Cort v Charman & Sons* [1981] ICR 816, EAT).

Disciplinary rules and procedure

9.33
An employer's disciplinary rules should make it clear to employees that he (or she) expects (indeed, insists upon) certain standards of conduct amongst employees, both in their relationships with one another and their immediate superiors, *and* in their dealings with customers, clients and members of the public. They should also be given to understand that socially-unacceptable conduct (fighting, physical assault, sexual harassment, licentiousness, racial abuse, obscene language, drunkenness, drug-taking, etc) will not be tolerated and will, in prescribed cases, lead to the summary dismissal of the offender. Failure to obey safety rules (eg by removing machine guards or indulging in dangerous 'horseplay') should also be added to the list.

The employer's disciplinary rules (some of which will be peculiar to the trade or industry in which the employer is engaged) must not only specify which offences will lead to summary dismissal, but must also described the procedure to be followed in the event of a breach of those rules, the number of stages in that procedure, and the person or persons to whom an employee can appeal if dissatisfied with any disciplinary decision (including dismissal) taken against him. Those rules and their accompanying procedures should also acknowledge the now statutory right of workers to be accompanied at the formal stages of a disciplinary (or grievance) procedure by a single companion of their own choosing (fellow-employee, shop steward or full-time trade union official) (as to which, see the *Note* to para. 9.9 above).

9.34

The dismissal of an employee contrary to the employer's clearly-laid-down rules for dealing with breaches of discipline will invariably (but not always) lead to a finding of unfair dismissal. Much will depend on whether the breach was serious or merely a technicality and whether the result would inevitably have been the same based on the information available to the employer at the material time (see Chapter 5, paras 5.93 to 5.99) (*Polkey v A E Dayton Services Ltd* [1988] ICR 142, HL). It is as well to point out here that, once the 'dispute resolution' provisions of the Employment Act 2002 come into force (September 2003), the employment tribunals will be empowered to disregard procedural mistakes, beyond certain statutory minimum procedures, in unfair dismissal cases, if following the full procedures would have made no difference to the outcome.

Grievances and procedure

9.35

An employee who is concerned about aspects of his (or her) work (pay, working hours, conditions of employment, etc) or a perceived infringement of his statutory employment rights has the right to refer such concerns to an immediate superior, and (if the contract so provides) to progressively higher levels of management, until they are resolved (whether or not to the satisfaction of the employee in question). The written statement must include (or be accompanied by) a note specifying, by description or otherwise, a person to whom the employee can apply for the purposes of seeking redress of any grievance relating to his employment and the manner in which any such application should be made. Where there are further steps consequent on any such application, the note must either explain those steps or refer to the provisions of a document explaining them which is reasonably accessible to the employee. The reader should note that, once the dispute resolution provisions of the Employment Act 2002 come into force, every employer, regardless of the size of his business or undertaking, will be duty-bound to develop and promulgate statutory minimum grievance procedures(GPs) accessible to all employees. See also the *Note* to para. 9.9 above.

Work outside the UK

9.36

A new recruit, who is to be posted overseas within one month of starting work, must be issued with the written statement of employment particulars *before* he (or she) leaves the UK. Furthermore, if the employee is to work outside the UK for more than one month, the statement must also contain particulars of:

- the period for which he (or she) is to work outside the UK;

- the currency in which remuneration is to be paid while the employee is working outside the UK;

- any additional remuneration payable to the employee, and any benefits to be provided to or in respect of him (or her) by reason of his being required to work outside the UK; and

- any terms and conditions relating to the employee's return to the UK.

(*Source*: ERA 1996, s.1(4)(k).)

STATEMENT OF CHANGES

9.37

If, after the initial statement is issued, there is any change in any of the particulars included in the statement, the employer must supply each of the employees concerned with a further written statement containing particulars of the change – and must do so not later than one month after the change in question (*Source*: ERA 1996, s.4).

Where only the name of the employer changes, no fresh statements have to be served. If the identity changes but nothing else, then it is sufficient for the employer to notify the employee in writing of the change in identity and restate the date on which the period of continuous employment began.

EXCLUDED CLASSES

9.38

A written statement of employment particulars need not be issued:

- to an employee who resigns or is dismissed within one month of starting work, but must be issued to an employee whose employment comes to an end (for whatever reason) after one month but before the end of the period of two months beginning with the date on which his (or her) employment began (*ibid* ss 2(6) and 198); or

- to a person employed as a seaman in a ship registered in the United Kingdom under a crew agreement the provisions and form of which are of a kind approved by the Secretary of State for Work & Pensions (*ibid* s.199(1)).

REMEDIES FOR FAILURE TO SUPPLY A WRITTEN STATEMENT OF EMPLOYMENT PARTICULARS

9.39

If an employer fails to supply an employee with a written statement, or issues a statement which is incomplete, the employee can refer the matter for determination by an employment tribunal. The tribunal has power to determine what particulars should have been included in the statement. Where the particulars have been supplied but are alleged to be wrong, the tribunal can confirm, amend or substitute other terms. A tribunal is entitled to hear oral evidence from both sides as to what they understood the correct position to be, and, if necessary, what they intended (*Boothferry BC v Boyle*, 19 December 1984, EAT).

Note: Once section 38 of the Employment Act 2002 comes into force (September 2003), an employer's evident failure to provide an employee with a written statement of employment particulars will prompt an employment tribunal to increase the amount of any award of compensation payable to that employee (arising out of an infringement of one or other of the employee's statutory rights), by the equivalent of between two and four weeks' pay.

9.40

An employer is likewise entitled to refer a written statement to tribunal where there is a dispute over its accuracy. The particulars as found by the tribunal will bind each party as if they had been included in the statement. A tribunal is now empowered to interpret the meaning of an agreement if the parties disagree as to what a term means. Thus if an employer fails to state what length of notice is required to terminate the employment and the tribunal finds on the evidence it should be the common law 'reasonable notice', it may go on to decide what is 'reasonable' (*Source*: Employment tribunals Extension of Jurisdiction (England & Wales) Order 1994; and the Employment tribunals Extension of Jurisdiction (Scotland) Order 1994).

In exercising its statutory powers, a tribunal will not rewrite or amend a binding contract. It will merely direct an amendment to or substitution for the particulars in dispute where there is an error or omission. It cannot make any monetary award.

9.41

The first task of an employment tribunal on a reference to it under section 11 of the 1996 Act (*References to employment tribunals*), is to:

- ascertain whether there are any express written or oral terms in the employee's contract;

- if there are none, then it must decide whether a term can be implied in all the circumstances which may include anything to be deduced from the conduct of the parties. If that fails to provide the answer, and there are factors pointing both ways, the term most favourable to the employee will usually be adopted;

- in the last resort, in a case where there is a mandatory requirement to provide particulars, eg notice periods or remuneration, a tribunal will need to determine what is 'reasonable' in the circumstances (*Eagland v British Telecommunications plc* [1992] IRLR 323, CA).

9.42
A tribunal may not invent terms in respect of non-mandatory requirements. For instance, if an employee claims sick pay during a lengthy absence, and there is nothing about it in the contract, and nothing can be deduced from the surrounding circumstances, a tribunal cannot decide that the employee should have been paid sick pay during his (or her) absence.

Effect of a declaration

9.43
Once a tribunal has made a declaration it becomes *res judicata* and all other courts and tribunals are bound by it. If the declaration is in favour of the employee, the new terms can be enforced by an employment tribunal or by a civil court. If other employees within the same organisation are affected by the declaration, the employer's final liability may be substantial. Indeed, the employer can be ordered to repay any sum properly payable to the employee, without limit as to the amount.

AMENDING THE EMPLOYMENT CONTRACT

9.44
An employer can amend an employee's contract of employment provided the employee is agreeable. Although an increase in an employee's annual holiday entitlement or the granting of more generous sickness benefits is unlikely to be challenged, an employee will be more than a little upset if his (or her) employer decides to cut his annual salary from, say, £20,000 to £15,000. Any such unilateral variation would be tantamount to a repudiation of the employee's contract and actionable as such.

9.45
Under the common law, an employer can achieve the same end by dismissing the employee with notice and re-employing him (or her) on terms which suit

the employer (as to which, see Chapter 8, paras 8.36 to 8.42). However, under statute law, the employee would be within his (or her) rights to resign (with or without notice) by virtue of his employer's repudiatory conduct and present a complaint of unfair 'constructive dismissal' – if the variation is serious and the employee objects to it (*Robertson v British Gas Corporation* [1983] ICR 351, CA). The dismissal will be unfair unless it is for one or other of the 'permitted' reasons (listed in Chapter 5 at para. 5.14). A variation of contract can be defended as being for 'some other substantial reason', if the change has been made for sound business reasons. It will nonetheless be necessary to demonstrate that there had been adequate consultation with the employee and every effort made to accommodate his (or her) objections (*Berriman v Delabole Slate Ltd* [1985] ICR 546, CA; *Ellis v Brighton Cooperative Society Ltd* [1976] IRLR 419, EAT; and *Evans v Elemeta Holdings Ltd* [1982] ICR 323, EAT).

TIME LIMITS

9.46
A complaint of an employer's refusal or failure to provide a written statement of employment particulars must be presented to the Secretary to the Tribunals within three months of that refusal or failure or, where appropriate, within three months of the 'effective date of termination' of the employee's contract of employment. A tribunal will not consider a reference or complaint presented 'out of time' unless satisfied that it was not reasonably practicable for the reference or complaint to have been presented sooner (see Chapter 3, paras 3.66 to 3.73).

9.47
If an employer has become insolvent or is adjudged bankrupt, his employees may recover some, but not all, of any monies owed to them at that time from the Secretary of State (in practice, the Department for Trade & Industry). If the latter refuses or fails to pay, the matter may be referred to an employment tribunal for a declaration as to what the Secretary of State should have paid and must pay (*Source*: ERA 1996, s.183). See also Chapter 15, paras 15.56 to 15.58.

Restrictive covenants

GENERAL INFORMATION

10.1
During their employment, it is inevitable that directors, senior managers, chemists, engineers, research staff, and others occupying strategic positions within an organisation, will have access to trade secrets, product formulations, development plans, marketing and pricing strategies, and other confidential matters relating to the employer's business. An employee who resigns or is dismissed could do serious damage to his (or her) (former) employer's business should he allow that information to fall into the wrong hands. To protect his position, the employer will often incorporate so-called restrictive covenants in the contracts of employment of all key personnel. Such a covenant will put the employee on notice that he or she must not divulge any such confidential information to unauthorised third parties and, in many cases, will impose a duty on the employee not to compete with his (former) employer after his employment ends and not to accept employment with another employer in the same trade or industry.

10.2
A restrictive covenant will usually be for a limited period and will restrict the employee's post-employment activities within a clearly defined geographical area. A covenant in 'restraint of trade' will only be enforceable if it is shown to be reasonable as between the parties, and that it is in the public interest. It is for the employer to demonstrate that it is reasonable in area and time in order to reasonably protect his business. A claim that such a restriction is not in the public interest must be proved by the employee (*Spencer v Marchington* [1988] IRLR 392, HC).

10.3
The principle was enunciated by Lord MacNaughten in this way: 'The public have an interest in every person's carrying on his trade freely: so has the individual. All interferences with the individual liberty of action in trading, and all restraints of trade of themselves, if there is nothing more, are contrary to public policy, and therefore void. That is the general rule. But there are exceptions... It is sufficient justification... if the restriction is reasonable... in reference to the interests of the parties concerned, and reasonable in reference to the interests of the public, so... as to afford adequate protection to the party

in whose favour it is imposed, while at the same time it is in no way injurious to the public' (*Maxim-Nordenfelt Gun Co v Nordenfelt* [1894] AC 535, HL).

THE GRANTING OF AN INJUNCTION

10.4
In considering the interests of the parties, the covenant must be necessary to protect some trade secret or to prevent some personal influence being exercised over customers to entice them away. It must be for no longer than is necessary to prevent the employee from enjoying the unfair advantage that he had obtained from the acquisition of the information (*Herbert Morris Ltd v Saxelby* [1916] 1 AC 688, HL; and *Roger Bullivant Ltd & Others v Ellis & Others* [1987] ICR 464, CA). Once it is established that the restraint in favour of a firm is reasonable, an injunction will be granted (subject to judicial discretion). It matters not that the customer has indicated that he (or she) no longer wishes to trade with the company but intends to deal with the ex-employee instead (*John Michael Design plc v Cooke & Foley* [1987] ICR 445, CA).

10.5
If an employer has been wrongfully dismissed, the employer will be unable to enforce a restrictive covenant, because he cannot take advantage of his own wrong. But the employee who brings about his (or her) own (premature) dismissal will still be bound by such a covenant (*Rex Stewart Jeffries Parker Ginsberg Ltd v Parker* [1988] IRLR 483, CA). But if an employee is entitled to, and does, resign because of his employer's repudiatory conduct (ie, 'constructive dismissal': see Chapter 2, paras 2.36 to 2.40), the employer loses the right to enforce any restrictive covenant against that employee. This principle was applied where an employer was in breach of his implied contractual duty of mutual trust and confidence, and the employee resigned (*General Bill Posting v Atkinson* [1909] AC 118, HL; and *Dairy Crest Ltd v Wise*, 24 September 1993, QBD).

The 'blue pencil' test

10.6
The general rule is that where a covenant is too wide, any attempt to enforce it in the courts will fail. But where it is possible to apply the 'blue pencil' test, eg by deleting parts, leaving the rest intact without the necessity of rewriting it, and the remaining part is separate and not part of a single covenant, it will be enforced (*Attwood v Lamont* [1920] 3 KB 571, CA). The severed parts must usually be of trivial importance, or merely be of a technical nature. They must not go to the main import or substance of the restraint. There has been a tendency in some cases, where justice demands it, for courts to ascertain the true intention of the parties and give effect to it, even though it involved some redrafting (*Mason v Provident Clothing & Supply Co Ltd* [1913] AC 724, HL; and *GFI Group Inc v Eaglestone* [1994] IRLR 119, QBD).

10.7

If a covenant is capable of being construed as giving a wider protection than is necessary or was intended, it will fail entirely. The 'blue pencil' cannot be applied (*Office Angels Ltd v Rainer-Thomas & Another* [1991] IRLR 214, CA). So where an employee covenanted not to engage in several different businesses, it was held not to be severable into parts which could be enforced and parts which could be ignored. To do so would require some of the terms to be rewritten. But where an outgoing partner covenanted not to engage in similar work or to compete with the partnership, it was held that the covenant was severable. The latter term was effective; the former was not (*Attwood v Lamont* [1920] 3 KB 571, CA; and *Ronbar Enterprises Ltd v Green* [1954] 2 AER 266, CA).

10.8

Sometimes the principle can act very harshly where the harm is likely to be great. An interior designer with five years' experience in the furniture business covenanted not to work in a similar job in the UK for 12 months after she left the company. 'Untold damage' could be done to the employer by disclosure of confidential pricing and certain other information if she joined a competitor. It was held to be an appropriate case to injunct her from doing so (*A & D Bedrooms Ltd v Michael & Hyphen Fitted Furniture Ltd*, 8 March 1983, CA).

10.9

Each case has to be considered on its own particular facts. Previous authorities are usually of little help in deciding what is 'reasonable'. They do not bind the judge (*Dairy Crest Ltd v Pigott* [1989] ICR 92, CA).

WHERE THE COVENANTOR IS VENDOR OR SHAREHOLDER

10.10

Where a business is acquired on terms that the former owners or shareholders (whatever the size of their holding or whether they are also employees) agree to a restriction on their future activities to protect the goodwill of the undertaking, different considerations apply (*Systems Reliability Holdings plc v Smith* [1990] IRLR 377, ChD).

10.11

A wider restrictive covenant will be upheld provided:

- it is legitimate for the purchaser to protect those interests; and

- the protection is no more than necessary.

Generally, the parties are the best judges of what is reasonable between them, and what price, in particular, should be paid for the restrictions. The court will shy away from trying to apply any sort of doctrine of 'proportionality', eg to establish whether the price is too low for the restriction (*Allied Dunbar (Frank Weisinger) Ltd v Weisinger (Case B)* [1988] IRLR 60, ChD).

APPLICATION OF THE PRINCIPLES

10.12
A solicitor's articled clerk agreed with his employers not to practise as a solicitor within seven miles of a stated place for an unlimited period. It was held that the covenant was reasonable. Any person who had served in such a position must have acquired information about the affairs and clients of the business. That puts him in a position of being able to impair gravely the goodwill of his employer's practice (*Fitch v Dewes* [1921] 2 AC 158, HL).

10.13
A distinction has to be drawn between two categories of employees. There are those who have direct dealings with clients and enhance the goodwill of the business through their skills and personalities. In such a case, the employer has an identifiable proprietary interest in that goodwill and has the right to protect it. And then there are employees who operate on a highly personalised basis and who have acquired a reputation for efficiency, integrity and trustworthiness. Those qualities attach themselves to the employee, not to the business. In the latter instance, the employer would have no proprietary interest that could be made the subject-matter of the restrictive covenant (*Marion White v Francis* [1972] 1 WLR 1423, CA; and *Cantor Fitzgerald (UK) Ltd v Wallace & Others* [1992] IRLR 215, QBD). It has been held that although the goodwill of a business might vest to a large degree in its staff, that did not make them an asset which could not be poached by competitors. So where four former employees set up in competition, a restriction, which sought to prevent then soliciting former colleagues to join them, was not enforceable (*Hanover Insurance Brokers Ltd & Another v Schapiro & Others, The Times,* 17 November 1993, CA).

10.14
Careful wording of a restrictive covenant is vital. In one case, a term sought to prohibit a company's shareholders from carrying on in business in competition with that firm for two years after they ceased to hold any shares. It was held that a former shareholder could not be restrained from becoming an employee of a company in competition. The covenant would apply only where he was setting up or operating his own firm (*WAC Ltd & Others v Whitlock* [1990] IRLR 22, CS).

INDIRECT RESTRAINTS OF TRADE

10.15
The same general principles apply to indirect restraints. An employee was required by his employers to join a pension scheme, a rule of which provided

that, should he become employed in any activity in competition with or detrimental to the employers' interests, he would forfeit his rights under the scheme. It was held that the doctrine of restraint extended to those affected by indirect means. On the facts, the prohibition was unreasonable and therefore void (*Bull v Pitney-Bowes Ltd* [1966] 3 AER 384, QBD).

10.16
Two companies manufacturing similar products were situated close to one another. They got together and agreed that neither of them would employ a person who had been employed by the other company within the previous five years. The restraint was held to be void as it extended to all employees whether they possessed confidential information or not. Furthermore, the restraint was not limited to the period when the companies were situated near to each other. Although an employee would not be a party to such an agreement, he could apply for a declaration that the agreement was void, on the grounds that it interfered with his right to seek and obtain employment (*Kores Manufacturing Co Ltd v Kolok Manufacturing Co Ltd* [1958] 2 AER 65, CA; and *Eastham v Newcastle United Football Club Ltd* [1963] 2 AER 139, ChD).

EQUITABLE RESTRAINTS

While employment subsists

10.17
It is an implied term in every contract of employment that an employee must serve his (or her) employer faithfully. Often, there is an express term to that same effect in the individual contract of employment. Before resigning, an employee may not make out a list of clients, or memorise their names for use at a later date. Doing so would amount to a breach of the duty of fidelity and would expose the employee to an action for damages (*Wessex Dairies Ltd v Smith* [1935] 2 KB 80, CA). So long as the employer/employee relationship persists, a worker can be restrained from setting up his (or her) own firm or working for a competitor. If what he is doing is harmful to his employer's legitimate interests, it does not matter that it is carried out in the employee's spare time. But an order will generally not be made where the effect would be to force the employee to continue working for the employer as an alternative to starving (*Hivac Ltd v Park Royal Scientific Instruments Ltd* [1946] 1 Ch. 169, CA).

10.18
The production manager of a newspaper resigned with just one month's notice instead of the 12 months required by his contract. He planned to start work with a competitor. The Court of Appeal held that the employers were entitled to an order restraining the manager from joining the other firm until the full 12 months had run their course. They had refused (as was their right)

to accept the ineffective notice and were prepared to pay him his salary for the 12 months, although not requiring him to work (*Evening Standard Co Ltd v Henderson* [1987] ICR 588, CA).

10.19
But where no work was to be provided ['Garden Leave'] and the employee joined or proposed to join a competitor during the notice period, it was held that the employer could rely on the employee's breach of obligation of good faith to restrain him. It had to be proved that the period was not excessive and that some harm would be sustained by the employer if his trade secrets or other confidential facts were relayed to the rival employer. The remedy of damages for breach of contract was always open to the employer (*Provident Financial Group plc & Another v Hayward* [1989] ICR 160, CA). Although an employee can be restrained during (and after) employment from disclosing confidential information, he will not be injuncted from informing statutory bodies or the Inland Revenue of any irregularities discovered in the course of his employment. It would be against public policy to do so and it matters not whether the employee had acted out of malice (*In re A Company* [1989] ICR 449, ChD).

Note: Since the coming into force on 2 July 1999 of the Public Interest Disclosure Act 1999 (the 'Whistleblowers' Act'), workers who make so-called 'protected disclosures' (alleging law-breaking or wrongdoing by their employers) have the legal right not to be dismissed, selected for redundancy, or subjected to any other detriment for doing so. For further particulars, please turn to Chapter 20.

After employment ends

10.20
Occasionally, because of an administrative error or otherwise, an employer will not have secured a covenant from an employee purportedly restricting that employee's post-employment activities. Even without such a covenant, an employee can nonetheless be restrained from setting up in competition (or using information) in appropriate circumstances. There is an implied term in every contract of employment that, after the employment ends, an employee will not use or disclose information about his (or her) former employer's business activities which is of such a high degree of confidentiality as to amount to a trade secret. But an employee *is* entitled to approach freely and canvass his former employer's customers, suppliers, or other contacts, as their names and addresses do not amount to a 'trade secret' (*Faced Chicken Ltd v Fouler & Another* [1986] IC 297, CA).

HOW ENFORCEABLE

10.21
These rights and duties are only enforceable in the ordinary courts. Usually proceedings take the form of an application for an interlocutory injunction,

ie for an order for a temporary ban until the full trial takes place. This generally has the effect of disposing of the action, as there is usually a delay of a year or two before the trial takes place – by which time, the problem will probably have resolved itself.

10.22
In deciding whether to grant an injunction, the court applies the 'balance of convenience' test, for example:

- whether there is a serious issue to be decided;

- whether damages would provide an adequate remedy to the employer; and

- whether the employer would be in an adequate position to compensate the employee for any damages should he lose at the full trial (*American Cyanamid v Ethic Ltd* [1975] AC 396, HL);

but it does not decide upon the relative strength of the cases unless 'the action cannot be tried before the period of restraint has expired, or [it] has run a large part of its course, that the grant of the interlocutory injunction will effectively dispose of the action... ' (per Balcombe LJ, *Lawrence David Ltd v Ashton* [1989] ICR 123, CA).

10.23
Where it is necessary to assess the likely outcome of proceedings it is nevertheless undesirable that there should be a prolonged preliminary battle, effectively proving the case at the interlocutory stage (*Lansing Linde Ltd v Kerr* [1991] ICR 428, CA).

Search orders

10.24
A useful means of obtaining the necessary evidence to establish whether there has been a breach of a restrictive covenant is to obtain a search order (previously known as an 'Anton Piller' order) from the court. A search order is defined in rule 25.1(1)(h) of the Civil Procedure Rules as an order under section 7 of the Civil Procedure Act 1997. Under such an order, the plaintiff (the employer), accompanied by a supervising solicitor (unless the order allows otherwise), is permitted to enter the defendant (the employee's) premises to search for, copy and/or retain, any and all documents belonging to the employer's business. The employer may then apply to the court for an order preventing the employee (or former employee), or any third party, from using or benefiting from the information contained in those documents – provided they are of a sufficiently high degree of confidentiality as to amount to a trade secret (*PSM International plc & Another v Whitehouse & Another* [1992] IRLR 279, CA).

Note: The term 'Anton Piller order' took its name from *Anton Piller KG v Manufacturing Processes Ltd* [1976] 1 All ER 779, CA.

TIME LIMITS

10.25
Claim must be brought before the ordinary courts within six years, after which they become 'statute-barred'.

11

Equal pay and sex discrimination

GENERAL INFORMATION

11.1

The Equal Pay Act 1970, as amended, together with the Sex Discrimination Acts 1975 and 1986, and the Equal Pay (Amendment) Regulations 1983, were enacted to render unlawful unreasonable and unjustified discrimination on grounds of sex or marital status. Behind the legislation lies Article 141 (formerly Article 119) of the Treaty of Rome, and Regulations and Directives made under that Treaty. As a result, this subject has become increasingly complicated and uncertain. The draftsmen of UK legislation, in following EC Directives, are 'required to patch new Flemish broadcloth upon the fine weave of our domestic law... (doing) the minimum damage to either fabric' (per Waite J, *McGrath v Rank Leisure Ltd* [1985] ICR 527, EAT).

11.2

European Union law is drawn in very wide and sweeping terms, and the European Court of Justice has to decide whether there has been a transgression of the Treaty on the facts of each case. The result is that there is now evolving a 'case law' similar to our own common law (see Chapter 8). As European law takes precedence over our own, it is always necessary to consider not only our own statutes and case law, but also the Treaty and decisions made under it. But the relevant European legislation must be clear before an English statute should be construed to conform to it (*Shields v E Coombes (Holdings) Ltd* [1978] ITR 473, CA; and *Roberts v Tate & Lyle Food & Distribution Ltd* [1983] ICR 521, EAT). The European Court has emphasised that there is a duty laid on national courts not to follow domestic legislation where it conflicts with European law. It is not necessary to wait until the law has been changed by legislative or constitutional means (*Nimz v Freie und Hansestadt Hamburg* [1991] IRLR 222, ECJ).

11.3

An added complication is that European law does not draw a line between equal pay and sex discrimination quite as explicitly as is done by the two UK statutes. A claim under Article 141 of the Treaty of Rome may be brought directly, where there is nothing in UK legislation which covers the relief sought by a litigant. Further, a worker employed in an 'organ of the State' (public servants, local authority employees, etc) can rely on certain Directives (*Secretary of State for Scotland & Greater Glasgow Health Board v Wright & Hannah* [1991] IRLR 187, EAT).

EQUAL PAY ACT 1970

11.4
So far as the Equal Pay and Sex Discrimination Acts are concerned, there is no overlapping of the rights and duties arising out of them. The distinction between them, which is very important when considering which Act applies in a particular case, is that the Equal Pay Act is concerned with instances where an employee:

- of one sex receives less favourable treatment than one of the opposite sex in respect of pay received under a contract with the same or an 'associated employer' (see Chapter 3, paras 3.95 to 3.97); or

- is treated less favourably than an employee of the opposite sex regarding a term in the contract of either. This would arise, for instance, where a man's contract entitled him to the benefit of a company car for his own use, whereas a woman's contract precluded such a right, or omitted any reference to such an entitlement;

always provided that:

- they are performing 'like work' (or work of a broadly similar nature – the differences between them being of no practical importance) in relation to terms and conditions of employment; work of equal value; or work rated as equivalent under a 'job evaluation scheme'.

(*Source*: EPA 1970, s.1(2).)

A 'job evaluation scheme' is a study undertaken to evaluate a job in terms of the demands made on a worker under various headings (for instance, effort, skill, decision) and to compare that job with others in an undertaking or group of undertakings (*Bromley & Others v H & J Quick Ltd* [1988] ICR 623, CA) (*Source*: EPA 1970, s.1(5)). The scheme itself must be prepared in an analytical way and must exclude any unfavourable treatment of either sex, that is to say, it 'must be based on the same criteria for both men and women and so drawn up so as to exclude any discrimination on grounds of sex' (*Bromley & Others v H & J Quick Ltd* [1988] ICR 623, CA EEC Directive 75/117)(*Source*: EPA 1970, s.2A(3)).

11.5
Under a job evaluation scheme, the values accorded to each element were converted into 'bands'. It was held that a tribunal was entitled to take the final position into account. It mattered not that the original values assigned to the two persons being compared under the scheme were different (*Springboard Sunderland Trust v Robson* [1992] ICR 554, EAT).

11.6

If no members of the opposite sex are employed on similar work, and/or no job evaluation study has been carried out, or if there is a non-discriminatory scheme in existence which does not show that the applicant's job has been rated as equal to a named comparator, the employee may apply to the tribunal for an independent expert – drawn from a panel of independent experts designated by the Advisory, Conciliation & Arbitration Service (ACAS) – to be appointed to carry out an evaluation study (*Pickstone & Others v Freemans plc* [1988] ICR 697, HL; and *Avon County Council v Foxall & Others* [1989] ICR 407, EAT) (*Source*: EPA 1970, s.2A(1)(a)).

11.7

The procedure is quite elaborate. A tribunal follows a number of steps, deciding:

- Whether there are 'no reasonable grounds for determining that' a woman's work is of equal value to that of the male comparator (or vice versa), eg Is it a hopeless case? If the claim is certain to fail, it will be dismissed at this point (*Leverton v Clywd County Council* [1989] ICR 33, HL).

- If not, and the employer raises the defence of 'genuine material difference', that defence will be considered at a preliminary hearing. If it succeeds, the case will stop (*Reed Packaging Ltd v Boozer & Another* [1988] ICR 391, EAT).

- If not, the tribunal must refer the claim to an independent expert for a report. After the expert has gone through several formalities, his (or her) report is filed in the tribunal.

- When accepted by the tribunal, the findings of fact set out in the report are binding on the parties, in the sense that no new evidence may be introduced to contradict them. It does not prevent the parties from making submissions on them (*Sheffield Metropolitan District Council v Siberry & Another* [1989] ICR 208, EAT).

- A full hearing will take place at which the parties may present their experts' reports. The recommendations made by an independent expert have no special status and are not binding. They will be considered by the tribunal which may accept or reject them (*Tennants Textile Colours Ltd v Todd* [1989] IRLR 3, CA (Northern Ireland); and *Aldridge v British Telecom Ltd* [1989] ICR 720, EAT).

Under the Sex Discrimination (Indirect Discrimination & Burden of Proof) Regulations 2002 (SI 2001/2660), once a complainant has established facts from which it may be presumed that she has been the victim of unlawful sex discrimination, the burden of proof shifts to the respondent employer. In short, it is then up to the employer to satisfy the employment tribunal that no such discrimination occurred.

11.8

When preparing his (or her) report, an independent expert must consider all the information supplied, including any representations by affected parties. Each party is then entitled to comment on the report. The expert must summarise those comments and give his (or her) conclusions, but must act fairly and take no account of the difference of sex. He (or she) should follow an analytical approach, in the sense of describing the process of dividing a physical or abstract whole into its constituent parts (*Bromley & Others v H & J Quick Ltd* [1988] ICR 623, CA). Each side is fully entitled to obtain its own expert's report and to present evidence to the tribunal. In the end, it will be for the tribunal to decide, in the light of all the evidence submitted, whether or not the employee's claim is substantiated.

11.9

Even if a person of the opposite sex is employed in the same capacity and place as the complainant and earns the same, the latter may nevertheless make a complaint that another worker of the opposite sex is performing work of equal value in another area of operations and is paid more. It matters not how the disparity arises, whether for historical reasons or otherwise (*Pickstone & Others v Freemans plc* [1988] ICR 697, HL) (*Source*: EPA 1970, s.1(2)(C)).

Essence of The Equal Pay Act 1970

11.10

The basic concept of the 1970 Act is that it requires that every term in a woman's (or man's) contract of employment must not be less favourable than that in a man's (or woman's) contract. This is achieved by importing 'an equality clause' into every contract of employment. Any term in a contract of employment that is inconsistent with that implied 'equality clause' has no effect and any favourable term that is omitted will be deemed to be included (*Source*: EPA 1970, s.1(1)).

11.11

In deciding whether any term is less favourable, a comparison must be made with a member of the opposite sex who is employed by the same or any 'associated employer' (as defined in Chapter 3, paras 3.95 to 3.97). It does not matter that the two employees, who are being compared, work on the same premises or even in different parts of the country. But where a woman seeks to compare her pay with a male worker who works at different premises, the 1970 Act provides that it is necessary for 'common terms and conditions of employment [to be] observed either generally or for employees of the relevant classes' (*Source*: EPA 1970, s.1(6)). The effect of the provision is to remove from consideration any special local conditions (eg a higher cost of living) or those which relate to geographical circumstances. What needs to be done is to pose the question: 'If a man was employed on the female's premises, doing work of equal value, would he be paid the same as the female, or the same as the comparator at the other premises?' (*British Coal Corporation v Smith & Others* [1994] IRLR 342, CA).

11.12

But where the two employees under comparison work at different establishments, three tests have to be applied:

- the applicant and her comparator must be typical of their groups and have no personal factors (such as 'red circling' or 'marking time');

- common terms and conditions must be observed within each establishment;

- there must be no difference caused by geographical influences where the derivation or historic basis for any variations result in different employment regimes at each place (*British Coal Corporation v Smith & Others* [1993] ICR 529, EAT).

(*Source*: EPA 1970, s.1(2)(c) & (6).)

11.13

A qualified nursery nurse sought to compare her worth with that of 11 male comparators doing work ranging from caretakers to clerks. They were employed at other establishments for the same employer, but under different contractual terms. It was held that she could bring herself within the section. She and her comparators were bound by the same 'Purple Book' terms of employment which set out the relevant scales (*Leverton v Clwyd County Council* [1989] ICR 33, HL). But the claim was defeated because the difference in the annual pay was due to a 'genuine material factor', namely, she worked for fewer hours each week and had longer holidays. In deciding whether a woman is entitled to equal pay with a man at another establishment, it is necessary to prove that, if a man were employed at her place of employment, he would be on the same terms and conditions as the man at the other premises, and that her work is of equal value (*British Coal Corporation v Smith & Others* [1994] IRLR 342, CA).

11.14

Under European Community law, a comparison may be made not only with a fellow employee of the opposite sex employed in the same undertaking, but also with a predecessor in the same job. The tribunal will have to take into account the time which had elapsed between the resignation (or dismissal) of the one and the appointment or recruitment of the other, and whether there had been any change in economic circumstances during that period (*McCarthys v Smith (No. 2)* [1980] ICR 672, CA).

11.15
In order to come within the provisions of the 1970 Act, it is not necessary to show that the employer intended to discriminate, merely that the effect was discriminatory. The equality clause 'operates to counteract all discrimination whether direct or indirect... it looks at the effect... not whether they are expressed in overtly discriminatory words or with any particular intention' (per Browne-Wilkinson J, *Jenkins v Kingsgate Ltd* [1981] ICR 715, EAT).

11.16
An 'indirect' discriminatory effect concerning pay arose where a provision in a collective agreement had the effect of favouring men. They were mainly full-time workers as opposed to women who were mostly part time. Only full-time workers were entitled to a severance payment on retirement. The European Court ruled that the provision had to be justified objectively on grounds other than sex (*Kowalska v Freie und Hansestadt Hamburg* [1992] ICR 29, ECJ). The European Court has further ruled that, as a party can rely on Article 141 directly, national legislation will not provide protection for any breach, where a provision has a more adverse effect against women (or men). It would have to be proved that the requirement was justified on objective grounds unrelated to sex (*Barber v Guardian Royal Exchange Assurance Group* [1990] ICR 616, ECJ). Statistical evidence which *prima facie* indicates that there is discrimination in pay between men and women in an organisation generally (and not just between a particular man or woman) will satisfy the burden of proof. The European Court has ruled that it is for the employer to show that the disparity is attributable to factors such as better job performance, and not to irrelevant factors such as the level of training received by an employee which has little relevance to the employee's ability to do the job in question (*Handels-og Kontorfunktionaererernes Forbund i Danmark v Dansk Arbejdsgiverforening* [1992] ICR 332, ECJ).

11.17
The mere fact that an employer is complying with a statutory regulation and has no power to depart from it, is not enough of itself to raise a defence where a requirement in that regulation is in breach of the Community law. The provisions and those that have come about as a result of consultations or agreements between various interested parties must have been screened to eliminate discrimination (*R v Secretary of State for Social Services & Others ex parte Clarke & Others* [1988] IRLR 22, QBD).

Defence of 'genuine material difference'

11.18
Once an employee has established a *prima facie* case of discrimination concerning pay or any other term in the contract, the employer can only

escape liability if he can prove that the variation is due to a genuine material factor, which is not a difference of sex (*Rainey v Greater Glasgow Health Board* [1987] ICR 129, HL) (*Source*: EPA 1970, s.1(3)). In an ordinary equal pay claim, the employer must prove that the genuine material difference applies, but in an equal value allegation, he need only show that it may be a defence (*McGregor v GMBATU* [1987] ICR 505, EAT). It may be shown, for instance, that the higher pay reflects longer service, which applies equally to both sexes and that it is not affected by past discrimination. It could be that the employee's pay has been 'red circled' for a legitimate reason (unrelated to sex). It would have to be shown that the lower salary would be paid to any successor employee, irrespective of sex.

11.19

Two women did work of equal value to that of a male comparator, but were paid less. All worked unsociable hours, with the women working the 'twilight' shift and the men on a system of rotating shifts. The Court of Appeal held that the defence of 'genuine material difference' succeeded. The men were paid extra for the additional inconvenience of working rotating shifts (*Calder & Another v Rowntree Mackintosh Confectionery Ltd* [1993] ICR 811, CA). Market forces, provided they are 'gender neutral', can also provide a 'material difference' defence. This was successfully raised where dinner ladies had established equal pay with some male council employees. When the work went out to competitive tender, it was necessary to reduce their pay in order to be competitive. Their claims for equal pay were rejected. If, on the other hand, a union were to negotiate a better deal for male employees at one establishment, who were performing work of equal value to women working at another, the defence would be likely to fail (*British Coal Corporation v Smith & Others* [1994] IRLR 342, CA; and *North Yorkshire CC v Ratcliffe & Others, The Times*, 11 May 1994, CA).

11.20

A tribunal is entitled to look beyond the 'personal equation'. It may consider economic factors connected with the efficient running of the business, provided they are objectively justified. The European Court of Justice has put it this way. It is up to the employer to show that 'the means chosen for achieving that objective correspond to a real need on the part of the undertaking, [and] are appropriate with a view to achieving the objective in question and are necessary to that end' (*Rainey v Greater Glasgow Health Board* [1987] ICR 129, HL; and *Bilka-Kaufhaus GmbH v Weber von Hartz* [1987] ICR 110, ECJ). This defence was not open to an employer who, having set salary levels which he later discovered were discriminatory, continued to pay at those rates. He did so without any justification apart from being advised to do so. It seems that if the comparator occupies a key position and it would cause immense harm should he leave, the employer could have relied on that fact (*McPherson v Rathgael Centre and Northern Ireland Office* [1991] IRLR 206, CA

(Northern Ireland)). But where the fixed rates of pay within an organisation were not discriminatory, but an administrative error resulted in a male comparator being paid more than a female employee, that oversight was held not to be actionable. It was not gender-tainted (*Yorkshire Blood Transfusion Service v Plaskitt, The Times*, 17 August 1993, EAT).

To whom does equal pay legislation apply?

11.21
The 1970 Act applies to any worker, whether an employee or one who works under a contract to execute personally any service or labour (full or part time), including serving members of the naval, military or air forces of the Crown, those serving a Minister of the Crown or employed in a government department (or in statutory bodies) and office holders (regardless of age or length of service). However, an equality clause does not operate in relation to terms:

- affected by compliance with any legislation regulating the employment of women; or

- affording special treatment to women in connection with pregnancy or childbirth.

Nor does it operate in relation to terms relating to a person's membership of (or rights under) an occupational pension scheme, being terms in relation to which (by reason only of any provision made by or under section 62 or 64 of the Pensions Act 1995) an equal treatment rule would not operate if the terms were included in the scheme.

(*Source*: EPA 1970, ss 1 & 6; SDA 1975, ss 7, 8 & 10.)

11.22
Article 141 of the Treaty of Rome has been held by the European Court of Justice to cover benefits made under a contractual scheme supplementing the State pension. The exclusion of part-timers from such benefits, which mostly affected women, was indirectly discriminatory, and breached the Article. To escape liability it was necessary to show that the scheme was based on objectively justified factors unrelated to any discrimination on the grounds of sex (*Bilka-Kaufhaus GmbH v Weber von Hartz* [1987] ICR 110, ECJ). The European Court of Justice has also held that benefits, including a (private) pension and redundancy pay, received by a prematurely dismissed man, were 'pay' within the meaning of Article 141. If the value of those benefits depended on different ages for men and women, that would be discriminatory. It has also been decreed that the German equivalent of statutory sick pay is 'pay' within the meaning of the Article (*Barber v*

Guardian Royal Exchange Assurance Group [1990] ICR 616, ECJ; and *Rinner-Kuhn v FWW Spezial-Gebaudereinigung* [1989] IRLR 493, ECJ).

11.23
An employer contracted out a private occupational scheme under which a person's statutory old age pension was deducted from the sum. The rate was otherwise the same for each sex. It was held not to be discriminatory against women. The situations were not identical. Article 141 cannot be interpreted to give women a two-fold benefit. That would be discriminatory against men (*Roberts v Birds Eye Walls Ltd* [1994] IRLR 29, ECJ).

Equal pay questionnaire

11.24
With the coming into force on 6 April 2003 of section 42 of the Employment Act 2002, an employee or other worker who believes that she (or he) is being paid less, or is employed on less favourable terms and conditions, than an employee of the opposite sex doing the same or broadly similar work (work of equal value, etc) may submit a questionnaire (Form EPA 7B) to her employer requiring him to demonstrate to her satisfaction (by completing and returning the questionnaire, with supporting evidence) that there has been no breach of the implied 'equality clause' in her contract of employment. An employer's refusal or failure to complete such a questionnaire and return it to the employee within the period prescribed by Regulations is admissible in evidence in any subsequent proceedings before an employment tribunal (as are the contents of the questionnaire itself, if duly completed and returned).

Note: For further information, the reader is commended to Web site www.womenand equalityunit.gov.uk/pay/update_question.htm.

SEX DISCRIMINATION ACT 1975

11.25
There are two parallel provisions affecting the issue of sex discrimination in employment. These are the law as laid down in EC Directives, and UK domestic legislation (*Garland v British Rail Engineering Ltd* [1982] ICR 434, HL). This can lead to complications. It is always necessary to look at the provisions of European legislation where there is a doubt whether UK law covers the situation or is overridden by European law (*Pickstone & Others v Freemans plc* [1987] ICR 867, CA – upheld by HL on different grounds). What may *not* be done is to distort the wording of the Sex Discrimination Act so as to have it accord with European law. So where the European Court of Justice ruled in an indirect discrimination case that 'attention should be directed less to the existence of a requirement... and more to the discriminatory result', it

was held that it was still necessary to apply the express provision of a 'requirement or condition' in the definition of indirect discrimination in the 1975 Act (*Bhudi & Others v IMI Refiners Ltd* [1994] ICR 307, EAT).

European law

11.26
Article 2(1) of Council Directive 76/207/EEC 'on the implementation of the principle of equal treatment for men and women as regards access to employment, vocational training and promotion, and working conditions' states that '... the principle of equal treatment shall mean that there shall be no discrimination whatsoever on the grounds of sex either directly or indirectly by reference in particular to marital or family status'. This is amplified by Article 5: 'Application of the principle of equal treatment with regard to working conditions, including the conditions governing dismissal, means that men and women shall be guaranteed the same conditions without discrimination on the grounds of sex'. Article 3(1) adds that the 'application of the principle of equal treatment means that there shall be no discrimination whatsoever on grounds of sex in the conditions, including selection criteria, for access to all jobs or posts...'.

11.27
Where a Directive requires a Member State to import the legislation into its domestic legislation, the Directive itself cannot be directly relied upon by an employee in the private sector. Only those employed in organs (or emanations) of the State can sue on it.

11.28
Where a measure adversely affects one sex (mostly women) compared to the opposite sex (mostly men) this would amount to indirect discrimination. But it would not be a violation of European law if it was shown:

- that the scheme was intended to achieve an appropriate policy;

- the means adopted were likely to achieve that objective; and

- the discriminatory effect was unavoidable.

(*Commission of the European Community v Kingdom of Belgium* [1993] IRLR 393, ECJ.)

11.29
It is not permissible to duplicate claims. An employee claimed discrimination under the Sex Discrimination Act 1986 but the case failed on its merits. It was held that it was not possible to launch further proceedings relying on the

same facts but based on Equal Treatment Directive No. 76/207 (*Blaik v Post Office* [1994] IRLR 280, EAT).

Part-time employees

11.30
It is acknowledged that many more women than men work part time. If there is any resultant discriminatory effect, that effect must be justified by factors other than a difference of sex. So when a group of part-time employees accompanied their full-time colleagues on a series of day-long training courses organised by their employer, they were paid only their standard rate of pay in spite of having put in longer hours than usual. One of their number complained of unlawful discrimination. The European Court of Justice held that her allegation was well founded. The employers could only escape liability if it could be shown that the difference between the amount paid to her and that received by the full-timers was justifiable on grounds other than sex (*Arbeiterwohlfahrt der Stadt Berlin e v Botel* [1992] IRLR 423, ECJ).

11.31
There was a similar ruling in *Gerster v Freistaat Bayern*, 2 October 1997, ECJ. The Bavarian State Civil Service operated a rule which required part-time employees to complete a longer period of service than their full-time colleagues before they could be considered for promotion. Given that 87 per cent of part-timers in the German Civil Service were women, the ECJ observed that the 'longer service' rule amounted to indirect discrimination unless it could be justified on grounds unrelated to sex. The Civil Service argued that, by definition, it would take longer for part-timers to acquire the skills and capabilities needed to qualify them for promotion. While accepting that this might be so, the ECJ held that unless a national court identified a special correlation between working hours, length of service and the acquisition of specified skills, a rule such as that imposed by the Bavarian State Civil Service would be in breach of the Equal Treatment Directive (76/207/EEC).

TYPES OF DISCRIMINATION

11.32
The Sex Discrimination Act 1975 (as amended) identifies three types of discrimination. These are: 'direct discrimination', 'indirect discrimination' and 'victimisation'. The 1975 Act, with certain exceptions, applies equally to men and women. It not only forbids discrimination on grounds of sex or gender reassignment (see *Note* below) but discrimination also against married persons in the employment field (see paras 11.52 to 11.56 below). The 1975 Act is, of course, primarily directed towards the protection of women (*Source*: SDA 1975, ss 1, 2, 3 & 4).

Note: The Sex Discrimination (Gender Reassignment) Regulations 1999 (SI 1999/1102), which came into force on 1 May 1999, extend the Sex Discrimination Act 1975 to cover discrimination on grounds of gender reassignment in employment and vocational training. Accordingly, it is nowadays unlawful for an employer to treat an employee (or job applicant) less favourably than he (or she) would treat other employees on the ground that the person in question intends to undergo, is undergoing or has undergone gender reassignment. It is similarly unlawful to deny such a person access to contractual sickness or injury benefits if absent from work while undergoing gender reassignment. The term 'gender reassignment' means a process which is undertaken under medical supervision for the purpose of reassigning a person's sex by changing physiological or other characteristics of sex, and includes any part of such a process.

Direct discrimination

11.33
Unlawful direct discrimination occurs when an employer or would-be employer treats a woman (or man) less favourably on the ground of her (or his) sex – by denying that person access to employment, promotion, transfer or opportunities for training, or by dismissing or selecting that person for redundancy simply because she is a woman (or he is a man). Direct discrimination can be established by what is said or can be inferred from all the circumstances (*Source*: SDA 1975, s.1(1)(a)). In determining whether there is direct discrimination, eg whether there is, in truth, any difference in the treatment of a woman compared to that of a man, it may be necessary in certain cases to discover the underlying reason for such treatment. An unmarried matron at a girl's school became pregnant and was dismissed because she declined either to marry the putative father or to leave voluntarily. It was held that the matron's subsequent dismissal did not amount to unlawful discrimination. It was the continuing and potentially damaging evidence of extra-marital activity that was the reason for her dismissal. The same treatment would have been accorded whatever the sex of the 'offender' (*Berrisford v Woodward Schools (Midland Division) Ltd* [1991] ICR 564, EAT).

As was pointed out earlier, it is also directly discriminatory and, therefore, unlawful to discriminate against a person for no other reason than that the person in question (employee or job applicant) intends to undergo, is undergoing or has undergone gender reassignment (*ibid* s.2A).

11.34
In deciding how an employer would treat a person of the opposite sex in identical circumstances, in the absence of direct evidence of past behaviour, a tribunal has to deal with a hypothetical situation. It has to draw inferences from the primary facts and reach a decision based on the balance of probabilities. A comparison may not normally be made between the treatment respectively accorded to a pregnant woman and a sick man, except, perhaps,

for very short-term employment (*Webb v EMO Air Cargo (UK) Ltd* [1993] ICR, HL 1994, ([1994] IRLR 482, ECJ).

Note: Under the Sex Discrimination (Indirect Discrimination & Burden of Proof) Regulations 2001 (SI 2001 / 2660), once a complainant has established facts from which it may be presumed that she has been the victim of unlawful sex discrimination, it is then for her employer to show that no such discrimination occurred.

11.35
A tribunal did not believe an employer who claimed that he was unaware that an employee was pregnant when he dismissed her. It was held that the tribunal was entitled to assume that the employer would have treated a male employee more favourably in similar circumstances, despite his protestations that he would have treated both equally (*Leeds Private Hospital Ltd v Parkin* [1992] ICR 571, EAT). There is a wide, grey dividing line between what is conceived to be the hypothetical treatment of the other sex. The mere fact that a woman dislikes an offensive display of female pictures in the workplace may not be enough in itself. A tribunal has to apply the norms of society at large and decide whether the woman has received less favourable treatment (*Stewart v Cleveland Guest (Engineering) Ltd*, *The Times*, 6 July 1994, EAT).

Indirect discrimination

11.36
Indirect discrimination occurs where the same requirement or condition is applied to both sexes, but:

- one sex is less likely to be able to comply with that requirement or condition than the other;

- it is not justified irrespective of sex;

- that it is a detriment to the person complaining because she (or he) cannot comply with it.

(*Source*: SDA 1975, s.1(1)(b).)

11.37
The distinction between direct and indirect discrimination can sometimes be difficult to discern. The test for the former propounded by Lord Goff in *James v Eastleigh Borough Council* [1990] ICR 554, HL is: '... would the complainant have received the same treatment from the [employer] but for his or her sex'; for example, where there is not necessarily an intention to discriminate but that is the effect of the action, or inaction, taken or not taken, by an employer. But there can be indirect discrimination which does not offend against the

law because, for instance, it is justified (*R v Birmingham City Council ex parte Equal Opportunities Commission* [1989] IRLR 173, HL).

11.38
It would seem that where a condition or requirement is imposed with the express intention of, say, excluding women from a job, then that would be direct discrimination. The defence of justification could not then be put forward. Furthermore, in both types of discrimination, like must be compared with like, where it is appropriate. A single woman's position must be compared with that of a single man or a group of women (of which an employee forms part) with a similar group of men (*Source*: EPA 1970, s.5(3)). This provision may not be relied upon where an employer fears that the consequence of not taking discriminatory action might be very serious, eg the possibility of young girls being sexually harassed. That there would be little risk were women to have contact with boys, was not a legitimate comparison (*Bain v Bowles & Others* [1991] IRLR 356, CA).

Ingredients of indirect discrimination

11.39
If a job specification contains a requirement or condition which can be complied with by most men, but not so by most women, it will be for the employer to justify that requirement or condition on grounds which have nothing to do with sex. For example, it is unlikely that as many women as men could comply with a requirement that they be at least 1.75 metres tall, or that they be able to lift and carry a sack weighing 50 kilograms or more. If lifting and carrying heavy weights is a routine feature of the job in question, well and good. But if it is only an occasional feature, an employer would have some difficulty in persuading an employment tribunal that his (or her) automatic exclusion of women from such work was justifiable.

11.40
In determining whether there is indirect discrimination it is necessary to establish the 'pool' from which the comparison is to be made. Generally the 'pool' must consist of members of both sexes who have the necessary qualifications and/or experience. It is permissible to restrict the pool to those with specialist qualifications or skills essential for the job in question (*Jones v University of Manchester* [1993] IRLR 218, CA). The imposition of a condition or requirement would be discriminatory if it is responsible for causing a considerable disparity in the proportions between the sexes. It is the proportion of the two sexes compared with each other that must be taken into account. So if 15 per cent of women only can comply with a particular job specification compared to, say, 40 per cent of men, the women have far less chance of securing the job. An employer could escape liability for an apparently discriminatory requirement

(eg all candidates must be at least 1.65 metres tall) if he could prove that it was justified (*Pearse v City of Bradford Metropolitan Council* [1988] IRLR 379, EAT; and *McCausland v Dungannon DC* [1993] IRLR 583, CA (Northern Ireland)).

11.41
Like must be compared with like. A school required its domestic staff (mostly women) to retire at 60. Gardeners and maintenance staff, on the other hand (mostly men) were permitted to stay on until 65. It was held that the employers had not discriminated, either directly or indirectly, against a female cleaner who was compulsorily retired at 60. Her position could not be compared to that of a gardener. In any event, the gardeners were kept on until 65 because of the difficulty in replacing them (*Bullock v Alice Ottley School* [1993] ICR 138, CA).

11.42
An employer seeking to rely on the defence of justification is entitled to show that there are 'objectively justified grounds which are other than economic, such as administrative efficiency, in an organisation which is not engaged in commerce or business' (per Lord Keith in *Rainey v Greater Glasgow Health Board* [1987] ICR 129, HL). There must be a real need for the measures adopted and they must be both appropriate and necessary. It has been held that, if the method of carrying out a scheme allows for the most economic and efficient use of available resources, being targeted at those most in need within a priority group, then although the effect might be discriminatory, this would be 'justifiable' (*Bilka-Kaufhaus GmbH v Weber von Hertz* [1987] ICR 110, ECJ; and *Cobb & Others v Secretary of State for Employment & Another* [1989] ICR 506, EAT).

11.43
A female teacher was required under her contract to coach badminton after school hours. When she adopted a child she was unable to continue with this duty, and her pay was reduced accordingly. Her complaint of unlawful sex discrimination failed because her employers established that the requirement was objectively justifiable when the discriminatory effect of the duty was balanced against their reasonable needs (*Briggs v North Eastern Education & Library Board* [1990] IRLR 181, CA (Northern Ireland)) (*Source*: SDA 1975 s.1(1)(b)(iii)).

11.44
What is *not* permissible is to take a decision based on wider social issues, however commendable or reasonable they may be. Only those necessary for the business of the employer are protected. A Member State is entitled to make legislative provisions that have a discriminatory effect on one sex, where the social and economic policies behind them justify such a course (*Greater Manchester Police Authority v Lea* [1990] IRLR 372, EAT; and *R v Secretary of State for Employment, ex parte Equal Opportunities Commission & Another* [1992] ICR 341, Div Ct).

11.45

'Detriment' is a very wide term and can encompass such acts as a supervisor subjecting an employee to discriminatory abuse if such abuse puts the person abused 'at a disadvantage'. Generally it is limited to matters about which a reasonable employee could justifiably complain. An employer should have regard to the feelings of an employee whom he knows to be particularly sensitive (*Ministry of Defence v Jeremiah* [1980] ICR 13, CA; and *Wileman v Minilec Engineering Ltd* [1988] IRLR 144, EAT). What a person cannot do, in seeking to prove that she (or he) has suffered 'a detriment', is to try to obtain enhanced rights where they are not available to anyone of either sex in her grade. A claim that the refusal to provide them is discriminatory, because of her personal circumstances, will fail (*Clymo v Wandsworth London Borough* [1989] ICR 250, EAT).

Pregnancy and childbirth

11.46

It is now established that a pregnant woman in long term employment who is absent from work on maternity leave may *not* be compared with a hypothetical man absent from work because of ill-health. As the European Court put it: 'The protection afforded by Community law to a woman during pregnancy and after childbirth could not be dependent on whether her presence at work during maternity was essential to the proper functioning of the undertaking in which she was employed' (*Webb v EMO Air Cargo (UK)* [1994] IRLR 482, ECJ). The European Court of Justice has also ruled that there would be a breach of the principle of equality of treatment under the Equal Treatment Directive if a female was refused employment on economic grounds because of her pregnancy. That there was no male candidate for the job was irrelevant. The main reason for the decision not to employ her related to a factor which applied exclusively to women (eg pregnancy). Reliance on that fact was direct discrimination (*Dekker v Stichting Vormingscentrum voor Jong Volwassenen Plus* [1992] ICR 325, ECJ). The logic behind the decision is that men and women are equally liable to become ill, but women have the additional impediment of being unable to do their jobs through pregnancy. It would therefore be unfair to compare them with the hypothetical 'sick' man. Special protection has to be given so that they are not put at a disadvantage by reason of their condition. The ruling would probably not apply if an employer were to refuse to employ a heavily pregnant woman to replace a woman absent from work on maternity leave if she too would be absent on maternity leave within weeks of taking up her temporary appointment (*Habermann-Beltermann v Arbriterwohlfahrt, Bezirksverband Ndb/Opfer* [1994] IRLR 364, ECJ; and *Webb v EMO Air Cargo (UK)* [1994] IRLR 482, ECJ).

11.47

A discretion is left to Member States as to the measures to be adopted to ensure the protection of women in connection with pregnancy and maternity to offset the disadvantages which women suffer in employment compared to men (*Habermann-Beltermann v Arbriterwohlfahrt, Bezirksverband Ndb/Opf er* [1994] IRLR 364, ECJ; *Webb v EMO Air Cargo (UK)* [1994] IRLR 482, ECJ; and *Hoffmann v Barmer Ersatzkasse* [1985] ICR 731, ECJ).

11.48
The European Court of Justice has also ruled that it was not discriminatory to dismiss a female who, having returned to work after maternity leave, was repeatedly absent through sickness, the origin of which lay in the childbirth. It was proved that the employers would have dealt in the same way with men who were similarly absent from work through sickness (*Handels-og Kontorfunktionaerernes Forbund i Danmark v Dansk Arbeijdsgiverforening* [1992] ICR 332, ECJ).

11.49
In *Brown v Rentokil* (Case C-394/96), the ECJ held that the dismissal of a *pregnant* woman – whose pregnancy-related illness incapacitated her for work for more than 26 weeks – was unlawful discrimination, notwith-standing a term in her contract of employment which stated that *any* employee absent from work because of sickness for more than 26 weeks, would be dismissed. Pregnancy, said the Court, was not comparable to a pathological condition. But it *was* a period during which there could arise 'disorders and complications' which were a specific feature of pregnancy. These could cause incapacity for work. So the dismissal of a *pregnant* employee due to such incapacity must be regarded as essentially based on the fact of her pregnancy and would, therefore, be unlawful direct discrim-ination on the grounds of sex. Had the woman been incapacitated for work *after* her maternity leave (for reasons connected with her having been pregnant or given birth), the fairness or otherwise of her dismissal would be determined by the general rules applicable to a dismissal on the grounds of illness or injury – so long as 'female and male workers' absences caused by incapacity for work were treated in the same way. It they were, there was no discrimination'.

Sexual orientation

11.50
In the well-publicised case of *Grant v South West Trains Limited* [1998] IRLR 206, brought under Article 141 (formerly Article 119) of the Treaty of Rome ('equal pay for equal work'), the ECJ held that discrimination on grounds of sexual orientation is not unlawful discrimination on grounds of sex. However, that analysis is set to change. The UK Government, along with other EU Member States, has until 2 December 2003 within which to introduce legislation implementing Council Directive 2000/78/EC – which

outlaws discrimination on the grounds of sexual orientation (as well as on the grounds of religion or belief, disability and age).

Victimisation

11.51
Discrimination can also occur by way of victimisation. This arises where an employee is treated less favourably for bringing or threatening to bring proceedings in respect of an alleged infringement of her (or his) rights under the 1975 Act, or the Equal Pay Act 1970, or sections 62 to 65 of the Pensions Act 1995 ('equal treatment rule' in occupational pensions schemes). This does not apply where the allegations are false and not made in good faith. Nor does it apply where there were other genuine factors which caused the person to treat the other less favourably, eg she was guilty of misconduct (*Source*: SDA 1975 s.4).

Discrimination against married persons

11.52
An employer discriminates against a married person of either sex:

(a) if he (or she) treats that person less favourably than he would do an unmarried person; or

(b) if he (or she) applies to that person a requirement or condition that he applies or would apply equally to an unmarried person but the proportion of married persons who can comply with that requirement is considerably smaller than the proportion of unmarried persons of the same sex who *can* comply with it; and

(c) which he (or she) cannot show to be justifiable irrespective of the marital status of the person to whom it is applied; and

(d) which is to that person's detriment because he (or she) cannot comply with it.

Note that the comparison in such cases must be made between persons of the same sex, that is to say between single women and married women, and single men and married men. It is not possible to cross the sexual divide by making a comparison between a married man and a single woman or a married woman and a single man (*Source*: SDA 1975, ss 3 & 5).

11.53
In deciding whether there is discrimination, a distinction has to be drawn between whether the decision was taken because the person was married or whether somebody else was a better candidate for a job, or for promotion, or

whatever the complaint is. In the case of a married woman, no consideration must be given to the fact that she has small children or might become pregnant and leave work to have children.

11.54
A married woman with several young children applied for a job as a waitress, but was rejected because the proprietor thought there was a strong risk that she might want to take too much time off work to attend to their needs. Her children might fall ill or there might be difficulty with babysitters. Her dismissal on those grounds was held to constitute unlawful discrimination under the 1975 Act. The employer was equating this one person with all women with young children. He should have reached a decision based on the woman's previous employment record. Had he made enquiries of former employers to establish whether they had found her to be unreliable? (*Hurley v Mustoe* [1981] ICR 490, EAT).

11.55
Part-time workers in a factory were selected for redundancy ahead of full-time workers. It was alleged that this indirectly discriminated against married women. They were more likely to have children to look after, and so be prevented from working full time. It was held that for proportional purposes their position should be compared with single women with children. There was no statistical evidence to support the proposition that their position was more adversely affected (*Kidd v DRG (UK) Ltd* [1985] ICR 405, EAT).

11.56
The same defences are available to an employer as in straightforward sex discrimination cases, including the defence that being single is a 'genuine occupation qualification' for the employment in question, although it is not easy to think of examples (but see paras 11.65 to 11.71 below). A married man applying for work in the UK or elsewhere within the EU (eg at an isolated construction site, where the workers are housed in temporary dormitory-style accommodation) might reject an offer of employment if informed that he would not be permitted to take his wife with him. But the imposition of such a rule would not normally amount to discrimination against married persons contrary to section 3 of the 1975 Act as the rule would apply equally to single men unhappy about being separated from their girlfriends or partners (although it should be emphasised that any such case would be decided on its merits) (*Source*: SDA 1975, ss 6(3)(a)&(b) & 48).

WHEN DISCRIMINATION IS UNLAWFUL

11.57
It is unlawful for an employer, in relation to employment by him (or her) at an establishment in Great Britain, to discriminate against a woman (or a man):

- In the arrangements made for determining who should be offered that employment. This might occur where a woman is 'filtered out' by a junior manager at an early stage in the interviewing process, even if the final selection of the most suitable candidate is made by someone at a more senior level – whether or not anyone was actually appointed to the vacancy in question (*Brennan v Dewhurst* [1984] ICR 52, EAT).

- In the terms on which an offer of employment is made, eg offering a male book-keeper a salary of, say, £20,000 a year; and a female, £18,000 a year (unless the difference in salary is justifiable on grounds other than sex).

- By refusing or deliberately omitting to offer her (or him) that employment.

It is likewise unlawful for an employer, in the case of a woman already employed by that employer at an establishment in Great Britain, to discriminate against her:

- in the way he (or she) affords her access to opportunities for promotion, transfer or training, or to any other benefits, facilities or services, or by refusing or deliberately omitting to afford her access to them; or

- by dismissing her, or subjecting her to any other detriment.

(*Source*: SDA 1975, s.6.)

11.58
Problems will often arise over questions put to candidates at interviews. If such questions are gender-stereotyped and have a demoralising effect on the job applicant so that her (or his) performance is undermined, that in itself can be a detriment amounting to discrimination. But there is nothing to prevent a prospective employer from exploring difficulties in the job to assess whether the interviewee will be able to cope with them (*Simon v Brimham Associates* [1987] ICR 596, CA; *Woodhouse v Chief Constable of West Yorkshire Police*, 27 July 1990, EAT).

11.59
The ramifications of the expression 'subjecting a person to a detriment' are extensive. It was held to apply when an employer refused to allow a woman with small children to work part time. She could have been accommodated at no great expense and without any significant disruption (*Home Office v Holmes* [1984] ICR 678, EAT).

Sexual harassment

11.60
The 1975 Act contains no definition of the expression 'sexual harassment'. The concept has evolved from two sources, (i) as a 'detriment' under the Sex

Discrimination Act 1975; and (ii) from a Recommendation of the European Commission on measures for the protection of the dignity of women (and men) at work. The Recommendation (which does not have the force of law) states that there should be no unwanted conduct of a sexual nature, whether physical, verbal or non-verbal (*Wadham v Carpenter Farrer Partnership* [1993] IRLR 374, EAT).

11.61
If a woman complains of unwanted sexual advances by a male colleague and the latter contends that the woman had consented to such advances, it will be for the tribunal to decide whether the employee's complaint was justified. Given that the public airing of such matters may cause embarrassment, the tribunals are empowered to hear evidence in private should the circumstances so warrant. There is power to make a so-called *restricted reporting order*, which forbids the identification of the parties until the tribunal's decision is promulgated (*Source*: Employment Tribunals (Constitution & Rules of Procedure) Regulations 1993, Schedule 1, para. 14[1]). The issue of acceptance or consent was raised in *Snowball v Gardner Merchant Ltd* [1987] IRLR 397. In that case, the EAT held that a complainant's attitude to matters of sexual behaviour was relevant and admissible for the purposes of determining the degree of injury to feelings she suffered (and hence the amount of compensation payable) as a consequence of her having been sexually harassed.

11.62
It would seem that a woman has the right to decide what causes her offence and what she finds unacceptable conduct in order to establish a harassment. The test of the objective 'reasonable employee' does not apply. In *Wileman v Minilec Engineering Ltd* [1988] IRLR 144, the EAT held that, in determining whether sexual harassment constituted a job, health or career-threatening detriment, an employment tribunal was entitled to take into account the fact that, on occasion, the complainant wore scanty and provocative clothes. In a more prominent case, a female teacher brought proceedings under the Sex Discrimination Act 1975 when she felt obliged to move to another school because of unremitting sexual harassment by two male colleagues. It was held that their conduct amounted to a 'detriment' and *was* actionable (*Porcelli v Strathclyde DC* [1986] ICR 564, CS).

11.63
A male employee was alleged by two women cleaners working in the same department to have sexually harassed them. He was suspended. At a disciplinary hearing, the allegation was unproved and he was returned to his old job. An allegation was made that it was discrimination to allow him back. A tribunal found that the claim of the earlier sexual harassment was substantiated (although unknown to the employers). But it ruled that it was not discrimination to permit the employee to return. The Act made it

necessary to look at the treatment and not at the consequence of that treatment. The man would have been allowed back whether the fellow employees were women or a man complaining of homosexual advances by a male employee (*Balgobin & Another v London Borough of Tower Hamlets* [1987] ICR 829, EAT).

11.64
The State is entitled to fix different ages at which men and women may draw their State pensions, but not the age at which they may be compulsorily retired (*Beets-Proper v F Van Lanschot Bankiers NV* [1986] ICR 706, ECJ). An employer provided redundancy terms, under which men and women could both receive a cash payment or an early retirement pension at the age of 55. This meant that the women received theirs five years earlier, and the men ten years earlier, than their State pensions. It was held that this was not discrimination. Both sexes were entitled to the same rights, and as the State was entitled to discriminate in fixing the age of retirement for each sex, that had to be disregarded (*Roberts v Tate & Lyle Industries Ltd* [1986] ICR 371, ECJ).

'Genuine Occupational Qualification'

11.65
Denying a person a job (or access to opportunities for promotion, transfer or training, or to any related benefits, facilities or services) on the grounds of sex is permissible in law if being of a particular sex is a 'genuine occupational qualification' (GOQ) for the vacancy or job in question (*Timex Corporation v Hodgson* [1982] ICR 63, EAT). For example, being a man might well be a GOQ for a job involving work in certain Middle Eastern countries whose laws, customs or cultural inclinations preclude any business dealings with women. Toilet and changing-room attendants is another example (*Source*: SDA 1975, s.7).

11.66
Although a job might require a measure of physical strength, it would be unlawful to deny that job to a woman simply because she is a woman. If physical strength or stamina is an important consideration, the only way to avoid a complaint of unlawful discrimination would be to apply the same aptitude tests to all job candidates, male as well as female. If lifting and carrying heavy weights is only an occasional feature of the work, there is no reason why a woman should not be capable of doing that work (even if that meant calling upon the help of one or other of her workmates when such an occasion arose). In *Etam plc v Rowan* [1989] IRLR 150, the EAT held that being a woman was not a 'genuine occupational qualification' for employment as a sales assistant in a women's clothes shop. A man could

quite happily carry out the bulk of the work without causing any inconvenience or embarrassment to customers. In a delicate situation, he could easily call upon one of his female colleagues for assistance. The same approach was adopted in an earlier case, that of *Wylie v Dee & Co* [1978] IRLR 103. There, a woman was refused a job as a sales assistant in a menswear shop because sales assistants were required, on occasion, to take a tape measure to a customer's inside trouser leg. The tribunal held that, should any customer be unhappy about being ministered to by a woman in that way, the assistant could always call for assistance from one of her male colleagues.

11.67

If a job involves working or living in a private house where there is likely to be a degree of physical or social contact with a person of the opposite sex living in the same house, or knowledge of intimate details of such a person's life, and where there might be reasonable objection, then discrimination on grounds of sex is permissible. The same applies where the nature of the job requires the holder to live in communal accommodation, which includes dormitories or other shared sleeping accommodation (including sanitary facilities) which, for reasons of privacy or decency should be used by men only, or by women only. However, a tribunal would need to be satisfied that the accommodation in question could not be altered or extended to overcome the difficulty and that the employer had acted reasonably in denying employment on such grounds (*Sisley v Britannia Security Systems Ltd* [1983] ICR 628, EAT) (*Source*: SDA 1975, s.7(2)).

11.68

There are corresponding and supplementary exceptions relating to gender reassignment. Accordingly, it is not *prima facie* unlawful to discriminate against a job applicant or existing employee on grounds of gender reassignment if a particular job involves the holder of the job being liable to be called upon to perform intimate physical searches pursuant to statutory powers (eg, immigration officials, customs officers, and the like); or if the job involves working or living in a private house where a person living in that house might reasonably object to the degree of physical or social contact (or knowledge of intimate details of such a person's life) which is a likely or inevitable feature of that job; or if the nature of the job requires a person undergoing gender reassignment to live in communal accommodation, which includes dormitories or other shared sleeping accommodation (including sanitary facilities) which, for reasons of privacy or decency should be used by men only, or by women only; or if the holder of the job provides vulnerable individuals with personal services promoting their welfare (or similar personal services) and, in the reasonable view of the employer, those services cannot be effectively provided by a person while that person is undergoing gender reassignment.

Discrimination on health and safety grounds

11.69
Section 51 of the 1975 Act allows that discrimination on grounds of sex is also permissible where the employment of women in certain activities and processes is prohibited by regulations made under (or saved by) the Health & Safety at Work, etc Act 1974. For example, pregnant women and women of 'reproductive capacity' must *not* be employed (or be allowed to continue working) in work which exposes them to lead or ionising radiations. However, reliance on section 51 has recently been challenged, and challenged successfully, before the European Court of Justice (ECJ). In *Mahlburg v Land Mecklenburg–Vorpommern* (2 February 2000), and in *Habermann-Beltermann v Arbeiterwohlfahrt, Bezirksverband Ndb/Obf e V* (No. c-421/92). In those cases, the ECJ ruled that it is not permissible to refuse to employ a new or expectant mother in work otherwise prohibited to her on health and safety grounds if the employment in question is intended to be *permanent* and she is the best candidate for the job. In short, such a candidate must be appointed to the vacancy for which she has applied and either be offered suitable alternative employment until she begins her maternity leave period or be suspended from work on full pay until the risks associated with what is essentially a temporary indisposition have passed and she is in a position (legally) to take up her duties.

Other exceptions

11.70
In certain limited instances, positive discrimination is allowed by a training body. It may limit one sex access to facilities for training, to redress any imbalance that existed during the previous 12 months (*Source*: SDA 1975, s.48).

11.71
The 1975 Act does not apply to the armed forces or to the various cadet corps. Nor does it apply to ministers of religion; to charitable organisations conferring benefits on persons of one sex only; to any sport, game or activity of a competitive nature where the physical strength, stamina or physique of the average woman puts her at a disadvantage to the average man; to the treatment of a person in relation to an annuity, life assurance policy, accident insurance policy or similar matter involving the assessment of risk, where the treatment was effected by reference to actuarial or other data from a source on which it was reasonable to rely; or to acts done for the purpose of ensuring the combat effectiveness of the naval, military or air forces of the Crown (*Source*: SDA 1975, ss 19, 43–45, 52 & 85).

PERSONS TO WHOM THE 1975 ACT APPLIES

11.72
The 1975 Act applies to a person of any age, whether an employee, an applicant for a job, or a person under a contract personally to execute any work or labour. Nor is length of service a limiting factor. For the current position relating to persons employed wholly or mainly outside Great Britain, please turn to Chapter 3, paras 3.74 & 3.75 (*Source*: RRA 1976).

11.73
The Act also applies to contract labour, eg to persons supplied by employment agencies, to partnerships, to trade unions and employers' organisations, to professional and trade bodies, to qualifying and vocational training bodies, to the Employment Service Agency and the Training Service Agency. It also applies to the police (but with some limited exceptions) and to the prison service. Midwifery is included. (*Source*: SDA 1975, ss 9, 11, 12, 14 to 16, 17,18 & 20.)

11.74
Those who unlawfully instruct others to discriminate are caught by the Act, as well as those who carry out such instructions, even in good faith. So too are those who pressurise others to discriminate (*Simon v Brimham Associates* [1987] ICR 596, CA). Employers and principals are (vicariously) liable for the unlawful acts of discrimination committed by their staff and agents during the employment. It matters not whether it is to their knowledge or not, unless they can prove that they have taken such steps as were reasonably practical to avoid such incidents occurring (*Source*: SDA 1975, ss 39–41).

Discrimination by barristers and advocates

11.75
Sections 35A and 35B of the 1975 (inserted by the Court & Legal Services Act 1990) point out that it is unlawful, in relation to any offer of pupillage or tenancy, for a barrister or barrister's clerk to discriminate against a woman in the arrangements which are made for the purpose of determining to whom it should be offered; in respect of any terms on which it is offered; or by refusing or deliberately omitting to offer it to her. The same rule applies to discrimination by an advocate in relation to taking on any person as his (or her) pupil.

Discriminatory advertisements

11.76
It is unlawful to publish or cause to be published an advertisement which indicates, or might reasonably be construed as indicating, an intention by a

person to do an act which is (or might be) unlawful under the 1975 Act. It is also a form of indirect discrimination to advertise job vacancies in any journal or magazine the majority of whose readers are female (or male) – unless being of a particular sex is a 'genuine occupational qualification' for the vacancy in question (*Source*: SDA 1975, ss 37 & 38). An advertisement which uses job titles such as (or is accompanied by an illustration depicting a) barmaid, waitress, chambermaid, flight stewardess, sales girl, etc might also be taken to indicate an intention to discriminate against men unless the accompanying copy contains a clear indication to the contrary. Publishers will also be liable under the Act if they allow such advertisements to be published in their newspapers or magazines. If illustrations are used in job advertisements, they should depict persons of both sexes.

QUESTIONS AND REPLIES

11.77
An employee (or job applicant) who believes that she (or he) has been discriminated against in contravention of the Sex Discrimination Act 1975, whether by her present employer or by a would-be employer, may question the person concerned asking him to explain why he has contravened her rights under the 1975 Act. The procedure is explained in the Sex Discrimination (Questions & Replies) Order 1975 (SI 1975/2048). The form prescribed by the Regulations is Form SD74, copies of which are available from the Equal Opportunities Commission or from any Job Centre or unemployment benefit office of the Department for Education & Employment) (*Source*: SDA 1975, s.74(2)(b)).

Note: Form SD74 is an eight-page document which not only provides space for preparing the questionnaire to be submitted, but also gives a great deal of practical advice both to the person aggrieved and to the person to whom the questions are directed. The document points out that an employer cannot be compelled to respond to the allegations made against him. However, the employer is cautioned that an employment tribunal may draw any such inference as is just and equitable from a failure, without reasonable excuse, to reply within a reasonable period, or from an evasive or equivocal reply, including an inference that the employer had unlawfully discriminated against the employee (or the rejected job applicant).

11.78
The questionnaire must be served within three months of the alleged act of discrimination, or within 21 days of an Originating Application (Form IT1) being sent to the Secretary to the Tribunals. A Chairman (or a tribunal) has power to extend the 21 days, and this will generally be granted where a reasonable explanation for the delay is given (*Williams v Greater London Citizens' Advice Bureaux* [1989] ICR 545, EAT). In appropriate circumstances, a further questionnaire may be served with leave. This will normally be given

where the information sought is not available in existing documents, so that an order for Discovery or Inspection would not be apt (*Carrington v Helix Lighting Ltd* [1990] ICR 125, EAT).

THE EQUAL OPPORTUNITIES COMMISSION

11.79
The Equal Opportunities Commission (EOC) is charged with the duty of eliminating unlawful discrimination, and is armed with several powers to enable it to carry out that duty. *First*, it may conduct formal investigations into cases where it believes that an employer's conduct contravenes the Sex Discrimination and Equal Pay legislation. If it does find a default it may issue a 'non-discrimination notice' requiring the employer to cease the discrimination or the alleged discriminatory practice. An employer who is served with a Non-Discrimination Notice must either comply with its terms or appeal to an employment tribunal within the next six weeks. An employer can also apply to the High Court for a Judicial Review (*Source*: SDA 1975, ss 53, 57, 67 & 68).

Note: If the tribunal finds that any of the requirements of a Non-Discrimination Notice are unreasonable (perhaps because they are based on incorrect findings of fact or for any other reason), it may quash the Notice or part of it. It may also substitute any other requirement (*Source*: SDA 1975, s.68(2)&(3)).

11.80
Second, the EOC may seek a declaration from an employment tribunal that an employer is engaging (or has engaged) in discriminatory practices, or has published a discriminatory advertisement, or has instructed another (eg an employment agency) to discriminate against job applicants on grounds of sex (or marital status) (*Source*: SDA 1975, s.73).

11.81
Third, the EOC may offer its services to any individual (employee, job applicant, or otherwise) who is preparing or planning to present a complaint of unlawful sex discrimination to an employment tribunal. It will do so where a question of principle is involved, or where it would be unreasonable to expect that person to act on her (or his) own behalf – bearing in mind the complexities that attend many such cases (*Source*: SDA 1975, s.75).

EOC Code of Practice

11.82
The Equal Opportunities Commission has produced a *Code of Practice for the Elimination of Discrimination on the Grounds of Sex and Marriage and the Promotion of Equality of Opportunity in Employment*, copies of which are available from The

Stationery Office. For information about other EOC publications, guidance notes, etc, the reader is commended to Web site www.eoc.org.uk.

REMEDIES

11.83
An employee (or aggrieved job applicant) may complain to an employment tribunal that her (or his) employer, or a particular employer, has discriminated against her on grounds of sex or marital status or that he has breached her rights under the Equal Pay Act 1970. If the complaint is upheld, the tribunal will make an order:

- declaring the rights of the complainant and the respondent (the employer) in relation to the act to which the complaint relates;

- requiring the respondent employer to pay to the complainant compensation of an amount corresponding to any damages he could have been ordered by a county court or by a sheriff court to pay to the complainant.

The tribunal may also make a recommendation that the respondent take within a specified period action designed to obviate or reduce the adverse effect on the complainant of any act of discrimination to which the complaint relates. Failure to comply with a recommendation without reasonable justification can lead to a further award of compensation or an increase in the existing award (Source: SDA 1975, s.65).

Note: In Sex Discrimination cases, a tribunal can award compensation for injury to feelings. Interest can also be awarded in the appropriate circumstances. The amount has to be kept moderate and calculated on the same basis as in defamation cases. A sum between £500 and £5,000 would be appropriate although the figure tends to rise yearly (*Bradford City Metropolitan Council v Arora* [1991] ICR 226, CA). Exemplary damages may not be awarded (*Deane v Ealing Borough Council & Another* [1993] ICR 329, EAT). But the power to award compensation does not arise if the discrimination is indirect and there was no intention to discriminate (*Source*: EPA 1970, ss 2(1A) & 2(5); SDA 1975 ss 65(a), (b) & (c), and 66(3)).

11.84
There is no upper limit on the amount of compensation that may be awarded in sex (race and disability) discrimination cases. Damages for loss of earnings, prospective loss of earnings and injured feelings and other losses are included in the compensation. The measure for damages is based on the principle that, as best as money could do it, the employee should be put into the position in which she would have been but for the employer's unlawful conduct. This is subject to the usual tests of evaluation of the loss of a chance, causation, remoteness of damage and a duty to mitigate (see Chapter 2, paras 2.57 to 2.64) (*Ministry of Defence v Cannock & Others, The Times*, 2 August 1994, EAT).

TIME LIMITS

Complaints under the Equal Pay Act 1970

11.85
In 'equal pay' cases, an Originating Application (Form IT1) must be sent to the Secretary to the Tribunals (in practice, the nearest Regional Office of the Tribunals) within six months of the alleged breach of the implied 'equality clause' or within six months of the effective date of termination of the employee's contract of employment.

11.86
Contrary to s.2(5) of the EPA 1970, which limits an award of arrears of pay and damages to the period of two years immediately preceding the date on which a complaint under the EPA is brought, the European Court of Justice (ECJ) in *Levez v T H Jennings (Harlow Pools) Ltd* (EOR 83), held that limiting an employee's entitlement to arrears of remuneration to a period of two years is in breach of the principle of equivalence under EU law. The only limit, said the ECJ, is the limit imposed by the relevant Member State's Statute of Limitations (ie, six years in England & Wales, and five years in Scotland & Northern Ireland). Legislation giving effect to the ECJ's decision in *Levez* (amending s.2(5) of the 1970 Act) is expected to come into force in July 2003.

11.87
Only one application concerning the same complaint may be made, unless a later application refers to different matters (*British Railways Board v Paul (qv)*). If proceedings are initially taken in the County Court and the question of the operation of the 'equality clause' arises, the case can be stopped and referred to an employment tribunal for a decision. The Secretary of State is also empowered to refer a case to the tribunal. There is no time limit on such referrals (*Source*: EPA 1970, s.2(3) & (4)).

Complaints under the Sex Discrimination Act 1975

11.88
A complaint under the 1975 Act must be 'presented' within three months of the matter complained of, or, if there is continuing discrimination, at any time. If the employee has (allegedly) been unlawfully dismissed, the complaint must be presented within three months of the effective date of termination of her (or his) contract of employment (*Lupetti v Wren's Old House Ltd* [1984] ICR 348 EAT; and *Barclays Bank plc v Kapur & Others* [1991] ICR 208, HL) (*Source*: SDA 1975, s.76(1)). If a complaint is presented 'out of time', a tribunal has power to adjudicate if, in all the circumstances, it is 'just and equitable' to do so (*Source*: SDA 1975, s.76(5)).

Racial discrimination

GENERAL INFORMATION

12.1
The Race Relations Act 1976 is almost identical in scope to the Sex Discrimination Act (see Chapter 11). Indeed, many of its provisions are worded similarly except for the substitution of the word 'race' or 'racial' for 'sex'.

12.2
Discrimination on 'racial grounds' means discrimination based on a person's colour, race, nationality, national or ethnic origins. 'Racial group' means any group of persons defined by reference to colour, race, nationality or ethnic or national origins. It has been held that Sikhs are covered by the 1976 Act but not Rastafarians. The former had a long history whereas the latter had existed for only 60 years (*Mandla & Another v Lee & Others* [1983] 2 AC 548, HL; and *Dawkins v Crown Supplies (PSA) Ltd* [1993] IRLR 284, CA) (*Source*: RRA 1976, s.3).

12.3
This Act also deals with various criminal offences which are rarely invoked; and provides for various civil causes of action. The latter are dealt with in the County Court (in England) or Sheriff's Court (in Scotland) (*Source*: RRA 1976, ss 43 to 52).

12.4
European law contains provisions against discrimination but, curiously, they are limited to discrimination on grounds of nationality as laid down in Article 7 of the Treaty of Rome. If another Article specifically prohibits discrimination, the wording of that other Article must be considered alone (*Ingetraut Scholz v Opera Universitaria di Cagliari & Another, The Times*, 29 March 1994, ECJ).

12.5
The Commission for Racial Equality (CRE) was set up by the 1976 Act. Like the Equal Opportunities Commission (EOC), the CRE is charged with the duty of eliminating discrimination at all levels and in every field. For these purposes, it has a variety of powers (see para. 12.32).

WHAT IS RACIAL DISCRIMINATION?

There are three types of racial discrimination rendered unlawful by the 1976 Act: 'direct' discrimination, 'indirect' discrimination and victimisation.

Direct discrimination

12.6
Direct discrimination arises where an employer (or other person), on racial grounds, treats a person (and this includes a company) less favourably than he (or she) treats or would treat other persons (including a company) (*Source*: RRA 1976, s.1(1)(a)).

12.7
But it is always necessary to compare like with like. So where two Indian nationals were refused employment when they declined to produce evidence of a right to work (which they had), it was not discriminatory. The same requirements were put to all non-British and non-EU subjects (*Dhatt & Another v McDonald's Hamburger Ltd* [1991] ICR 238, CA) (*Source*: RRA 1976, s.3(4)). Furthermore, it is essential to allege and prove that the treatment received was less favourable on the grounds of race or colour than would be the case with others not of the claimant's group. It is not sufficient to establish that the treatment was poor or deplorable. The alleged discriminator may dislike the claimant as a person, or he might treat all deplorably, irrespective of background (*Chapman & Another v Simon* [1994] IRLR 124, CA).

12.8
It is necessary to see whether there is any departure from the requirement of equality of treatment and not that the effect of the treatment produces different results. Some employers failed to follow their own equal opportunities policy when they refused to allow a complainant to see his references when considering him for promotion. It was held that there was no evidence to show he had been treated unfavourably in comparison to other applicants (*Quereshi v London Borough of Newham* [1991] IRLR 264, CA).

Indirect discrimination

12.9
Indirect racial discrimination occurs when an employer imposes a condition or requirement which acts as an absolute bar to selection if a job applicant (or candidate for promotion, transfer or training) is unable to satisfy that requirement or condition; and if

- the number of persons in the racial group to which the applicant belongs who can comply with that requirement or condition is considerably smaller than that of others not of that group; and

- the requirement or condition is not justified on non-racial grounds;

- it is to the applicant's detriment because he(or she) cannot comply with it;

but, where there is discrimination affecting a racial group, only the Commission for Racial Equality (see para. 12.32 below) can bring proceedings (*Perera v Civil Service Commission* [1983] ICR 428, CA) (*Source:* RRA 1976, s.1(1)(b)).

12.10
To establish whether a condition or requirement has a discriminatory effect on an applicant, it is necessary:

- to identify the ethnic group to which the applicant belongs;

- to consider the extent of the geographic area to be taken into account when considering the relative proportions; and

- to establish what was the condition or requirement which that group in that area could not comply with (*Tower Hamlets LBC v Qayyum, The Times*, 2 May 1988, EAT).

If there are several conditions or requirements to be satisfied, the importance attached to each by an employer (or prospective employer) will also be relevant in deciding whether there has been discrimination (*Meer v London Borough of Tower Hamlets* [1988] IRLR 399, CA). A company can escape liability for a discriminatory condition or requirement by proving 'on the balance of probabilities' (see Chapter 2, paras 2.13 to 2.17) that it was justifiable for non-racial reasons, eg that it is necessary for reasons of health or safety, or for some other non-racial reason (*Gurmit Singh Kambo v Vaulkhard, The Times*, 7 December 1984, CA). A company which insisted on its production-line employees having short hair in compliance with food hygiene regulations was held not to have discriminated against a Sikh who was refused employment because of his insistence (for cultural and religious reasons) on wearing his hair long (*Panesar v Nestlé Co Ltd* [1980] ICR 144, CA).

12.11
However, a genuine belief in the justification of a particular condition or requirement is not enough. An objective test must be applied and a balance struck between the reasonable needs of the party applying the condition or requirement and the discriminatory effect it had on the complainant. It has to be 'capable of being justified... 'without regard to' the colour, race, etc of the applicant' (*Orphanos v Queen Mary College* [1985] IRLR 349, HL) (and see Chapter 11, paras 11.39 to 11.45 for analogous provisions in the Sex Discrimination Act 1975). Thus, the governors of a Church of England

school were held to be justified in imposing a requirement that candidates for the post of head teacher had to be committed communicants, even though that requirement effectively ruled out most Asians. The person appointed would quite often be required to administer the sacrament at communion (*Board of Governors of St. Matthias Church of England School v Crizzle* [1993] ICR 401, EAT).

12.12

The phrase 'cannot comply' means that an applicant must prove that, in practice, persons of his racial group cannot accept a requirement which is inconsistent with their customs and cultural traditions (*Mandla & Another v Lee & Others* [1983] IRLR 209, HL). So a Sikh whose religion requires him to wear a turban was prevented from taking a job as a bus conductor by a company rule that all conductors must wear the regulation uniform cap. As there was no *prima facie* justification for the rule (eg on grounds of health, safety or hygiene), the rule was tantamount to unlawful indirect discrimination. There must be a comparison with persons where the relevant circumstances are the same, or are not materially different. It does not matter whether there is no intention to discriminate; it is unlawful if the effect is to discriminate (*R v Birmingham City Council ex parte EOC* [1989] IRLR 173, HL) (*Source*: RRA 1976, s.3(4)).

12.13

An employer in Italy refused to take into account the previous employment in public service in Germany of a former German citizen. It was held by the European Court of Justice that this was unjustified indirect discrimination under Article 48 of the Treaty of Rome which reads as follows: '1. Freedom of movement for workers shall be secured within the Community...' and again: '2. Such freedom shall entail the abolition of any discrimination based on nationality between workers of the Member States as regards employment, remuneration, and other conditions of work and employment' (*Ingetraut Scholz v Opera Universitaria di Cagliari & Another, The Times*, 29 March 1994, ECJ). See also the *Note* to para. 12.16 below.

Victimisation

12.14

There can also be discrimination by way of victimisation. This arises where a person is treated less favourably because he (or she) has brought proceedings or given evidence or information under the Race Relations Act 1976, or has alleged an infringement of his rights under that Act. However, this does not apply where the alleged victim makes a false allegation or one not made in good faith (see also Chapter 11, para. 11.51) (*Source*: RRA 1976, s.2(1) s.2(2)).

12.15

To prove victimisation it is necessary to consider the reasons behind the act or omission complained of, and to decide whether those reasons were justified on non-racial grounds. Consequently, it is important to identify the person who took the relevant decision and to question him (or her) about his motives (*Aziz v Trinity Street Taxis Ltd & Others* [1988] ICR 534, CA; and *Subasinghe-Sharpe v London Borough of Brent*, 5 December 1991, EAT).

DISCRIMINATION AGAINST JOB APPLICANTS AND EMPLOYEES

12.16

It is unlawful for a person, in relation to employment by him at an establishment in Great Britain (but see *Note* below) to discriminate against a job applicant on racial grounds:

- in the arrangements made for the purposes of determining who should be offered that employment; or

- in the terms on which that employment is offered; or

- by refusing or deliberately omitting to offer that employment.

It is likewise unlawful for an employer, in the case of a person employed by him (or her) at an establishment in Great Britain, to discriminate against that employee on racial grounds:

- by denying the same terms and conditions of employment to that employee as are available to other employees doing the same or equivalent work;

- by withholding (or denying access to) opportunities for promotion, transfer or training, or any other benefits, facilities or services; or by refusing or deliberately omitting to afford the employee access to them; or

- by dismissing or subjecting the employee to any other detriment.

(*Source*: RRA 1976, s.4(1) & (2).) See also para. 12.22 below.

Note: In a recent case, the EAT held that sections 4 and 8 of the 1976 Act – which only permit complaints under the Act to be brought by persons employed at (or seeking employment at) an establishment in Great Britain (and Northern Ireland) – conflict with Article 48 of the Treaty of Rome ('freedom of movement of workers'). In the case in question, a Mr Bossa, an Italian national living in the UK, answered an advertisement in the British press placed by Alitalia, the Italian airline. The airline was seeking to recruit flight attendants to be based in Italy. During his interview at Gatwick airport, Nordstress Limited (the company contracted by Alitalia to interview candidates on their behalf) informed Mr Bossa that they were forbidden by the Italian authorities to recruit Italian nationals living outside Italy and to take them back to Italy. The EAT held that Article 48 of the Treaty applies to all citizens of the European Economic Area (ie the EU plus Iceland, Norway and Liechtenstein) and has both 'horizontal' and 'vertical' direct effect. It could therefore be relied on by both public and private sector employees and job applicants discriminated against on the grounds of their nationality or national origins. In short, Article 48 overrides any conflicting provisions in UK domestic legislation. The EAT upheld Mr Bossa's appeal and referred his case back to the employment tribunal (*Bossa v Nordstress Limited*, EAT 571/96).

12.17
In *de Souza v Automobile Association* [1986] ICR 514, CA) a black employee overheard two other employees discussing him in a racially-derogatory way. The Court of Appeal held that that was not of itself actionable. It is the effect of such conduct that has to be considered. The complainant would need to show that he had been subjected to a detriment, eg that what he had overhead had adversely affected his health and general well-being or his ability to carry out his duties efficiently.

Note: Under section 4A of the Public Order Act 1986, it is a criminal offence, punishable by a fine of up £5,000 and/or imprisonment for a term not exceeding six months, for any person, with intent to cause a person harassment, alarm or distress, to use threatening, abusive or insulting words or disorderly behaviour, or to write or display graffiti which is threatening, abusive or insulting. The 1986 Act (amended in this instance by the Criminal Justice & Public Order Act 1994) applies equally to offences committed within the workplace.

GENUINE OCCUPATIONAL QUALIFICATION

12.18
There are circumstances in which discrimination on racial grounds is lawful where being of a particular racial group is a 'genuine occupational qualification' for a particular job or occupation. Thus, in the interests of authenticity, it is permissible for the proprietors or managers of a Chinese restaurant to restrict their recruitment of waiters to persons who are either themselves Chinese or of Chinese appearance.

The same applies where a job involves participation in a dramatic performance or some other form of entertainment, or as a model, or where personal services promoting the welfare of people of a particular racial group are provided. See also Chapter 11, paras 11.65 to 11.68 (*Source*: RRA 1976 s.5).

12.19
A local authority sought to restrict two appointments to Afro-Caribbean or Asian applicants to perform functions of an essentially managerial and administrative nature. The Court of Appeal held that being Afro-Caribbean

or Asian was not a genuine occupational qualification for either job, as the persons doing those jobs would not be dealing directly with the client base and would not therefore be providing 'personal services'. In short, they would not be working at a level where language and cultural understanding was important (*London Borough of Lambeth v Commission for Racial Equality* [1990] IRLR 231, CA).

12.20
A person was required for the post of nursery worker to deal with children of primarily Afro-Caribbean origin. A white man was rejected because it was thought that a person from the same ethnic background as the children would be more suitable. It was held that as the work *did* involve the provision of 'personal services', the employers were not in breach of the 1976 Act. They *were* entitled to take into account the type of person who would most effectively provide the services required (*Greenwich Homeworkers Project v Marroll (Case A)*, 19 October 1990, EAT).

TO WHOM DOES THE 1976 ACT APPLY?

12.21
The Act applies to a person of any age, whether an employee, an applicant for a job, or a person under a contract personally to execute any work or labour. Nor is length of service a limiting factor. For the current position relating to persons employed wholly or mainly outside Great Britain, please turn to Chapter 3, paras 3.74 & 3.75 (*Source*: RRA 1976).

12.22
For the purposes of the 1976 Act, a person is deemed to be employed at an establishment in Great Britain provided that he (or she) does at least part of his work within Great Britain. This rule applies even where the work is done mainly elsewhere. Thus, an employee who ordinarily works outside Great Britain (eg, in another EEA Member State), who is sent (albeit temporarily) to work in Great Britain, enjoys the same protection under the 1976 Act as persons who ordinarily work inside Great Britain (*ibid* s.5, as amended by the Equal Opportunities (Employment Legislation) (Territorial Limits) Regulations 1999 (SI 1999/3163).

Note: Article 3(1)(g) of Council Directive 96/71/EC of 16 December 1996 'concerning the posting of workers in the framework of the provision of services' (The 'Posted Workers' Directive), which came into force in the UK on 16 December 1999, requires every Member State to ensure that employment legislation concerning equality of treatment between men and women and other provisions on non-discrimination are extended to 'posted workers', that is to say, workers who, for a limited period, carry out their work in the territory of that State, having been posted there in certain circumstances by an undertaking established in another Member State.

Persons employed on ships registered in Great Britain, or on aircraft or hover craft registered in the United Kingdom and operated from Great Britain, are also protected unless their work is wholly outside the territorial waters (*Wood v Cunard Line Ltd* [1990] IRLR 281, CA). In determining whether a person works 'wholly outside Great Britain', it is necessary to consider what was contemplated by the parties at the time of making the contract of employment. Subsequent unforeseen events are not relevant (*Deria v General Council of British Shipping* [1986] ICR 172, CA).

12.23

The Act also applies to contract labour, eg to those who are supplied by some third party, to partnerships where there are six or more partners, to trade unions and employers' organisations, to professional and trade bodies, to vocational training bodies, to the Employment Service Agency, the Training Service Agency and to the police. It also applies to barristers (or barristers' clerks) and to advocates minded to offer pupillages or tenancies. An employment tribunal has the power to adjudicate where there is a complaint of discrimination by a qualifying body relating to a decision by that body, except where there is a right of 'appeal or proceedings in the nature of an appeal' from such a decision. The essential feature of such an appeal is the independence of the appellate body, the ability of an aggrieved to make oral representations to it, and the fairness of the proceedings (*Khan v General Medical Council* [1993] ICR 627, EAT) (*Source*: RRA 1976 ss 7, 10, 11, 12, 13 to 16, 26A, 26B and 54(2)).

12.24

Those who give instructions to discriminate unlawfully on racial grounds are also caught by the 1976 Act, as are those who put pressure on others (such as an Employment Agency) to do likewise. Employers and principals are vicariously liable for the unlawful acts of their employees or agents in the course of their employment unless they can prove that they took such steps as were reasonably practicable to avoid the discrimination. Employers should make their 'equal opportunity policies' known to their staff, complemented by adequate supervision and training (*Balgobin & Another v LB of Tower Hamlets* [1987] ICR 829, EAT) (see Chapter 11, para. 11.74) (*Source*: RRA 1976 ss 30, 31 & 32).

12.25

A post office worker had written racist comments on an envelope addressed to his neighbours. It was held that it was not done in the course of his employment. This was a personal act of his, unrelated to his work (*Irving & Another v Post Office* [1988] IRLR 144, CA).

12.26

Those who help others to breach the 1976 Act are also liable provided they do so knowingly. But it is a defence, for example, for an employment agency or newspaper publisher to show that they had acted on an assurance given by an employer, or whomever, that there would be no breach of the 1976 Act and that it was reasonable for them to have relied on that assurance (*Source*: RRA 1976, s.33).

12.27
It is unlawful to impose a requirement or condition which results in an act of unlawful racial discrimination, or to publish an advertisement which clearly indicates an intention to discriminate. Acts done by a Minister of the Crown, or a Government Department, or on behalf of the Crown, by a statutory body or a person holding a statutory office, are all within the scope of the Act (*Source*: RRA 1976 ss 28, 29 & 75).

12.28
The provisions do not apply to the armed services. Disputes within the services can only be dealt with by their own internal disciplinary bodies. Discriminatory provisions in charitable instruments are void but acts done to safeguard national security are exempt (*Source*: RRA 1976, ss 34, 39, 42, & 75(2)(c),(8)&(9)). Any act done pursuant to a condition or requirement contained in a statutory instrument is immune except in respect of indirect discrimination. To escape liability for indirect discrimination, it must be shown that, in the exercise of discretion in the performance of public duties, a non-discriminatory approach had been adopted where reasonably possible (*Hampson v Department of Education & Science* [1990] ICR 511, HL) (*Source*: RRA 1976 s.41).

European Union law

12.29
There is some overlap between the European law and that of our domestic legislation. Article 48 of the Treaty of Rome prohibits discrimination on the grounds of nationality in employment. In one respect the effect of Article 48 may be nullified by Article 223 which states that no Member State can be obliged to supply information, the disclosure of which would be contrary to its essential security interests. So documents in the possession of the State need not be supplied to an aggrieved person to enable him (or her) to mount a case against any organ or emanation of the State (*R v Secretary of State for Transport & Civil Aviation Authority ex parte Evans & Commission for Racial Equality*, 2 December 1991, Div Ct). But see the *Note* to para. 12.16 above.

Positive discrimination

12.30
In certain limited instances, positive discrimination is allowed by a training body in affording a racial group access to facilities for training. But this can only be done to redress an imbalance that has existed throughout the

previous 12 months. The same rules apply to employers and trade unions in respect of access to training. However, it was held that this duty does not extend to an obligation to provide English lessons to a Thai croupier to enable him to qualify as a manager (*Mecca Leisure Group plc v Chatprachong* [1993] ICR 688, EAT) (*Source*: RRA 1976, ss 37 & 38).

QUESTIONS AND REPLIES

12.31
An employee (or job applicant) who believes that he (or she) has been discriminated against in contravention of the Race Relations Act 1976, whether by his own employer or by a would-be employer, may question the person concerned asking him to explain why he has contravened his rights under the 1976 Act. The procedure is explained in the Race Relations (Questions & Replies) Order 1977 (SI 1977/842). The form prescribed by the Regulations is Form RR65, copies of which are available from any Job Centre or unemployment benefit office of the Department for Education & Employment, or from the Commission for Racial Equality (CRE)(*Source*: RRA 1976, s.65).

Note: Form RR65 is an eight-page document which not only provides space for preparing the questionnaire to be submitted, but also gives a great deal of practical advice both to the person aggrieved and to the person to whom the questions are directed. The document points out that an employer cannot be compelled to respond to the allegations made against him (or her). However, the employer is cautioned that an employment tribunal may draw any such inference as is 'just and equitable' from his failure, without reasonable excuse, to reply within a reasonable period, or from an evasive or equivocal reply, including an inference that the employer had unlawfully discriminated against the employee (or the rejected job applicant).

The questionnaire must be served within three months of the alleged act of discrimination, or, within 21 days of an Originating Application (Form IT1) being sent to the Secretary to the Tribunals. A Chairman (or a tribunal) has power to extend the 21 days, and this will generally be granted where a reasonable explanation for the delay is given (*Williams v Greater London Citizens' Advice Bureaux* [1989] ICR 545, EAT). In appropriate circumstances, a further questionnaire may be served with leave. This will normally be given where the information sought is not available in existing documents, so that an order for Discovery or Inspection would not be apt (*Carrington v Helix Lighting Ltd* [1990] ICR 125, EAT).

THE COMMISSION FOR RACIAL EQUALITY (CRE)

12.32
The Commission for Racial Equality (CRE) has identical duties and powers to the Equal Opportunities Commission. These are explained in Chapter 11, at paras 11.79 to 11.81) (*Source*: RRA 1976 ss 43–52 & 58–65).

Code of Practice

12.33
The CRE has issued a *Code of Practice for the Elimination of Racial Discrimination and the Promotion of Equal Opportunity in Employment*, copies of which can be purchased from the Stationery Office. The code recommends (*inter alia*) that employers should declare their commitment to equal opportunities within their organisations and nominate a senior manager with the responsibility to ensure that the policy is carried out. There should be discussions with employees about the implementation of the policy, together with training, and guidance on the legal implications. The criteria used to select staff should be reviewed to ensure that the selection process is not discriminatory. The composition of the staff should be analysed according to ethnic origins and positive steps taken to encourage racial groups to train for work in areas in which they are under-represented. The Code suggests also that deliberate acts of discrimination be treated as disciplinary offences.

REMEDIES AND TIME LIMITS

12.34
The remedies available for a breach of the 1976 Act are the same as those for discrimination on grounds of sex, marital status or gender reassignment (see Chapter 11, paras 11.83 & 11.84). With the coming into force, on 3 July 1994, of the Race Relations (Remedies) Act 1994, there is no longer an upper limit on the amount of compensation which may be awarded in such cases.

A complaint of unlawful racial discrimination must be presented to an employment tribunal with three months of the alleged discriminatory act or, as appropriate, within three months of the 'effective date of termination' of the complainant's contract of employment (*Source*: RRA 1976 ss 56 & 68).

Disability discrimination

GENERAL INFORMATION

13.1
The Disability Discrimination Act 1995, which came into force on 2 December 1996, contains provisions very similar to those in the Sex Discrimination and Race Relations Acts 1975 and 1976. The new statute, which (for the time being at least) does *not* apply to firms or businesses with fewer than 15 people on the payroll, makes it unlawful for an employer to discriminate against job applicants and employees because they are disabled. The 1995 Act is 'policed' and (where appropriate) enforced by the Disability Discrimination Commission established under the Disability Rights Commission Act 1999.

13.2
There is no upper limit on the amount of compensation that may be awarded by an employment tribunal for an infringement of an employee's (or job applicant's) rights under the 1995 Act (as to which, see 13.18 & 13.19 below).

MEANING OF 'DISABILITY' AND 'DISABLED PERSON'

13.3
For the purposes of the 1995 Act, a person is disabled (or has a disability) if he (or she) has a physical or mental impairment which has a substantial and long-term effect on his ability to carry out normal day-to-day activities.

The expression 'mental impairment' includes an impairment resulting from, or consisting of, a mental illness, but only if the illness is a clinically well-recognised illness. The effect of an impairment (physical or mental) is a long-term effect if:

- it has lasted at least 12 months;

- the period for which it lasts is likely to be at least 12 months; or

- it is likely to last for the rest of the life of the person affected.

If an impairment ceases to have a substantial adverse effect on a person's ability to carry out normal day-to-day activities, it is to be treated as continuing to have that effect if that effect is likely to recur. Furthermore, an impairment is to be taken to affect the ability of the person concerned to carry out normal day-to-day activities only if it affects one of the following:

- mobility;
- manual dexterity;
- physical co-ordination;
- continence;
- ability to lift, carry or otherwise move everyday objects;
- speech, hearing or eyesight;
- memory or ability to concentrate, learn or understand; or
- perception of the risk of physical danger.

The Act and the accompanying code of practice (see para. 13.16 below) point out that a person who has a progressive condition, which is likely to change and develop over time (such as cancer, multiple sclerosis, muscular dystrophy, and the HIV infection) will be taken to have an impairment which has a substantial adverse effect on his (or her) ability to carry out normal day-to-day activities if the condition is likely to result in his having such an impairment (*ibid* Schedule 1).

Severe disfigurement

13.4
A severe disfigurement (facial or otherwise) falls within the meaning of 'disability' unless it consists either of a tattoo (which has not been removed) or a piercing of the body for decorative and other non-medical purposes, including any object attached through the piercing for such purposes (*ibid* Schedule 1, para. 3, as modified by the Disability Discrimination (Meaning of Disability) Regulations 1996 [SI 1996/1445] referred to in the following paragraphs as 'the 1996 Regulations').

Addictions and other conditions excluded

13.5
A person who is addicted to alcohol, nicotine or any other substance is not thereby a disabled person within the meaning of the 1995 Act – unless the addiction in question (in the case of an addiction to drugs) was originally the result of the administration (or mal-administration) of medically prescribed drugs or other medical treatment (1996 Regulations, Reg. 3).

Also excluded from the scope of the Act are the following personality disorders:

(a) a tendency to set fires;

(b) a tendency to physical or sexual abuse of other persons;

(c) exhibitionism; and

(d) voyeurism.

Seasonal allergic rhinitis (hay fever) does not amount to a disability unless the condition aggravates the effect of another condition.

Status of registered disabled persons

13.6
Persons hitherto registered as disabled, under the (now repealed) Disabled Persons (Employment) Act 1944 & 1958, will be deemed to have disabilities, and hence to be disabled persons for the purposes of the 1995 Act, for an initial period of three years from 2 December 1996. After that period has elapsed, any such person will be deemed to have had a disability and to have been disabled during those three years. A certificate of registration (issued under regulations made under section 6 of the 1944 Act) will be conclusive evidence that the person to whom it was issued is (or was) a disabled person.

UNLAWFUL DISCRIMINATION

Discrimination in recruitment

13.7
It is unlawful for an employer to discriminate against a disabled job applicant by taking steps (whether overt or covert) to ensure that no disabled person is interviewed or short-listed for employment within the organisation (however well-qualified that person may be for the vacancy under consideration). If an employer is prepared to recruit disabled persons, it is nonetheless unlawful for him (or her) to do so on terms and conditions which are less favourable than those which would otherwise be offered (or have been offered) to able-bodied persons appointed to (or occupying) the same or similar positions.

13.8
An employer has, of course, every right to refuse to employ a person with a particular disability, if the nature of the work to be done (or the associated risks to health and safety) would make it impossible or highly dangerous for the job applicant to do that work. The same would apply if there is no possible way to modify the work equipment or to adapt it for use by a person with that particular disability, or to make that work equipment more

accessible to the employee (without incurring enormous and unacceptable costs). Should an employer's refusal to employ a particular disabled person be referred to an employment tribunal, it will be for the employer to show that the job applicant's disability militated against his (or her) being offered the job in question.

13.9
Use of expressions, such as 'dynamic', 'energetic', 'alert', 'pleasant appearance', etc – in advertisements lodged in newspapers and magazines or in cards posted in the windows of employment agencies, and the like – could be interpreted as showing an intention to discriminate on grounds of disability and might well be submitted in evidence before an employment tribunal. The same would apply to advertisements, job specifications etc; which call for unnecessary qualifications or skills which bear little relation to the duties of the jobs in question. Any newspaper proprietor or manager of an employment agency or business who knowingly publishes or publicises a patently discriminatory advertisement is guilty of an offence under the 1995 Act. The penalty on summary conviction is a fine of up to £5,000 (*ibid* section 57).

Discrimination in employment

13.10
It is unlawful for an employer to discriminate against any disabled person in his (or her) employ by paying that person a lower wage or salary than that paid to an able-bodied person doing the same or similar work or by offering other less favourable terms and conditions of employment. To deny a disabled person the same opportunities for promotion, transfer and further training as are available to able-bodied persons is also discriminatory and unlawful.

An employee who believes that he (or she) has been discriminated against in this way has no need to resign in order to obtain redress from an employment tribunal. It would be a foolhardy employer indeed who would respond to such a challenge to his (or her) authority by victimising or disciplining the employee. That too is unlawful and could lead to a further hearing before a tribunal and an award of a substantial award of compensation (as to which, please turn to Chapter 6, notably paras 6.17 to 6.19).

Dismissing the disabled employee

13.11
It should be stressed that a disabled person is not immune from dismissal. But, it *is* inadmissible in law and automatically unfair to dismiss a disabled person (or select him or her for redundancy, ahead of more suitable candidates – able-bodied or otherwise) because the employee in question is disabled, and for no

other reason. If the employee is dismissed for a permitted reason, including redundancy (eg misconduct, incompetence, etc), an employment tribunal is nonetheless likely to scrutinise the reasons for dismissal very carefully. A disabled person's inability to match the performance of able-bodied persons doing the same or similar work will not necessarily be indicative of 'incompetence' if the quality of the work produced is not in dispute.

13.12
Employers should be cautious about dismissing an absentee employee on grounds of ill-health, even if that employee has exhausted his (or her) entitlement to occupational sick pay, without first obtaining an up-to-date medical opinion on the nature of the employee's illness, and the likelihood of his returning to work in the medium or long-term future. A decision to dismiss should be based on the need for the work to be done (and the disruption and cost associated with the employee's continued absence) and may be justifiable on those grounds alone. As was mentioned earlier, a disabled employee has no immunity from dismissal. As always, the ultimate test will be that of 'reasonableness'.

EMPLOYER'S DUTY TO MAKE ADJUSTMENTS

13.13
An employer is duty-bound to make whatever 'adjustments' are reasonable and appropriate so as to ensure that job specifications, working hours, starting and finishing times, and his (or her) policies in relation to performance assessment, recruitment, promotion, transfer or access to training, do not needlessly put disabled persons at a disadvantage relative to their able-bodied colleagues.

13.14
The same general rules applies to any physical features of the employer's premises which inhibit access to an employee's work-bench or desk or which make it difficult for a disabled person to move freely about those premises. Chairs and desks may need to be modified or adapted. The On/Off buttons on a machine may likewise need to be relocated. Telephones may have to be fitted with a voice-enhancing device for use by an employee who is deaf or partially deaf; and so on. If some of the work a disabled person is employed to do is relatively insignificant but, nonetheless, beyond the employee's capabilities, the employer will need to consider assigning that part of the employee's work to another employee. In some situations, the code of practice alluded to earlier (see also para. 13.16 below) suggests that it might well be appropriate to provide a reader or interpreter.

13.15
Although an employer cannot be expected to go to inordinate lengths to accommodate a disabled employee, or to invest large sums of money in modifying his

premises or work equipment, he may well be required to satisfy an employment tribunal (in response to a complaint of unlawful discrimination) that he had done all that he reasonably could in the circumstances.

CODES OF PRACTICE AND GUIDANCE

13.16
The reader is referred to the following codes of practice and guidance, both of which are available from The Stationery Office (Tel: 0870 600 5522). These are:

- *A Code of Practice for the Elimination of Discrimination in the Field of Employment Against Disabled Persons or Persons Who Have Had a Disability*; and

- *Employing Disabled People: A Good Practice Guide for Managers and Employers*.

A list of related DRC publications, leaflets, etc can be accessed and downloaded from Web site: www.drc.gov.uk/drc/informationandlegislation/page312.asp

OBTAINING REDRESS

Questions and replies

13.17
An employee (or job applicant) who believes that he (or she) has been discriminated against in contravention of the Disability Discrimination Act 1995, whether by his own employer or by a would-be employer, may question the person concerned, asking him to explain why he has contravened his rights under the Act. The procedure is explained in the Disability Discrimination (Questions & Replies) Order 1996 (SI 1996/2793). The form prescribed for this purpose, with its accompanying Notes, is Form DL56, copies of which will be supplied free of charge by telephoning the Disability Rights Commission Helpline on 08457 622 633, or from any Job Centre or unemployed benefit office (*Source*: DDA 1995, s.67).

Note: Form DL56 not only provides space for preparing the questionnaire to be submitted, but also gives a great deal of practical advice both to the person aggrieved and to the person to whom the questions are directed. The document points out that an employer cannot be compelled to respond to the allegations made against him. However, the employer is cautioned that an employment tribunal may draw any such inference as is 'just and equitable' from his failure, without reasonable excuse, to reply within a reasonable period, or from an evasive or equivocal reply, including an inference that the employer had unlawfully discriminated against the employee (or the rejected job applicant).

The questionnaire must be served within three months of the alleged act of discrimination, or, within 21 days of an Originating Application (Form IT1) being sent to the Secretary to the Tribunals. A Chairman (or a tribunal) has power to extend the 21 days, and this will generally be granted where a reasonable explanation for the delay is given (*Williams v Greater London Citizens' Advice Bureaux* [1989] ICR 545, EAT).

Complaint to an employment tribunal

13.18
An employee (or would-be) employee who believes that he (or she) has been unlawfully discriminated against on grounds of disability may complain to an employment tribunal. Such a complaint must be presented within three months of the alleged unlawful act or (if the employee has been dismissed) within three months of the effective date of termination of his contract of employment.

13.19
If the complaint is upheld, the tribunal will make a declaration to that effect and will order the employer to pay compensation to the complainant (which may include compensation for injury to feelings), the amount of which will be calculated by applying the principles applicable to the calculation of damages in claims in tort or (in Scotland) in reparation for a breach of statutory duty. The tribunal may also recommend to the employer that he (or she) take appropriate steps to remedy the situation which initiated the complaint in the first place (bearing in mind that the employee who brought the complaint may be still in the employer's employment). In short, the tribunal may recommend to the offending employer that he adapt, modify or adjust certain features of the workplace to review any discriminatory effect. If an employer fails to comply with any such recommendation, the tribunal may increase the amount of compensation payable to the employee (*ibid* section 8).

RELATED PROVISIONS AND LEGISLATION

Occupational pension schemes

13.20
Under section 6 of the 1995 Act, every occupational pension scheme will be taken to include a 'non-discrimination rule' relating to the terms of admission to (or membership of) such a scheme. The rule effectively requires the trustees (or managers) of the scheme to refrain from doing (or omitting to do) any act which, if done by an employer, would amount to unlawful discrimination under the 1995 Act.

Companies Act 1985

13.21
Paragraph 9 of Schedule 7 to the Companies Act 1985, requires every company which employs an average of more than 250 people per week (including part-timers, but excluding persons employed wholly or mainly outside the UK) to include in the directors' report attached to its annual accounts a statement outlining its policy in relation to the employment, training, career development and promotion of registered disabled persons.

Chronically Sick and Disabled Persons Act 1970

13.22
Section 8A of the Chronically Sick & Disabled Persons Act 1970 (as amended) imposes a duty on the owners and developers of proposed new offices, shops, factories, retail parks, and the like, to consider the needs of disabled persons when designing the means of access to (and within) such premises, including the means of access to (and the provision of) suitable parking facilities, toilets, cloakrooms and washrooms. Section 29A of the Town & Country Planning Act 1971 requires local authorities to draw the attention of persons seeking planning permission for such developments to the relevant provisions of the 1970 Act and to the *Code of Practice for Access for the Disabled to Buildings*. Any person injured as a direct consequence of a builder or developer's failure to comply with the 1970 Act may face a claim for damages in the ordinary courts.

CASE LAW

13.23
To date, the tribunals have identified asthma, epilepsy, post traumatic stress disorder, ureteric colic and clinical depression as conditions capable of amounting to a 'disability' within the meaning of the 1995 Act. But, as was pointed out by the EAT in *O'Neill v Symm & Co Ltd* [1998] IRLR 933, this does not mean that such conditions will always amount to a disability. The acid test is whether the condition in question has a long term adverse effect on an employee's (or would-be employee's) ability to carry out normal day-to-day activities. In each case, it is for a tribunal to determine whether that test is satisfied. The fact that an employee is taking medication or controlling his condition through the use of inhalers (as is the case with asthmatics) does not mean that the employee is not disabled (*Jones v Cadstart Ltd*, COIT 2101363/96). Furthermore, as the 1995 Act itself points out, a progressive condition (such as cancer, multiple sclerosis or muscular dystrophy, or infection by the human immunodeficiency virus (HIV)), which has an effect (but not a substantial adverse effect) on a person's

ability to carry out normal day-to-day activities, will be deemed to have such a substantial adverse effect if that is the likely end result (*ibid* Schedule 1, para. 8(1)).

13.24
It is as yet uncertain whether a stress-induced illness falls within the definition of 'disability' under the 1995 Act (see para. 13.3 above). In *Walker v Northumberland County Council* [1995] IRLR 35 (brought before the 1995 Act came into force) an employee who had suffered two nervous breakdowns, as a direct consequence of being subjected to a health-endangering workload, accepted an out of court settlement from his employers. It was held that he might well have claimed unfair constructive dismissal on the grounds that his employers had breached their common law and implied contractual duty of care. In *O'Neill v Symm & Co Ltd* (*qv*), an employment tribunal held that ME (or myalgic encephalomyelitis) – a condition capable of being caused or exacerbated by stress – could be characterised as a 'disability', but the decision of the tribunal was by no means conclusive.

13.25
Case law confirms that an employer's refusal to employ disabled persons in certain hazardous jobs is justifiable if there is no practicable or cost effective way of making any adjustments or arrangements to eliminate or minimise the risks associated with the work in question, or to eliminate risks which are likely to compound or aggravate the disabilities in question. Thus, the London Underground Limited was held to have been justified in refusing to employ a job applicant suffering from depression because of the possible side effects from the medication he was receiving and the risks to the safety of the travelling public (*Toffel v London Underground Ltd*, IDS Brief 609).

13.26
A employee who had been absent from work for 18 months with a work-related back injury was dismissed when medical evidence confirmed that he would be unlikely to return to work within the foreseeable future. The man complained that he had been unlawfully discriminated against on the grounds of his disability. An employment tribunal (and the EAT which heard his appeal) disagreed. They found that he had been no less favourably treated than would any other sick or injured employee who had been absent from work for a similar period. The Court of Appeal rejected that line of reasoning. 'In deciding whether the reason for less favourable treatment does not (or would not) apply to others, it is simply a case of identifying others to whom the reason does not (or would not) apply. The test of less favourable treatment is based on the reason for the treatment of the disabled person and not on the fact of his disability. It does not, said the Court, turn on a like-for-like comparison of the treatment of the disabled person and of others in similar

circumstances. Thus, it is not appropriate to make a comparison of the cases in the same way as in the Sex Discrimination and Race Relations Acts. There is no express provision in the Disability Discrimination Act, said the Court, which requires a comparison of the cases of different persons in the same or not materially different circumstances. In short, the questions to be asked are these: Why was the employee dismissed? Was it for a reason related to his disability? If so, could the employer justify dismissing the employee for that reason? If 'No', the employer's actions amounted to unlawful discrimination under section 5(1) of the 1995 Act (*Clark v TDG Limited t/a Novacold* [1999] IRLR 318, CA).

13.27
But there can be no discrimination under the 1995 Act if an employer had no prior knowledge of an employee's disability. A woman suffering from chronic fatigue syndrome (ME) was dismissed because of her poor health and attendance record. On her self-certificates for illness, she claimed to be suffering from an (unspecified) viral illness. As her employers were unaware of the true nature of her illness, they could not be held to have treated her less favourably for a reason related to her disability (*O'Neill v Symm & Co Ltd* [1998] IRLR 933, EAT).

13.28
There was a similar outcome in *Ridout v TC Group* [1998] IRLR 628. There, a woman suffering from photosensitive epilepsy (and who had previously disclosed that fact in her job application) was interviewed by her prospective employer under fluorescent lighting. She later complained that the employer had failed to make reasonable adjustments to the lighting in the room in order to accommodate her disability. The EAT upheld the employment tribunal's decision that the employer had not been in breach of his duty to make reasonable adjustments to the lighting in the interview room. No reasonable employer, said the EAT, could be expected to know of the deleterious effects of fluorescent lighting unless the woman had taken the trouble to forewarn him of those effects.

13.29
In *Kenny v Hampshire Constabulary* [1999] IRLR 76, a man suffering from cerebral palsy needed help when using the toilet. He complained that his employers had failed to comply with their statutory duty under section 6 of the Disability Discrimination Act to make such arrangements or adjustments as were necessary or appropriate to enable him to use the toilet during working hours. In evidence, it was revealed that, in spite of their best efforts, his employers had been unable to find sufficient volunteers from amongst the employee's workmates and had been unable to find funds sufficient to secure the services of a carer. The EAT pointed out that an employer's duty under section 6 of the 1995 Act was to provide job-related assistance and to make

such structural alterations to the premises as would enable a disabled employee to move freely about the employer's premises. That duty did not extend to providing toilet assistance or transport to and from work.

Maternity, adoption, parental, paternity and other 'family friendly' rights

OVERVIEW

14.1
In recent years, the Government has acknowledged that the working parents of young children often find it difficult to strike a balance between their obligations as parents and their duties as employees. Pregnant employees and new mothers, of course, have long since had the right to take up to 40 weeks' maternity leave during the weeks and months preceding and following childbirth, and the right also to return to work with their former employers at the end of their maternity leave periods. From 6 April 2003, that period of leave increased to 52 weeks, a right also available to one or other of the parents of a child placed with them for adoption. Other 'family friendly' rights include the right to periods of parental and paternity leave, time off for dependants, and the right of parents of young children to apply to their employers for more flexible working arrangements. Pregnant employees also enjoy the right to paid time off work for ante-natal care, a transfer (in prescribed circumstances) from night work to day work, payment of their normal wages or salaries if suspended from work on maternity grounds; and the right (along with breastfeeding mothers and women who have recently given birth) to be provided with suitable rest facilities for use during the working day).

This chapter is in seven parts:

Part 1: Rights in pregnancy and maternity
Part 2: Adoption leave and pay
Part 3: Parental leave
Part 4: Paternity leave and pay
Part 5: Flexible working
Part 6: Time off for dependants
Part 7: Other rights in pregnancy and maternity

PART 1: RIGHTS IN PREGNANCY AND MATERNITY

14.2
Legislation governing the rights of employees before and after childbirth is currently to be found in Part VIII of the Employment Rights Act 1996, as substituted by section 7 and Schedule 4 (Part 1) of the Employment Relations Act 1999 and 'fleshed out' by the Maternity & Parental Leave etc Regulations 1999 (SI 1999/3312), which latter were amended (on 24 November 2002) by the Maternity & Parental Leave (Amendment) Regulations 2002 (SI 2002/2789). The law regulating an employee's entitlement or otherwise to statutory maternity pay (SMP) or the state maternity allowance (MA) is to be found in Parts II and XII of the Social Security Contributions & Benefits Act 1992, and in Regulations made under (or saved by) that Act. The 1992 and 1996 Acts apply to persons employed in England, Scotland and Wales. Cognate legislation covers persons employed in Northern Ireland.

Expected week of childbirth on or after 6 April 2003

14.3
The reader should note that this Part discusses the rights of those pregnant employees only whose expected weeks of childbirth (EWCs) begin or began *on or after* 6 April 2003. An employee in this category is entitled to take up to 26 weeks' ordinary maternity leave, supplemented, if she qualifies, by a further period of up to 26 weeks' additional maternity leave (the latter period starting on the day immediately following the day on which her ordinary maternity leave period ends). Under the old rules, which continue to apply to employees whose EWCs began *before* 6 April 2003, a pregnant employee is entitled to take up to 18 weeks' ordinary maternity leave, supplemented (if she qualifies) by a period of up to 29 weeks' additional maternity leave (the latter period starting with the Sunday of the week in which childbirth occurred). From 6 April 2003, the standard or lower rate of SMP, payable to an employee in respect of the seventh and subsequent weeks of her maternity pay period, increased to £100 a week or 90 per cent of her average weekly earnings, whichever is the lower of those amounts (as to which, see paras 14.39 & 14.40 below).

Meaning of 'childbirth'

14.4
Section 235(1) of the 1996 Act defines *childbirth* as meaning the birth of a living child or the birth of a child whether living or dead after 24 weeks of pregnancy. The *expected week of childbirth* is the week beginning on Sunday and ending at midnight on the following Saturday, specified in the Certificate of

Expected Confinement (Form MatB1) as being the week in which childbirth is expected to occur.

ORDINARY MATERNITY LEAVE

14.5
Every pregnant employee expecting a baby on or after 6 April 2003 is entitled to take up to 26 weeks' ordinary maternity leave, whether she is in full-time or part-time employment and regardless of her length of service at the material time. If she is healthily pregnant, she has the right also to decide when her maternity leave period is to begin (subject to the proviso that, unless she gives birth prematurely, she may not begin her maternity leave earlier than the beginning of the 11th week before her EWC). Although a pregnant employee may delay the start of her ordinary maternity leave period until the very last minute, that period of leave begins immediately if she is absent from work with a pregnancy-related illness at any time during the four weeks immediately preceding her EWC (see para. 14.11 below).

Notification of intention to take maternity leave

14.6
Once she has made up her mind, a pregnant employee must inform her employer by the end of the 15th week before her EWC of the date on which she intends her maternity leave period to begin (in writing, if her employer insists). At the same time, she must specify her EWC and (if asked to do so) produce for her employer's inspection a certificate of expected confinement (Form Mat B1 or the equivalent) signed by her doctor or registered midwife. If for one reason or another, an employee is unable to give the required advance notice by the end of that 15th week, she must do so as soon as is reasonably practicable. If she later changes her mind about the date on which she intends to start her maternity leave, she must give her employer at least 28 days' advance notice of the revised start date. The employee's maternity leave period begins on the notified date, unless she gives birth or is taken ill with a pregnancy-related illness before that notified date, as to which see paras 14.9 to 14.11 below.

Note: Form Mat B1 (*Maternity Certificate*) is the standard form of certificate issued by doctors and midwives, although any form of certificate signed by a doctor or registered midwife, and couched in similar terms, will satisfy the legal requirement. Form Mat B1 is in two parts. Part A nominates the week in which childbirth is expected to occur; while Part B (Mat B2) certifies the date on which childbirth actually occurred.

14.7

An employee, who neglects (or wilfully refuses) to give the prescribed advance notice of the date on which she intends to start her maternity leave, runs the risk of forfeiting her right to maternity leave and, very possibly, her right (if any) to SMP.

14.8

An employer who has been correctly informed of an employee's pregnancy and EWC, and of the date on which she intends to start her maternity leave, must respond in writing within the next 28 days. In doing so, he must inform her of the date on which her full entitlement to maternity leave ends. By 'full entitlement' is meant her entitlement to ordinary maternity leave or, where appropriate, her entitlement to both ordinary and additional maternity leave). If he fails to reply in those terms within that 28-day period, he may not prevent her returning to work sooner than the due date and may not legitimately dismiss or discipline her for returning to work later than expected. The reader should note also that, with the coming into force on 6 April 2003 of the Maternity & Parental Leave (Amendment) Regulations 2002, an employer may no longer write to an employee towards the end of her ordinary maternity leave period asking her to confirm whether or not she intends to return to work at the end of her additional maternity leave period.

Premature birth

14.9

If an employee gives birth prematurely (that is to say before her EWC and before the date on which she intended to begin her maternity leave, whether or not she had already notified her employer of that intended start date), her ordinary maternity leave period begins with the day on which childbirth occurs. But she risks forfeiting her entitlement to ordinary maternity leave (and, where appropriate, SMP) unless she informs her employer as soon as is reasonably practicable that she gave birth on such-and-such a date.

14.10

If she has not done so already, she must also inform her employer of her EWC (supported by a Form Mat B1, if her employer asks her to produce that document or its equivalent), bearing in mind that it is her EWC, not the actual date of birth, which determines her entitlement, if any, to SMP and additional maternity leave. It is useful to note that one side of Form Mat B1 is a 'Certificate of Expected Confinement'; the other, a 'Certificate of Confinement'. If an employee gives birth prematurely, she should ask her doctor or midwife to sign both sides of the form before sending it off to her employer.

Note: An employee whose baby is stillborn within the first 24 weeks of pregnancy has no legal right to maternity leave (but will usually qualify for statutory sick pay (SSP) and, very likely, occupational sick pay, for so long as it takes for her to recover and return to work). But, if the stillbirth occurs *after* 24 weeks of pregnancy, she retains her right to ordinary maternity leave and, if she qualifies, to additional maternity leave .

Pregnancy-related illness

14.11

If a pregnant employee falls ill (or is still ill) with a pregnancy related illness at any time on or after the beginning of the fourth week before her EWC, her ordinary maternity leave period must begin immediately (regardless of the date on which she had otherwise intended to start her leave). If she has been receiving SSP in respect of her illness, those payments must cease, to be replaced (if she qualifies) by SMP. No further payments of SSP are permissible during the maternity pay period, even if the employee does not qualify for SMP during that period. In these circumstances also, she must notify her employer as soon as is reasonably practicable that she is absent from work wholly or partly because of pregnancy.

Note: A pregnant employee who is on sick leave (because of an illness or injury that has nothing to do with her being pregnant) may continue to draw statutory sick pay or invalidity benefit until her *notified leave date* (ie, the date on which she intended her maternity leave period to begin) or until her baby is born, whichever occurs sooner.

Application of terms and conditions during ordinary maternity leave

14.12

An employee who takes ordinary maternity leave is entitled, during that period of leave, to the benefit of all the terms and conditions of employment that would have applied but for her absence (other than her right to be paid her normal wages or salary), and is bound, during that period, by any obligations arising under those terms and conditions.

If, for example, an employee's entitlement to paid annual holidays or occupational sick pay (or, indeed, a pay rise) is determined by reference to her length of service, her absence on maternity leave counts as part of her total period of continuous employment. If her employer pays pension contributions while she is at work, he must continue to pay those contributions at the same level while she is absent on ordinary maternity leave (that is to say, based on her normal wages or salary). However, unless she volunteers otherwise, her own pension contributions must be based only on the amount of any contractual remuneration or SMP actually paid to her during her maternity leave (*per* section 23 and Schedule 5 to the Social Security Act 1989). The point is that, save for the suspension of her right to be paid her normal wages or salary, an absentee employee's remaining terms and conditions of employment (as well as her statutory right to four weeks' paid annual holidays) prevail throughout her ordinary and additional maternity leave periods.

Return to work after ordinary maternity leave

14.13

An employee returning to work after her ordinary maternity leave has the right to do so in the job she occupied before that period of leave began (that is to say, in her original job) – unless, as is explained in the next paragraph, she takes four or more weeks' parental leave before returning to work. If she intends to return to work on the day following the day on which her ordinary maternity leave period comes to an end, she need do no more than turn up for work on the day in question. However, different rules apply if she wishes to return to work before the due date (see para. 14.16 below). While it would be sensible for an employee approaching the end of her ordinary maternity leave period to keep in touch with her supervisor or head of department, to ensure that everything is in readiness for her return to work, this is by no means a legal requirement. However, a woman who has decided not to return to work after childbirth must give her employer the notice of termination required by her contract of employment.

14.14

A woman who takes up to four weeks' parental leave immediately after the end of her ordinary maternity leave period retains her right to return to work in her original job on the same terms and conditions as if she had not been absent. But, if she takes more than four weeks' parental leave at that time, she may have to forego that right and accept an offer of suitable alternative employment if it is not reasonably practicable for her employer to permit her to return to her original job. It is as well to point out that a woman who wishes to take a period of parental leave immediately after her ordinary (or additional) maternity leave period must apply to take that leave at least 21 days before the end of her maternity leave period. A woman does not qualify to take a period of parental leave, of whatever duration, at the end of her ordinary maternity leave (or at any other time) unless she has completed one or more years' continuous service by the time the requested period of parental leave is set to begin (as to which, see paras 14.61 to 14.87 below).

14.15

A woman's ordinary maternity leave period will usually end after 26 weeks (unless she has a contractual right to a longer period of leave), but must continue for so long as may be necessary to accommodate the 'compulsory maternity leave period' referred to in the next paragraph. If she is prevented by illness from returning to work at the end of her ordinary maternity leave, she must comply with such procedures for notifying sickness absence as are laid down in her contract of employment or in any associated document. An employer does not have the right to postpone an employee's return to work after the end of her ordinary (or, indeed, her additional) maternity leave period) (*ibid* regulation 11).

An early return to work?

14.16
But if an employee plans to return to work early – bearing in mind that she may not lawfully do so within the compulsory maternity leave period, that is to say, within two weeks of giving birth (or within four weeks of that date if she works in a factory (*per* section 205, Public Health Act 1936) – she must give her employer at least 28 days' notice of her intentions, although there is no need for her to do so in writing. If she returns to work unannounced and earlier than the due date, or after having given less than 28 days' notice, her employer has every right to send her home and to insist that she delay her return to work until those 28 days have elapsed or until the end of her ordinary maternity leave period, whichever occurs sooner. An employer has no right to delay an employee's return to work beyond the end of her ordinary maternity leave period. An employee who is denied her right to return to work after that period will be treated in law as having been unfairly dismissed and may pursue the matter before an employment tribunal.

Dismissal during ordinary maternity leave

14.17
Section 99 of the 1996 Act (supported by Regulation 20 of the Maternity & Parental Leave etc Regulations 1999 (as now amended)) cautions employers that it is unlawful and automatically unfair to dismiss an employee (or select her for redundancy) during her ordinary (or additional) maternity leave period if the reason (or, if more than one, the principal reason) for her dismissal or selection is that she is (or was) pregnant or had given birth to a child, or because she had exercised her statutory rights in relation to pregnancy and childbirth. She has the right also to be provided with a written statement explaining the reasons for her dismissal (as to which, see paras 14.37 & 14.38 below).

Redundancy during ordinary maternity leave

14.18
If an employee is made genuinely redundant during her ordinary maternity leave, her employer is nonetheless duty-bound to offer her

suitable alternative employment before her employment under her old contract comes to an end. The alternative employment must begin on the day following the day on which her previous employment ended and, to be 'suitable', must involve work that is both suitable and appropriate for her to do in the circumstances (given her qualifications, experience and skills) and on terms and conditions of employment not substantially less favourable to her than those that would have applied had she continued to be employed in her original job. In short, she should enjoy the same or equivalent status or seniority under the new contract, work in the same location (if not in the same department or section), receive the same or a comparable rate of pay, and be entitled to the same annual holidays, the same sickness benefits; and so on (*ibid* regulation 10).

14.19
If an employee is made redundant during her ordinary maternity leave period without being offered suitable alternative employment, or without being consulted about the suitability of any available vacancies, her dismissal will be held to have been unfair. If she believes that she has been unfairly treated, she has the right to pursue her case before an employment tribunal. If the tribunal finds in her favour or believes that she was selected for redundancy principally because she was pregnant or because she had given birth to a child (or for a connected reason), it will order her employer to pay a substantial award of compensation – the more so if she elects to pursue her complaint under the Sex Discrimination Act 1975.

14.20
If the employer's defence is that there was no suitable alternative employment to offer the employee, or that she had unreasonably refused an offer of what would ordinarily be considered to be suitable alternative employment, or that there was nothing untoward about the employer's motives in selecting her for redundancy, the case will be decided on its merits.

14.21
An employer should be extremely cautious about dismissing an employee (for a reason other than redundancy) during her ordinary (or additional) maternity leave period – bearing in mind that her contract of employment subsists during her absence and that she is accordingly entitled to the same consideration as any person who is absent from work on holidays or sick leave. To dismiss an employee *in absentia* will usually be held unfair – the more so if the evidence shows that she was not told about the reasons for her dismissal, had not been forewarned of the likelihood of her being dismissed, and not been afforded an opportunity either to put her side of the case or to appeal against her employer's decision to dismiss her – issues of procedural fairness re-emphasised by the House of Lords in *Polkey v Dayton Services Limited* [1987] IRLR 503.

Note: Unless dismissed for an unlawful or inadmissible reason (or for a reason connected with her having been pregnant or given birth to a child), an employee dismissed during her maternity leave period for a reason other than redundancy (eg, misconduct) will not normally qualify to bring a complaint of unfair dismissal unless employed by her employer for a continuous period of at least one year ending with the effective date of termination of her contract of employment. However, there is nothing to prevent her pursuing her complaint (regardless of her length of service) if she is convinced that the real reason for her dismissal was an unlawful or inadmissible reason; as to which latter, please turn to the section titled **Dismissal** elsewhere in this handbook (notably the paragraphs headed *Inadmissible and unlawful reasons for dismissal*).

ADDITIONAL MATERNITY LEAVE

14.22

In addition to her right to a minimum of 26 weeks' ordinary maternity leave, a woman who has been continuously employed for 26 weeks or more by the end of the 15th week before her EWC, is entitled to take up to 26 weeks' additional maternity leave beginning on the day immediately following the day on which here ordinary maternity leave period ends. Furthermore, she has the right to return to work at the end of (or, subject to certain conditions, during) that additional maternity leave period.

Note: For the meaning of the expression continuously employed, please turn to Chapter 3, paras 3.27 to 3.37.

Notification procedure

14.23

An employee who qualifies for additional maternity leave has no need to inform her employer in advance that she intends to take advantage of that right; nor need she inform her employer (as was the case under the previous regime) that she intends to exercise her right to return to work after her additional maternity leave period ends. As was explained earlier, the only advance notice she need give her employer (before the end of the 15th week before her EWC) is notice confirming that she is pregnant (with supporting documentation) and specifying the date on which she intends to start her maternity leave. Her additional maternity leave period commences automatically on the day immediately following the day on which her ordinary maternity leave period ends.

Contractual rights during additional maternity leave

14.24

The Maternity & Parental Leave etc Regulations 1999 (as amended) make it clear that an employee's contract of employment persists during her additional maternity leave period although not necessarily to the same extent as her contractual rights during her ordinary maternity leave period.

14.25
Regulation 17 of the 1999 Regulations (as amended) states that, during her additional maternity leave, an employee is entitled to the benefit of her employer's implied obligation to her of trust and confidence and to any terms and conditions relating to:

(a) notice to terminate her employment;

(b) compensation in the event of redundancy; or

(c) disciplinary and grievance procedures.

In short, if she is dismissed during her additional maternity leave, she must be paid her normal wages or salary during the notice period (or money in lieu of notice), as well as any accrued entitlement to holiday pay. If she is made redundant (assuming that her employer is unable to offer her suitable alternative employment (see para. 14.29 below), she must also be paid any entitlement to statutory redundancy pay, plus any 'top up' payment by way of severance pay (to which she would otherwise be entitled under her contract). If she is liable to disciplinary action or dismissal (for a reason unconnected with the fact that she is on maternity leave), or has a grievance against her employer, she is entitled to be treated in the same way as any other employee facing dismissal or intent upon pursuing any such grievance.

14.26
During her additional maternity leave, an employee is also duty-bound not to disclose to unauthorised third parties any confidential information relating to her employer's business affairs (trade secrets, pricing policy, marketing strategy, etc); must not accept any gifts or benefits in breach of her implied contractual duty of trust and confidence; and must not participate in any other business in competition with her employer. If she decides not to exercise her right to return to work, she must give her employer the notice to terminate her employment as laid down in her contract of employment.

Dismissal during additional maternity leave

14.27
Section 99 of the 1996 Act (supported by Regulation 20 of the now amended Maternity & Parental Leave etc Regulations 1999 (*qv*)) cautions employers that it is unlawful and automatically unfair to dismiss an employee (or select her for redundancy) during her additional (or ordinary) maternity leave

period if the reason (or, if more than one, the principal reason) for her dismissal or selection is that she had given birth to a child, or because she had exercised any of her statutory rights in relation to pregnancy and childbirth. For further particulars, please see Chapter 5, paras 5.21 to 5.25. See also paras 14.37 & 14.38 below.

14.28
If an employee is dismissed during her additional period of maternity leave (for a reason other than redundancy), it will be for an employment tribunal to decide whether her dismissal was fair bearing in mind that the tribunal is likely to question her employer's motives in dismissing her *in absentia* and his (or her) failure to follow the correct procedure when doing so. If the tribunal finds that the employee was dismissed for an unlawful or inadmissible reason, it will make a declaration to that effect and will order the employer either to reinstate or re-engage the employee in her former or a suitable alternative job or pay her an additional award of compensation (over and above the basic and compensatory awards of compensation for unfair dismissal) (as to which, see Chapter 5, paras 5.157 to 5.164).

Redundancy during additional maternity leave

14.29
An employee made redundant during her additional maternity leave period is entitled to the same consideration as an employee made redundant during her ordinary maternity leave period. In short, she is entitled to be offered suitable alternative employment beginning on the day immediately following the day on which her previous employment ended, and on terms and conditions of employment not substantially less favourable to her than those that would have applied had she continued to be employed in her original job. If challenged concerning the alleged non-availability of suitable alternative employment, it will be for the employer to satisfy an employment tribunal that no such alternative work was available.

Right to return to work after additional maternity leave

14.30
An employee returning to work after her additional maternity leave is entitled to do so in the job in which she was employed before her ordinary maternity leave period began (but see para. 14.31 below), unless it is not reasonably practicable for her employer to permit her to return to work in that job, in which latter situation, she is entitled to return to work in another job which is both suitable for her and appropriate for her to do in the circumstances. Whether she returns to work in her original job or in a 'suitable and appropriate' alternative job, she must be permitted to do so:

(a) on a salary or wage (or rate of pay) not less favourable to her than the remuneration that would have been applicable to her had she not been absent from work at any time since the commencement of her ordinary maternity leave period;

(b) with her seniority, pension and associated rights as they would have been if the period (or periods) of her employment prior to her additional maternity leave period were continuous with her employment following her return to work; and

(c) on terms and conditions no less favourable to her than those that would have applied but for her absence from work (*ibid* Reg. 18).

14.31

An employee who takes a period of parental leave of four weeks or less, immediately after the end of her additional maternity leave, retains her right to return to work in her original job unless it would not have been reasonably practicable for her to have returned to that job at the end of her additional maternity leave period and it is still not reasonably practicable for her to do so at the end of that period of parental leave. If she takes more than four weeks' parental leave immediately after the end of her additional maternity leave, she is entitled to return to her original job or, if that is not reasonably practicable, to a similar job on terms and conditions no less favourable to her than those to which she was entitled in her original job. For further particulars, please turn to *Part 4: Parental Leave* below (paras 14.61 to 14.87).

Exercise of right to return after additional maternity leave

14.32

An employee who intends to return to work at the end of her additional maternity leave period need do no more than turn up for work on the due date. However, if she intends to return to work early, that is to say, *before* the end of that period, she must notify her employer at least 28 days beforehand that she intends to return to work on that earlier date. If an employee's return to work is delayed because of illness or injury, she need do no more than inform her employer of that fact (in accordance with her employer's rules in relation to sickness absence) and provide the necessary evidence of incapacity.

Note: Employers should note that they no longer have the statutory right to delay an employee's return to work after childbirth (for whatever reason); nor do would-be-returning employees forfeit their right to return to work if illness or injury intervenes to prevent them doing so within four weeks of the notified date. Those provisions of the Employment Rights Act 1996 have long since been repealed.

An early return to work?

14.33

An employee who wishes to return to work before the end of her additional maternity leave period must inform her employer of that decision at least 28 days before the date in question. If the employee returns to work early and unannounced, without having given that prescribed period of notice, her employer has every right to send her home and to insist that she delay her return until those 28 days have elapsed or until the end of her additional maternity leave period, whichever occurs sooner. She has no right to be paid if she ignores her employer's instructions and remains at work during the notice period.

Failure to permit a return to work treated as a dismissal

14.34

An employee who is denied her statutory right to return to work after either of her ordinary or additional maternity leave periods will be treated in law as having been unfairly dismissed if her dismissal is solely or mainly attributable to the fact that she exercised her right to maternity leave or took advantage of the benefits of her terms and conditions of employment to which she was entitled during either period of leave. In short, her employer will need to satisfy an employment tribunal that he had a legitimate reason for dismissing the employee (unconnected with her having taken advantage of statutory maternity rights) and that he had acted fairly and reasonably in doing so.

14.35

If an employer can satisfy an employment tribunal that the employee's original job was no longer available because of redundancy and that he (or she) had acted fairly and lawfully in selecting her for redundancy – there being no suitable available vacancy to offer her, or that she had been offered suitable alternative employment by an associated employer which she had either accepted or unreasonably refused – her dismissal will be held to have been fair (*ibid* section 81).

Note: If the evidence before an employment tribunal shows that the employee was selected for redundancy for an inadmissible reason (eg, because of her sex or for reasons connected with her having taken advantage of her statutory rights in connection with pregnancy or childbirth, including her right to maternity leave), her dismissal will be held to have been inadmissible and unfair (*ibid* regulation 20(2)).

14.36

Finally, an employee who has been denied her right to return to work after additional maternity leave will not be held to have been unfairly dismissed:

(a) if, immediately before the end of her additional maternity leave period (or immediately before her dismissal, if her additional maternity leave ended with her dismissal) the number of persons employed by her employer (including the employee herself) added to the number employed by any associated employer, did not exceed five; and

(b) her employer (who may be the same employer or a successor) can satisfy the tribunal that it was not reasonably practicable either to permit her to return to work in her original job or to offer her suitable alternative employment or for an associated employer to offer her a job of that kind (*ibid* section 96(2)).

As was indicated earlier, the alternative employment (or job) offered to an employee who has been denied her right to return to work in her original job, must involve work that is both suitable and appropriate for her to do (given her qualifications, experience and skills) and must be on terms and conditions of employment not substantially less favourable to her than those that would have applied had she been permitted to return to work in her original job. In short, she should enjoy the same or equivalent status or seniority, be employed in the same place (if not in the same department or section), receive the same or a comparable rate of pay, and be entitled to the same annual holidays, the same sickness benefits; and so on.

WRITTEN STATEMENT OF REASONS FOR DISMISSAL

14.37
An employee who is dismissed (for whatever reason), either while pregnant or after having given birth (in circumstances in which her ordinary or additional maternity leave period ends by reason of the dismissal) must be provided by her employer with a written statement explaining the reasons for her dismissal – regardless of her working hours or length of service at the relevant time and regardless of whether she has asked to be issued with such a statement. Furthermore, the statement must be given or sent to the employee within 14 days of the date on which her dismissal took place (*Source:* s.92(4), ERA 1996).

14.38
A complaint to an employment tribunal, concerning an employer's refusal or failure to provide the written statement (within the prescribed 14-day period), or that the statement provided was inadequate or untrue, must be presented within three months of the effective date of termination of the employee's contract of employment (see Chapter 3, paras 3.66 to 3.71). If the employee's complaint is upheld, her employer will be ordered to pay the employee a sum equivalent to two weeks' pay without limit as to the

amount *(Ladbroke Entertainments Ltd v Clark* [1987] ICR 585, EAT) *(Source:* s.93, ERA 1996). Where appropriate, the tribunal will also make a declaration as to what it finds the employer's real reasons were for dismissing the employee – bearing in mind that a complaint arising out of an employer's failure to provide a written statement will very likely be heard at the same time as a complaint of unfair or unlawful dismissal *(ibid)*.

The written statement of reasons for dismissal referred to in the previous paragraph is admissible in evidence in proceedings before a tribunal or court *(ibid* s.92(5)).

STATUTORY MATERNITY PAY (SMP)

14.39

A pregnant employee who has worked for her employer for 26 weeks or more by the end of the 15th week before her EWC and who has average weekly earnings equal to or greater than the current (2003/04) 'lower earnings limit' for National Insurance purposes (ie, £77), is entitled to be paid up to 26 weeks' statutory maternity pay (SMP) during her maternity pay period. The 'maternity pay period' is the period of up to 26 weeks that begins on the day immediately following the day on which she starts her maternity leave, and ends with the payment week immediately preceding the day on which she returns to work. If she resigns (or is dismissed, for whatever reason) part-way through her maternity pay period, her employer must nonetheless continue to pay her SMP until the maternity pay period ends. Different rules apply if an employee does some work for her employer, if she starts work with another employer, if she is taken into legal custody, or if she or her baby dies during that same pay period. Readers can obtain advice on these and related SMP issues by telephoning the Employer's Helpline on 08457 143 143.

14.40

An employee who qualifies for SMP is entitled to be paid 90 per cent of her average weekly earnings for each of the first six weeks of her maternity pay period, and the lower of 90 per cent of her average weekly earnings or £100 for each of the remaining 20 weeks of that same period. An employee who does not qualify for SMP may nonetheless qualify for the State maternity allowance (MA) or a payment from the Social Fund. For further particulars, including the right of employers to recover 92 per cent of the amount of SMP lawfully paid to an employee (or the full amount, plus 4.5 per cent, in the case of 'small employers'), the reader is commended to the Inland Revenue's Help Book *(Pay and Time off work for parents)*(Ref. E15(2003)), copies of which are available free of charge from the Employer's Orderline on 08457 646 646.

INTERACTION OF CONTRACTUAL AND STATUTORY RIGHTS

14.41
An employee who has a contractual as well as a statutory right to maternity leave may take advantage of whichever of those rights is the more favourable to her (not both). The same applies if she has a contractual right to be paid the whole or part of her normal wages or salary during her ordinary maternity leave period. In that event, her employer may offset SMP (if any) paid to that employee against the amount paid under her contract (and *vice versa*), but only in respect of weeks in which both the contractual and statutory amounts are due. For example, an employee may be entitled under her contract to 32 weeks' paid maternity leave, but her employer cannot insist that she delay her return to work until the end of that contractual entitlement, as that would deny her legal right to return to work (on full pay) at the end of her 26-week ordinary maternity leave period.

CHANGE OF EMPLOYER

14.42
If there has been a change of employer (for example, in circumstances in which there is no break in the mother-to-be or new mother's period of continuous employment), the new employer (who may be an associate or successor employer) inherits her former employer's contractual and statutory obligations in relation to that employee including her right to maternity leave and pay, and her right to return to work after childbirth. If her former employer had started paying her SMP before the change in ownership, her new employer must continue paying SMP until her maternity pay period ends.

PART 2: ADOPTION LEAVE AND PAY

14.43
From 6 April 2003, an employee who has been newly-matched with a child for adoption, or whose partner has been newly-matched with a child for adoption, or who is one of a couple who have been newly matched with a child for adoption (in each case, by an approved adoption agency), and who has been continuously employed by his or her employer for 26 weeks or more leading into the week in which notification of being matched occurred, has the right to take up to 26 weeks' ordinary adoption leave, followed immediately by up to 26 weeks' additional adoption leave. An employee with average earnings of £77 or more per week will qualify to be paid statutory adoption pay (SAP) during his or her ordinary adoption leave period. The

relevant legislation is to be found in the Paternity & Adoption Leave Regulations 2002 (SI 2002/2788) which came into force on 8 December 2002. By definition, the right to adoption leave is not available to a step-father or mother who adopts his or her partner's children.

14.44
It is as well to point out that the right to take up to 52 weeks' adoption leave is available to those eligible employees only who were informed on or after 6 April 2003 that they had been matched with a child for adoption – unless the notification occurred before 6 April 2003, but the child was not actually placed with them (or their partners) until 6 April 2003 or later. Furthermore, the right to adoption leave is available to one member only of a couple (whether married or otherwise) who have had a child placed with them for adoption – in which event, it is up to the adoptive parent or parents to decide which of them takes the adoption leave. However, the other partner may be entitled to take one or two weeks' paid paternity leave during the eight weeks following adoption and up to 13 weeks' unpaid parental leave, as to which please turn to Part 3 (**Parental leave)** and Part 4 (**Paternity leave)** below.

Disrupted placement in the course of adoption leave

14.45
An employee who has already begun a period of adoption leave, in anticipation of being placed with a child, may remain on adoption leave for up to eight weeks (or, where appropriate, for a further eight weeks) if, for one reason or another, the expected placement does not occur or if the child dies or is returned to the adoption agency under section 30(3) of the Adoption Act 1976 or section 30 of the Adoption (Scotland) Act 1978.

Notification procedure

14.46
To exercise his (or her) right to adoption leave, an employee must (within seven days of the date on which he was notified of having been matched with a child for adoption) inform his employer (in writing, if requested to do so) of his intention to take ordinary adoption leave, specifying:

(a) the date on which the child is expected to be placed with him for adoption; and

(b) the date on which he has elected to take adoption leave (which may begin either on the date on which the child is placed with him for adoption or no more than 14 days before the expected placement date).

Where his employer requests it, the employee must also produce documentary evidence (letters, certificates, etc) issued by the adoption agency confirming the name and address of the agency, the name and date of birth of the child, the date on which the agency informed him that he had been matched with that child and the date on which the agency expects to place the child with him.

14.47
Employees who have correctly notified their employers of the date on which they intend to start their adoption leave may change their minds, so long as they inform their employers at least 28 days beforehand of the revised start date.

14.48
An employer, who has been correctly notified of the date on which an employee intends to start his or her adoption leave, must write to the employee in question, within the next 28 days, setting out the date in which the employee would be expected to return to work on completion of his or her full entitlement to adoption leave.

Statutory rights during and after adoption leave

14.49
While absent from work on adoption leave, an employee has rights similar to those available to employees on maternity leave. In short, an employee absent from work on adoption leave has the right:

- if made redundant during his or her ordinary or additional adoption leave period, to be offered suitable alternative employment under a new contract of employment to begin on the day immediately following the day on which his or her previous contract of employment came to an end;

- to the continuation of certain contractual rights and duties while absent from work on adoption leave (save for the right to be paid his or her normal wages or salary while absent on adoption leave);

- to return to work after adoption leave in his or her original (or in a substantially equivalent) job;

- to ask for more flexible working arrangements on his or her return to work (as to which, see Part 5, paras 14.88 to 14.99 below; and

- not to be dismissed, selected for redundancy, victimised, or subjected to any other detriment for exercising or asserting his or her rights under the Paternity & Adoption Leave Regulations 2002.

Employees on adoption leave, who wish to return to work earlier than the date on which they are otherwise due to return, must notify their employers of the proposed earlier date of return at least 28 days beforehand. Should they fail to do so, their employers are within their rights to delay their return until those 28 days have elapsed or until the date on which they are otherwise due to return, whichever occurs sooner.

Claims and remedies

14.50
Eligible employees who are denied their entitlement to adoption leave, or who are dismissed, selected for redundancy, victimised, or subjected to any other detriment for asserting their rights under the Paternity & Adoption Leave Regulations 2002, may complain to an employment tribunal and will be awarded appropriate compensation if their complaints are upheld.

STATUTORY ADOPTION PAY

14.51
An employee who qualifies for adoption leave, and who has average weekly earnings equal to or greater than the current (2003/04) 'lower earnings limit' for National Insurance contributions purposes (ie, £77 a week, or £333 a calendar month), will normally qualify for up to 26 weeks' Statutory Adoption Pay (SAP) during his or her ordinary adoption pay period. The adoption pay period is the period that begins on the day immediately following the day on which an employee begins his or her ordinary adoption leave.

14.52
Unlike SMP (see paras 14.39 & 14.40 above), there is just the one standard rate of SAP. That rate is £100 a week or 90 per cent of the relevant employee's average weekly earnings, whichever is the lower of those amounts. An employer who has lawfully paid SAP to an employee may reclaim 92 per cent of the amount paid by deducting the amount in question from payments of employees' and employers' NI contributions made to the Collector of Taxes at the end of each tax month. Employers who are eligible for small employers' relief may recover 100 per cent of the amount of SAP paid, plus an additional amount (currently 4.5 per cent) in compensation for the employer's portion of NI contributions paid on SAP. For further information, the reader is commended to Inland Revenue Help Book E16(2003)(*Pay and time off work for adoptive parents*) available free of charge from the Employer's Orderline on 08457 646 646).

PART 3: PATERNITY LEAVE AND PAY

14.53

Legislation relating to the right of a child's biological father (or the mother's present husband or partner) or of an adoptive parent to take one or two weeks' paid or unpaid paternity leave during the eight-week period following birth or adoption is to be found in the Paternity & Adoption Leave Regulations 2002 (SI 2002/2788), which came into force on 8 December 2002. It should be emphasised that an eligible employee may elect to take one week's paternity leave or two consecutive weeks' paternity leave (either, but not both). There is no provision for either period of leave to be taken in instalments (ie, odd days). It should be noted also that the right to paternity leave is not restricted to men. For example, if a couple has jointly adopted a child, one of them (male or female, if eligible) may elect to take up to 52 weeks' adoption leave while the other (if eligible) may take paternity leave.

14.54

To be eligible for paternity leave, an employee must:

(a) have been continuously employed by his (or her) employer for a period of not less than 26 weeks by the beginning of the 14th week before the mother's expected week of childbirth (EWC) (or would have been continuously employed for that prescribed minimum period, but for the fact that the child was either born before the beginning of that 14th week or was stillborn after 24 weeks of pregnancy or has died); or

(b) in the case of an adopted child, have been continuously employed by his or her employer for 26 or more weeks by the end of the week in which the child was placed with him or her and/or his or her wife or partner for adoption; and

(c) have or expect to have responsibility for the child's upbringing; and

(d) be the child's biological father or the mother's husband or partner; or, in the case of an adopted child, the adopter's spouse or partner.

Employees claiming paternity leave must, if asked to do so by their employers, provide a form of self-certificate as evidence that they meet the eligibility conditions listed above. To that end, employers may either design their own form of self-certificates or use either of the Inland Revenue's model forms of self-certificate (Form SC3 [Birth] or Form SC4 [adoption]) available on request from the Employer's Orderline on 08457 646 646.

14.55

It is as well to point out that when a child is placed with an individual or with a couple for adoption, only one of them (male or female) is entitled to adoption leave (see paras 14.43 & 14.44 above). It is up to the couple in question to decide which of them is to take adoption leave. The other partner (if eligible) will have the right to take one week or two consecutive weeks' paternity leave.

Timing of paternity leave

14.56
An employee who qualifies for paternity leave must take his or her full entitlement to either one or two consecutive weeks' leave:

    (a) within 56 days of the child's date of birth or, if the child was born prematurely, within the period from the actual date of birth up to 56 days after the mother's expected week of childbirth (EWC); or

    (b) in the case of an adopted child, within 56 days of the date on which the child was placed with him or her and/or his or her partner for adoption (whether that date occurs sooner or later than expected).

It should be noted that paternity leave can start on any day of the week beginning with the date on which the child is born or placed with the adopter for adoption or from the first day of the expected week of the child's birth, or from a chosen number of days or weeks after the date of the child's birth or adoption (whether this is earlier or later than expected) so long as the selected start date ensures that the full period of leave is completed within the prescribed 56-day period. Only one period of paternity leave is available, regardless of the number of children born or placed with an individual or couple for adoption.

Notification procedure

14.57
To exercise their right to paternity leave, eligible employees must inform their employers of their intentions either by the end of the 15th week before the mother's expected week of childbirth (EWC) or, in the case of an adoptive parent or a couple who are adopting, within seven days of the adopter or adopters being notified by an approved adoption agency that he, she or they have been matched with a child. At the same time, an employee must:

    (a) specify the mother's EWC or the date on which the child is expected to be placed for adoption;

    (b) whether he (or she) wishes to take one or two weeks' paternity leave; and

    (c) when he (or she) wants that period of leave to start.

Employees who have correctly notified their employers of the date on which they intend to start their paternity leave may change their minds about that start date so long as they inform their employers of that change of mind at least 28 days before the revised start date (or as soon as is reasonably practicable, if circumstances dictate that they are not in a position to give 28 days' advance notice).

Statutory paternity pay

14.58

To qualify for statutory paternity pay (SPP) during his or her paternity leave, an eligible employee must have average weekly earnings equal to or greater than the current 'lower earnings limit' for National Insurance purposes. For 2003/04, that lower earnings limit is £77 per week. SPP is payable at the same standard (or lower) rate as statutory maternity pay (SMP), ie, £100 a week or 90 per cent of the employee's average weekly earnings at the time, whichever is the lower of those amounts. Employers who have lawfully paid SPP to an employer will (as is the case with payments of SMP) be able to recover an amount equal to 92 per cent of the amount paid by deducting it from PAYE tax and NI contributions routinely remitted to the Inland Revenue at the end of each income tax month. Small employers (the total of whose NI contributions did not exceed £40,000 during the preceding tax year) will, on the other hand, be able to recover 100 per cent of the amount of SPP paid, plus a further 4.5 per cent to recoup the additional NI contributions paid on such payments. These figures are reviewed every year.

Return to work after paternity leave

14.59

Employees returning to work after a period of paternity leave have the legal right to do so in the jobs they held immediately before that period of leave began, without any loss of seniority or pension rights, or any other terms and conditions that would have prevailed but for their absences from work.

Claims and remedies

14.60

Eligible employees who are denied their entitlement to paternity leave, or who are dismissed, selected for redundancy, victimised, or subjected to any other detriment for asserting their rights under the Paternity & Adoption Leave Regulations 2002, may complain to an employment tribunal and will be awarded appropriate compensation if their complaints are upheld.

PART 4: PARENTAL LEAVE

14.61

Legislation giving employees (in their capacities as parents or adoptive parents) the right to take up to 13 weeks' unpaid parental leave (or up to 18 weeks' unpaid parental leave, in the case of a child awarded a disability living allowance) is to be found in Part III of the Maternity & Parental Leave etc Regulations 1999 (SI 1999/3312), as amended by the Maternity & Parental Leave (Amendment) Regulations 2001 (SI 2001/4010), implementing Council Directive 96/34/EC of 3 June 1996 'on the framework agreement on parental leave'.

14.62
Before the 1999 Regulations were amended, the right to take a period of unpaid parental leave was restricted to the parents of children born to (or placed with them for adoption) on or after 15 December 1999. Following a challenge mounted by the TUC, and the likelihood of proceedings before the European Court of Justice (ECJ), the UK Government conceded that the right to parental leave should have been made available to *all* employed parents with children under the age of five on 15 December 1999 as well as to adoptive parents of children under the age of 18, who were placed with them for adoption before that date. For further information about the restored rights of previously 'disenfranchised parents', see paras 14.85 & 14.86 below.

14.63
The right to parental leave is available only to those employees who have been continuously employed with their respective employers for a period of one year or more and who are either the parents of a child under the age of five (or under the age of 18, if the child has been awarded a 'disability living allowance) or who adopted a child on or after that date.

Nature of the right

14.64
The parents of a child under the age of five may (as employees) each take up to 13 weeks' unpaid leave during the first five years of the child's life (that is to say, up to and including the child's fifth birthday). If the mother gives birth to twins, the entitlement applies to each of those children.

The parents of a child placed with them for adoption may likewise (as employees) each take up to 13 weeks' unpaid parental leave during the first five years following the adoption or until the child turns 18, whichever occurs sooner.

The parents of a disabled child (that is to say, a child who has been awarded a disability living allowance) may each take up to 18 weeks' unpaid parental leave until and including the child's 18th birthday.

14.65
A week's leave, for these purposes, is a period of absence from work which is equal in duration to the period for which an employee is normally required to work in any week. For an employee whose working hours (under his or her

contract) vary from week to week, a week's parental leave is a period of absence from work which is equal in duration to the total of the employee's contractual working hours in any one year divided by 52. An employee who takes parental leave for a day or two at a time, will have taken a full week's parental leave when the aggregate of those days equates to the number (or average number) of days in a week in which he or she is normally required to work. Overtime hours should not be included in calculations unless an employee is required under his or her contract to work a specified number of overtime hours each week.

14.66
When dealing with a first request for parental leave, an employer has the right to ask for documentary evidence of parental responsibilities in the form of a full birth certificate or adoption papers, or (in the case of a disabled child) evidence that a child has been awarded a disability living allowance. An employer may decline a request for parental leave until such time as that evidence is produced for his inspection.

How much leave can be taken at a time?

14.67
The amount of parental leave that can be taken at any one time is a matter for negotiation and agreement between employees and their employers. If there is nothing in an employee's contract of employment (eg, in the written statement of employment particulars, a staff or works handbook, or in a company policy document) concerning an employee's right to parental leave – including the amount of parental leave that may be take at any one time – the default (or fallback) provisions outlined in Schedule 2 to the 1999 Regulations will apply (as to which, see paras 14.78 to 14.82 below).

14.68
Collective and workforce agreements can also be used to determine procedures for dealing with requests for parental leave, the amount of leave that may be taken at any one time; and so on. If an employee's terms and conditions of employment are determined by a collective agreement between the employer and a recognised independent trade union (and those terms are imported into each employee's contract of employment), that same forum may be used to give practical effect to an employee's statutory right to parental leave. A workforce agreement may be used for parental leave purposes if the terms and conditions of employees (or certain identifiable groups of employees) are not otherwise determined by agreement with a recognised independent trade union.

14.69
An employer wishing to conclude a workforce agreement on parental leave must oversee the conduct of a secret ballot for the election of an appropriate number of

employee representatives to negotiate the agreement with him. The number of representatives to be elected is a matter for the employer, depending on the size of the workforce or of the group of employees to be covered by the agreement. The employer must ensure that every employee is afforded an opportunity to vote in the ballot and to put his or her name forward as a candidate for election as an employee representative. The employer must provide the necessary facilities and must ensure that votes are counted fairly and accurately.

14.70
To be valid, the resultant workforce agreement must be in writing; must be signed by the negotiating parties; must be shown to all affected employees (together with a guide explaining what the agreement means); and must last for no longer than five years. The agreement should (advisedly) lay down procedures for applying for parental leave, indicate how much leave may be taken at any one time; and, where appropriate, explain the circumstances in which the employer may postpone a request for parental leave (including the employee's right to take that postponed leave at a later date). If negotiations fail to produce a workforce agreement, the fallback parental leave scheme explained below automatically applies.

14.71
Any term in a contract of employment (or in a collective or workforce agreement) that purports to override or undermine an employee's statutory right to parental leave is null and void. However, there is nothing to prevent an employer providing more generous parental leave provisions, including a period of paid parental leave.

Contractual and statutory rights during parental leave

14.72
Although the continuity of an employee's period of employment is not broken by periods of unpaid parental leave, the only contractual rights that prevail during such absences are those relating to notice periods, severance payments (that is to say, payments in excess of statutory redundancy pay), and access to the employer's disciplinary or grievance procedures. Both parties to the employment contract are bound by their mutual and implied contractual duty of trust and confidence. From the employee's standpoint, this means that, during any period of parental leave, the employee must not work for any other employer and must not disclose to any unauthorised person confidential information relating to his (or her) employer's trade secrets, business activities, etc (see Chapter 10).

14.73
Apart from the express and implied contractual rights referred to in the previous paragraph, all other terms and conditions of employment (eg, the

right to be paid, accrual of occupational sickness benefits, holidays in excess of the statutory minimum, occupational pension rights, etc) are held in suspense when an employee is absent from work on parental leave. An employer may, of course, choose to override these statutory limitations and may, for example, continue to allow an employee the use of a company car or mobile phone during his or her absence on parental leave.

14.74
An employee's statutory rights remain undisturbed during parental leave, including the right not to be unfairly or unlawfully dismissed, the right to be paid a statutory minimum redundancy payment if dismissed for redundancy, and the entitlement to accrue paid annual leave under the provisions of the Working Time Regulations 1998.

Returning to work after parental leave

14.75
An employee who takes parental leave for a period of four weeks or less (other than immediately after taking additional maternity leave)(see para. 14.77 below) is entitled to return from leave to exactly the same job that he (or she) held before that period of leave began. That same rule applies if (having completed a minimum of one year's service) a woman takes parental leave for a period of four weeks or less immediately after the end of her *ordinary* maternity leave period.

14.76
An employee who takes parental leave for a period of more than four weeks is likewise entitled to return from leave to the job in which he (or she) was employed before that period of absence began – unless it was not reasonably practicable for his employer to permit him (or her) to return to that job; in which case, the employee has the right to return to another job that is both suitable for him and appropriate for him or her to do in the circumstances. That same rule applies if a woman takes more than four weeks' parental leave immediately after her *ordinary* maternity leave period.

14.77
An employee who takes parental leave for a period of four weeks or less immediately after her additional maternity leave period is entitled to return from leave to the job in which she was employed before her maternity absence began – unless it would not have been reasonably practicable for her to return to that job if she had returned at the end of her additional maternity leave period, and it is still not reasonably practicable to permit her to do so at the end of that period of parental leave.

Note: As is demonstrated in Part 1 above (*Rights in Pregnancy & Maternity*), an employee who is made redundant during her ordinary or additional maternity leave periods has the right to be offered suitable alternative employment under a contract that takes effect on the day following the day on which her original contract came to an end. Should she accept such an offer, her right to return to work after her ordinary or additional maternity leave is a right to return to work in that alternative job (not the job she held before her absence began). If the same employee takes parental leave immediately after either of her ordinary or additional maternity leave periods, it is the alternative job (not her original job) to which she has the qualified right to return.

THE PARENTAL LEAVE FALLBACK SCHEME

14.78
In the absence of any alternative arrangements (negotiated individually or under the terms of a collective or workforce agreement), the so-called 'fallback scheme' outlined in Schedule 2 to the 1999 Regulations comes into play. There is anecdotal evidence that most small- to medium-sized firms have adopted the fallback scheme.

14.78
Under the fallback scheme, an employee may take parental leave in blocks (or tranches) of one week or more, unless the child in question is entitled to a disability living allowance, in which case the leave may be taken in single days or periods of less than one week. No more than four weeks' parental leave may be taken in any one year. For these purposes, a year is the period of 12 months which begins on the date on which the employee first became entitled to take parental leave in respect of the child in question (that is to say, either the day following the date on which the employee completed 12 months' continuous service with his (or her) employer, or the date on which the child was born or placed for adoption, whichever occurs later).

14.79
Employees seeking parental leave under the fallback scheme must (if asked to do so) provide their employer with evidence of parental responsibility (in the form of a birth certificate, adoption papers or evidence that a child has been awarded a social security disability living allowance). Such evidence need only be produced on the first occasion that a parent submits a request for parental leave (although, strictly speaking, an employer has the right to demand such evidence each time the same employee seeks further tranches of parental leave). The procedure may, of course, be repeated in the case of a second or subsequent child.

14.80
As a rule, a request for parental leave must specify the dates on which the period of leave is to begin and end, and must be submitted to the employer at

least 21 days before the date on which the requested period of leave is to begin. If the applicant is a father-to-be, the request for leave must be made at least 21 days before the beginning of the expected week of childbirth (EWC), and must specify that EWC and the duration of the intended period of leave. If a period of parental leave is to begin on the date on which a child is to be placed for adoption with an employee, the request for leave must be submitted at least 21 days before the beginning of the week in which the placement is to occur, and must specify the week in question and the duration of the intended period of leave. An employer's unreasonable refusal to agree to a request for parental leave will very likely be scrutinised by an employment tribunal, the more so if an employee's child was born prematurely or the intended adoption date was unexpectedly brought forward.

14.81
The fallback scheme allows that an employer may postpone the intended start date of a requested period of parental leave for a period of up to six months. This is permissible if the employee's absence from work during that period is likely to cause undue harm to the employer's business. Such a situation might arise if a key worker has asked for parental leave at a very busy time of the year or if a number of employees have asked for overlapping periods of parental leave, leaving the employer seriously understaffed. However, postponement is not permissible if the requested period of parental leave is intended to begin on the day of a child's birth or on the day on which a child is to be placed with an employee for adoption.

14.82
Within seven days of receiving a request for a period of parental leave, an employer intent on postponing that period of leave must write to the employee explaining his reasons for the postponement and setting out alternative dates for the beginning and end of that leave. Before doing so, the employer must discuss the postponement with the employee and agree alternative start and finishing dates. A postponed period of parental leave must be of the same duration as the period of leave originally requested. An employee may take the postponed period of leave, even if the revised start date occurs after the child's fifth birthday (or after the fifth anniversary of the date on which the child was placed with the employee for adoption; or, in the case of a child entitled to a disability living allowance, after the child's 18th birthday).

Unfair dismissal

14.83
An employee will be treated in law as having been unfairly dismissed if the reason (or principal reason) for the dismissal or selection for redundancy was

that the employee had taken (or sought to take) parental leave. The same rule applies if the employee was dismissed or selected for redundancy for refusing to sign a workforce agreement or (as appropriate) for performing or proposing to perform or carry out his (or her) legitimate functions or activities as a workforce representative or as a candidate for election as such a representative (see Chapter 5).

Detrimental treatment

14.84
An employee has the right also not to be punished, victimised or subjected to any other detriment (demotion, transfer, loss of promotion prospects, forfeiture of opportunities for training, etc) for exercising or proposing to exercise his (or her) statutory right to parental leave, or for refusing to sign a workforce agreement, or (where appropriate) for performing or proposing to perform his functions or activities as a workforce representative or as a candidate for election as such a representative. For further particulars, please see Chapter 6.

RIGHTS OF DISENFRANCHISED PARENTS

14.85
As indicated in para. 14.62 above, the rights of parents effectively disenfranchised by the 1999 Regulations, as originally enacted (including those who have since changed jobs and are now working for different employers), were reinstated on 10 January 2002 by the Maternity & Parental Leave (Amendment) Regulations 2001. What this means is that the parents of a child born or placed with them for adoption *before* 15 December 1999, and who have (or had) been continuously employed by their present (or a previous) employer for one year or more during the period from 15 December 1998 to 9 January 2002, inclusive, may take the parental leave previously denied to them (so long as they do so by 31 March 2005) – even if (in the case of employees who have since changed employers) they have yet to complete one year's continuous service with their new employers.

14.86
Disenfranchised parents 'deemed' (in the circumstances described) to have worked for their present employers for the minimum qualifying period of one year, will forfeit their restored entitlement to parental leave until and unless they produce the child or children's birth certificates (or adoption papers) and, in the case of a disabled child, confirmation that the child has been awarded a disability living allowance. Disenfranchised parents who resigned or were dismissed from their previous jobs on or after 15 December 1999 must also produce evidence supporting their assertion that they had

worked for a previous employer for one year or more during the period from 15 December 1998 to January 9, 2002, inclusive.

Further information

14.87
The Department of Trade & Industry (DTI) has published a booklet titled *Parental Leave: A Guide for Employers and Employees* (Ref URN 99/1193), copies of which may be obtained (free of charge) from the DTI's Publication Orderline on 0870 1502 500 (e-mail: publications@dti.gsi.gov.uk).

PART 5: FLEXIBLE WORKING

14.88
Although employees returning to work after maternity leave have no statutory right to do so on a part-time or job-sharing basis, recent amendments to the Employment Rights Act 1996 mean that the parents (or adoptive parents) of children under the age of six, or of disabled children under the age of 18, who have been continuously employed for 26 or more weeks, now have the right (without penalty) to *apply* to their employers for a more flexible pattern of working hours. In short, they have the right to seek to vary their contracts of employment so as to enable them to spend more time with their children. Their employers may not reject any such application 'out of hand', but must consider the implications and be prepared to offer sound business reasons if they decide to reject it. If, on the other hand, an employer agrees to accommodate the employee's request, the variation in the employee's terms and conditions will be permanent and irreversible.

14.89
It is as well to point out that the right to apply for flexible working is restricted to parents, foster parents, etc who are 'employees' in the strict legal sense of the word; that is to say, to persons employed under contracts of employment or service. For the time being at least, agency workers (or 'temps'), who are supplied by employment agencies to client employers, have no right to request a more flexible pattern of working hours.

The relevant legislation is to be found in sections 80F to 80I of the Employment Rights Act 1996 (as inserted by section 47 of the Employment Act 2002); the Flexible Working (Procedural Requirements) Regulations 2002 (SI 2002/3207); and the Flexible Working (Eligibility, Complaints & Remedies) Regulations 2002 (SI 2002/3236).

Meaning of 'flexible working'

14.90
Section 80F of the Employment Rights Act 1996 defines an application for 'flexible working' as meaning a request for a change in an employee's terms and conditions of employment involving staggered daily starting and finishing times (or flexi-time), shorter working hours, a shorter working week, a system of annualised hours, job sharing, term-time working, self-rostering, and so on. The legislation also allows that, in appropriate circumstances (given the nature of their work), employees may ask to work from home.

Eligibility

14.91
However, the right to apply for a more flexible pattern of working hours (or more flexible working arrangements) is restricted to those individuals who are the parents, adopters, guardians or foster parents of children under the age of six (or 18, in the case of children who have been awarded a disability living allowance) or who are either married to or the partners of such persons.

14.92
An employee who is the parent or guardian, etc of a child under the age of six (or 18) will not be eligible to submit an application for flexible working unless he or she:

(a) has been continuously employed by his or her employer for at least 26 weeks at the time the application is made;

(b) submits that application at least two weeks before the child's sixth birthday (or the child's 18th birthday, if disabled);

(c) has or expects to have responsibility for the child's upbringing;

(d) has a genuine need to work more flexibly in order to have more time to care for the child; and

(e) has not submitted an earlier application to work flexibly within the previous 12 months.

Contents of employee's application

14.93
Applications for flexible working must be submitted in writing and must:

(a) state that it is such an application;

(b) specify the change applied for and the date on which it is proposed the change should become effective;

(c) explain what effect (if any) the employee thinks making the change applied for would have on his (or her) employer and how, in the employee's opinion, any such effect might be dealt with; and

(d) explain his or her relationship to the child in question.

Employees applying for flexible working should be given to understand that any resultant and agreed variation in their terms and conditions of employment will be permanent and irreversible. In other words, they may not later change their minds, even if no longer responsible for the care and upbringing of the child or children in questions. To that end, they should consider the financial implications (eg, a drop in pay, if their applications are accepted).

Procedure

14.94
On receipt of an employee's written application for flexible working, an employer has 28 days within which to accept that application or to arrange a meeting with the employee. The purpose of the meeting is to consider the employee's application and its implications, and to discuss any compromise arrangements. The employee has the right to be accompanied at the meeting by a working colleague of his or her own choosing, or by a shop steward or full-time trade union official. The meeting must be postponed if the employee is absent on holidays or sick leave, or for up to five days if the person nominated to accompany the employee at the meeting is temporarily unavailable.

14.95
Within 14 days of the meeting, the employer must write to the employee either:

• agreeing to the proposed new work pattern and its start date; or

• confirming any compromise arrangement discussed and agreed at the initial meeting; or

• explaining in precise terms why his or her application has been rejected.

An employee whose application for flexible working has been rejected must nonetheless be reminded of his or her right to appeal against that decision, and the procedure for doing so. An employee who chooses to appeal must do so in writing within 14 days of receiving the employer's letter. The appeal must be heard within the next 14 days. At the appeal hearing, the employee again has the right to be accompanied by a fellow-employee of his or her own choosing, or by a shop steward or full-time trade union official. Within 14 days of the appeal hearing, the employer must convey his decision to the employee in writing. If the appeal has been upheld, the employer's letter must specify the contract variation agreed to and the date from which it is to take effect. If the employee's appeal has been dismissed, the letter must set out the grounds on which the dismissal is based.

Grounds for rejecting an application for flexible working

14.96
Section 80G of the Employment Rights Act 1996 states that an employer who has received an application for flexible working may only refuse the application for one or more of the following reasons:

(a) the burden of additional costs;

(b) detrimental effect on the ability to meet customer demand;

(c) inability to reorganise work among existing staff;

(d) inability to recruit additional staff;

(e) detrimental impact on quality or performance;

(f) insufficiency of work during the periods the employee proposes to work;

(g) planned structural changes; or

(h) such other grounds as may be specified in regulations made by the Secretary of State for Trade & Industry

and must be prepared to explain those reasons before an employment tribunal should the need arise.

Complaints to an employment tribunal

14.97
An employee whose application for more flexible working has been rejected out of hand (without the benefit either of an initial meeting or an appeal hearing), or if the employer has been dilatory in dealing with the employee's application (or has made it plain that he is not prepared to discuss it), or if the employee believes that the employer's dismissal of the application was based on grounds other than those listed in the preceding paragraph (or on inaccurate information not fully explored at the initial or appeal meeting) may complain to an employment tribunal, but must do so within three months of the employer's rejection or refusal to entertain the application.

14.98

If an employment tribunal finds such a complaint to be well-founded, it will make a declaration to that effect and may order the employer both to reconsider the employee's application and to pay such compensation to the employee as the tribunal considers to be just and equitable in all the circumstances (subject to a maximum of eight weeks' pay).

Further information

14.99

A DTI booklet (Ref. PL520) entitled *Flexible Working: the right to request and the duty to consider,* may be downloaded from Web site www.dti.gov.uk/er/individual/flexwork-pl520.pdf. DTI-designed forms for use by employees and employers in flexible working 'situations' are available on Web site www.dti.gov.uk/er/individual/flexforms.htm. The booklet and accompanying forms may also be obtained from the DTI's Publications Orderline on 0870 1502 500.

PART 6: TIME OFF FOR DEPENDANTS

14.100

Every employee (regardless of his or her age, length of service or working hours) has the right to be permitted a reasonable amount of *unpaid* time off work to care for dependants (per section 57A, Employment Rights Act 1996, as inserted by section 8, Schedule 4, Part II, Employment Relations Act 1999).

This statutory right, which came into effect on 15 December 1999, applies to a situation in which an employee needs time off work to take action which is necessary:

(a) to provide assistance on an occasion when a dependant falls ill, gives birth, or is injured or assaulted;

(b) to make arrangements for the provision of care for a dependant who is ill or injured;

(c) in consequence of the death of a dependant;

(d) because of the unexpected disruption (or termination) of existing arrangements for the care of a dependant;

(e) to deal with an incident at school involving one of the employee's children.

14.101

For obvious reason, an employee cannot be expected to give his (or her) employer advance warning of his need to take time off work in the circumstances described above. However, he must inform his employer of the situation as soon as is reasonably practicable (either by telephoning from home as soon as possible or, if suddenly called away from work, by notifying his supervisor or immediate manager of the situation before leaving the premises).

14.102
It should be pointed out that, in the absence of any contractual arrangement to the contrary, an employee's right to take time off for dependants does not extend to dealing with other types of domestic emergency, such as a boiler explosion or gas leak, although employers would undoubtedly be prepared to be reasonable in such cases.

Meaning of 'dependant'

14.103
For these purposes, a 'dependant' is an employee's wife, husband, partner, child, parent, or some other person living in the same household as the employee (other than as a tenant, lodger or boarder) who reasonably relies on the employee for assistance if he or she falls ill or is injured or assaulted, or to make arrangements for the provision of care in the event of illness or injury. The definition would also include a parent, grandparent, aged aunt or other close relative (whether or not living in the same household as the employee, but nearby) who is dependant on the employee for routine care and assistance.

14.104
A live-in nanny or 'au pair' would also qualify (especially if living at a considerable distance from home), as would an elderly neighbour living alone who has no immediate family to call upon in an emergency. It is not yet clear whether a person sharing accommodation with an employee and one or two others (either as a live-in partner or friend) would fall within this category. In such circumstances, it is up to the employer to exercise a degree of judgement when asked to make a decision in the matter.

14.105
It would be open to an employer to take disciplinary action against any employee who breaches his (or her) implied contractual duty of trust and confidence by abusing the right to time off in circumstances which do not warrant such time off.

How much time off is reasonable?

14.106
Section 57A of the 1996 Act makes the point that an employee has the right to take a reasonable amount of unpaid time off work *to provide assistance* in a

genuine emergency, *to make arrangements* for the care of a dependant, or *to collect a child from school* if he (or she) has had an accident or has been involved in some other incident. That right does not include taking extended leave of absence to care for an injured dependant or sick child or to wind-up a deceased relative's affairs. Should there be any dispute as to what does and what does not constitute a reasonable amount of time off (given the circumstances), the matter should be dealt with through the usual 'grievance' channels (or, if need be, by an employment tribunal). In some circumstances, it would not be unreasonable to require an employee to 'dip into' his or her annual holiday entitlement.

Complaint to an employment tribunal

14.107
A complaint of an employer's refusal or failure to permit an employee to take time off for dependants must be lodged with an employment tribunal within three months of the date on which that refusal or failure occurred. Should the employee's complaint be upheld, the tribunal will make a declaration to that effect and will order the employer to pay the employee such compensation as it considers to be 'just and equitable' in the circumstances. Employees have no need to resign in order to pursue their rights in these circumstances.

Protection from detriment

14.108
Section 47C of the 1996 Act (supplemented by regulation 19 of the Maternity & Parental Leave etc Regulations 1999) cautions that an employee has the right not to be subjected to any detriment by any act, or by any deliberate failure to act, by his (or her) employer, done because the employee took or sought to take time off for dependants under section 57A of that Act. On a successful complaint to an employment tribunal, the employer would be ordered to pay the disadvantaged employee an appropriate amount of compensation, including compensation for the loss of any benefit which would otherwise have been available to the employee but for the employer's actions (or failure to act). See also Chapter 6.

Unfair dismissal

14.109
An employee who is dismissed or selected for redundancy will be held to have been unfairly dismissed if the reason (or, if more than one, the principal reason) for his (or her) dismissal or selection was that he had taken or sought to take time off for dependants under section 57A of the 1996 Act. A complaint of unfair dismissal in such circumstances (if upheld) would result in the

employer being ordered to pay the employee a substantial amount of compensation (comprising a basic award of a maximum £7,800, a compensatory award of up to £53,500 and, where applicable, an additional award of between 26 and 52 weeks' pay). A complaint of unfair dismissal in such circumstances may be presented regardless of the employee's age or length of service at the material time. For further particulars, please turn to Chapter 5.

Further information

14.110
For further information, the reader is commended to DTI publication: *Time off for dependants: A guide for employers and employees* (Ref. URN 99/1186), copies of which are available, free of charge, from the DTI's Publications Orderline on 0870 1502 500 (e-mail: publications@dti.gsi.gov.uk).

PART 7: OTHER RIGHTS IN PREGNANCY AND MATERNITY

Ante-natal care

14.111
A pregnant employee who has, on the advice of her doctor (or registered midwife) made one or more appointments to attend at any place for the purpose of receiving ante-natal care, is entitled to be permitted by her employer to take paid time off during her normal working hours to enable her to keep those appointments. Before allowing time off for such purposes, her employer has the right to require the employee to produce for his inspection a Certificate of Expected Confinement (Form Mat B1), signed by her doctor or registered midwife, as well as evidence in the form of an appointment card (or similar) confirming that she has made one or more appointments to attend at an ante-natal clinic. However, the employer cannot insist on inspecting either document until after the employee has made her first visit to the clinic (*Source*: ss 55 & 56, ERA 1976).

14.112
A pregnant employee, who has been denied her statutory right to paid time off work in the circumstances described above, may complain to an employment tribunal, but must do so within three months of the date of the appointment concerned, or within such further period as the tribunal considers reasonable. If her complaint is upheld, the tribunal will order the employer to pay the employee a sum equivalent to her loss or the value of her time during the period when she was refused time off. If the tribunal finds that the employer had failed to pay the employee the whole or part of any wages or salary to which she was entitled in respect of any such time off, it

will also order the employer to pay the amount which it finds due to her (*Source*: ERA 1996, s.57).

Suspension on maternity grounds

14.113
An employee is suspended from work on maternity grounds if, in consequence of any relevant health and safety legislation or a recommendation contained in a code of practice issued and approved under section 16 of the Health & Safety at Work etc Act 1974, she is suspended from work by her employer because she is pregnant, or has recently given birth or is breast-feeding a child.

14.114
Before being suspended from work in the circumstances described above, the employee has the right to be offered suitable alternative work by her employer (if such is available). To be suitable, the alternative work must be both suitable and appropriate (in the light of the employee's qualifications, skills and experience) and on terms and conditions which are no less favourable to her than the corresponding terms and conditions of her usual job.

14.115
If there is no suitable alternative work for the employee to do (or she has not unreasonably refused an offer of suitable alternative work), she must be suspended from work on full pay until such time as it is safe for her to resume her normal duties. If there is any disagreement, the employee may refer the matter for determination by an employment tribunal. Any such reference or complaint must be presented within three months of the day in respect of which payment was denied or, in the case of an employer's failure to offer suitable alternative employment, within the period of three months beginning with the first day of the suspension period. A complaint presented 'out of time' will not normally be heard unless the tribunal is satisfied that it was not reasonably practicable for the complaint to be presented within the prescribed three-month period.

14.116
If an employment tribunal finds that the employer had failed to pay the remuneration to which the employee was entitled during the period of her suspension on maternity grounds, it will order the employer to pay the employee the amount which it finds is due to her. If the finding is that the employer had failed to provide the employee with suitable alternative work, the tribunal will make an award of compensation to be paid by the employer to the employee – the amount of which shall be such as the tribunal considers 'just and equitable'.

14.117
Restrictions on the employment (or continued employment) of pregnant women are to be found in the code of practice accompanying the Control of Lead at Work Regulations 2002, and in Schedule IV to the Ionising Radiations Regulations 1999. Furthermore, regulations 16 & 18 of the Management of Health & Safety at Work Regulations 1999 (*qv*) state that the risk assessment necessarily carried out by every employer must include an assessment of the risks facing pregnant employees, new mothers and employees who are breastfeeding. If there are any significant risks arising out of their working conditions or from the products or processes to which they are exposed, they must either be transferred to more suitable work or, if that is not possible, be suspended from work on full pay for so long as is necessary. The risks in question may be related to the physical, biological or chemical agents to which any such employee is, or may be, exposed (including those specified in Annexes I and II of Council Directive 92/85/EEC 'on the introduction of measures to encourage improvements in safety and health at work of pregnant workers and workers who have recently given birth or are breastfeeding'). An employer who fails to comply with his (or her) duties under the regulations referred to above is guilty of an offence and liable to prosecution and a heavy fine.

Replacement employees

14.118
A person employed specifically to replace an employee who has been suspended from work on maternity grounds may be dismissed (for 'some other substantial reason') once the person he (or she) has been employed to replace returns to normal working – subject to the proviso that the replacement employee must be made aware of the nature of his (or her) employment at the very outset (in writing) and must be informed in clear and unequivocal terms that dismissal will take place once the permanent employee returns to work. However, the test of 'reasonableness' will nonetheless apply (*Source*: ERA 1996, s.106(3) & (4)).

Restrictions on night work

14.119
If a new or expectant mother works at night and produces a certificate signed by her doctor (or registered midwife) to the effect that working at night could be detrimental to her health and safety (or, in the case of a pregnant employee, to that of her unborn child), her employer must either transfer her to daytime work (without loss of pay) or suspend her on full pay for the period specified in the certificate. Non-compliance with this requirement is an offence under

the Health & Safety at Work etc Act 1974 (*Source*: Reg. 17, Management of Health & Safety at Work Regulations 1999).

Rest facilities – new and expectant mothers

14.120
Regulation 25(4) of the Workplace (Health, Safety & Welfare) Regulations 1992 requires every employer to provide suitable rest facilities for the use of employees who are pregnant or breastfeeding, or who have given birth within the previous six months. In a large establishment, the facilities may consist of a small well-ventilated room equipped with (or adjacent to) a toilet and washbasin and be furnished with one or two daybeds. In the smaller business, a clean and comfortable reclining chair in a curtained-off area may suffice, so long as any employee making use of the facility is assured of a measure of privacy. Wherever possible, the rest area or facility set aside for these purposes should be situated as near as possible to the washrooms and toilets used by other (female) employees. A failure to provide this facility is an offence under the Health & Safety at Work etc Act 1974, which could lead to prosecution and the imposition of a fine.

Dismissing a maternity leave replacement

14.121
Dismissing a replacement employee, recruited to replace an employee who is absent from work on maternity, parental or adoption leave, will not present a problem so long as the replacement had been informed in writing, when first recruited, that he or she would be dismissed on the return to work of the permanent incumbent. In short, the dismissal of a replacement employee in those circumstances would be treated in law as a dismissal 'for a substantial reason of a kind such as to justify the dismissal of an employee holding the position which the replacement employee held'. However, the test of 'reasonableness' will nonetheless apply (*ibid* s.106(1), (2) & (4)).

Miscellaneous statutory rights

SUSPENSION ON MEDICAL GROUNDS

15.1
Current health and safety legislation empowers Employment Medical Advisers (EMAs) and appointed factory doctors to suspend any employee from work on medical grounds if the employee's exposure to certain hazardous substances at the workplace poses a particular risk to his (or her) health. An employee suspended from work on medical grounds is entitled to be paid his (or her) normal wage or salary during the suspension period for a maximum of 26 weeks or until such time as the EMA or factory doctor declares that it is safe for that employee to return to work (whichever occurs sooner). To qualify for payment during a period of suspension on medical grounds, the employee must:

- have been continuously employed for a minimum period of one month ending with the day immediately preceding the day on which the suspension period begins;

- not otherwise be incapable of work by reason of disease or bodily or mental disablement;

- remain 'on standby' (that is to say, must be readily contactable and available to return to work at short notice) in case his (or her) employer finds other work for him to do; and

- not have unreasonably refused any such offer of suitable alternative work – whether or not the work in question is of a kind which he (or she) is normally required to do under the contract of employment.

(*Source*: ERA 1996, s.65.)

15.2
The Regulations under which employment medical advisers and factory doctors have the right to suspend employees are:

- the Control of Lead at Work Regulations 2002 (SI 2002/2676) – exposure to lead (including lead alloys, any compounds of lead, and lead as a constituent of any substance or material);

- the Control of Substances Hazardous to Health Regulations 2002 (SI 2002/2677) – exposure to one or other of the substances listed in Schedule 5 to the Regulations;

- the Ionising Radiations Regulations 1999 (SI 1999/3232) – exposure to electromagnetic or corpuscular radiation capable of producing ions and emitted from a radioactive substance or from a machine or apparatus that is intended to produce ionising radiation or in which charged particles are accelerated by a voltage of not less than five kilovolts; and

- the Management of Health & Safety at Work Regulations 1999 (SI 1999/3242) – exposure to processes or working conditions, or to physical, biological or chemical agents, which could involve risk, by reason of her condition, to the health and safety of a new or expectant mother, or to that of her baby.

Note: A woman suspended from work on maternity grounds (as distinct from medical grounds) has no need of a qualifying period of employment and has the right to be paid her normal wages or salary throughout her period of suspension unless she has unreasonably refused an offer of suitable alternative employment made to her by her employer. For further information, please turn to Chapter 14, paras 14.113 to 14.117.

An employee need not necessarily be ill or incapable of work in order to be suspended from work on medical grounds; but may be displaying symptoms (headaches, fatigue, skins problems etc) commonly associated with exposure to the hazardous substances in question.

Dismissal of a replacement employee

15.3
A person employed specifically to replace an employee who has been suspended from work on medical grounds may be fairly dismissed (for 'some other substantial reason') once the person he (or she) has been employed to replace returns to normal working – always provided that the replacement employee is made aware at the very outset (preferably in writing) of the circumstances of his (or her) employment and is informed that dismissal will take place once the permanent employee returns to work. However, the test of 'reasonableness' will nonetheless apply (*Source*: ERA 1996, s.106(3) & (4)).

Complaints

15.4
An employee who has been suspended from work on medical grounds may complain to an employment tribunal that his (or her) employer has refused or failed to pay him the whole or part of his normal wages during the period of suspension. Such a complaint must be presented within three months of the

alleged refusal or failure (or within such further period as the tribunal considers reasonable in a case where it is satisfied that it was not reasonably practicable for the complaint to have been presented within that period of three months).

If such a complaint is upheld, the employer will be ordered to pay the employee the amount of remuneration which it finds is due to him (or her) (*Source*: ERA 1996, s.70).

TIME OFF WORK

15.5
The rights of employees to be allowed a reasonable amount of paid or unpaid time off work during normal working hours are to be found in the Trade Union & Labour Relations (Consolidation) Act 1992, the Employment Rights Act 1996, and in regulation 25 of the Transnational Information & Consultation of Employees Regulations 1999 (SI 1999/3323). The right to paid (or unpaid) time off work is available in prescribed circumstances to:

- trade union officials;
- trade union members;
- officials or members of prescribed public bodies;
- redundant employees (to look for work or arrange training);
- safety representatives (trade union-appointed or otherwise);
- pregnant employees needing ante-natal care;
- employees attending to the needs of dependants;
- pension scheme trustees;
- employee representatives (collective redundancy and TUPE consultations);
- young persons aged 16, 17 or 18 who are undertaking study or training leading to a 'relevant qualification';
- members of 'special negotiating bodies' (SNBs) and European Works Councils (EWCs) and 'information and consultation representatives';
- a worker ('employee' or otherwise) accompanying another worker at any formal stage of a disciplinary or grievance procedure.

With one exception (namely, the employee under notice of redundancy, who must have 'notched up' two years' continuous service), the right to time off work is available to all relevant employees, regardless of their age, length of service or working hours at the material time.

15.6
The right to be *paid* during time off work is available to all but two of the categories listed above. Trade union members given time off during working hours to attend trade union-organised meetings (or whatever) are *not* entitled to be paid while absent from their work stations or desks. The same applies to employees who are justices of the peace or members of certain public bodies.

The amount of time off to be allowed (in the circumstances summarised above) must be 'reasonable'. A dispute over whether the amount of time off allowed was reasonable or unreasonable may well lead to proceedings before an employment tribunal.

Time off for trade union duties

15.7
Trade union officials (shop stewards, works convenors, and the like) must be paid their normal wages or salary when granted time off to carry out their official duties or when undergoing approved training in relevant aspects of industrial relations. To qualify, the official in question must be an official of an independent trade union recognised by the employer for the purposes of collective bargaining.

15.8
The statute provides that the amount of time off which an employee is to be permitted to take... and the purposes for which, the occasions on which and any conditions subject to which time off may be so taken are those that are reasonable in all the circumstances having regard to the (recently updated) ACAS Code of Practice 3: *Time off for Trade Union Duties & Activities* (*Source*: TULRA 1992, s.170(3)). The phrase 'reasonable in the circumstances' covers the nature, extent and purposes of the time already being taken off (*Wignall v British Gas Corporation* [1984] IRLR 493, EAT).

15.9
The way that the tribunals approach these provisions was summarised by Slynn J in *Sood v GEC Elliott Process Automation Ltd* [1980] ICR 1, EAT: 'It seems to us that when questions involving industrial relations arise, a union official may well be entitled, as part of his duties, to take part in the planning of strategy and in discussing with other workers who are at the time negotiating with their employers, so long as the latter employers are associated with a particular trade union official's own employees. Nor do we accept the argument that a trade union official is only entitled to take time off for the purpose of negotiating where the employers have laid down the particular industrial relations structure ... the test is whether the time off is required to enable the official to carry out his duties in relation to a matter which arises in

relations between employees and management. We do not consider that the mere exchange of information between the trade union officials themselves necessarily qualifies, even if those officials represent workers in a particular group of companies'. See also *London Ambulance Service v Charlton & Another* [1992] IRLR 510, EAT.

15.10

Trade union officials who work shifts are not entitled to be paid when carrying out those of their official duties which occur outside normal shift-working hours; nor have they any legal right to take time off work in lieu of the time spent carrying out those duties. But if they work nights and their official duties occur during the day, it probably would be reasonable to give them the night off and pay them, to enable them to carry out those duties (*Hairsine v Kingston-upon-Hull City Council* [1992] ICR 18, EAT).

15.11

An employee minded to complain about his (or her) employer's refusal to allow him time off work to carry out his duties as a trade union official (or about his employer's failure to pay him during such time off) must do so within three months of the alleged refusal or failure (or, if that is not reasonably practicable, as soon as possible). If the complaint is upheld, the tribunal will make a declaration to that effect, and will order the employer to pay to the employee such amount of compensation as it considers 'just and equitable in all the circumstances' (*Source*: TULRA 1992, ss 168, 171 & 172).

15.12

The award of compensation will comprise:

* the wages that have been wrongly withheld; and

* compensation for any other injury sustained (eg hurt feelings).

But a tribunal cannot order an employer to allow time off for a special occasion or at a specified level, nor can it impose conditions. But any observations made of what it considers to be reasonable time off are likely to be taken into consideration at a later complaint (*Corner v Buckinghamshire County Council* [1978] IRLR 320, EAT).

15.13

In assessing the amount of lost wages, the tribunal will include premiums for duties that the employee was contractually bound to perform, eg for shift work. But any extra payment for non-compulsory overtime, even if regularly undertaken, would not be recoverable (*McCormack v Shell Chemical UK Ltd* [1979] IRLR 40, EAT; and *Davies & Alderton v Head Wrightson Teesdale Ltd* [1979] IRLR 170, EAT).

Time off for trade union activities

15.14

The right to a reasonable amount of time off work to participate in the activities of an independent trade union extends to any member (as opposed to an official) of such a union, so long as that union is recognised by the employer as having bargaining rights in relation to terms and conditions of employment, etc. The trade union activities must not of themselves comprise industrial action and may only take place at 'an appropriate time', that is to say, at a time during normal working hours in accordance with arrangements agreed with or consent given by the employer. However, an employer is *not* duty-bound to pay trade union members who have asked for (and been granted) time off to participate in such activities. See also Chapter 5, para. 5.26)(*Source*: TULRA 1992, s.170).

15.15

The ACAS *Code of Practice: Tine off for trade union duties and activities* states that the type of trade union activities for which a reasonable amount of (unpaid) time off work should be permitted during working hours are:

- attending workplace meetings to discuss and vote on the outcome of negotiations with the employer;

- meeting full-time officials to discuss issues relevant to the workplace;

- voting in properly-conducted ballots on industrial action;

- voting in union elections.

And again: 'The amount and frequency of time off should be reasonable in all the circumstances'. Although the statutory provisions apply to all employers without exception as to size and type of business or service, trade unions should be aware of the wide variety of difficulties and operational requirements to be taken into account when seeking or agreeing arrangements for time off, for example:

- the size of the organisation and the number of workers;

- the production process;

- the need to maintain a service to the public;

- the need for safety and security at all times.

15.16

The refusal by an employer must be unreasonable before a member has a remedy. Thus, if the purpose of the time off is to plan industrial action, or foment unrest, then an employer can refuse to allow it. Indeed, he may be able to dismiss without it being held to be unfair (*Oxford & County Newspapers & Another v McIntyre & Shipton*, 29 July 1986, EAT) (*Source*: TULRA 1992, s.170(2)).

15.17
An employee who has been denied his (or her) statutory right to time off work (or, if qualified, who has not been paid in respect of such time off) may complain to an employment tribunal. The complaint must be presented within three months of the employer's refusal (or failure to pay) or, if this is not reasonably practicable, within such further period as is reasonable in the circumstances. If the complaint is upheld, the tribunal will:

- make a declaration to this effect; and

- award compensation for any injury sustained, eg hurt feelings.

(*Source*: TULRA 1992, ss 170(4), 171 & 172.)

Time off for public duties

15.18
Employers must allow those of their employees who are justices of the peace or members of certain public bodies a reasonable amount of time off work to enable them to carry out their official duties. Although an employee has no legal right to be paid at such times, an employer's refusal to pay could be construed as a refusal to allow time off, the more so if an employee simply cannot afford to take time off without pay. This view was endorsed by Slynn J in *Corner v Buckingham County Council* [1978] ICR 836. There, he remarked that 'in considering where there has been refusal to grant time off, the [employment] tribunal can look at the conditions subject to which an employer is prepared to grant time off (including conditions relating to pay) and could say that they really amounted to a refusal to allow time to be taken'.

15.19
In deciding whether the time off is reasonable, the following factors must be taken into account:

- how much time off is needed to enable an employee to carry out his (or her) public duties;

- how much time off is required to carry out a particular duty;

- how much time off has already been permitted (eg time off for trade union duties and activities); and

- the circumstances of the employer's business and the effect the employee's absence (or further absence) would have on it.

(*Source*: ERA 1996, s.50(4).)

15.20

A balancing act has to be carried out, and each case has to be decided on its own particular facts. However, there is no obligation on the employer to rearrange the duties of an employee to enable him (or her) to make up for the time lost (*Ratcliffe v Dorset CC* (1978) IRLR 191, EAT).

15.21

A complaint relating to an employer's refusal or failure to allow time off work for public duties must be presented to an employment tribunal within the time limits described in para. 15.17 above. If the complaint is upheld, the tribunal will make a declaration to that effect and may make an award of compensation to be paid by the employer to the employee. The amount of compensation will be such as the tribunal considers 'just and equitable' in the circumstances, having regard to the employer's default in failing to permit the employee to take time off, and any loss sustained by the employee which is attributable to the matters to which the complaint relates (*Source*: ERA 1996, s.51).

Time off during redundancy notice

15.22

To qualify for the right to paid time off work during his (or her) notice period, a redundant employee must have been continuously employed for at least two years at the (projected) effective date of termination of his (or her) contract of employment. If the employee has been given less than the *statutory* notice period, his (projected) length of service must be calculated to the end of that longer notice period. The purpose of the time off is to enable the employee to look for work elsewhere or to make arrangements for retraining after the employment comes to an end. As the penalty for refusing paid time off work in these circumstances is a maximum 40 per cent of a week's pay, it follows that an employer should allow up to two days' time off work (consecutive or in the aggregate) during the employee's notice period (*Source*: ERA 1996, ss 52 & 53).

15.23

A complaint of an employer's failure to allow time off in the circumstances described, or to pay the employee his (or her) normal wages or salary at such times, must be presented to an employment tribunal within three months of the alleged refusal or failure to pay (or within such further period as the tribunal considers reasonable). If the complaint is upheld, the tribunal will make a declaration to that effect and may order the employer to pay the employee the amount which it finds is due to him, subject to a maximum of two day's pay (*Source*: ERA 1996, s.54).

Time off for safety representatives and representatives of employee safety

15.24
The subject of health and safety at work (and the eponymous 1974 Act) is considered in Chapter 23. Trade union-appointed safety representatives and elected representatives of employee safety, have certain statutory functions to perform. Their employer must permit them to take such time off work (with pay) as is reasonable and necessary to enable them to carry out those functions – and paid time off also for the purposes of undergoing such training in aspects of those functions as may be reasonable in all the circumstances (*Source*: Safety Representatives & Safety Committees Regulations 1977 (Reg. 4(2)) & Health & Safety (Consultation with Employees) Regulations 1996 (SI 1996/1513) (Reg. 7(2)).

15.25
According to the Health and Safety Commission's *Approved Code of Practice: Safety Representatives & Safety Committees*, the functions of safety representatives include encouraging co-operation between their employer and the workforce in promoting and developing essential measures to ensure the health and safety of employees; and bringing to the employer's notice... any unsafe or unhealthy conditions or working practices, or unsatisfactory arrangements for welfare at work, which come to their attention whether on an inspection or day to day observation. Copies of the code (ISBN 0 7176 1220 1) are available from HSE Books (see Chapter 23, para 23.14).

Note: The code of practice (or *Brown Book*) referred to above relates to the role and functions of trade union-appointed representatives, although there can be little difference between those and the functions of employee-elected representatives.

15.26
A complaint of an employer's refusal or failure to permit time off work in the circumstances described (or to pay an employee his [or her] normal wages or salary during such time off) must be presented to an employment tribunal within three months of the alleged refusal or failure (or within such further period as the tribunal considers reasonable in a case where it is satisfied that it was not reasonably practicable for the complaint to be presented within the prescribed three-month period) (*Source*: Safety Representatives & Safety Committees Regs 1977, Reg. 11; and Health & Safety (Consultations with Employees Regs 1996, Sch. 2).

15.27
If such a complaint is upheld, the tribunal will make a declaration to that effect and will order the employer to pay compensation to the complainant of such amount as it considers just and equitable, having regard to the

employer's default in failing to permit time off and to any loss sustained by the employee which is attributable to that failure. In the case of a failure to pay a representative his (or her) normal wages or salary during such time off, the tribunal will order the employer to pay the employee the amount which it finds is due to him.

Time off for ante-natal care

15.28
The right of a pregnant employee to be permitted a reasonable amount of paid time off work to enable her to keep one or more appointments at an ante-natal clinic (or similar establishment), on the recommendation of her doctor or registered midwife, is discussed earlier in Chapter 14 (paras 14.111 & 14.112).

Time off work – pension scheme trustees

15.29
Under section 16 of the Pensions Act 1995 an employee may be nominated and appointed by his (or her) colleagues to represent their interests as members of a relevant occupational pension scheme (that is to say, a scheme established under a trust by their employer). Every such *pension scheme trustee* has the legal right to be permitted a reasonable amount of paid time off work to enable him (or her) to perform his duties as such a trustee or to undergo training relevant to the performance of those duties. Just how much time off is reasonable is a matter of common sense and judgement. When considering a request for time (eg to attend a meeting of the trustees of the pension scheme) an employer is entitled to consider the effect the employee's absence from his desk or workbench is likely to have on the business, but must be mindful also that an employee-elected trustee should not be too circumscribed in the exercise of his legitimate functions.

15.30
A pension scheme trustee who believes that he (or she) is not being reasonably treated in the matter of time off work, or who is aggrieved at his employer's refusal or failure to pay him his normal wages or salary at such times, may present a complaint to an employment tribunal. The complaint must be presented within three months of the alleged refusal of failure (or, if the employee has resigned or been dismissed) within three months of the effective date of termination of the employee's contract of employment. If the complaint is upheld, the tribunal will make a declaration to that effect and will order the employer to pay to the employee such compensation as is considered appropriate in the circumstances (*Source*: ERA 1996, ss 58, 59 & 60).

Time off work – employee representatives

15.31
Under the Collective Redundancies & Transfer of Undertakings (Protection of Employment) (Amendment) Regulations 1999 (SI 1999/1925), trade union-appointed and/or employee-elected *employee representatives* have the right to be consulted by their employers when 20 or more redundancies are mooted (collective redundancies) or when proposals are afoot for the sale or transfer of the whole or part of the employer's business or for the acquisition of the whole or part of another employer's business (as to which, see Chapter 4, paras 4.41 to 4.51, and (in relation to transfers of undertakings) Chapter 22, paras 22.21 to 22.26).

15.32
Employee representatives in the circumstances described above have the legal right to be permitted a reasonable amount of paid time off work to enable them to carry out their functions efficiently. An employer who denies them that right (or who refuses or fails to pay them their normal wages or salary during such time off as is granted) will be called upon to explain his intransigence before an employment tribunal. If the complaint against him is upheld, he (or she) will be ordered to pay an appropriate amount of compensation. It must be emphasised that an employee attempting to exercise his (or her) statutory rights in this context has no need to resign in order to obtain redress for an alleged breach of those rights. A complaint must nonetheless be presented to the Secretary to the Tribunals within three months of the alleged failure to allow time off or within three months of the employer's refusal or failure to pay. If the employee has resigned (or been dismissed), the three-month period begins to run from the effective date of termination of the employee's contract of employment (as to which, see Chapter 3, paras 3.15 to 3.26).

Time off for young persons for study or training

15.33
An employee aged 16 or 17, who is not receiving full-time secondary or further education, and who has not achieved (*inter alia*) grades A* to C in at least five GCSE subjects, has the right to be permitted by his (or her) employer to take a reasonable amount of paid time off work in order to undertake study or training leading to an academic or vocational qualification likely to enhance the employee's employment prospects. That same right extends to any 18-year-old employee who began his studies before his (or her)18th birthday (*Source*: ERA 1996, s.63A, as inserted, with effect from 1 September 1999, by the Teaching & Higher Education Act 1998).

Note: For a full list of the standards of achievement encompassed by section 63A of the 1996 Act (unfortunately, too numerous to reproduce here), the reader is commended to the Right to Time Off for Study or Training Regulations 1999 (SI 1999/986), copies of which are available from The Stationery Office (Telephone 0870 600 5522). The text of the Regulations may be freely downloaded from the Stationery Office's Web site: www.hmso.gov.uk.

15.34
The amount of time off to be permitted in the circumstances described in the preceding paragraph, and the occasions on which any conditions subject to which time off may be so taken, are those that are reasonable given the requirements of the employee's study or training balanced against the employer's business circumstances and the effect that the employee's absences would have on the efficient running of the business (*ibid*).

15.35
An employer's refusal or failure to allow a young person in his employ to take time off for study or training (or a refusal to pay the employee for such time off) may be referred to an employment tribunal. If such a complaint is upheld, the tribunal will make a declaration to that effect and will order the employer to pay the employee an amount equivalent to the amount he would have been paid had he been permitted to take time off or, if the employee had been granted time off, but without pay, the amount that the tribunal finds is due to the employee in respect of that time off.

Time off – members of SNBs and EWCs

15.36
With the coming into force on 1 February 2000 of the Transnational Information & Consultation of Employees Regulations 1999 (*qv*) – implementing Council Directive 94/45/EC of 22 September 1994 'on the establishment of a European Works Council or a procedure in Community-scale undertakings, etc' – employees who are members of a 'special negotiating body' (SNB) or of a European Works Council (EWC), or who are 'information and consultation representatives' have the right to be permitted such time off work (with pay) as is necessary to enable them to carry out their functions as such members or representatives. That same right extends to employees canvassing for election as such a member or representative.

15.37
An employee (*qua* member, representative or candidate), who is refused paid time off work in the circumstances described in the previous paragraph, may complain to an employment tribunal. If his (or her) complaint is upheld, the employer in question will be ordered to pay an appropriate amount of compensation.

ITEMISED PAY STATEMENT

15.38
Every employee (part-time, full-time, seasonal or casual) is entitled to receive an itemised pay statement on every occasion that he (or she) receives a pay packet or pay statement (weekly, fortnightly, monthly, or whatever). The statement must itemise:

- the gross amount;

- the amount of each fixed deduction authorised by the employee (SAYE schemes, trade union dues, mortgage payments, etc);

- the amount of any variable deductions and what each is for (PAYE, National Insurance and pension contributions, etc);

- the net amount paid (after deductions);

- details of how the net amount is paid (by cash or cheque, or by credit transfer to one or more named banks or building societies).

(*Source*: ERA 1996, ss 8 to 10.)

15.39
Separate particulars of each fixed deduction need not be shown in a pay statement if, but only if, the aggregate amount is shown *and* the employer has already provided the employee with a so-called 'standing statement of fixed deductions'. The latter statement must be amended or updated as often as may be necessary and reissued to the employee (if not amended or updated in the meantime) at least once every 12 months.

15.40
An employee, regardless of his (or her) age or length of service at the material time, may refer the matter to an employment tribunal if his employer fails to provide an itemised pay statement (or issues a pay statement which does not comply with the statutory requirements). Any deductions from an employee's wages or salary, which are not explained in an accompanying pay statement, will be treated by the tribunal as 'unnotified deductions'. In short, the tribunal may order the employer to refund any and all such deductions from the employee's pay over the period of up to 13 weeks immediately preceding the date on which the employee's Originating Application (Form IT1) was received by the Secretary to the Tribunals.

15.41
It is important to note that an employee has no need to resign from his (or her) employment in order to obtain redress from an employment tribunal. An employer who reacts to any such challenge to his authority by dismissing

the employee in question, runs the risk of being summoned before a tribunal yet again and of being ordered to pay the employee a very substantial amount of compensation indeed, as to which see Chapter 5, paras 5.44 & 5.45 (*Source*: ERA 1996, s.104).

15.42
References or complaints to an employment tribunal in the circumstances described above must be presented within three months of the employer's refusal or failure to provide an itemised pay statement (or one which is incomplete). If the employee has been dismissed or is no longer employed, the complaint must be presented within three months of the effective date of termination of the employee's contract of employment. A complaint presented 'out of time' will not be heard unless a tribunal is satisfied that it was not reasonably practicable for it to have been presented sooner.

GUARANTEE PAYMENTS

15.43
An employee who is not provided with work by his (or her) employer, throughout a day on which he is ordinarily required to work, has the legal right to be paid a 'guarantee payment' in respect of that and any subsequent 'workless days' – subject to a maximum of five 'workless days' in any period of three consecutive months. From 1 February 2003, the maximum guarantee payment is £17.30 a day (which figure is adjusted each year in line with the September on September change in the retail price index). If an employee earns less than an average £17.30 a day, the employer need only pay the lower amount (*Source*: ERA 1996, ss 28 to 35).

15.44
An employer's failure or inability to provide work must have been prompted by:

- a diminution in the requirements of the employer's business for work of the kind which the employee is employed to do (eg a dramatic downturn in orders); or

- some other occurrence (such as a power failure, fire, flood, non-delivery of raw materials, etc) affecting the normal working of the employer's business in relation to work of the kind which the employee is employed to do.

However, an employer is not obliged to make guarantee payments to any of his employees if his (or her) inability to provide them with work is due to a strike, lock-out or other industrial action prompted by other employees (or by persons employed by an 'associated employer') – even if the employees seeking guarantee payments are not directly involved in the dispute in question.

Qualifying conditions

15.45
To qualify for a guarantee payment in respect of a workless day, an employee must have worked for his (or her) employer for a period of at least one month ending with the day immediately preceding the day in question. Furthermore, if asked to do so, the employee must keep himself available for work (ie must remain 'on standby') on the off-chance that his employer may have suitable alternative work for him to do. An employee who does not remain on standby or who reasonably refuses an offer of alternative work (even if the work in question is not of the type he is ordinarily required to do under his contract of employment) will forfeit his right to a guarantee payment.

15.46
If a shift or night worker's working hours begin and end before and after midnight, the 'workless day' will be the day on which the major portion of the shift falls. If the hours on either side of midnight are the same, the workless day will be the day on which the shift ends.

Complaints

15.47
A complaint concerning an employer's refusal or failure to pay a guarantee payment in respect of any day must be lodged with the nearest local or regional office of the Employment Tribunals Service within the period of three months beginning with the day in question. Should such a complaint be upheld, the employer will be ordered to pay the employee the amount of guarantee which it finds is due to him (or her)(*ibid* s.34).

Cautionary note

15.48
It is as well to point out that an employer has no automatic right to lay off any employee without pay when business is slack (or for any other reason) unless that right has already been conceded by employees in their contracts of employment. In the absence of any such contractual right (express or otherwise), laying off an employee without pay is a breach of contract which could lead to a claim for damages before a court or tribunal or to enforced resignation and a complaint of unfair constructive dismissal. If an employee has a contractual right to be paid the whole or part of his (or her) normal wages or salary when laid off, any guarantee payment in respect of a 'workless day' may be offset against any payment of wages or salary in respect of that same day, and vice versa.

DAMAGES FOR BREACH OF CONTRACT

15.49
Nowadays, employment tribunals share jurisdiction with the county courts to entertain claims for damages arising out of a breach of contract which arise or remain on the termination of an employee's contract of employment – eg dismissal without the appropriate notice ('wrongful dismissal') or dismissal in breach of an employer's own contractual procedures for terminating employment.

15.50
Damages can generally be divided into three types:

- ordinary damages to compensate the aggrieved for the loss he has sustained, eg the amount of wages, holiday entitlement and so forth;

- aggravated damages for injury to feelings which are compensatory in nature, although difficult to evaluate;

- exemplary damages that are punitive – intended to deter a defendant rather than compensate a plaintiff.

(*Duffy v Eastern Health & Social Services Board* [1992] IRLR 251, Fair Employment Tribunal (Northern Ireland).)

15.51
It matters not that the defendant's behaviour was high-handed, malicious, insulting or oppressive. Exemplary damages may only be awarded where:

- the defendant was motivated by a search for profit; or

- they are specifically authorised by statute; or

- the defendants are exercising some form of governmental function – extending, in appropriate circumstances, to the acts of local authorities.

(*Broome v Cassel & Co* [1972] AC 1029, HL; and *Bradford City Metropolitan Council v Arora* [1991] ICR 226, CA.)

15.52
Where a statute directs that an award should be made, *inter alia*, for injury to feelings – such as in claims relating to unjustified disciplinary action – generally the amount should be modest. If the statute specifies a minimum award, that would be an appropriate amount provided there are no other aggravating features. Damages should be akin to those in claims for defamation (*Bradley & Others v National & Local Government Officers' Association* [1991] ICR 359, EAT).

15.53

Except in well-defined circumstances, there is a general principle that, when assessing damages, credit must be given for benefits received. It has been held that this precept does not apply in wrongful dismissal claims, where the benefit is an accelerated pension (*Hopkins v Norcross plc* [1994] IRLR 11, CA). Where money is paid in lieu of notice, it may be net or gross at the employer's discretion. However, whatever the basis of the calculation, it is in fact a sum tendered to avoid a claim being pursued in the courts or in a tribunal. Similarly, if compensation for future loss of income is offered to avoid litigation, it may be gross or net (see Chapter 8, paras 8.43 to 8.45 (*Dietman v Brent LBC* [1988] IRLR 299, CA).

Interest on awards

15.54

Except for awards under the Equal Pay and Sex Discrimination Acts (see next paragraph), a respondent employer, who fails to pay an award of compensation to a former employee within 42 days of promulgation of the tribunal's decision, must pay interest on that award. The rate is the same as in the civil courts (*Source*: Employment Tribunals (Constitution & Rules of Procedure Regs 2001 (SIs 2001/1170 & 2001/1171)).

15.55

Interest on awards under the Sex Discrimination and Equal Pay Acts accrue from the day after promulgation of the tribunal or court's decision. But interest is not payable if the full amount of the award is paid within 14 days of promulgation. Further a tribunal is entitled at its discretion to make an order for the payment of interest from the date when it finds that the act of discrimination occurred, or from the mid-way point of the period in respect of which a financial award is calculated (*Source*: Sex Discrimination & Equal Pay (Remedies) Regulations 1993 (SI 1993/2798)).

INSOLVENCY OF EMPLOYER

15.56

An employer's insolvency will usually result in the automatic (possibly formal) dismissal of some or all of his workforce – given that the company or organisation in question must then cease trading and go into liquidation. In such circumstances, Part XII of the Employment Rights Act 1996 allows that an employee may recover the following amounts from the Secretary of State for Employment:

- up to eight weeks' arrears of pay (including guarantee payments, any payment due to the employee as a trade union official in respect of his or her right to paid time off work, payments due in respect of a period or periods of suspension on medical grounds, and any remuneration due to the employee under a 'protective award')(as to which latter, see Chapter 4, paras 4.52 to 4.55);

- payment for any statutory period of notice to which the employee was entitled to at the time of his (or her) dismissal;

- payment in respect of up to six weeks' holiday which accrued due to the employee during the period of 12 months immediately preceding the dismissal or insolvency;

- any 'basic award' of compensation for unfair dismissal awarded by an employment tribunal, which remains unpaid;

- any reasonable sum by way of reimbursement of a fee or premium paid by an apprentice or articled clerk.

For these purposes, the current (2003/04) upper limit on the amount of a week's pay is £260. Subject to that upper limit, the sum payable must represent the actual loss to the employee during the weeks in question, after deduction of tax and National Insurance contributions (*Westwood v Secretary of State for Employment* [1985] ICR 209, HL).

15.57
The Secretary of State will pay the amount due to an employee out of the National Insurance Fund; but is entitled to make a deduction in respect of any social security benefits received by the employee during the relevant period (*Westwood v Secretary of State for Employment* [1985] ICR 209, HL).

(*Source*: ERA 1996, Part XII.)

Complaints to an employment tribunal

15.58
A former employee may complain to an employment tribunal if the Secretary of State has refused to make a payment under the 'insolvency provisions' of the 1996 Act or has paid a smaller sum than was allegedly due. Such a complaint must be presented within three months of the refusal or underpayment. If the complaint is upheld, the tribunal will make a declaration that the Secretary of State is in default and will determine what amount ought to have been paid. A complaint presented 'out of time' will not be entertained unless the tribunal is satisfied that it was not reasonably practicable for it to have been presented within the prescribed three-month period (*Source*: ERA 1996, s.188).

WRITTEN STATEMENT OF REASONS FOR DISMISSAL

15.59
An employee who has been dismissed by his (or her) employer, and who had been continuously employed for one or more years ending with the effective date of termination of his contract of employment (as to which, see Chapter 3, paras 3.15 to 3.26), has the right to demand a written statement explaining the reasons for his dismissal. The written statement which must be provided within the next 14 days is admissible in evidence in any proceedings before an employment tribunal or court, as is the employer's refusal or failure to provide the statement (*Source*: ERA 1996, s.92).

Note: A woman who is dismissed (for whatever reason) while pregnant or on maternity leave, must be provided with written reasons for her dismissal, whether or not she has asked for such reasons. For further particulars, please turn to Chapter 14, paras 14.37 & 14.38).

15.60
It does not matter that the employee knew perfectly well why he (or she) had been dismissed: he has the right to have documentary proof of the reasons for his dismissal – which can be relied on should the employee decide to present a complaint of unfair dismissal to an employment tribunal (*McBrearty v Thompson t/a Highfield Mini-Market*, 9 April 1991, EAT).

15.61
The employer should explain to a former employee, in broad terms, what were the true reasons for the latter's dismissal. An employer, who wishes to rely on the contents of a letter previously sent to the employee setting out those reasons, is entitled to do so, provided he (or she) encloses a copy of that earlier letter with the written statement. There will be a technical breach if he fails to do so. It matters not that the reason for dismissal was good or wholly misconceived – provided it was the true reason operating on the employer's mind (*Gilham v Kent County Council* [1985] ICR 233, CA; and *Harvard Securities plc v Younghusband* [1990] IRLR 16, EAT).

15.62
If an employer tells a former employee that the reason for his (or her) dismissal was redundancy, when, in truth, the employee was dismissed for being a trouble-maker (and might well have been validly dismissed for that reason), the employee will be entitled to be compensated. Although not obliged to provide detailed reasons, an employer must provide information sufficient to enable the employee to understand what prompted the dismissal. Particular events on which reliance is placed should be identified, eg 'You were dismissed for misconduct arising out of the events of March 3, when you punched such-and-such a manager on the nose' (*Walls v The City Bakeries*, 24 February 1987, EAT).

15.63

Where there is a genuine dispute over whether an employee had been dismissed or resigned, and the employer reasonably believes that there had been no dismissal, a failure to supply written reasons will generally not attract any remedy (*Broomsgrove v Eagle Alexander Ltd* [1981] IRLR 127, EAT; and *Banks v Lavin*, 20 October 1989, EAT).

Complaint to an employment tribunal

15.64

An employer who unreasonably refuses or fails to provide a written statement of reasons for dismissal (eg there being evidence of a deliberate or intentional withholding of the information), will be ordered to pay the employee two weeks' gross pay, without limit as to the amount (*Ladbroke Entertainments Ltd v Clark* [1987] ICR 585, EAT) (*Source*: ERA 1996, s.93).

15.65

A complaint that an employer has refused or failed to provide written reasons for dismissal must be presented to the Secretary to the Tribunals within three months of the 'effective date of termination' of the employee's contract of employment (as to which, see Chapter 3, paras 3.15 to 3.26). A complaint presented 'out of time' will not normally be heard unless the tribunal is satisfied that it was not reasonably practicable for the complainant to have acted sooner (*Source*: ERA 1996, s.93).

RIGHTS TO TRADE UNION MEMBERSHIP

15.66

A trade union may not lawfully deny membership to an individual, or expel an existing member – *unless* that individual or member does not belong (or no longer belongs) to the particular trade, industry or profession or occupation which the union represents. But an applicant or member may be excluded or expelled if he (or she) does not live (or no longer lives) in that part of Great Britain in which the trade union operates or does not work for (or no longer works for) the only employer with whom the union has dealings. Conduct is another factor which may justify the exclusion or expulsion of a would-be or existing member – so long as that conduct does *not* relate to membership or non-membership of another trade union, or to employment with a particular employer (or at a particular place), or to his or her membership or non-membership of a particular political party.

15.67

Nor can an individual or existing member be excluded or expelled from membership for failing to support (or for voicing opposition to) a strike organised by the union itself or by another trade union, or for doing (or refusing to do) something for which he (or she) could not lawfully be disciplined by any other trade union (*Source*: TULRA 1992, ss 174 to 177).

Time limits and penalties

15.68
A person who believes that he (or she) has been unlawfully excluded or expelled from a trade union may present a complaint to the Secretary to the Tribunals within six months of the exclusion or expulsion or, if that is not reasonably practicable, within such further period as is reasonable (*Source*: TULRA 1992, s.175).

15.69
If an employment tribunal finds such a complaint to be well-founded, it will make a declaration to that effect. The complainant then has six months within which to apply for an award of compensation to be paid to him (or her) by the union (but must not apply until four weeks have elapsed from the date of the tribunal's declaration). If the trade union admits or re-admits the complainant to membership within those four weeks, the union will be ordered to pay the complainant such compensation as it considers to be just and equitable in the circumstances, subject to a minimum of £5,700. If the trade union has not admitted or re-admitted the complainant within those four weeks, the complainant may apply directly to the Employment Appeal Tribunal (EAT). In such circumstances, the EAT will order the trade union to pay compensation of between £5,700 and £61,300 (being the aggregate of the current (2003/04) maximum basic and compensatory awards for unfair dismissal). Either award of compensation may be reduced to the extent that the complainant caused or contributed to his (or her) exclusion or expulsion but *not* so as to reduce the award to below £5,700 (*Source*: TULRA 1992, s.176).

UNJUSTIFIED DISCIPLINARY ACTION BY UNION

15.70
Akin to the right of a member not to be unjustifiably expelled from membership of his (or her) trade union is his right under sections 64 and 65 of the Trade Union & Labour Relations (Consolidation) Act 1992 not to be unjustifiably disciplined by that same trade union (eg by withdrawal of benefits, suspension, imposition of a fine, or whatever):

• for failing to participate in or support (or for voicing opposition to) a strike or other industrial action (whether by members of the union or by others); or

- for refusing to contravene, for a purpose connected with such a strike or other industrial action, a requirement imposed by or under the contract of employment; or

- for making a *bona fide* assertion (whether before a court or tribunal, or otherwise) that his union (including any official or representative or a trustee of its property) has contravened, or is proposing to contravene a requirement which is, or is thought to be, imposed by or under the rules of the union or any other agreement or by or under an Act of Parliament (whenever passed) or any rule of law; or

- for encouraging or assisting a person to comply with his (or her) contract of employment; or

- for contravening a requirement imposed by (or in consequence of) a determination which infringes his (or her) or another individual's right not to be unjustifiably disciplined; or

- for failing to agree, or for withdrawing agreement, to a deduction from his (or her) wages (under a check-off arrangement) in respect of his trade union dues; or

- for resigning (or proposing to resign) from the union or from another union, or for becoming or proposing to become (or for refusing to become or for being) a member of another union; or

- for working with (or proposing to work with) individuals who are not members of the union, or who are (or are not) members of another union; or

- for working with, or proposing to work with, an employer who employs (or has employed) individuals who are not members of the union or who are (or are not) members of another union; or

- for requiring the union to do anything which the member in question is entitled to require the union to do by or under any provision of the Trade Union & Labour Relations (Consolidation) Act 1992.

(*Source*: TULRA 1992, ss 64 & 65.)

A recommendation from a branch to the central committee that a member should be expelled from a union does not fall within the meaning of unjustifiable discipline. There must be a final decision to expel the member (*Transport & General Workers Union v Webber* [1990] ICR 711, EAT).

Time limits and remedies

15.71
A claim must be presented to the Secretary to the Tribunals within three months of the matter complained about, or if that is not reasonably practicable,

within such further period as is considered reasonable in the circumstances. An attempt to pursue an internal appeal or otherwise attempt to have the union decision reversed or reconsidered might be treated as a valid ground for delay (*Source*: TULRA 1992, ss 66 & 67).

15.72
The tribunal will make a declaration that there has been unlawful disciplinary action, and:

- provided the union agrees to withdraw the disciplinary action, will award such compensation as it considers to be 'just and equitable in the circumstances, subject to a maximum of £61,300 (being the agggregate of the current [2003/04] maximum basic and compensatory awards for unfair dismissal);

- where the union refuses to withdraw the disciplinary action, or fails to take all steps necessary for the reversal of anything done for the purpose of giving effect to the unlawful action, then the matter must go to the Employment Appeal Tribunal (EAT). Compensation is the same as above, subject to a minimum basic award of £5,700 (2003/04) (*ibid* s.67(8));

but, in both instances, it will be subject to reduction for contributory fault (see Chapter 5, paras 5.146 to 5.152) or for a failure to mitigate loss (see Chapter 2, paras 2.57 to 2.64) (*Source*: TULRA 1992, s.176). An appeal from the decision of an employment tribunal (on a point of law) lies to the Employment Appeal Tribunal.

15.73
There must be full compliance with these requirements. A union wrote to the applicant's employers notifying them that he had been expelled and that no further deductions in respect of union dues were to be taken from his pay or sent to them. The expulsion of the applicant was reversed, but no action was taken on the notification. This resulted in an award of compensation by the EAT (*Leese v Food From Britain*, 4 March 1991, EAT).

15.74
A union expelled some of its members who had refused to take part in industrial action. Thereafter, members of the local branch had written objectionable articles about them to frighten them. It was held that £2,250 (the minimum at that time) was the appropriate measure of damages for injury to feelings. The remedy had to relate to the expulsion itself – not to any subsequent conduct on the part of others (*Bradley & Others v National & Local Government Officers Association* [1991] ICR 359, EAT).

UNLAWFUL REFUSAL OF ACCESS TO EMPLOYMENT

15.75
It is unlawful for a prospective employer (whether under pressure from a trade union or otherwise) to refuse to employ a person either because that person is, or is not, a member of a trade union or because he (or she) has refused to accept a requirement to become or remain a member of a particular union, or of any union. It is also unlawful to require a job applicant (or new recruit) to accept a deduction from his or her) pay or to demand a payment from any such person as an alternative to trade union membership (*Source*: TULRA 1992, s.137).

15.76
It is similarly unlawful for an employment agency to refuse to provide its services to people who are (or are not) members of a trade union or to accept instructions from an employer not to supply job applicants who fall within either category. It is also unlawful to publish an advertisement (or notice circulated privately) which indicates, or might reasonably be understood as indicating, an intention to discriminate on trade union grounds. A subsequent refusal to interview (or advance the name of a job applicant) who responds to such an advertisement will be deemed to be unlawful discrimination on trade union grounds (*Source*: TULRA 1992, s.138).

15.77
These provisions do not apply to employment (or access to employment) in relation to police service; to service as a member of the naval, military or air forces of the Crown; to employment as master or as a member of the crew of a fishing vessel where the employee is remunerated only by a share in the profits or gross earnings of the vessel; to employment wholly outside Great Britain; to employment on a ship registered at a port outside Great Britain; or to employment in respect of which a Minister of the Crown has issued a certificate exempting that employment for the purpose of safeguarding national security (*Source*: TULRA 1992, ss 274, 275, 280, 284 & 285).

15.78
A person denied access to employment because of his (or her) membership or non-membership of a trade union may present a complaint to an employment tribunal, but must do so within three months of the alleged unlawful act (or, if that is not reasonably practicable, within such further period as the tribunal considers reasonable). If the complaint is upheld, the offending employer and/or employment agency (and/or a person or trade union joined or sisted to the proceedings) will be ordered to pay compensation of up to £53,500. An employment tribunal may also recommend that the respondents do what needs to be done to put matters to rights for the complainant. If that recommendation is ignored, the

tribunal may increase the amount of compensation payable (*Source*: TULRA 1992, ss 139 to 142).

Access to employment denied on grounds of sex, race or disability

15.79
It is unlawful for an employer to discriminate against a job applicant – on grounds of sex, marital status, gender reassignment, race, colour, national or ethnic origins, nationality or disability – by refusing to interview, short-list or employ any such person regardless of that person's qualifications, experience or evident suitability for the vacancy in question. It is also unlawful to discriminate against such a person by offering less favourable terms and conditions of employment or by withholding opportunities for promotion, transfer or training. For further particulars, please turn to Chapters 11, 12 and 13.

REHABILITATION OF OFFENDERS

15.80
People who break the law, and who are convicted and sentenced by the courts, will often have difficulty securing employment. Some offences (eg speeding offences) will not necessarily stand in the way of a person who is looking for work; others (street crimes, shoplifting, etc) will undoubtedly have a more serious effect. A man with three serious convictions for fraud is unlikely to be offered employment as a cashier in a bank or financial insti-tution. A woman with a string of convictions for shoplifting would probably have some difficulty securing employment as a floorwalker or shop assistant in a department store.

15.81
The Rehabilitation of Offenders Act 1974 (ROOA 1974) acknowledges that it would be unfair for a convicted person to be forever precluded from obtaining employment in the field of his (or her) choice. The Act provides for the rehabilitation of persons who have been convicted of certain crimes, so long as they do not commit further offences during a specified 'rehabili-tation period'. At the end of that period, their convictions become 'spent'. This means that, at the end of the 'rehabilitation period' (five, seven or ten years, as appropriate – see *Note* below) such a person need not disclose details of the conviction in question when applying for work, filling out job applications or answering questions at an employment interview. In short, a person with a 'spent' conviction may effectively lie at an employment interview if asked the question: 'Have you been convicted of any offences?' (*Source*: ROOA 1974, s.4).

Note: Details of the rehabilitation periods for particular sentences, and for certain sentences confined to young persons, are to be found in s.5, Tables A and B, of the 1974 Act.

15.82
It is unfair of an employer to dismiss an employee on discovery that the employee in question had refused to reveal details of a 'spent' conviction when first recruited – unless the employee falls within one of the *Exceptions* listed overleaf. An employer who uses fraud, dishonesty or a bribe, to uncover details of an employee's previous convictions, is guilty of an offence and liable on summary conviction to a fine of up to £5,000 and/or imprisonment for a term not exceeding six months (*Source*: ROOA 1974, s.9).

Sentences excluded from rehabilitation

15.83
Sentences excluded from rehabilitation under the 1974 Act are:

- a sentence of imprisonment for life;

- a sentence of imprisonment, youth custody, detention in a young offender institution, or corrective training, for a term exceeding thirty months;

- a sentence of preventive detention;

- a sentence of detention during Her Majesty's pleasure, or for life, or under section 205(2) or (3) of the Criminal Procedure (Scotland) Act 1975, or for a term exceeding 30 months, passed under section 53 of the Children & Young Persons Act 1933 (young offenders convicted of grave crimes) or under section 206 of the said Act of 1975 (detention of children convicted on indictment) or a corresponding court-martial punishment;

- a sentence of custody for life.

Exceptions

15.84
But there are exceptions to the general rule. The right to conceal details of 'spent' convictions does *not* apply to solicitors, barristers, advocates, legal executives, chartered (or certified) accountants, actuaries, teachers in higher education, doctors, chartered psychologists, dentists, dental hygienists (or dental auxiliaries), veterinary surgeons, nurses, midwives, ophthalmic opticians, dispensing opticians, pharmaceutical chemists, teachers, persons in professions to which the Professions Supplementary to Medicine Act 1960 apply, registered osteopaths or registered chiropractors. The same applies to any office or employment concerned with the provision to persons aged

under 18 of accommodation, care, leisure and recreational facilities, schooling, social services, supervision or training, being an office or employment of such a kind as to enable the holder to have access, in the course of his (or her) normal duties to such persons, and any other office or employment the normal duties of which are carried out wholly or partly on the premises where such provision takes place.

15.85
'Spent' convictions must also be disclosed in relation to judicial appointments, appointments in the police force (or as a traffic warden), the ownership of an independent school, dealerships in securities, and to the managers (and trustees) of unit trust schemes. The same applies to regulated employments (eg to persons dealing in firearms), and to any person applying to the police or to a court of summary jurisdiction for a licence to keep explosives. A person seeking a Gaming Board Licence must also reveal details of any and all convictions, 'spent' or otherwise (*Sources*: ROOA 1974; Rehabilitation of Offenders Act 1974 (Exceptions) Order 1975 (SI 1975/1023); the Rehabilitation of Offenders Act 1974 (Exceptions) (Amendment) Order 1986 (SI 1986/1249)); and the Rehabilitation of Offenders Act 1974 (Exceptions) (Amendment) Order 2002 (SI 2002/441).

TRADE UNION RECOGNITION

15.86
If an employer recognises an independent trade union to any extent, for the purpose of collective bargaining, the union acquires certain rights, such as the right to be consulted on redundancy dismissals. The officials and members of that union likewise acquire the right to paid/unpaid time off work for trade union duties and activities, discussed earlier in this chapter. Collective bargaining means negotiations relating to or connected with one or more of the matters specified in Chapter 7 (at para. 7.17). A recognition agreement union does not need to be in writing or be formally agreed (*Source*: TULRA 1992, ss 168, 178, 188 & 196).

15.87
It is a question of fact and degree whether there is 'recognition'. It requires 'mutuality, that is to say, that the employer acknowledges the role of union' which 'may be... express or implied'. The course of conduct must be 'clear and unequivocal... over a period', and 'there may be partial recognition, that is to say, recognition in certain respects but not in others' (*NUGSAT v Albury Brothers Ltd* [1978] ICR 62, EAT (affirmed on appeal, [1979] ICR 86, CA). Mere discussion with a union over matters specified in para. 7.17 is not sufficient; it must be established that an employer is willing to negotiate with a view to reaching agreement in one of those areas.

15.88

An employer was a member of a trade association. The latter had effected agreements with a trade union relating to the terms and conditions for those working in the trade. The employer used it as the basis of an agreement with his own workforce. It was held that that alone was insufficient to establish 'recognition' (*Peart & Co Ltd v TASS Craft Section*, 16 December 1988, EAT).

Compulsory recognition

15.89

Since the coming into force on 6 June 2000 of Part 1, Chapter 5A and Schedule A1 to the Trade Union & Labour Relations (Consolidation) Act 1992 – inserted by s. 1 and Schedule A1 to the Employment Relations Act 1999 – employers with 21 or more people on the payroll are duty-bound to respond to a valid request for recognition from an independent trade union. Such a request will be admissible if (*inter alia*) 10 per cent of the workers in the proposed bargaining unit are members of the trade union in question. The request may be rejected if the employer has reason to believe that a majority of workers in the proposed bargaining unit would not be in favour of the union negotiating terms and conditions of employment on their behalf.

15.90

Should the trade union be dissatisfied with that rejection, it may refer the matter for adjudication by the Central Arbitration Committee (CAC). If the CAC is persuaded that more than 50 per cent of the workers constituting the relevant bargaining unit are in favour of recognition, it will make a compulsory recognition order (binding on both parties, and enforceable by the courts). If not so persuaded, the CAC will order that a secret ballot be conducted and will appoint an independent scrutineer to oversee the conduct of the ballot. If a majority of the workers who cast their votes in the ballot vote in favour of recognition, and that majority comprises at least 40 per cent of those entitled to vote, the CAC will declare the union to be recognised as having collective bargaining rights in respect of pay, working hours and holidays. A CAC booklet explaining the rules and procedures attendant upon a trade union request for recognition (entitled *Trade Union Recognition & Derecognition*), may either be accessed and downloaded from the CAC's Web site: www.cac.gov.uk/publications/publicathead.htm or may be obtained free of charge (together with related publications) from the CAC's London Office on 020 7251 9747.

TRANSFER OF AN UNDERTAKING

15.91

Under the Transfer of Undertakings (Protection of Employment) Regulations 1981 (SI 1981/1794, as amended), an employer proposing the sale or transfer or his (or her) business (or part of that business), or the acquisition of another business, is duty-bound to consult representatives of any recognised independent trade union and/or employee-elected representatives about his proposals and the effect the relevant transfer is likely to have on affected employees. Long enough before the transfer, to enable purposeful consultations to take place, the employer must inform those representatives of:

- the fact that the relevant transfer is to take place;

- when, approximately, it is to take place, and the reasons for it;

- the legal, economic and social implications of the transfer for the affected employees;

- the measures which he (or she) envisages he will, in connection with the transfer, take in relation to those employees or, if he envisages that no measures will be so taken, that fact; and

- if the employer is the transferor, the measures which the transferee envisages he (or she) will, in connection with the transfer, take in relation to such of those employees as become employees of the transferee after the transfer or, if he envisages that no measures will be so taken, that fact.

15.92
The defence of 'not reasonably practicable' is available to an employer who fails to forewarn and consult the relevant employee representatives. For a breach, the 'appropriate compensation' is a maximum of 13 weeks' pay for every affected employee (*Source*: TUPE Regs 1981, Reg. 10(11)). For further particulars, please turn to Chapter 22.

TRADE UNION DUES AND THE 'CHECK-OFF' SYSTEM

15.93
An employer must not deduct trade union dues (ie, membership subscriptions) from a worker's pay (in accordance with check-off arrangements previously agreed with a trade union) unless he has received written authorisation from each of the workers concerned (*per* section 68, Trade Union & Labour Relations (Consolidation) Act 1992, as amended by the Deregulation (Deduction from Pay of Union Subscriptions) Order 1998).

Note: Itemised pay statements necessarily issued to employees must identify deductions in respect of trade union dues (as to which, please see paras 15.38 to 15.42 above).

15.94
Before 23 June 1998, when the Deregulation Order referred to in the previous paragraph came into force, a written notice authorising the deduction of

union dues from a worker's pay had to be renewed once every three years. This is no longer necessary. Any written authorisation given before 23 July 1998 (a so-called 'preserved authorisation') which has not yet expired remains valid for a period of three years from the date on which it was given (unless withdrawn in the meantime). But any renewal of that authorisation will be subject to the new arrangements.

15.95
An employer may write in the following terms to any worker of his who has signed a preserved authorisation (as outlined in the Schedule to the 1998 Order):

DEDUCTION OF TRADE UNION SUBSCRIPTIONS FROM PAY

Following the coming into force of the Deregulation (Deduction from Pay of Union Subscriptions) Order 1998, you no longer need to re-authorise payments of trade union subscriptions by 'check-off' (deduction from pay by your employer) every three years and your employer need not give you advance written notice of any increase in the rate of deductions. The law continues to require your written authorisation before check-off can start and you continue to have the right to stop paying by check-off at any time, by giving notice in writing to your employer.

This notice affects you if you pay your union subscription by check-off and you gave your authorisation before the date on which the Order came into force.

If you are content for the new arrangements to apply to you, you need do nothing.

If, however, you wish the previous arrangements to continue to apply to you, you must give notice to that effect in writing to your employer at [*name and address of employer*] within 14 days of receiving this notice.

If you do so, your current authorisation will expire three years after you gave it, but any subsequent authorisation will be subject to the new arrangements.

15.96
If a worker writes to his (or her) employer asking him to stop deducting union dues from his wages or salary, the employer must act on that request on the worker's next pay day or (if the request was not received in time) as soon as 'reasonably practicable' after that pay day (*ibid*).

15.97
Under section 68A of TULRA 1992, a worker may complain to an employment tribunal that his employer has deducted union dues from his pay in contravention of these requirements. The complaint must be presented

within the period of three months beginning with the date on which the unauthorised deduction was made or (if there have been a number of such deductions) the date on which the last of those deductions was made. If the complaint is upheld, the tribunal will make a declaration to that effect and will order the employer to make restitution.

Political fund contributions

15.98

Although content to have his membership subscription (or union dues) deducted from his pay packet under a 'check-off' arrangement, a worker may be less than happy about contributing to the union's political fund. To ensure that no such contributions are deducted from his (or her) pay, the worker must first write to his trade union in the following terms (*ibid* section 84):

To: (Name of Trade Union)

POLITICAL FUND (EXEMPTION NOTICE)

I give notice that I object to contributing to the Political Fund of the Union, and am in consequence exempt, in manner provided by Chapter VI of Part I of the Trade Union & Labour Relations (Consolidation) Act 1992, from contributing to that fund.

Signature of Member:

Address: ....Date: ....

The next step is to write to his employer confirming that he has written to his trade union in the terms outlined above and certifying that he is exempt from any obligation to contribute to his trade union's political fund. The employer must respond on the first payday on which it is reasonably practicable for him to do so – by seeing to it that no amount representing any such contribution is deducted from the worker's pay (*ibid* section 86).

15.99

A worker, who has instructed his (or her) employer to cease deducting political fund contributions from his pay, may complain to an employment tribunal if his employer has ignored his instructions or has responded by refusing to deduct *any* union dues from the worker's pay (while continuing to operate a 'check-off' arrangement for other members of the same trade union). If the complaint is upheld, the tribunal will make a declaration to that effect and will order the employer to repay the amount wrongly deducted from the worker's pay. Non-compliance with the terms of such an order (within the next four weeks) will prompt a further complaint to a tribunal and an order directing the employer to pay the worker the equivalent of two weeks' pay (*ibid* section 87, as substituted by section 6 of the Employment Rights (Dispute Resolution) Act 1998).

15.100
Breach of these provisions entitles an employee to apply to an employment tribunal for restitution. The application (or complaint) must be 'presented' within three months of the relevant unlawful deduction, or within such further period as the tribunal considers reasonable. If the tribunal finds the complaint to be well-founded, it will order the employer to repay the amount in question.

DEDUCTIONS FROM PAY

15.101
As a rule, an employer has no right to deduct money from the wages or salary of an employee (or to demand a payment in respect of breakages, cash shortages, damaged goods, or whatever) without that employee's express permission. There are, of course, exceptions to this rule, which are explained below.

15.102
Any such deduction (or demand for payment) will be void and unenforceable (and the monies recoverable) unless:

- the employer's right to make that deduction (or demand for payment), and the circumstances in which such a deduction (or demand) might be made, is clearly laid down in writing in the employee's contract of employment (either the written statement of terms of employment issued in accordance with sections 1 to 7 of the Employment Rights Act 1996 or in some associated document, signed and dated), a copy of which must have been supplied to the employee in advance of any such deduction (or demand); or

- the employee had previously given his (or her) consent in writing to the making of that deduction (or demand).

Any term in a contract of employment (or related document) which authorises the employer to make deductions (or demands for payment) will apply only to incidents or events which occurred *after* the employee's authorisation or agreement was given or obtained. In short, an employer cannot require an employee to give retrospective consent to the deduction of money from his or her pay (or to make a payment) in respect of an incident (such as a breakage or cash shortage) which occurred before that consent was given.

The provisions are to be found in Part II of the Employment Rights Act 1996 ('*Protection of Wages*').

Exceptions

15.103
The obvious exceptions are deductions from pay authorised or demanded by statute. An employer does not need an employee's prior written consent before deducting PAYE income tax or National Insurance contributions from the employee's wages or salary.

Furthermore, the rule restricting the right of an employer to deduct money from an employee's pay (or to make a demand for payment) does not apply:

- to the recovery or reimbursement of overpaid wages or salary, or to any overpayment in respect of business expenses incurred by the employee in the course of his (or her) employment;

- to third party requests for deductions (eg pension contributions, etc) in accordance with any relevant provision in the employee's contract of employment;

- to attachment of earnings (or garnishee) orders made by a court under the Attachment of Earnings Act 1971 or related legislation;

- to deductions (or payments) made (or required) in respect of an employee's participation in a strike or other form of industrial action;

- to deductions or demands for payment in response to a court or tribunal order requiring the payment of a specified amount to the employee's employer.

(*Source*: ERA 1996, ss 13 & 14.)

15.104
The expression 'wages' (or, for that matter 'salary') applies to all emoluments, however classified, including shift allowances, overtime payments, bonuses, commission, sickness and holiday pay, etc – but not to advances, loans, expenses, pensions or redundancy payments or any other payments made other than in the employee's capacity as an employee. It also covers sums 'whether payable under the employee's contract or otherwise'. It has been held to embrace discretionary but legitimately-expected commission payments, unless there is evidence that the agreement to make such payments has been withdrawn (*Kent Management Services Ltd v Butterfield* [1992] ICR 272, EAT).

15.105
The correct way to assess deductions from pay in respect of absences from work due to industrial action is to approach the problem on a 'breach of

contract' basis. For how many days' work annually did the employers pay the employee his (or her) salary? If the employee was contracted to work 200 days a year, but was absent on strike for ten of those 200 days, the appropriate deduction would be one-twentieth (or five per cent) of the employee's annual salary (*Smith & Others v London Borough of Bromley*, 5 April 1991, Cty Ct).

15.106

The non-payment of any sum due and payable to an employee would be deemed to be an unauthorised deduction and, therefore, recoverable under Part II of the Employment Rights Act 1996. To escape liability the employer would have to satisfy an employment tribunal that the deduction fell within the category of lawful deductions listed in para. 15.97 above (*Delaney v Staples (t/a De Montfort Recruitment)* [1992] ICR 483, HL).

15.107

Further, where there is a dispute over the justification of a deduction made within the Act, a tribunal will have to decide whether it is sustainable. For instance, if an employer deducts the cost of repairs to a motor car, for which an employee is liable, the sum must be justified and reasonable. Any figure above that sum is irrecoverable (*Fairfield Ltd v Skinner* [1992] ICR 836, EAT).

15.108

An employment tribunal has jurisdiction to entertain complaints under Part II of the Employment Rights Act 1996. Where it finds a complaint to be well-founded it will make a declaration to that effect and will order the employer to repay the unlawful deduction. Such a complaint must be 'presented' to a tribunal within three months of the alleged unlawful deduction or (if the deduction is one of a series of such deductions) within three months of the last of those deductions; or, if that is not reasonably practicable, within a reasonable period thereafter.

15.109

An employment tribunal also has jurisdiction to deal with 'breach of employment contract' claims, including claims arising out of an employer's failure to give the correct notice of termination ('wrongful dismissal'). That jurisdiction is shared with the County Court, although claims for damages in excess of £25,000 are still the exclusive preserve of the County Court.

15.110

The wording of Part II of the 1996 Act (which has replaced similar provisions in the now-repealed Wages Act 1986) can lead to curious results. If a tribunal has ruled that an employer had unlawfully made a deduction in respect of a loan made to an employee, because he had not obtained the employee's prior written authorisation to the making of that deduction, the employer will not only be ordered to repay the money deducted but will also be debarred from recovering the deducted amount in any other proceedings before a civil court (*Delaney v Staples (t/a De Montfort Recruitment)* [1992] ICR 483, HL).

15.111
An employee may refuse to accept any unilateral variation in the terms and conditions of his (or her) employment, eg a cut in the rate of pay. Because an employer can impose such a variation, an employee has the choice either to accept the repudiation (by resigning and pursuing a complaint of unfair constructive dismissal) or by continuing to work under protest. This happened to an employee who was shortly afterwards made redundant. The EAT held that he could recover the amount that had been unlawfully 'deducted' from his wages. By protesting about the cut in his pay, the employee had not 'affirmed' the variation in his contract (*MacRuary v Washington Irvine Ltd*, 17 March 1994, EAT).

15.112
If an employee has certified to his (or her) employer that he has resigned his membership of a trade union, the employer must cease deducting union dues from the employee wages on the next payday after notification, or as soon as reasonably practicable thereafter. An employer's failure to respond will be deemed to be a contravention of the employee's rights under Part II of the Employment Rights Act 1996, thereby entitling the employee to apply to the tribunal for reimbursement of the amount (or amounts) unlawfully deducted (*Source*: TULRA 1992, s.68).

Cash shortages and stock deficiencies

15.113
As is the case with other types of deductions or demands for payment, an employer cannot legitimately deduct money (or demand a payment) in respect of cash shortages or stock deficiencies unless his (or her) right to do so and the circumstances in which he can exercise that right are clearly and unequivocally laid down in the employee's contract of employment. Alternatively, the employee must have agreed in writing to the making of any such deduction or demand *before* any incident or event which would otherwise prompt the employer to make such a deduction or demand for payment. In other words, any consent given after the event is void and unenforceable (*Source*: ERA 1996, ss 17 to 21).

15.114
The amount deducted from an employee's pay packet on a particular payday must not exceed one-tenth of the *gross* wages or salary due to the employee on that payday. The same rule applies whatever the amount of money owed, even if the employer has deducted a number of cash shortages or stock

shortages directly attributable to the same employee. In short, the total amount recoverable may have to be recovered by a series of deductions from the employee's pay packet (none of which may exceed the prescribed maximum 10 per cent on any one payday).

15.115

A *demand for payment* in respect of a particular cash shortage or stock deficiency must be preceded by a letter or memorandum addressed to the employee in question informing him (or her) of the total amount payable in respect of that cash shortage or stock deficiency and of the payday (or sequence of paydays) on which such payments are to be made. Second and subsequent demands for payment must also be made in writing and must be given on the payday on which payment is required. Any demand for payment on a day other than a payday will be null and void. As with deductions from pay, the amount payable by an employee on any one payday must not exceed one-tenth of the employee's gross pay on that payday (*Source*: ERA 1996, s.18).

15.116

Furthermore, an employer is debarred from making any deduction (or demand from payment) in respect of a cash shortage or stock deficiency which has remained undetected for 12 or more months. In other words, an employer has 12 months within which to recover (or begin to recover) the amount of any previously undetected cash shortage or stock deficiency. Any deductions (or demands) made 'out of time' will be unlawful and recoverable before an employment tribunal (*Source*: ERA 1996, ss 18(2) & (3) and 20(2) & (3)).

Monies outstanding on the termination of employment

15.117

Should a person in retail employment resign or be dismissed before he (or she) has repaid the full amount of any monies owed to the employer in respect of cash shortages or stock deficiencies, the employer may (in accordance with a previously-agreed arrangement, *but not otherwise*) either deduct all or part of the amount outstanding from any final payment of wages or salary due to the employee, or demand repayment of that outstanding amount. In the event of a refusal or failure to pay, the employee may have no option but to sue for recovery in the ordinary courts (*Source*: ERA 1996, s.22).

Complaints to tribunals

15.118

If an employer has made an unauthorised deduction from an employee's wages or salary, the employee may present a claim for reimbursement to an employment tribunal. The complaint or claim must be 'presented' within three months of the date on which the relevant unauthorised deduction or payment was made. The time limit may be extended where it was not reasonably practicable for the employee to present his (or her) complaint within the prescribed three months, and it was done as soon as reasonably practicable thereafter (*Source*: ERA 1996, ss 23 to 26). If the employee's complaint is upheld, the tribunal will make a declaration to that effect and will order the employer to reimburse the full disputed amount. In certain cases, the tribunal will direct that any amount owed to the employee in respect of a cash deficiency or stock shortage is to be reduced by the amount of any unauthorised deduction or payment, in spite of the fact that the employer had already been ordered by the tribunal to reimburse that same amount to the employee (*Source*: ERA 1996, s.23).

15.119
As with a number of other statutory rights in employment, an employee, who believes that one or other of his (or her) statutory rights have been infringed, may complain to an employment tribunal without having to resign his (or her) job in order to do so. If the employer responds to any such challenge to his authority by dismissing that employee (or selecting him or her for redundancy), the dismissal will be automatically unfair (regardless of the age or length of service of the employee in question) and will almost certainly result in the employer being ordered to pay a substantial amount of compensation (*Source*: ERA 1996, s.104). For further particulars, please turn to Chapter 5 (paras 5.44 & 5.45).

REFERENCES FOR FORMER EMPLOYEES

15.120
An employer is under no legal obligation to provide an employee with a reference. If he (or she) does so, care should be taken not to provide a reference which is patently untrue. Indeed, it might be highly damaging to an employee's prospects if the reference is given out of vindictiveness or malice, or out of sheer incompetence. It is essential to provide a 'careful reference'. An employer is in a unique position to know the character, skill and diligence of a former employee.

15.121
A former employer provided an untrue reference for a former employee 'so strikingly bad as to amount to... a 'kiss of death' to his career in insurance'. It was held that there was a failure to exercise due care and skill in the preparation of the reference. This entitled the employee to compensation for the loss he had sustained (*Spring v Guardian Assurance plc & Others* [1994] ICR 596, HL).

15.122

Employers are duty-bound to provide written reasons for dismissal in certain circumstances (see paras 15.59 to 15.65 above). Problems could arise if a sympathetic reference contradicts the information provided in a written statement of reasons for dismissal. In *Castledine v Rothwell Engineering Ltd* [1973] IRLR 99, a dismissed employee produced a reference supplied by his former employer which stated that he 'had carried out his duties satisfactorily, often under difficult conditions'. The written statement of reasons for dismissal, supplied by the same employer, claimed that the employee had been dismissed on grounds of incompetence. When confronted with such conflicting evidence, the employment tribunal had no difficulty in concluding that the employee's dismissal had been unfair.

15.123

In *Coote v Granada Hospitality Ltd (No. 2)* [1999] ICR 943 EAT, a woman who had been denied a reference by her former employers (seemingly as a punishment for taking proceedings against them for alleged sex discrimination – which later prompted an out of court settlement) was awarded substantial damages because of her resultant inability to find work. Her former employer's actions (even after she had left their employment) amounted to unlawful victimisation under the Sex Discrimination Act 1975.

15.124

With the coming into force on 1 March 2000 of the Data Protection Act 1998, employers are duty-bound to disclose the contents of references (whether given in confidence or otherwise) issued by former employers, if asked to do so by an employee to whom any such reference relates. That duty does not, however, extend to references issued by the employer himself. For further information on 'data protection' issues, please turn to Chapter 21.

Fixed term employees

OVERVIEW

16.1

With the coming into force on 1 October 2002 of the Fixed-term Employees (Prevention of Less Favourable Treatment) Regulations 2002, employees on fixed-term or task-related contracts, or on contracts intended to come to an end on the occurrence or non-occurrence of a particular event, have the right not to be treated less favourably than comparable permanent employees working in the same establishment. In short, they have the right to be paid the same as those employees and to enjoy equivalent terms and conditions of employment (albeit, in appropriate circumstances, on a *pro rata* basis) including equal access to their employers' occupational pension schemes.

16.2

Fixed-term employees have the right also to be afforded equal access to opportunities for transfer, promotion or developmental training, and must be informed of any suitable vacancies that may arise within the establishment in which they work. On completion of four years' continuous employment under one or a series of consecutive fixed-term contracts, a fixed-term employee automatically acquires permanent status when that or the last of those contracts is renewed, unless their employers have objective reasons for continuing to employ that employee on a fixed-term basis. Amendments to the Social Security Contributions & Benefits Act 1992, and the Employment Rights Act 1996, mean that fixed-term employees engaged on contracts lasting (or expected to last for three months or less) now have access to certain rights previously denied to them under those statutes. Finally, the insertion of redundancy waiver clauses in fixed-term contracts of two years or more is no longer permissible.

16.3

The 2002 Regulations, which implement EU Council Directive 99/70/EC of 28 June 1999 'concerning the framework agreement on fixed-term work', give employees on fixed-term or task-related contracts the right to compare the terms and conditions on which they are employed with those enjoyed by comparable permanent employees working in the same establishment; to seek a written explanation from their employers for what they perceive to be less favourable treatment; and to refer the issue to an employment tribunal if dissatisfied with the explanation proffered by their employers. On completion of four years continuous under one or more consecutive fixed-term contracts, an employee automatically acquires permanent status within the employing organisation.

Regulations apply only to 'employees'

16.4
The reader should note that the 2002 Regulations apply to those workers only who are 'employees' in the strict legal sense of the word, that is to say, to persons employed under contracts of employment or service. They do *not* apply to workers who are hired on an 'as and when required' basis, who are free, without penalty, to accept or reject any offer of occasional or short-term work that happens their way. Nor do the regulations apply to students undergoing work experience, or to agency 'temps', to persons employed under fixed-term contracts that are contracts of apprenticeship; or to persons who are genuinely self-employed. That said, it is arguable that the majority of people (notably youngsters paying their way through college or university) who are engaged to work in factories, offices, super-markets, department stores, shops, hotels, restaurants, and the like, for an agreed number of weeks or months (or, in some instances, years) are not only employees, but fixed-term employees, given the clear evidence of mutuality of obligation and control that is characteristic of a contract of employment. The same applies to people engaged to replace permanent employees who are absent on maternity, parental or sick leave; and to employees hired to complete a particular task or project (for however short or long a period).

Meaning of 'fixed-term' contract

16.5
A 'fixed-term contract is a contract of employment that, under its provisions, is intended to terminate:

(a) on the expiry of a specific term (one, two, three months, or whatever);

(b) on the completion of a particular task (eg, the installation and testing of a new computer system);

(c) on the occurrence or non-occurrence of any other specific event (other than the achievement of normal retiring age) – such as the return to work of an employee after extended sick, maternity or adoption leave or (in the case of the non-occurrence of a specific event), the cancellation of a contract for goods or services.

Meaning of 'comparable permanent employee'

16.6

An employee is a comparable permanent employee in relation to a fixed-term employee if, at the time when the treatment that is alleged to be less favourable to the fixed-term employee takes place, both employees are employed by the same employer and are engaged in the same or broadly similar work (having regard, where relevant, to whether they have a similar level of qualifications and skills). Further, the permanent employee must either work or be based at the same establishment as the fixed-term employee or (if there is no comparable permanent employee working at that establishment who satisfies those requirements) works or is based at a different establishment within the same organisation and satisfies those requirements.

Objective grounds for less favourable treatment

16.7

As was indicated in the preamble above, fixed-term employees have the right to be paid the same as comparable permanent employees working in the same establishment and to be employed on the same terms and conditions as those other employees albeit, in appropriate circumstances, on a pro rata basis. If, for example, a comparable permanent employee has the right under his (or her) contract to six weeks' paid annual holidays, a fixed-term employee employed for just three months, would be entitled to one-and-a-half weeks' holidays during that three-month period. The same pro rata principle would need to be applied in relation to other benefits (such as the use of a company car, free medical insurance, permanent health insurance, access to an occupational pension scheme, annual rail season tickets, clothing allowances, low-interest loans, and so on).

16.8

Employers may justify the less favourable treatment of fixed-term employees if they can demonstrate to the satisfaction of an employment tribunal that there are objective grounds for such treatment, eg if the cost of offering a fixed-term employee a particular benefit is disproportionate when compared to the benefit the employee would receive, or that there is no practical way of offering the same benefits to a fixed-term employee on a pro rata basis. For example, an employer may be able to justify a refusal to offer a company car to a fixed-term employee on a three-month contract (whose comparator has a company car) if the cost of doing so is high and the employee's need to travel on business can be accommodated in some other more cost-effective way. Alternatively, less favourable treatment may be acceptable under the 2002 Regulations if the terms of a fixed-term employee's contract of employment, taken as a whole (or as a 'package'), are at least as favourable as those enjoyed by a comparable permanent employee working at the same establishment. In the final analysis, it will be for an employment tribunal to determine whether a fixed-term employee has been treated less favourably than a comparable permanent employee working in the same establishment. See also para. 16.19 (*Further information*) below.

Complaints of less favourable treatment

16.9
Fixed-term employees have the right under the 2002 Regulations to challenge their employers' refusal or failure to acknowledge their rights under those Regulations by demanding a written statement from their employers asking the latter to explain why they are being treated less favourably than comparable permanent employees. An employer's refusal or failure (without reasonable excuse) to provide that statement within the next 21 days, as well as the contents of any statement that *is* provided, is admissible in evidence in proceedings before an employment tribunal.

Amendments to primary legislation

16.10
Until 1 October 2002, access to certain statutory rights (payments under the Employers' Statutory Sick Pay Scheme) was denied to employees on fixed-term contracts lasting or expected to last for three months or less. With the concomitant repeal of these and related provisions in both the Social Security Contributions & Benefits Act 1992 and the Employment Rights Act 1996, all fixed-term employees, regardless of the duration (or expected duration) of their contracts, are now entitled (subject to the usual qualifying conditions) to statutory sick pay (SSP) when incapacitated for work; guarantee payments in respect of workless days; and payment of their normal wages or salary if suspended from work on medical grounds. Furthermore, they are henceforth required to give and are entitled to receive the prescribed minimum statutory notice to terminate their contracts of employment.

Redundancy waiver clauses no longer permissible

16.11
Section 197 of the 1996 Act has also been repealed. What this means is that the insertion of a redundancy waiver clause in a fixed-term contract lasting or expected to last for two or more years will be void and unenforceable unless the contract in question (or, in the case of successive renewals, the most recent renewal of that fixed-term contract) was agreed before 1 October 2002, and the agreement to exclude any right to a statutory redundancy payment was entered into and took effect before 1 October 2002.

Right to be informed of suitable vacancies

16.12
Fixed-term employees working alongside comparable permanent employees in the same establishment have the right to compete on equal terms when vacancies are advertised or posted on company notice boards. To that end, their employers are duty-bound to inform fixed-term employees (eg, by e-mail or internal memos) of suitable available vacancies within their establishments, and at the same time as those details are circulated or made available to permanent employees.

Acquiring permanent status

16.13
Under the 2002 Regulations, the use of successive fixed-term contracts will be limited to a maximum of four years. If a fixed-term contract (which may be a stand-alone contract or one of a succession of fixed-term contracts) is renewed after that four-year period (ignoring any period of continuous employment that began before 10 July 2002 – being the date on which the UK Government should have implemented Council Directive 99/70/EC), it will be treated in law as a permanent contract, unless its use for a longer period can be objectively justified. In such circumstances, the employee in question may write to his (or her) employer asking for written confirmation that he (or she) is now in permanent employment or setting-out objective reasons for his continued status as a fixed-term employee. If the employer does not respond in writing within the next 21 days, the employee may refer the matter to an employment tribunal for adjudication, without having to resign in order to do so.

16.14
With a view to preventing fixed-term employees building up sufficient service to qualify for statutory rights otherwise dependent on qualifying periods of continuous employment (eg, the right not to be unfairly dismissed) many employers operate a system of successive fixed-term contracts, with breaks of one or more weeks between each, in the (often mistaken) belief that this tactic destroys continuity of service. Section 212(3) of the Employment Rights Act 1996 clearly states that continuity is preserved if an employee is absent from work in circumstances such that, by arrangement or custom, he (or she) is regarded as continuing in the employment of his employer for any purpose. In *Ford v Warwickshire County Council* [1983] IRLR 126, the House of Lords held that the interval between the termination of a teacher's fixed-term contract at the end of every summer term and its renewal at the beginning of the autumn term did not break the continuity of his period of employment. If a fixed-term employee is informed (or is given to understand) on the termination of his

contract that he will be re-engaged under a second fixed-term contract in (sic) 'one of two weeks' time', the likelihood is that there will be no break in the continuity of his period of employment; the more so, if this happens more than once.

16.15

Notwithstanding the foregoing, the 2002 Regulations allow that, in certain situations, fixed-term employees will not acquire permanent status on completion of four years' continuous service under one or more fixed-term contracts if, under the terms of a collective or workforce agreement they and their employers accept that there are objective reasons for continuing to employ them under fixed-term or task-related contracts. Guidance notes produced by the Department of Trade & Industry (see para. 16.19 below) suggest that such an agreement would be appropriate in the case of actors, professional sports people, and similar, who are traditionally employed under a series of fixed-term contracts.

Termination and non-renewal of a limited-term contract

16.16

Section 95 of the Employment Rights Act 1996, as amended by the 2002 Regulations, states that the expiry and non-renewal (under the same contract) of a 'limited-term' contract – which is the collective term for a fixed-term contract, a 'task-related contract', and a contract that provides for its termination on the occurrence or non-occurrence of a particular event – is a dismissal in law. Subject to the usual age and service qualifications (ie, one year's continuous service and under normal retiring age at the effective date of termination), a person employed under a limited-term contract, that expires without being renewed (whether under the same contract or otherwise), may not only challenge the fairness of his or her dismissal before an employment tribunal but may also (in accordance with section 92 of the 1996 Act) request a written statement of reasons for dismissal, which latter must be supplied within the 14 days. It is as well to add that no such qualifying conditions apply if a fixed-term employee is dismissed or selected for redundancy simply for being a fixed-term employee or for presuming to assert his or her statutory rights under the 2002 Regulations.

Unfair dismissal and the right not to be subjected to a detriment

16.17

Fixed-term employees, who are dismissed, selected for redundancy, disciplined, victimised, or subjected to any other detriment, for asserting their rights under the 2002 Regulations, or for questioning or challenging any alleged infringement of those rights (either before an employment tribunal or otherwise), may complain (or yet again complain) to an employment tribunal and will be awarded appropriate compensation should their complaints be upheld. Such complaints must be presented within three months of the effective date of termination of their contracts.

Written statement of employment particulars

16.18
The written statement of initial employment particulars (or 'contract') necessarily issued to every new employee under sections 1 to 7 of the Employment Rights Act 1996 (see Chapter 9, paras 9.3 *et seq*) must, if the employment is not intended to be permanent, specify the period for which the employee's employment is expected to continue or, if it is for a fixed term, the date when it is to end.

Further information

16.19
A detailed Guide to the 2002 Regulations (including further guidance on the *pro rata* principle and advice on what may or may not constitute objective grounds for the less favourable treatment of fixed-term employees) may be accessed and downloaded from Web site www.dti.gov.uk/er/fixed/fixed-pl512.htm. The Guide in booklet form (Ref. PL512) may also be obtained from the DTI's Publications Orderline on 0870 1502 500, or by e-mail from publications@dti.gsi.gov.uk.

Part-time workers

OVERVIEW

17.1
With the coming into force on 7 April 2000 of the Part-time Workers (Prevention of Less Favourable Treatment) Regulations 2000 (SI 2000/1551), any part-time worker who is treated less favourably (or believes that he (or she) has been treated less favourably) than a comparable full-time worker is entitled to demand and receive from his employer a written statement explaining the reasons for such treatment. If dissatisfied with his employer's explanations, the part-time worker may seek redress from an employment tribunal. A part-timer who is dismissed, selected for redundancy or subjected to any other detriment for exercising or asserting his statutory rights under the Regulations, or for bringing proceedings before an employment tribunal, may complain (yet again) to a tribunal and will be awarded such compensation as the tribunal considers to be 'just and equitable' in all the circumstances.

17.2
The 2000 Regulations implement EC Directive 97/81/EC of 15 December 1997 'concerning the Framework Agreement on part-time work concluded by UNICE, CEEP and the ETUC', the purpose of which latter is 'to provide for the removal of discrimination against part-time workers and to improve the quality of part-time work'. It is also designed 'to facilitate the development of part-time work on a voluntary basis and to contribute to the flexible organisation of working time in a manner which takes into account the needs of employers and workers'.

Previous legislation

17.3
Since 6 February 1995 (when the Employment Protection (Part-time Employees) Regulations 1995 (SI 1995/31) came into force), part-time employees (that is to say, individuals employed under contracts of employment) have enjoyed the same statutory rights as their full-time contemporaries. In short, the qualifying period for access to those statutory rights is the same for part-timers as it is for full-time employees. The 1995 Regulations were prompted in large part by the decision of the House of Lords in *R v Secretary of State for Employment, ex parte the Equal Opportunities Commission* [1994] ICR 317.

Their Lordships held that the provisions of the then Employment Protection (Consolidation) Act 1978, which differentiated between part-time and full-time employees, contravened Article 119 (now Article 141) of the Treaty of Rome.

The 2000 Regulations

17.4
Unlike the 1995 Regulations (referred to in the previous paragraph), the 2000 Regulations apply to all 'workers'. In other words, they apply not only to persons employed under contracts of employment or apprenticeship but also to casual or seasonal workers, freelancers, agency 'temps', homeworkers and others who, while not 'employees' in the strict legal sense, undertake to do or perform personally any work or services for an employer – whether the contracts under which they are employed are express (that is to say, oral or in writing) or implied. Such a worker is usually said to be engaged under a contract *sui generis* (that is to say, 'of its own kind'). The Regulations do not, however, apply to individuals who are genuinely self-employed. Furthermore, they add a new dimension by requiring employers to review the terms and conditions on which part-time workers are employed, compare them with the terms and conditions and contractual benefits available to 'comparable full-time workers', and make the necessary adjustments, adopting (where appropriate) the principle of *pro rata temporis*.

Note: The principle of *pro rata temporis* means that where a comparable full-time worker receives (or is entitled to receive) pay or any other benefit, a part-time worker employed under the same type of contract must receive (or be entitled to receive) not less than the proportion of that pay or other benefit that the number of his (or her) weekly hours bears to the number of weekly hours worked by that full-time worker (*ibid* Reg. 1(1)).

Meaning of 'full-time' and 'part-time' worker

17.5
Under the 2000 Regulations a 'full-time worker' is a person who is paid wholly or partly by reference to the time he (or she) works and, having regard to the custom and practice of the employer in relation to workers employed under the same type of contract, is identifiable as a full-time worker. A 'part-time worker', on the other hand, is a person who works under the same type of contract as a full-time worker, but works fewer hours than that full-time worker. On reflection, no more precise definition is possible. A person ('employee' or otherwise), who works (say) a 40-hour, five-day week in a particular organisation, will ordinarily be regarded as a full-time worker within that organisation. A worker in the same organisation, who is employed under the same type of contract as that full-time worker, but works fewer than 40 hours a week, is a part-time worker (*ibid* Reg. 2).

Meaning of 'comparable full-time worker'

17.6
It follows that, for the purposes of the 2000 Regulations, a worker is a 'comparable full-time worker' in relation to a part-time worker if, at the time when the alleged less favourable treatment occurred, both of those workers were employed by the same employer at the same establishment, worked under the same type of contract, carried out the same or broadly similar work, and possessed (where relevant) the same or a broadly similar level of qualification, skills and experience.

If there is no comparable full-time worker at the establishment in question, a part-time worker may compare his (or her) treatment with that received by a 'comparable full-time worker', working at another establishment (branch office, factory, depot, warehouse, etc) situated elsewhere within the same organisation (*ibid*).

17.7
Workers employed under the following types of contract are not employed under the same types of contract:

(a) employees employed under a contract of employment that is not a contract of apprenticeship;

(b) employees employed under a contract of apprenticeship;

(c) workers who are not employees;

(d) workers who are not employees but are employed under a fixed-term contract;

(e) any other description of worker that it is reasonable for the employer to treat differently from other workers on the ground that workers of that description have a different type of contract.

For example, (a) is not the same type of contract as (b); (c) not the same as (a); (d) not the same as (b); and so on.

LESS FAVOURABLE TREATMENT

17.8
Part-time workers must not be treated less favourably than comparable full-time workers solely because they work part-time – unless different treatment is justified on objective grounds. This means that a part-time worker must be paid the same hourly rate of pay as a comparable full-time worker. A different hourly rate of pay may be justifiable on performance-related grounds, so long

as a worker's performance is measured fairly and consistently under a performance appraisal scheme (*ibid* Regs 5 to 7).

Note: A full-time worker who becomes a part-time worker, following a termination or variation of his (or her) previous contract, whether of the same type or not, must be treated as if there were a comparable full-time worker employed under the terms that applied to him immediately before the variation or termination. The same applies if a former full-time worker returns to work part-time with his former employer in the same or a similar job within 12 months of the termination of his previous contract, whether or not the contract under which he is re-engaged is the same type of contract or a different or varied contract (*ibid* Regs 3 & 4).

Terms and conditions of employment

17.9
It is not uncommon for employers' occupational sick pay schemes to provide more generous benefits to full-time workers (eg full salary or wages for a period of up to three months in every 12-month period). By the same token, it is not unusual for part-time workers to receive no more than their entitlement to statutory sick pay (SSP) when incapacitated for work on grounds of illness of injury. Such a sweeping differential is no longer acceptable, or justifiable. When calculating the rate of *occupational* sick pay (or maternity pay), or the length of service required to qualify for such payments, or the period over which such contractual payments are made, part-time workers must not be treated less favourably than comparable full-time workers in the same employment. Indeed, any differential treatment could give rise to allegations of unlawful sex discrimination, let alone a complaint to an employment tribunal under the 2000 Regulations. That same general prohibition applies to differential treatment in relation to occupational maternity and parental leave schemes, annual holiday entitlements (in excess of the statutory minimum entitlement), unpaid career breaks; access to occupational pension schemes, access to opportunities for training and promotion, redundancy selection criteria, and so on – unless that different treatment is justifiable on objective grounds (*ibid* regulation 3).

Other benefits

17.10
Other benefits available to comparable full-time workers, such as health insurance, subsidised mortgages and staff discounts, should be applied to part-time workers on a pro rata basis, unless their exclusion is justified on objective grounds. Some benefits, such as health insurance, company cars, luncheon vouchers, and the like, are 'indivisible'. Although it may not be possible to provide such benefits pro rata, that is not of itself an objective justification for withholding them. However, the disproportionate cost to the employer of providing such benefits may prove to be objectively justifiable.

One way of overcoming the problem of company cars is to calculate the financial value of the benefit to a comparable full-time worker and apply that value pro rata (eg, in the form of a car allowance) to the part-time worker. See also para 17.20 below (*Further information*).

17.11
In future, employers will need to scrutinise the relative terms and conditions of their full-time and part-time workers and eliminate any discrepancies or anomalies that cannot be justified on objective grounds. In determining whether a part-time worker has been treated less favourably than a comparable full-time worker, the principle of *pro rata temporis* (referred to earlier in this section) may be applied – unless it is inappropriate. It would be inappropriate, for example, to apply that principle to basic rates of pay, overtime payments (but see next paragraph), access to pension schemes, opportunities for training, transfer or promotion, career break schemes, enhanced maternity or parental leave schemes, or redundancy selection criteria.

Exception in relation to overtime payments

17.12
The new Regulations acknowledge that part-time workers have no right to premium payments in respect of overtime work until such time as their working hours (including overtime hours) during a particular pay reference period exceed the number of hours ordinarily worked by comparable full-time workers in that same period. But, once that point is reached, premium payments, for hours worked in excess of those full-time hours, must be the same as those paid to comparable full-time workers (*ibid* Reg. 3(4)).

Written statement of reasons for less favourable treatment

17.13
Any part-time worker, who considers that he (or she) is being treated less favourably than a comparable full-time worker, may ask his employer for a written statement explaining the reasons for that treatment. The employer must provide that statement within the next 21 days (*ibid* Reg. 4).

17.14
A failure to provide that written statement, without reasonable excuse, is admissible in evidence before an employment tribunal. Furthermore, when entertaining a complaint of less favourable treatment, the tribunal may draw any inference from that failure as it considers just and equitable (including an inference that the employer has infringed the complainant's statutory rights). The same applies if the explanation given in the written statement is evasive or equivocal (*ibid*).

Note: There is no need for a separate written statement if a part-time 'employee' who has been dismissed has already requested and received a written statement of reasons for dismissal under section 92 of the Employment Rights Act 1996 (as to which, please turn to Chapter 14, paras 14.37 to 14.38 and Chapter 15, paras 15.59 to 15.65, elsewhere in this book (*ibid* Reg. 4(4)).

UNFAIR DISMISSAL AND DETRIMENTAL TREATMENT

17.15
A part-time worker (other than a worker who is not an 'employee') who is dismissed or selected for redundancy will be treated in law as having been unfairly dismissed or selected if the reason (or, if more than one, the principal reason) for his (or her) dismissal or selection was that he:

(a) had complained to an employment tribunal about an alleged infringement of his rights under the 2000 Regulations;

(b) had asked his employer for a written statement of the reasons for his less favourable treatment;

(c) had given evidence or information in proceedings before an employment tribunal brought by another worker;

(d) had alleged (in good faith) that his employer had infringed the 2000 Regulations;

(e) had refused (or proposed to refuse) to forego a right conferred on him by the 2000 Regulations; or

(f) that his employer believed or suspected that the worker had done (or intended to do) any of the things mentioned in (a) to (e) above.

(*ibid* Reg. 5(1), (3) & 4.)

17.16
A part-time worker who has been victimised, disciplined or subjected to any other detriment, including termination of his (or her) contract on any of the grounds (a) to (f) specified in the previous paragraph, has the right to refer the matter to an employment tribunal without having to resign in order to do so (*ibid* Reg. 5(2), (3) & (4)).

Complaints to employment tribunals, etc

17.17
A part-time worker (regardless of his [or her] age or length of service at the material time) may complain to an employment tribunal that his employer has infringed his statutory rights under the 2000 Regulations – either by

subjecting him to a detriment (including termination of his contract) or some other punishment, or (in the case of an employee) by dismissing him or selecting him for redundancy. Such a complaint must be presented within three months of the alleged detrimental treatment or, if the employee has been dismissed or made redundant, within three months of the effective date of termination of his contract of employment. A tribunal may consider a complaint which is out of time if, in all the circumstances of the case, it considers that it is just and equitable to do so.

17.18

If a complaint of unlawful detrimental treatment is upheld, the tribunal will make a declaration to that effect and may order the employer to pay compensation to the worker and/or recommend that the employer take appropriate corrective action (within a specified period) to obviate or reduce the adverse effect of any matter to which the worker's complaint relates. A failure to take such corrective action will prompt the tribunal either to increase the amount of compensation already awarded to the worker or (if no compensation had previously been awarded) order the employer to pay compensation to the worker. The amount of compensation awarded in such circumstances will be such amount as the tribunal considers just and equitable, and will include compensation for the loss of any benefit which the worker might reasonably be expected to have had but for his employer's infringement of his rights under the 2000 Regulations (or the employer's failure to take the recommended corrective action) (*ibid* Reg. 6).

17.19

A worker (*qua* employee) who has been dismissed (or selected for redundancy), in contravention of the 2000 Regulations, will be treated as having been unfairly dismissed (regardless of his or her age or length of service at the material time) and will be awarded compensation comprising a basic and compensatory award (maximum £7,800 and £53,500, respectively) and, where appropriate, an additional award of compensation of between 26 and 52 weeks' pay (as to which, please turn to Chapter 5, paras 5.158 *et seq* elsewhere in this book (*ibid* Reg. 5(1))).

Further information

17.20

The Department of Trade & Industry (DTI) has published a guide to the Part-time Workers Regulations 2000 titled *The Law & Best Practice: A detailed guide for employers and part-timers*, copies of which are available free of charge from the DTI Publications Orderline on 0870 1502 500 (e-mail: publications@dti.gsi.gov.uk) or by accessing Web site www.dti.gov.uk/er/pt-detail.htm.

Working time regulations 1998

GENERAL INFORMATION

18.1
The Working Time Regulations 1998 (which came into force on 1 October 1998) implement Council Directive 93/104/EC of 23 November 1993 ('concerning certain aspects of the organisation of working time') and Council Directive 94/33/EC of 22 June 1994 ('on the protection of young people at work'). The 1998 Regulations have since been amended by the Working Time Regulations 1999 (SI 1999/3372), the Working Time (amendment) Regulations 2001 (SI 2001/3256) and, more recently, by the Working Time (Amendment) Regulations 2002 (SI 2002/3128).

SUMMARY

18.2
The 1998 Regulations apply to all workers over compulsory school age regardless of the nature of the contractual arrangements between them and the people who employ them. In short, they apply not only to 'employees' in the strict legal sense of the word, but also to casual, seasonal and temporary workers, agency workers, freelancers, and the like (but not self-employed persons) who undertake to do or perform personally any work or service for an employer (usually on an 'as and when required' basis), even if only for a day or two here or there.

18.3
Under the 1998 Regulations (as amended):

(a) adult workers (ie, workers aged 18 and over) have the right not to be employed for more than an *average* 48 hours a week (calculated over a reference period of 17 weeks – which reference period may be increased to 26 weeks by their employer (but only in prescribed circumstances), or to up to 52 weeks under a collective or workforce agreement;

(b) adolescent workers (ie, workers under the age of 18), may not lawfully be employed for more than eight hours a day, or for more than 40 hours a week (including overtime hours), with no provision for averaging;

(c)   adult workers may not lawfully be employed at night for more than an *average* eight hours in any 24-hour period, calculated over a reference period of 17, 26 or 52 consecutive weeks (see (a) above), or, if engaged in hazardous activities, for more than eight hours in any 24-hour period;

(d)   adolescent workers may not lawfully be employed at night (other than in prescribed circumstances) between the hours of 10.00 pm and 6.00 am (or between 11.00 am and 7.00 am, if their contracts require them to work after 10.00 pm),with no provision for averaging;

(e)   night workers are entitled to free initial and follow-up health assessments (or, if under the age of 18, free initial and follow-up health and capacities assessments);

(f)   every worker is entitled to a minimum weekly rest period of 24 hours (or 48 hours in every fortnight); or, if under the age of 18, a minimum weekly rest period of 48 consecutive hours;

(g)   every worker is entitled to a daily rest period of a minimum 11 consecutive hours; or, if under the age of 18, a daily rest period of a minimum 12 consecutive hours;

(h)   every worker is entitled to a minimum 20-minute rest break during the course of any working day or shift lasting or expected to last for more than six hours; or, if under the age of 18, a minimum 30-minute rest break during the course of any working day or shift lasting, or expected to last, for more than four-and-a-half hours;

(i)   every worker is entitled to a minimum four weeks' paid holidays in every holiday year (and to accrued holiday pay on the termination of his or her employment, even if employed for no more than one or two days).

For these purposes, an 'adolescent worker' is a worker who has lawfully left school (that is to say, is over compulsory school age) but has not yet had his or her 18th birthday. It follows that an 'adult worker' is a worker aged 18 years and over.

18.4
The Regulations are enforced both by the employment tribunals (in relation to an employee's statutory rights to rest breaks, paid annual holidays, etc); and by the Health & Safety Executive (in relation to the limits on weekly working time, night work, etc).

Excluded categories

18.5
Save for the right to four weeks' paid annual holidays, managing executives and other workers with autonomous decision-making powers (including

workers, such as travelling sales representatives whose working hours comprise a mix of standard and voluntary hours) do not enjoy the protection otherwise afforded to all workers by the 1998 Regulations. The same is true of family workers, and persons officiating at religious ceremonies in churches and religious communities. They too are nonetheless entitled to a minimum of four weeks' paid holidays each year.

18.6
The Regulations do not yet apply to workers employed in air, rail, road, sea, inland waterway and lake transport; or to doctors in training; or to specific activities of the armed forces, the police, fire brigades, ambulance services, customs and immigration officers, the prison service, the coast guard, or to lifeguard crews and other voluntary rescue services (although some of these exceptions are currently being challenged through the courts by representative trade unions). Moves are also afoot to extend the protection afforded by the 1998 Regulations to so-called non-mobile workers in the road and rail transport industries. The amending legislation is expected to come into force on 1 August 2003.

THE WORKING WEEK

1. Adult workers

18.7
Adult workers (ie, workers aged 18 and over) may agree to work more than an average 48 hours a week so long as they do so individually, voluntarily and in writing. To be valid, the opt-out agreement must remind the worker in question of his (or her) statutory right to rescind that agreement on giving his employer an agreed period of notice (of not less than seven days nor more than three months). It must be emphasised that an adult worker's statutory right to refuse to work more than an average 48-hour week cannot be overridden by a collective or workforce agreement or by any contrary provision in his contract of employment (Reg. 5).

18.8
Following amendments introduced by the Working Time Regulations 1999 (SI 1999/3372), employers are not required to keep detailed records of the weekly hours worked by people who have opted-out of the maximum average 48-hour week (although they must be able to produce those agreements on request). However, they must keep records sufficient to satisfy a Health and Safety Inspector (or local authority Environmental Health Officer) that the working hours of all other workers do not exceed the statutory maximum. See also para. 18.43 below.

18.9

An adult worker's average weekly hours are to be calculated over a static or rolling reference period of 17 weeks or, in special circumstances, 26 weeks. Employers may extend the standard 17-week reference period to one of 26 weeks in the case of workers sent to distant locations whose patterns of work vary from location to location and who may need to work long hours to complete a given task in the shortest possible time. The same extended reference period may be appropriate in the case of dock workers, security guards, postal workers, hospital and care workers, workers in the media, gas, water and electricity industries, farm workers, and so on. Calculations must not include those working days during which an employee is absent from work because of sickness, annual holidays or maternity leave). See also para. 18.41 below, which allows for the further extension of the 17-week reference period to one of up to 52 weeks under the terms of a workforce or collective agreement.

2. Young workers

18.10

Young workers under the age of 18 (who are over compulsory school age) may not be employed for more than eight hours a day or for more than 40 hours in any week (including overtime hours). These limits are absolute. Unlike their adult counterparts, workers aged 16 and 17 have no legal right to opt-out of those limits (whether they wish to or not); nor, unlike adult workers, may their workings hours be averaged over a 17-week or longer reference period. An exception to these rules is permissible if a young worker is occasionally required to undertake work which is necessary either to maintain continuity of service or production, or to respond to a surge in demand for a service or product, so long as there is no adult worker available to perform the work and performing the work would not adversely affect the young person's education or training (Reg. 5A).

NIGHT WORK

18.11

The expression 'night work', in relation to a worker, means a period of not less than seven hours that includes the period between midnight and 5.00 am.

1. Adult workers

18.12

An adult 'night worker' is a worker aged 18 and over who normally works three or more hours of his (or her) daily working time at night, or who is likely during night time to work such proportion of his annual working time as may be specified in a collective or workforce agreement. Adult night-workers may not be assigned to work at night for more than an average eight hours in any period of 24 consecutive hours, calculated over a reference period of 17 consecutive weeks. If, on the other hand, a night worker is engaged in especially hazardous work, or in work involving heavy physical or mental strain, it is the employer's responsibility to ensure that he (or she) does not work more than eight hours in any 24-hour period during which he performs night work (Reg. 6).

18.13
Night work is regarded as involving special hazards (or heavy physical or mental strain) if it is identified as such in a collective or workforce agreement (see paras 18.41 & 18.42 below) or in the risk assessment exercise necessarily carried out by every employer in accordance with Regulation 3 of the Management of Health & Safety at Work Regulations 1999 (SI 1999/3242).

Free health assessments

18.14
An employer must not assign any adult worker to night work without first providing him (or her) with the opportunity of a free health assessment (unless the worker in question has already had a health assessment prior to being assigned to night work on an earlier occasion and the employer has no reason to believe that the previous assessment is no longer valid). Further opportunities for free health assessments must be provided at regular intervals so long as the night worker continues to work at night. If a doctor advises that a worker is suffering from health problems associated with his (or her) working at night, and it is possible to transfer the worker to suitable alternative work during the day shift, the employer must transfer the worker accordingly (Reg. 7(1)). See also para. 18.17 below.

2. Young workers

18.15
Young workers under the age of 18 must not be employed at night during the so-called 'restricted period', ie, the period between 10.00 pm or 6.00 am (or, if their contracts provide for them to work after 10.00 pm, during the period from 11.00 pm and 7.00 am). Workers in hotels, restaurants, bars, and the like may be employed after 10.00 pm or 11.00 pm, as the case may be, in order to maintain continuity of service or if there is a surge in demand for a service – so long as there are no adult workers available to do the work and their working hours do not extend into the period between midnight and 4.00 am. Even so, they must be supervised by at least one adult worker and, if not permitted to take their normal rest breaks or rest periods (see paras 18.19 to

18.25 below), must be allowed an equivalent period of compensatory rest. These rules do not apply to young workers employed in hospitals or similar establishments or in connection with cultural, artistic, sporting or advertising activities, so long as they too are allowed the prescribed rest breaks and rest periods (Reg. 6A).

Free health and capabilities assessments

18.16
An employer must not assign any young worker to work during the 'restricted period' (see previous paragraph) without first ensuring that he (or she) has the opportunity of a free assessment of his health and capabilities (unless the young worker in question had received such an assessment on a previous occasion and the employer has no reason to believe that the previous assessment is no longer valid). Repeat assessment opportunities must nonetheless be provided at regular intervals (Reg. 7(2)). See also next paragraph.

Transfer to day work

18.17
If an employer is advised by a doctor that a worker is suffering from health problems, which the doctor considers to be connected with the fact that the worker works at night (or, in the case of a young worker, work during the restricted period), and it is possible to transfer the worker to suitable alternative day work, the employer must transfer the worker accordingly (Reg. 7(6)).

Note: If a new or expectant mother works at night and produces a certificate signed by her doctor (or registered midwife) to the effect that working at night could be detrimental to her health and safety (or, in the case of a pregnant employee, to that of her unborn child), her employer must either transfer her to daytime work (without loss of pay) or suspend her on full pay for the period specified in the certificate. Non-compliance with this requirement is an offence under the Health & Safety at Work etc Act 1974 (*Source*: Regulation 17, Management of Health & Safety at Work Regulations 1999). For further particulars, see Chapter 14, para. 14.119.

Pattern of work

18.18
Employees engaged in monotonous work (or in work which is carried out at a pre-determined rate) must be given adequate rest breaks if the work they do is such as to pose a risk to their health and safety. Production-line workers could well fall into this category (Reg. 8).

DAILY REST

18.19
Adult workers (that is to say, workers aged 18 and over) are entitled to a rest period of at least 11 consecutive hours in each period of 24 consecutive hours. However, this does not apply to a situation in which a shift worker changes shift and cannot take a daily rest period between the end of one shift and the start of the next one. Nor does it apply to a worker engaged in work (such as catering or cleaning) that occurs at different times of the day and is split up over the day. In such circumstances, the employer must nonetheless allow that shift worker to take an equivalent period of compensatory rest or, if that is not possible, 'appropriate protection' (Regs 9(1), 20 & 22).

18.20
For a young person under the age of 18, the prescribed minimum daily rest period is 12 consecutive hours – although that minimum period may be interrupted if the young person is engaged in activities involving periods of activity that are split up over the day or of short duration. In exceptional circumstances, a worker under the age of 18 may be required to do work otherwise done by an adult during his (or her) rest period if the need for him to do so is prompted by unusual or unforeseeable circumstances – so long as that work is of a temporary nature and must be performed immediately. In such a situation, the employer must nonetheless allow that young worker to take an equivalent period of compensatory rest within the following three weeks (Regs 9(2) & 23).

WEEKLY REST PERIOD

18.21
In addition to his (or her) right to a minimum rest period of at least 11 hours in every period of 24 consecutive hours, an adult worker must be afforded at least one full day off work (that is to say, 24 consecutive and uninterrupted hours) in every period of seven consecutive days. Alternatively, an adult worker must be permitted two such days off work – separate or consecutive – in every period of 14 consecutive days, if the employer prefers the latter alternative approach. This provision does not, however, apply to an adult shift worker when he (or she) changes shift and cannot take a weekly rest period between the end of one shift and the start of the next one. The employer must nonetheless allow that worker to take an equivalent period of compensatory rest or, at the very least, afford him 'appropriate protection' (Regs 10(1) & (2), 20 and 22).

18.22
A young worker under the age of 18 is entitled to two days off work (preferably consecutive) in each seven-day period during which he (or she) works for his employer (Reg. 10(3)).

The beginning of any such period of seven or 14 consecutive days will either be as laid down in any collective or workforce agreement applicable to the workers in question or, in the absence of any such agreement, midnight between Sunday and Monday.

REST BREAKS

18.23

Adults who work more than six hours a day are each entitled to a rest break during the working day of at least 20 uninterrupted minutes. Workers under the age of 18, who work more than four-and-a-half hours a day, are entitled to a rest break of at least 30 minutes' duration during the course of that working day or shift. Workers have the legal right to spend their rest breaks away from their desks or workstations (already a requirement under current health and safety legislation for persons employed in prescribed hazardous activities or processes) (Reg. 11).

18.24

In exceptional circumstances, a worker under the age of 18 may be required to do work otherwise done by an adult during his (or her) rest break if the need to do so is prompted by unusual or unforeseeable circumstances – so long as that work is of a temporary nature and must be performed immediately. In such a situation, the employer must nonetheless see to it that the young worker in question is allowed, and takes, an equivalent period of compensatory rest within the following three weeks (Regs 11(4) & 23).

18.25

The terms and conditions under which rest breaks are to be provided and granted may be contained in any related provision in either or both of a collective agreement or a workforce agreement (as to which, see paras 18.41 & 18.42 below).

PAID ANNUAL HOLIDAYS

18.26

Every worker, part-time, full-time, temporary, seasonal or casual), other than a worker in an excluded category (see paras 18.5 & 18.6), is entitled to a minimum of four weeks' paid holidays in every holiday year. That entitlement begins to accrue from day one of a worker's contract. The previous 13-week 'waiting period' has long since been abolished. It follows that a worker is entitled to accrued holiday pay on the termination of his or her employment, even if termination occurs within a day or two of the date on which he or she first started work. Workers must take their full four weeks' entitlement to paid holidays (or their accrued entitlement, in the case of workers recruited part-way though a holiday year) during the holiday year in which they fall due. That holiday entitlement may not be replaced by a payment in lieu under any circumstances (except on the termination of the worker's employment) nor may unused holidays be carried forward or 'rolled-over' into the next holiday year (Reg. 13).

18.27
The 'holiday year' is the period of 12 consecutive months which begins on such date during the calendar year as may be provided for in a collective agreement or a workforce agreement, or as may be specified in the written statement of terms and conditions of employment necessarily issued to employees in accordance with sections 1 to 7 of the Employment Rights Act 1996. In the absence of any such agreement or alternative provision, the holiday year will either be the period of 12 consecutive months which begins on 1 October 1998 (and each subsequent anniversary of that date) or, if the employee's employment begins after 1 October 1998, on the date on which his (or her) employment begins (and each subsequent anniversary of that date).

18.28
Public and bank holidays may be incorporated into the four weeks' paid holiday entitlement unless the contract stipulates (or has always stipulated) otherwise. In short, an employer may not presume to include public and bank holidays in an employee or other worker's holiday entitlement if that employee has previously enjoyed the contractual (or implied contractual) right to paid annual holidays *in addition to* bank and public holidays.

Holidays during extended sick leave or maternity leave

18.29
Strictly speaking, a worker forfeits his (or her) entitlement to paid annual holidays if he (or she) is unable to take his full statutory entitlement due to illness or injury which unavoidably keeps him away from work for the whole or major portion of the relevant holiday year. However, as was pointed out by the Employment Appeal Tribunal (EAT) in *Kigass Aero Components v Brown* (EAT/481/00), there is nothing in the 1998 Regulations to prevent workers on extended sick leave (maternity leave, adoption leave, or whatever), taking their statutory entitlement to four weeks' paid annual holidays (or money in lieu of those holidays) during their enforced absences from work, the more so if they would otherwise be unable to take those holidays (or what remains of those holidays) in the holiday year in which they fall due.

18.30
The only requirement, said the EAT in *Kigass*, is that the workers in question give their employers the required advance notice of the date (or dates) on

which they intend those holidays to start, whether or not they actually take those holidays or are physically in any condition to do so (as to which, see para. 18.32: *Notification of intention to take holidays*). The fact that a worker on extended sick leave may or may not have exhausted his or her entitlement to SSP or occupational sick pay, said the EAT, is irrelevant.

18.31

Readers should note that absentee workers (notably employees) continue to accrue an entitlement to four weeks' paid annual holidays so long as they remain in their employers' employment. This is as true of employees on extended sick leave (as in the *Kigass* case above) as it is of employees on maternity leave, adoption leave, or on extended leave of absence without pay (eg, study leave). If their absences from work during the whole or major part of a holiday year would prevent them taking the statutory holidays otherwise due to them in that holiday year, they too would be entitled to lay claim to holiday pay before their return to work. The only requirement is that they serve notice on their employers of the date or dates on which they intend their holidays to start – the amount of notice in such cases being the notice required by their contracts of employment or, in the absence of any collective or work-force agreement to the contrary, the notice prescribed by Regulation 15(4) of the 1998 Regulations (see para. 18.32 below). So far as maternity and adoption leave is concerned (see Chapter 14, Parts 1 & 2), the reader will be aware that an employee who qualifies for both ordinary and additional maternity or adoption leave might well be absent from work for up to 52 weeks, even longer if she (or he) chooses to take up to four weeks' unpaid parental leave at the end of her additional maternity leave or (her or his) additional adoption leave periods – and longer still if illness or injury intervenes to prevent the employee returning to work on the due date.

Timing of annual holidays

Notification of intention to take holidays

18.32

In the absence of any contractual or long-established procedure to the contrary, a worker wishing to take some or all of his (or her) holiday enti-tlement during a particular holiday year must give advance notice to his employer equal to twice the required holiday period. Thus, a worker wanting to take two weeks' paid holiday must give his employer at least four weeks' advance notice of the date on which he intends those holidays to start. Should the employer be unable to accede to the worker's request (perhaps for opera-tional reasons, or because too many people have asked to take their holidays at the same time) he must give the worker at least two weeks' notice of his refusal to allow that worker to begin his holidays on the date in question (ie, notice equivalent to the number of days or weeks' leave requested by the worker in the first place). An employer who postpones a worker's requested period of leave must nonetheless see to it that the worker is permitted to take that requested period of leave (and the remainder of any leave due to him) before the end of the relevant holiday year.

Note: In practice, most employers have well-developed procedures relating to the notification and timing of annual holidays. To avoid the inevitable disruption caused by people wishing to take their holidays (or part of their holidays) at the same time, employers will often draw up their holiday rosters at the beginning of a holiday year. Employers also have the right to limit the number of days' or weeks' holidays that their workers may take at any one time, subject to the proviso that their workers must be permitted to take their full statutory entitlement to paid holidays in the holiday year in which they fall due.

Holidays during the first year of employment

18.33
Under the 1998 Regulations, as originally enacted, a worker whose period of employment began *before* 25 October 2001, and part-way through a holiday year, was entitled to anticipate the holidays to which he (or she) was entitled during the remainder of that holiday year, on the assumption that he would remain in his employer's employment until the end of that holiday year. If the worker's employment came to an end (for whatever reason), the employer would have the right to recover any overpaid holiday pay from the worker's final pay cheque (so long as that right is clearly laid down in the worker's contract; as to which, see paras 18.38 & 18.39 below).

18.34
However, with the coming into force on 25 October 2001 of the Working Time (Amendment) Regulations 2001, the rules have changed. Under the 1998 Regulations, as now amended, a worker's entitlement to paid holidays during his (or her) first year of employment may be calculated *monthly in advance*; that is to say, at the rate of one-twelfth of the worker's full statutory entitlement to four weeks' paid holidays during a complete holiday year (with fractions of a day rounded-up to the nearest half day). In short, during their first year of employment, workers may only take the holidays that have accrued due to them, at the time they choose (or are permitted) to take those holidays (unless their contracts state otherwise).

Note: The 'monthly in advance' rule (described above) for calculating a worker's entitlement to paid holidays during his (or her) first year of employment may not appeal to employers whose holiday years run from, say, 1 January to 31 December. Rather than adopt that procedure in its entirety, there is nothing in the 1998 Regulations (as amended) to prevent an employer adopting the same or a similar piecemeal approach to holidays for new recruits during the remainder of the employer's holiday year (rather than the 12-month period that constitutes the worker's first year of employment).

Incorporating holiday pay in a worker's wages

18.35
The practice adopted by many employers of incorporating an element for statutory holiday pay in a worker's wages or salary, and then paying them nothing when they physically take their holidays, quit their jobs or are dismissed, was castigated recently by the EAT in *MPB Structure Ltd v Munro* (EAT/1257/01) as being contrary to the spirit of the 1998 Regulations, and void. 'It is clear to us', said the EAT, 'that the basic theme or aim of the Regulations is to ensure that workers obtain appropriate holiday leave and to do so they must have the necessary funds. We consider that, by placing the onus of retaining the funds from week to week for holiday purposes [on the worker], there may well arise the problem of adequate funding at the time of the holiday leave being taken. This could become compounded if sufficient service in any one year had not been served so as to build up a sufficient entitlement to be paid the equivalent of a week's pay during the holiday period. We consider that the only way that the provisions of the 1998 Regulations and, indeed, their spirit can be met, is for holiday pay to be paid as and when the holiday is taken, at the appropriate rate'.

18.36
In light of the EAT's decision in *MPB Structure Ltd v Munro*, which (at the time of writing) remains unchallenged, employers contemplating incorporating an element for statutory holiday pay in a worker's wages or salary should think again. Furthermore, as was pointed out by the Court of Appeal in *Blackburn & Others v Gridquest Ltd* [2002] IRLR 604, an employer cannot unilaterally decide that a week's pay is a payment not only for the hours worked during a week but also includes an element for holiday pay. 'The weekly payment', said the CA, 'can only be held to include an amount for something else, such as holiday pay, if that is agreed between employer and employee. The claim [by the employers in the present case] that holiday pay was in fact paid amounts to an assertion that the employer can decide unilaterally what is included in the weekly payment. Regulation 16(5) [of the Working Time Regulations 1998] does not confer that right upon an employer'. In reaching its judgement in the *Blackburn* case, the CA declined to address that of the EAT in *MPB Structure Ltd v Munro* (*qv*), as there was no reference in that earlier judgement to Regulation 16(5) of the 1998 Regulations.

18.37
Given the circumstances that prompted the EAT's ruling in *MPB Structure Ltd v Munro*, it may be (repeat, *may* be) acceptable to incorporate an element for holiday pay (sick pay, or whatever) in the wages of those casual, seasonal or temporary workers who rarely spend more than two or three days at a time working for a particular employer. However, in light of the CA's decision in

the *Blackburn* case (see previous paragraph), they should see to it that the workers in question are made aware of (and accept) that arrangement before they actually start work. Ideally, this should be done in writing. Furthermore, to avoid a situation in which workers make unfavourable comparisons with the wages paid to other workers doing the same or similar work within the same organisation, employers should make it clear to those casual workers (again, preferably, in writing) precisely what percentage or element of their hourly or daily rate of pay constitutes a payment in respect of holiday pay. That element should not be less than 8.33 per cent. In other words, if the standard rate of pay for a particular job is, say, £5 an hour, a casual worker doing the same job, whose wages include an element for statutory holiday pay, should be paid a minimum of £5.42 an hour.

Payment of accrued holiday pay on termination

18.38
Any worker who resigns or is dismissed (whether summarily or otherwise, and for whatever reason) part-way through a holiday year, without having exhausted his (or her) full accrued entitlement to paid holidays, must be paid accrued holiday pay on the termination of his employment. If, on the other hand, the worker in question has taken more holidays than were due to him, his employer may deduct the excess from the worker's final payment of wages or salary (so long as there is a term in the worker's contract to the effect that such a deduction will be made on termination)(*ibid* Reg. 14(4).

18.39
That view was restated by the Employment Appeal Tribunal in *Hill v Chappell* (EAT 1250/01). There, a Miss Hill had quit her job after six months' service, having already taken three weeks' paid holidays. As she had only accrued half of her full year's entitlement to four weeks' paid holidays, her employers deducted the equivalent of one week's pay from her final pay cheque. The Employment Appeal Tribunal (EAT) held that, in the absence of an express term to that effect in her contract, her employers had no authority to make such a deduction. In their defence, her employers had relied on section 14(4) of the Employment Rights Act 1996 which authorised employers to deduct any overpayment of wages or salary from a worker's pay cheque without prior written consent. Maybe so, said the EAT; but Miss Hill's excess holiday pay was not an 'overpayment' within the meaning of section 14(1). She had applied for and had been permitted to take three weeks' paid holiday, in keeping with her rights under the Working Time Regulations 1998. Had her employers wished to 'claw back' any overpaid holiday pay on the termination of her employment, they should have included a clause to that effect in her contract.

ENTITLEMENTS UNDER OTHER PROVISIONS

18.40

If an employee is already entitled to minimum rest periods, rest breaks or annual holidays under his (or her) contract of employment, those terms will prevail – so long as they accord with the employee's minimum statutory rights under the Working Time Regulations 1998. If one or other (or all) of those terms are less beneficial to the employee, the 1998 Regulations will take precedence in respect of that term (or those terms) and will be 'deemed' to be imported into the employee's contract of employment. In short, an employee may take advantage of whichever right is, in any particular respect, the more favourable. However, any term in a worker's contract (or in a collective or workforce agreement) that purports to override or undermine his or her rights (or the employer's statutory obligations) under the 1998 Regulations is void and unenforceable (Reg. 15).

COLLECTIVE AND WORKFORCE AGREEMENTS

18.41

Save for the restrictions on the employment of young persons at night (see paras 18.15 to 18.17 above), the rights of workers (or an identifiable group of workers) under the 1998 Regulations – in relation to night work, daily and weekly rest periods, and rest breaks – may be modified or excluded by a collective agreement or by a workforce agreement. Either type of agreement may also (for objective or technical reasons, or for reasons concerning the organisation of work) modify the reference period for determining the length of the average working week by substituting for the prescribed period of 17 weeks, a period not exceeding 52 weeks (Reg. 21).

Meaning of 'workforce agreement'

18.42

An agreement is a 'workforce agreement' for the purposes of the 1998 Regulations if:

(a) it is in writing;

(b) it specifies the date on which it is to take effect;

(c) it has been signed either by a majority of the workforce (by excluding those whose terms and conditions of employment have otherwise been agreed in a collective agreement) or by their elected representatives;

(d) before the agreement was made available for signature, copies – together with any notes for guidance – had been distributed to all affected employees for their consideration;

(e) in the case of an agreement signed by the majority of affected employees, it specifies a date, no later than five years after the date in (b) above, in which it will cease to have effect.

RECORDS

18.43

An employer must maintain adequate records of the working hours and periods of employment of day workers, shift workers and night workers so as to satisfy health and safety inspectors that there has been no abuse of an employee's rights under the Working Time Regulations 1998. Details of opportunities for health assessments (and/or of 'health and capacities' assessments) must also be committed to writing. All such records must be maintained for at least two years (Reg. 8).

ENFORCEMENT BY HEALTH AND SAFETY EXECUTIVE

18.44

Responsibility for enforcing those provisions of the 1998 Regulations which relate to maximum weekly working hours, the upper limits on night time working, health assessments, patterns of work and the maintenance of adequate records, rests with the Health & Safety Executive. Inspectors have the right to enter and inspect an employer's premises, to talk to employees and take statements, and to examine records. If there is evidence of non-compliance, a friendly warning may be followed by an improvement or prohibition notice and, ultimately, prosecution. The penalty for non-compliance (in the appropriate circumstances) is a fine of up to £20,000 or, if a conviction is obtained on indictment, a fine of an unlimited amount (Regs 26 & 27).

COMPLAINTS TO AN EMPLOYMENT TRIBUNAL

18.45

Workers denied their statutory rights to minimum daily and/or weekly rest periods, rest breaks during the day, or paid annual holidays may complain to an employment tribunal. Any such complaint must be 'presented' to the Secretary to the Tribunals (in practice, the nearest local or regional office of the employment tribunals) within three months of the date of the employer's refusal or failure to comply, or within such further period as the tribunal considers reasonable, in the light of the worker's explanation for the delay (Reg. 28A).

18.46

If the worker's complaint is upheld, the tribunal will make a declaration to that effect and will order the employer to pay compensation to the worker of such amount as it considers 'just and equitable' in the circumstances. If the complaint arose out of the employer's failure to pay the worker in respect of his (or her) entitlement to four weeks' annual holidays, the tribunal will also order the employer to pay the worker the amount which it finds to be due.

RIGHT NOT TO SUFFER DETRIMENT

18.47
Section 45A of the Employment Rights Act 1996 (as inserted by regulations 2(1) and 31(1) of the 1998 Regulations) cautions employers that a worker has the right *not to be disciplined or subjected to any detriment* at the hands of his (or her) employer:

- for refusing (or proposing to refuse) to comply with a requirement imposed (by the employer) in contravention of the Working Time Regulations 1998; or

- for refusing to forego a right conferred by those Regulations; or

- for failing to sign a workforce agreement for the purposes of those Regulations; or

- for bringing proceedings against his employer to enforce a right conferred on him by those Regulations; or

- for alleging that the employer had infringed such a right.

DISMISSAL FOR ASSERTING A STATUTORY RIGHT

18.48
A worker who is dismissed (or selected for redundancy) for asserting his (or her) statutory rights under the Working Time Regulations 1998, or for challenging his employer's refusal or failure to acknowledge those rights, may present a complaint of unfair dismissal to an employment tribunal regardless of his age or length of service at the material time. For further details, please turn to Chapter 5, paras 5.37 to 5.39).

CASE LAW

18.49
In *Sindicato de Médicos de Asistencia Pública (Simap) v Conselleria de Sanidad y Consumo de la Generalidad Valenciana* (C-303/98), the ECJ held that workers (such as doctors) who are required to be 'on call' (that is to say, readily contactable) during certain hours of the day or night, are not to be regarded as 'working' unless they are actually called-out and at their place of work. The

Court also held that consent to work more than an average 48-hour week must be given individually and in writing, and *not* by trade union representatives under the terms of a collective agreement.

18.50
In *Bowden & Others v Tufnells Parcels Express Limited* (Case No. 1102254/98), the employment tribunal held that the 1998 Regulations did *not* apply to office workers employed by a road transport business. Proposals to correct this and related anomalies affecting 'non-mobile workers' have since been adopted by the European Commission, although amendments to Working Time Directive 93/104/EC have yet to put in an appearance.

18.51
In *Barber v R J B Mining UK Limited* [1999] IRLR 308, the High Court held that there was an implied term in every contract of employment that, in the absence of a voluntary 'opt-out', a worker cannot lawfully be required to work more than an average 48 hours a week. This contractual right enabled the employees in question to bring their breach of contract case before the High Court. As the employees in question had already worked more than that average number of hours during the rolling 17-week reference period, the High Court declared that they had every right to reduce their weekly hours or, if need be, stop work for a time until the average fell within the 48-hour limit.

18.52
In *Clark v Oxfordshire Health Authority* [1998] IRLR 125, the contract under which a 'bank nurse' was engaged imposed no duty on her employers to provide her with work. Nor did it impose any duty on her to accept any offer of work that was forthcoming. She was nonetheless a 'worker' and was entitled to the protection afforded by the 1998 Regulations (working hours, rest breaks and rest periods, etc) when she was at work.

National minimum wage

19.1
With the coming into force on 1 April 1999 of the National Minimum Wage Regulations 1998 (SI 1998/584) (made under the National Minimum Wage Act 1998), every UK worker aged 18 and over now has the statutory right to be paid no less than the national minimum wage (NMW) appropriate to his or her age.

19.2
Since 1 October 2003, the national minimum wage (NMW) for workers aged 22 and over has been £4.20 an hour – or £3.60 an hour, during their first six months of employment, for workers in receipt of 'accredited training' for 26 days or more during those first six months. For workers aged 18 to 21, inclusive, the NMW is £3.60 an hour. At present, there is no NMW for workers age 16 or 17. These rates are reviewed annually. Certain payments made to workers (such as overtime premium payments, shift allowances, cost of living allowances, 'weighting' allowances, and the like) do not count towards the NMW; nor do most benefits in kind. Some deductions from pay also do not count. For further details, please turn to paras 19.12 to 19.18 below.

Note: The term 'accredited training' means training undertaken with a *new* employer during normal working hours (at or away from the workplace) which leads to a vocational qualification approved by the Secretary of State for Education. It does *not* apply to in-house training devised and provided by employers.

19.3
A refusal or failure to pay the appropriate NMW is an offence, the penalty for which, on summary conviction, is a fine of up to £5,000 for each offence. Inland Revenue enforcement officers have the right to enter an employer's premises and to inspect wage records. A failure to keep adequate or accurate records, or an attempt to obstruct inspectors in the exercise of their functions, will also lead to prosecution and a fine of up to £5,000.

19.4
Workers are not entitled to be paid the NMW in respect of meal or refreshment breaks (whether paid or unpaid); nor when they are travelling from their homes to their regular places of work (and *vice versa*); nor if they are on standby or on-call at their homes (or are entitled to be at home),

even if paid a standby or on-call allowance. It follows that workers who are travelling from one assignment to another, as part of their regular duties (eg, as sales representatives) must be paid the NMW for the time spent travelling, as must workers who are required to be on standby or on-call at or near their places of work (eg, doctors in hospitals). See also paras 19.24, 19.31 and 19.32 below.

19.5
Workers who are dismissed, selected for redundancy, or subjected to any other detriment, for questioning or challenging their employer's refusal or failure to pay the NMW, or for bringing proceedings before a tribunal or court, will likewise be entitled to compensation (see also Chapter 5, paras 5.46 & 5.47). Indeed, a worker who suspects that he or she is being paid less than the NMW may write to his or her employer demanding to see the relevant wage records, and must be supplied with those records within the next 14 days. An employer who fails to comply with such a request will be ordered to pay the worker in question a sum equivalent to 80 times the appropriate NMW, as well as compensation for the shortfall in pay.

PRACTICAL GUIDANCE

Meaning of 'worker'

19.6
A 'worker' is a person who does work for an employer, either under a contract of employment or under a contract *sui generis* (that is to say, of its own kind). In short, the term encompasses employees, seasonal and casual workers, freelancers, agency 'temps', pieceworkers (or output workers), workers paid entirely on commission, and homeworkers. All such workers must be paid no less than the appropriate NMW rate. As a 'rule of thumb' a worker's employer is the person (or organisation) who (or which) pays a worker's wages or salary, and deducts payments in respect of PAYE Tax and NI contributions. It is important to note that workers over normal retiring age or the State Pension Age (60 or 65, as the case may be) must also be paid the appropriate NMW.

19.7
The only category of person who is not a 'worker' in this sense, and who does not qualify for the NMW, is the self-employed person. The genuinely self-employed person is engaged under a contract *for* services to carry out a specific task or activity in return for an agreed fee. The self-employed person prepares his (or her) own annual accounts for submission to the Inland Revenue, pays his own taxes and National Insurance contributions, submits his own invoices (preferably on a pre-printed form), is (where

appropriate) registered for VAT, provides his own tools and equipment, and is not under the direction or control of any other person. An employer would be well-advised to demand proof of 'self-employed' status from any person who holds himself out to be self-employed.

19.8
Employers who choose to categorise some or all of their workers as 'self-employed', in order to avoid paying the appropriate NMW rate, are liable to prosecution and heavy fines – unless they are in a position to convince Inland Revenue enforcement officers that the workers in question are indeed self-employed.

19.9
Agency 'temps' are usually employed by the employment business which hires them out to client employers. It is the employment business (not the client employer) that is responsible both for paying a 'temp's' wages (within clearly-defined time limits) and for ensuring that their workers are paid the appropriate NMW rate.

Excluded categories

19.10
The NMW need not be paid until their 19th birthdays to 18-year-old apprentices who began their apprenticeships at 16 or 17. Nor need it be paid to apprentices age 19 and over during the first 12 months' of their apprenticeships or until their 26th birthdays, whichever occurs sooner. An 'apprentice', for these purposes, is a person who is either employed under a contract of apprenticeship or who is taking part in the Government's Modern Apprenticeship programme.

19.11
Also excluded from the NMW during their placements with employers are 'sandwich course' students, students obtaining work experience, teacher trainees, and trainees on Government-funded schemes (such as the 'New Deal', 'Work-based learning for adults', and so on).

Note: Also excluded are members of the armed forces, share fishermen, voluntary workers (who receive no pay for their time apart from genuine expenses), and prisoners.

But, those exclusions do *not* apply to students taking a 'gap year' between school (or college) and university. Nor do they apply to students undertaking post-graduate studies (whether taking up employment independently or as an adjunct to their studies). All such people must be paid no less than the appropriate NMW rate during their employment .

DEDUCTIONS AND PAYMENTS THAT DO OR DO NOT COUNT

19.12
As was mentioned in the preamble above, there are some payments included in a worker's gross wages or salary (such as overtime premium payments and shift allowances) that do *not* count towards the NMW; and there are others that do. Likewise, there are certain benefits in kind and deductions from pay (or payments made to an employer) which must be excluded from calculations. There is, for example, no upper limit on the amount of rent that an employer may charge a worker for 'live-in' accommodation (a not uncommon feature of employment in the hotel and leisure industries). However, as is explained below (see paras 19.16 to 19.18) that portion of the rent paid by a worker, which exceeds a specified hourly, daily or weekly amount, does *not* count towards the NMW. In short, the excess amount must be deducted from the worker's gross wages or salary in order to establish whether the worker in question is being paid the appropriate NMW rate.

19.13
Other deductions (or payments by a worker) that do *not* count include deductions in respect of meals compulsorily purchased by a worker from his or her employer; and deductions in respect of uniforms or protective clothing and equipment. The object of the exercise here is to ensure that employers do not use deductions from pay (or demands for certain payments from workers) as a means of 'clawing-back' (or reducing the effect of) the NMW.

Deductions and payments that do not count

19.14
The following components of a worker's gross wages or salary in a particular pay reference period (week, fortnight or month) do *not* count as part of the NMW:

- overtime premium payments;
- shift allowances;
- premium payments for work carried out on a bank or public holiday;
- unsociable hours payments;
- 'danger money';
- 'standby' or 'on call' allowances;
- travel allowances;
- 'cost of living' allowances (eg, 'London weighting' payments);
- payments carried forward from a previous pay reference period.

Benefits in kind provided by an employer (whether taxable or not) do *not* count towards the NMW. These include:

- a company car;
- petrol, oil and lubricants;
- meals (or the notional value of such meals) if, as is unlikely, a worker is required by his (or her) contract to take his meals in a staff or works canteen;
- luncheon vouchers (or the notional value of such vouchers);
- the employer's contributions to an occupational pension plan;
- relocation expenses;
- free health insurance; and
- that part of the rent charged by an employer for live-in accommodation (see paras 19.16 to 19.18 below) that exceeds a specified hourly, daily or weekly amount.

Furthermore, tips paid directly to a worker (or distributed amongst fellow workers), which are not paid through the payroll, do not count towards the NMW. The same applies to deductions from pay (or payments made to an employer) in respect of protective clothing and equipment, uniforms, dry cleaning or laundry costs, tools, etc.

Deductions and payments that do count

19.15
Deductions or payments that *do* count towards the NMW include:

- incentive payments, bonuses, commission, tips, gratuities and service charges collected centrally by the employer and distributed to a worker through the payroll (but not otherwise);
- deductions in respect of PAYE tax and NI contributions;
- a worker's pension contributions;
- a fine imposed in accordance with a worker's contract for misconduct (including authorised deductions in respect of cash shortages or stock deficiencies);
- deductions in respect of overpaid wages or salary (or overpaid expenses);
- deductions (or payments) in respect of live-in accommodation up to a prescribed maximum (see paras 19.16 to 19.18 below);
- voluntary deductions in respect of trade union dues, private health insurance, membership of a social club;

- deductions or payments in respect of meals voluntarily purchased by a worker from a staff or works canteen; and

- deductions in respect of goods and services *voluntarily* purchased by a worker from his or her employer.

Live-in accommodation

19.16
Live-in accommodation is a common feature of employment in the hotel and leisure industry, both for the convenience of employers and that of workers. Although technically there is no upper limit on the amount of rent that a worker may be required to pay for live-in accommodation, the 1998 Regulations make it clear that employers will not lessen the effect of the NMW Regulations by charging more than a prescribed amount for such accommodation.

19.17
Currently (2003/04), the most that an employer may offset against the NMW by way of accommodation charges is 57 pence for each hour of a worker's contractual weekly hours or £22.75 a week, whichever is the lower of those two amounts. It follows that, if a worker works a 35-hour week, the maximum amount of rent he (or she) pays weekly for live-in accommodation that may be offset against his NMW is £19.95. If a 30-hour week, £17.10; and so on.

19.18
If a worker occupies live-in accommodation for less than a whole week (eg, five days a week), the maximum daily amount that may be offset against the NMW is whichever is the lower of 57p per hour for each of the worker's contracted (or average) daily hours or £3.25. A day for these purposes is the period from midnight to midnight.

CATEGORIES OF WORKER

19.19
Most workers in industry and commerce can be categorised as salaried or hourly-paid. Other categories include seasonal workers, casual workers, workers paid wholly or mainly by commission, agency 'temps', and homeworkers.

Salaried workers

19.20
The ranks of salaried workers traditionally include senior executives, managers, accountants, clerks, secretaries, etc, most of whom are paid at regular monthly

intervals by cheque or credit transfer to their bank accounts. A salaried worker's pay usually remains the same month after month (unless absent from work because of illness or injury or on maternity or parental leave, or on approved leave of absence without pay). A salaried worker's pay will also encompass meal and rest breaks, and annual holidays.

19.21
Many salaried workers (especially those in the middle and higher echelons of management) are not paid for overtime working, it being a feature of their contracts that they work such additional hours as may be necessary for the more efficient performance of their duties. Given that salaried jobs are no longer the exclusive preserve of 'white-collar' workers, there will, of course, be salaried workers who are relatively lowly-paid (eg, in the region of £7,500 to £10,000 per annum), whose hourly rate of pay in a particular pay reference period may dip below the appropriate NMW rate – the more so if the worker in question regularly works overtime hours (paid or otherwise) or is paying more than £22.75 a week in rent for 'live-in' accommodation provided by his or her employer. As was explained earlier, there are a number of payments or deductions from pay which do not count towards the NMW.

EXAMPLE

Twenty-four-year-old Sally Brown works as a trainee manager at a small London Hotel. She earns a salary of £9,500 a year, and is contracted to work a five-day, 40-hour week (including meal and rest breaks). She is also paid a London'weighting allowance' of £45 a month. She is paid monthly in arrears and receives all her meals free of charge. She lives full time in accommodation provided by her employer. The monthly rental of £250 is deducted from her salary. Sally often works overtime when the hotel is busy or there are staff shortages. She is paid time-and-a-quarter for all overtime hours in excess of 173 hours a month.

Sally's gross salary for May 2003 (ie, before the deduction of PAYE tax and NI contributions), was made up as follows:

Regular monthly pay (£9,500 divided by 12):	£791.66
Overtime Pay (25 hours @ £5.71/hour):	£142.75
London 'weighting allowance':	£45.00
Gross Pay:	£979.41
LESS Rent of £250	

Was Sally paid less than the correct NMW for May 2003? To answer that question, Sally's overtime premium payments (£28.50) must be disregarded, as must her 'weighting allowance' (£45) and all rental payments in excess of £22.75 a week (or £98.58 a month), ie, £151.42. These 'specified reductions' effectively reduce Sally's gross pay for May 2003 from £979.41 to £754.49. As Sally worked a total of 198 hours during May, her hourly rate of pay for NMW purposes was just £3.81 an hour. As the correct NMW for her age is £4.20 an hour, her employer will need to pay her a further £77.20 (ie, 198 x £0.39) for that month, in order to make up the difference.

Hourly-paid workers

19.22
As the term implies, hourly-paid workers are paid for the number of hours they work each week or month (whatever the pay reference period). They are traditionally paid overtime for all hours worked in excess of their standard (or contractual) working hours, but are not normally paid for meal and rest breaks. If they work a system of shifts, they may be paid a shift allowance. If they work normally on a bank or public holiday (or on a rest day), they may be paid at a higher hourly rate for such work or they may have a contractual right to an equivalent amount of paid time off work to be taken at an agreed later date. If employed under a contract of employment, their terms and conditions of employment (including working hours, rate of pay, shift allowances, overtime premium payments, and the like) must be explained in the written statement of employment particulars necessarily issued to each of them within two months of the date on which their employment began.

Note: The expression pay reference period' means the period (not exceeding one month) in respect of which wages or salaries are normally paid (monthly, weekly, fornightly, or whatever). Some workers, notably casual workers (many of whom are hired on an 'as and when required' basis) will have a pay reference period of one day. Workers who are paid less frequently than once every month (eg, every three months) nonetheless have a pay reference period of one month. In short, the maximum pay reference period for any worker (under the 1999 Regulations) is one month.

19.23
Hourly-paid workers must be paid no less than the appropriate NMW rate for all hours worked in the standard pay reference period. Working hours do not include recognised meal and rest breaks (even if the worker is paid during such breaks, or works throughout a recognised meal or rest-break), absences from work occasioned by annual holidays, sick leave, maternity leave, parental leave, time off for dependants, and so on. Nor do they include time when a worker is engaged in a strike or other form of industrial action (including a 'go slow' or 'work to rule'). Whether or not a worker is entitled to be paid all or part of his (or her) wages when sick or injured will depend on the terms of his contract (although he will have the qualified

right to be paid statutory sick pay at such times). Payments in respect of maternity leave and annual holidays are regulated by statute (notably the Employment Rights Act 1996 and the Working Time Regulations 1998)(See Chapters 14 and 18).

19.24
An hourly-paid worker who is on standby or 'on-call', at or near his (or her) workplace (or who is at work, as required, but is not actually provided with work, or is unable to work because of a machine or plant breakdown) must be paid no less than the NMW for that time. The same applies when a worker is travelling between jobs, but not when he is travelling from and to his home and place of work.

Piece-workers and 'output' workers

19.25
There are workers who do not receive a basic wage, but are paid entirely on the basis of the work they do, the sales (or number of telephone calls) they make or the goods they produce. Such people may work from home or in premises provided by their employer. Unless (as is unlikely), they are genuinely self-employed, every such worker must be paid no less than the appropriate NMW wage rate for every hour worked (based on what their employer agrees is a fair estimate of the hours they work). The NMW rules for piece-workers, output workers, and the like, are complicated. Interested employers are advised to acquire a copy of the DTI's *Detailed Guide to the National Minimum Wage* (Ref. URN 99/662), copies of which are available from the address given at the end of this chapter.

RECORDS

19.26
Regulation 38 of the 1998 Regulations imposes a duty on employers to keep records 'sufficient to establish that he is remunerating [workers] at a rate at least equal to the national minimum wage'. Those records must be kept in a form which enables the information about a worker in respect of any one reference period to be produced in a single document. Furthermore, the employer must keep those records (either in paper form or on a computer or computer disk) for a rolling three-year period and must make those records available either to a worker (on request) (see para. 19.29 below) or to an Inland Revenue enforcement officer (on demand). An employer who fails to keep such records, or who keeps or produces false or inaccurate records, is guilty of an offence and liable on summary conviction to a fine of up to £5,000 – for each and every such offence.

ENFORCEMENT AND PENALTIES FOR NON-COMPLIANCE

19.27
The National Minimum Wage Act 1998 and its accompanying regulations are policed and enforced by Inland Revenue enforcement officers. Section 14 of the 1998 Act cautions employers that enforcement officers have the power to enter an employer's premises (at reasonable times), to inspect and take copies of pay records, to require an explanation of any such records, to ask questions, and to talk to workers. Enforcement officer can also issue enforcement notices requiring an employer to pay the appropriate rate of NMW to identified workers or to make up the shortfall between the NMW and the wages actually paid to those workers (backdated as appropriate). A failure to comply with the terms of an enforcement notice will prompt the issue of a penalty notice requiring the recalcitrant employer to pay £7.20 a day to each affected worker for every day of continued non-compliance.

19.28
There are a number of criminal offences under the 1998 Act, each of which attracts a penalty of up to £5,000 – for each offence. These are:

- a refusal or wilful neglect to pay the appropriate NMW rate;

- a failure to maintain adequate and accurate payroll records and time sheets;

- keeping false or inaccurate records;

- intentionally obstructing an Inland Revenue enforcement officer in the exercise of his or her authority; and

- refusing or neglecting to give information to an Inland Revenue enforcement officer.

The reader should note that, once the National Minimum Wage (Enforcement Notices) Bill becomes law, Inland Revenue enforcement officers may issue enforcement notices on employers known to have failed to pay the correct NMW to those of their workers who have since left their employ. The Bill, which was laid before Parliament on 21 November 2002, is to have retrospective effect.

Complaints by workers

19.29
Workers who know (or suspect) that they are not being paid the appropriate NMW rate have the right to ask to see their payroll records. Any such request must be made in writing. An employer who fails or refuses to produce those

records within 14 days, or who prevaricates or refuses to make those records available, will be ordered by an employment tribunal to pay the worker in question an amount equal to 80 times the appropriate NMW rate. A worker may also apply to a tribunal or county court for the recovery of any amount of wages or salary which fell short of the NMW. Any such application must be lodged with the nearest Regional Office of the Employment Tribunals on Form IT1 within three months of the employer's alleged refusal or failure.

19.30

Workers have no need to resign in order to pursue their statutory rights before an employment tribunal. If denied their right to be paid no less than the appropriate NMW rate, they may complain to an employment tribunal and/or invoke the assistance of an Inland Revenue enforcement officer. An employer who dismisses such a worker, or selects him (or her) for redundancy, or subjects him to some other detriment (eg, by demoting or transferring him, withholding a promised pay rise, or by denying opportunities for overtime, etc) – for challenging or questioning the employer's refusal or failure to pay the NMW (before a tribunal or court, or otherwise), or for asserting his statutory rights – will be ordered to pay the worker a substantial amount of compensation. See also Chapter 5, paras 5.46 & 5.47.

Case law

19.31

In *British Nursing Association v The Inland Revenue (NMW Compliance Team)* [2002] IRLR 240, the Court of Appeal held that homeworkers, employed by a Nursing Agency to deal with out-of-hours calls from clients (or would-be clients) between 8.00 pm and 9.00 am at night, were entitled to be paid the NMW for each of those 13 hours notwithstanding that they received very few calls between 11.30 pm and 5.00 am and spent most of their time watching television, sleeping or carrying out their domestic chores. They were not on standby or 'on call' in the strict legal sense, as their homes *were* their places of work, and they had to be there between 8.00 pm and 9.00 am to answer any and all incoming calls.

19.32

In a not dissimilar case, that of *Wright v Scottbridge Construction Limited* [2001] IRLR 589, a Mr Wright worked a seven-day, 98-hour week as a nightwatchman. However, he was paid for just 28 of those 98 hours, on the basis that his duties did not take up more than four hours a night. Indeed, his employers provided him with a bed and had told him that he could sleep, watch television, read, or do whatever, for the remaining 10 hours of his night-time shift. When pressed, his employers acknowledged that Mr Wright's primary role as nightwatchman was to ensure that their premises were secure and to respond speedily if the intruder or fire alarms were to ring. At no point, said the EAT, could Mr Wright be said to be off duty. Although he spent most of his time asleep, he was 'at work' and was therefore entitled to be paid the NMW wage for each of his 98 weekly hours. The employers were ordered to pay Mr Wright 24 weeks' back-pay and to adjust his weekly pay to the correct NMW amount.

Further information

19.33
The Department of Trade & Industry's (DTI) *Detailed guide to the national minimum wage* (Ref. URN99/662) may be obtained without charge from the DTI Publication Orderline, ADMAIL 528, London, SW1W 8YT (telephone 0870 1502 500, fax: 0870 1502 333, or e-mail: publications@dti.gsi.gov.uk).

For further assistance on the national minimum wage, employers should call NMW Enquiries on 0845 6000 678 or write to the following address:

NMW Enquiries
Freepost PHQ1
Newcastle upon Tyne
NE98 1ZH

Employers may also visit the DTI's National Minimum Wage Web site at www.dti.gov.uk/er/nmw

Public interest disclosures

20.1
Under the Public Interest Disclosure Act 1998, which came into force on 2 July 1999, any worker who makes a so-called protected disclosure has the right not to be dismissed, selected for redundancy or subjected to any other detriment (demotion, forfeiture of opportunities for promotion or training, etc) for having done so. Any term in a contract of employment or other document (such as a 'worker's contract') which purports to undermine or override a worker's right to make a protected disclosure is null and void.

Note: The relevant provisions of the 1998 Act (commonly referred to as 'the Whistleblower's Act') have been inserted as Part IVA (sections 43A to 43L) of the Employment Rights Act 1996. Those relating to a worker's right not to be dismissed, selected for redundancy or subjected to any detriment for making a protected disclosure are to be found in sections 47B, 103A and 105 of the 1996 Act. The latter Act is hereinafter referred to as 'the 1996 Act'.

Meaning of 'protected disclosure'

20.2
Section 43A of the 1996 Act defines 'protected disclosure' as meaning a qualifying disclosure, that is to say, any disclosure of information which, in the reasonable belief of the worker making the disclosure, tends to show one or more of the following:

(a) that a criminal offence has been, is being or is likely to be committed;

(b) that a person has failed, is failing or is likely to fail to comply with a legal obligation to which he (or she) is subject;

(c) that a miscarriage of justice has occurred, is occurring or is likely to occur;

(d) that the health and safety of an individual has been, is being or is likely to be endangered;

(e) that the environment has been, is being or is likely to be damaged; or

(f) that information tending to show any matter falling within any one of the preceding paragraphs has been, or is likely to be deliberately concealed.

It is important to note the use of the word 'worker', in this context. A worker is a person who is either an employee in the accepted sense (that is to say, a person employed under a contract of employment) or a person who works personally for another person under some other form of contractual arrangement (perhaps as a freelance operator, a trainee, a casual labourer, or agency worker). The term does not however apply to a person who is genuinely self-employed.

20.3
A worker prompted to make a disclosure about alleged wrongdoing by (or within) the organisation for which he (or she) works may do so:

(a) to his employer (either directly or in accordance with established procedures for dealing with such allegations) or to another person whom the worker reasonably believes to be solely or mainly responsible for the alleged unlawful or criminal conduct;

(b) to a legal adviser (if made in the course of obtaining legal advice);

(c) to a Minister of the Crown (if the disclosure is made in good faith, and the worker in question is employed by a Government-appointed person or public body);

(d) to the appropriate enforcing authorities (such as the Health & Safety Executive, the Commissioners of the Inland Revenue, the Environmental Agency, etc (see below));

(e) (subject to certain conditions) to some other person or agency, if the disclosure relates to an exceptionally serious failure on the part of the worker's employer or some other person; or

(f) (subject to certain conditions) to some other person or agency (eg, the media, or a professional body responsible for policing standards and conduct in a particular field).

Disclosure to employer or other responsible person

20.4
A worker may make a qualifying disclosure directly to his (or her) employer, or to some other person whom he reasonably believes to be solely or mainly responsible for the alleged wrongdoing, and will enjoy the protection available to him under Part IVA of the 1996 Act, so long as he acts in good faith (*ibid* section 43C).

20.5
If an employer has developed or authorised a simple and readily accessible procedure to encourage workers to air their concerns about alleged wrongdoing

within his organisation (eg, breaches of health and safety legislation), then those procedures should be exhausted before a worker takes it upon himself (or herself) to air those concerns or allegations elsewhere (see paras 20.8 to 20.10 below). He may choose, on the other hand, to present his allegations of wrong-doing directly to the appropriate enforcing authorities (so long as he does so in good faith and reasonably believes those allegations to be substantially true).

20.6
An employer's in-house procedures for dealing with allegations of wrong-doing are unlikely to inspire confidence unless they involve other members of the workforce or workforce representatives elected or appointed by their peers to deal with such issues and make representations to their employer. A reasonable employer will, of course, respond positively to qualifying disclo-sures about supposed criminal activities or other wrongdoing within his organisation. So long as those disclosures were made in good faith, it would be wholly irresponsible (not to mention costly) for an employer to react by disciplining the worker or workers concerned, or by dismissing them or subjecting them to some other detriment.

Disclosure to the 'appropriate authorities'

20.7
A worker who makes a qualifying disclosure to a prescribed person or body – such as the Health & Safety Executive, the Inland Revenue, HM Customs & Excise, the Environment Agency, the Audit Commission, the Director General of Fair Trading, and the like (see *Note* below) – will enjoy the protection afforded by the 1998 Act, so long as he (or she) does so in good faith and reasonably believes that the allegations of wrongdoing he is making are substantially true (*ibid* section 43F).

Note: A list of the persons and descriptions of persons prescribed for the purposes of section 43F of the 1996 Act is to be found in the Schedule to the Public Interest (Prescribed Persons) Order 1999 (SI 1999/1549) and is reproduced in DTI Booklet URN 99/511 (*Guide to the Public Interest Disclosure Act 1998*), copies of which are available free of charge from the DTI's Publications Orderline (Telephone: 0870 1502 500).

Disclosure in other cases

20.8
A worker who makes a qualifying disclosure to some other person or body (other than his employer or the appropriate enforcing authority) will enjoy the protection of the law, if he (or she):

(a) made the disclosure in good faith;

(b) reasonably believed that the information disclosed, and any allega-tions contained in it, were substantially true;

(c) did not make the disclosure for purposes of personal gain;

(d) reasonably believed (at the time he made the disclosure) that he would have been punished, dismissed, selected for redundancy or subjected to some other detriment had he made the disclosure to his employer or to the appropriate enforcing authority;

(e) (in the absence of an appropriate enforcing authority), reasonably believed that his employer would have concealed or destroyed any incriminating evidence; or

(f) had previously made the same or a similar disclosure to his employer or the appropriate enforcing body without avail.

Whether or not it was reasonable for the worker to have made the qualifying disclosure to a person or body other than his (or her) immediate employer (or the appropriate enforcing authority) will depend in large part on the identity of the person or body to whom the disclosure was made. An employment tribunal will also consider the seriousness of the alleged wrongdoing (and the likelihood of its happening again), whether the disclosure in question contained information in breach of the employer's duty of confidentiality to another person (eg, a customer or client), the employer's or the prescribed enforcing authority's response (or failure to respond) to a previous disclosure of the same (or substantially similar information), and whether, in making the same or similar allegations to his employer on a previous occasion, the worker had complied with any procedure whose use by him was authorised by his employer (*ibid* section 43G).

20.9
Challenging an employer's failure to pay the appropriate national minimum wage, or to comply with his (or her) duties under the Working Time Regulations 1998, or to provide personal protective equipment, or for discharging toxic chemicals into the environment, or for defrauding the Inland Revenue etc, may not achieve the desired result if made directly to the person allegedly responsible for such breaches of the law, or if doing so is likely to prompt the concealment of any damaging documents or other evidence before the relevant authorities have had an opportunity to make their own assessments of the situation.

20.10
A worker might also be concerned about the risk to his livelihood, the more so if his previous allegations on the same or a similar theme have been dismissed out of hand or 'swept under the carpet', or he has been warned 'to keep his mouth shut'. Whether influenced by such considerations or otherwise, a worker has the right to make his disclosures about alleged wrongdoing to the body, person or authority responsible for investigating

and enforcing the particular law which the worker reasonably believes has been (is being or is about to be) broken.

Disclosures about exceptionally serious failures

20.11
A worker who has made a qualifying disclosure (eg, to a newspaper) about an *exceptionally serious failure* (either by his or her employer or by some other person) will enjoy the protection afforded by the Employment Rights Act 1996 if, but only if, he:

(a) made the disclosure in good faith;

(b) reasonably believed that the information disclosed, and any allegations contained in it, were substantially true;

(c) did not make the disclosure for purposes of personal gain; and

(d) if, given the circumstances, it was reasonable for him to have made the disclosure.

Whether or not the failure in question was exceptionally serious is a matter of fact, not of opinion. In other words, a worker's reasonable belief that a particular failure was exceptionally serious will not be enough. The failure must in fact have been exceptionally serious.

20.12
In determining whether or not it was reasonable for the worker to have made the disclosure in question, an employment tribunal will have regard in particular to the identity of the person or organisation to whom the disclosure was made (*ibid* section 43H). All of which suggests that a worker would be well-advised to obtain legal advice before make a qualifying disclosure which, if aired in the public domain, could not only undermine his right not to be dismissed or subjected to a detriment for doing so but could also lead to his being sued in defamation.

Other forms of protection

20.13
It should be remembered that the Employment Rights Act 1996 offers considerable protection to employees who allege (in good faith) that their employer has infringed their statutory rights under that Act, the Trade Union & Labour Relations (Consolidation) Act 1992, or the Working Time Regulations 1998. Under the National Minimum Wage Act 1998, for example, Inland Revenue enforcement officers have the right to question workers and to act on any information supplied by those workers concerning their employer's alleged failure

to pay the appropriate national minimum wage rate. There are any number of similar examples, all of which complement a worker's rights under the 'Protected Disclosures' provisions of the 1996 Act (eg, the right of employees under section 100 of that same Act to bring to their employer's attention (by reasonable means) circumstances connected with their work which they reasonably believe to be harmful or potentially harmful to health or safety).

COMPLAINT TO AN EMPLOYMENT TRIBUNAL

20.14
A worker may complain to an employment tribunal that he (or she) has been penalised, victimised or subjected to some other detriment for making a protected disclosure. Should the worker's complaint be upheld, his employer will be ordered to pay him such compensation as the tribunal considers appropriate in the circumstances (including compensation for the loss of any benefit that the worker might reasonably be expected to have enjoyed) but for his employer's conduct or failure to act.

20.15
A worker (as 'employee') who has been dismissed (or selected for redundancy) for making a protected disclosure may complain to an employment tribunal and will be awarded a substantial amount of compensation if his (or her) complaint is upheld. A worker who is not an employee in the strict legal sense, but whose detrimental treatment amounted to a termination of his contract, may likewise complain to an employment tribunal, and will also be awarded compensation if his complaint is upheld. It is as well to point out that there is no upper limit on the amount of compensation that may be awarded in such cases.

20.16
Complaints to an employment tribunal, in the circumstances described above, must be presented within three months of the effective date of termination of an employee's contract of employment, or within three months of the alleged detrimental treatment (including, in the case of a worker who is not an employee, detrimental treatment amounting to a termination of the worker's contract). Such complaints may be presented regardless of the worker's age or length of service at the material time.

Data protection

OVERVIEW

21.1

Under the Data Protection Act 1998, employers who store and process personal data about their employees – whether in a computerised, paper-based or other relevant filing system – must ensure that the data in question serves a legitimate purpose; that it is kept under 'lock and key'; and that it is not deliberately or unwittingly disclosed to unauthorised third parties. Employees, for their part, have the right to be informed of the nature and scope of the data held on their personal files, the source of that data (*Who provided it?*), and the names or job titles of the people to whom that data has been or may be disclosed. They have the right also (on payment of a fee of up to £10) to inspect and take copies of most (if not all) of the documents concerning personal data about them that is held in their employers' filing systems. Although the term 'employee' is used throughout this section, it is as well to point out that the 'data protection' and 'subject access' provisions of the 1998 Act apply equally to casual, seasonal and temporary workers who may or may not be 'employees' in the strict legal sense of the word.

21.2

Employees may challenge the relevance or accuracy of any personal data about them that is held on their employers' files and may apply to the High Court or county court for an order directing their employers to rectify, block, erase or destroy that data and any other personal data which contains an expression of opinion which appears to the court to be based on inaccurate data. But see paras 21.19 to 21.21 below.

Note: 'Processing', in relation to information or data, whether done manually or by computer, means obtaining, recording, or holding the information or data; or carrying out any operation or set of operations on that information or data, including organising, adapting, altering, retrieving, disclosing, erasing or destroying it.

MEANING OF 'RELEVANT FILING SYSTEM'

21.3

The term 'relevant filing system' encompasses any non-automated or manual filing system that is structured either by reference to individuals or by reference to criteria relating to individuals, and that is assembled in such a way that specific information relating to a particular individual is readily accessible. Arguably, the contents of the typical personnel file are neither 'structured'; nor 'readily accessible'. Indeed, some commentators have expressed the view that, because they are unstructured, such files fall outside the scope of the 1998 Act. Others have argued, equally cogently, that they do not. Wiser counsel urges employers to err on the side of caution by applying the 1998 Act's 'data protection principles' (paras 21.9 to 21.11 below) to all personal data which relates to individual employees.

21.4
Although the processing of personal data on a computer in a coded format may be appropriate from the point of view of security, it does not relieve employers of their statutory duty to disclose that data when an employee asks to see it. Coded data must, of course, be translated into plain English (and a hard copy produced) before it is made available to the employee.

MEANING OF 'PERSONAL DATA'

21.5
'Personal data' means data or information relating to a living person (whether employee or worker, job applicant or former employee) who can be readily identified from that data (or from any other data held by, or likely to come into the possession, of that individual's employer (or former employer), including any expression of opinion about that individual and any indication of the employer's intentions in respect of that individual. But see paras 21.16 to 21.18 below.

Sensitive personal data

21.6
The 1998 Act lays down rules concerning the processing of so-called 'sensitive personal data' – that is to say, data that consists of information relating to a person's racial or ethnic origins, or to his (or her) religious beliefs, political opinions, trade union membership, physical or mental health, sexual life, or criminal convictions.

21.7
An employer may not process sensitive personal data about an employee (or reveal such data to a third party) without the employee's express consent, preferably in writing, unless the data in question is needed for legal reasons or in compliance with an employer's statutory duties. Indeed, the 1998 Act allows that the 'processing' of data about an employee's racial or ethnic origins may be justified if the employer's aim is to monitor the effectiveness of his equal opportunities policy.

21.8

Job application forms that require a would-be employee to reveal sensitive data should explain why that information is needed. For example, in certain trades and industries involving exposure to specified hazardous substances, health and safety legislation effectively requires women of 'reproductive capacity' to disclose whether they are pregnant or are breast-feeding or have recently given birth. Such information will need to be kept on file for obvious reasons (at least for so long as it remains relevant). Job applicants who have a liability to epileptic seizures, or who are insulin-treated diabetics, or who have a alcohol or continuing drug dependency, or who have suffered from a psychotic illness within the previous three years, may not be employed to drive large vehicles; and so on. The Rehabilitation of Offenders Act 1974 also requires job applicants (and, in some cases, existing employees) who are applying for appointment or transfer to particular occupations to disclose details of any and all criminal convictions (including 'spent' convictions).

THE EIGHT 'DATA PROTECTION PRINCIPLES'

21.9

The 1998 Act lists eight data protection principles that differ slightly in subject-matter and content from the seven principles laid down in the now-repealed 1984 Act. Under the 1998 Act, personal data about an individual (whether 'processed' by automated or non-automated means):

1. must be processed fairly and lawfully;

2. must be obtained for one or more specified lawful purposes;

3. must be adequate, relevant and not excessive in relation to the purposes for which it is processed;

4. must be accurate and, where necessary, kept up to date;

5. must not be kept longer than is necessary;

6. must be processed in accordance with the rights of employees (or former employees);

7. must be safeguarded (by appropriate technical or organisational measures) against unauthorised or unlawful processing, and against accidental loss, damage or destruction; and

8. must not be transferred to a country or territory outside the European Economic Area unless that country or territory ensures an adequate level of protection for the rights and freedoms of data subjects (this principle is new in the 1998 Act).

21.10

In brief, an employer should only process personal data if the information held on an employee's file (computerised or otherwise) is necessary or justifiable:

- for the purposes of entering into a contract of employment (employee's name, address, age, sex, marital status, number of dependants, schooling, academic qualifications, employment history, etc); or

- in the context of an employee's (or employer's) statutory or contractual rights, duties or obligations (eg, doctor's sick notes, attendance records, performance appraisals, disciplinary records and warnings, health assessments, information about accidents, injuries or diseases); or

- for PAYE tax, National Insurance, or occupational pension scheme purposes.

Personal data about an employee or worker should only be kept on file for so long as is strictly necessary. It follows that personnel files should be 'laundered' at regular intervals to remove extraneous, invalid, irrelevant or out of date information (particularly important in the case of former employees). If an employee asks for inaccurate, false or irrelevant material to be removed from his (or her) personal file, the employer should comply, unless of course he disagrees with the employee's assessment of that information; in which event, the matter may be referred to the High Court or a county court for determination, although the latter option will not be available in relation to data held in manual or paper-based filing systems in existence before 24 October 1998 (see paras 21.19 to 21.21 below).

21.11

Finally, and most importantly, an employer must ensure that appropriate security measures are in place to prevent personal data held on computer or in paper-based filing systems falling into the wrong hands. As indicated earlier, sensitive personal data should not be kept on file without the express permission of the individual(s) concerned unless there is an overriding legal or practical requirement for the retention of such data.

ACCESS TO PERSONAL DATA

21.12

Under the 'subject access' provisions of the 1998 Act, employees have the right (at reasonable intervals and without undue delay, and on payment of a fee of up to £10) to be informed about any personal data concerning them that is held by their employers either electronically (that is to say, in a computerised format) or in their manual or paper-based filing systems. They have the right also to examine that data and to ask for the correction, updating or erasure of any data that they consider to be inaccurate or irrelevant. What constitutes *reasonable* access will depend on the particular circumstances. But two or three times a year would not be unreasonable.

Note: If revealing the source of contentious information on an employee's file means disclosing the identity of the person who provided that information in the first place, the employer must first obtain the permission of that person before doing so. If that permission is withheld, the employer must edit the information in such a way as to omit that person's name or other identifying particulars.

21.13

An employee should not expect to be given access to personal data at a moment's notice. He (or she) may have to wait up to 40 days (the maximum under the 1998 Act), before that information is supplied. An employer who refuses to supply such data (or needlessly delays issuing that data) is guilty of an offence and liable on summary conviction to a fine of up to £5,000.

Evaluating an employee's capabilities

21.14

Information held on computer or on an employee's personnel file, which expresses an opinion about that employee's capabilities, character, attitudes, conduct, performance, etc must be disclosed to that employee on request.

21.15

Furthermore, an employee may challenge his (or her) employer's *sole* reliance on the computerised processing of his personal data to evaluate his work performance, capabilities, reliability, conduct, etc – the more so if decisions stemming from that automated evaluation are likely to have a significant impact on the employee's prospects for advancement or career development within the employing organisation. In short, the employee has the right to demand an intelligible explanation of the logic involved in such decision-taking and may write to his employer requiring him to ensure that no such decision is to be taken based solely on a computerised evaluation of his personal data.

Information that need not be disclosed

21.16

The definition of *personal data* in the 1998 Act includes any indication of an employer's intentions with respect to an individual employee – which, at first sight, would appear to suggest that an employee is entitled to know whether he (or she) has been earmarked for a pay rise, promotion, redundancy, disciplinary action or dismissal. However, that is not the case. Schedule 7 to the Act (*Miscellaneous Exemptions*) makes it clear that employees have no statutory right to demand to see (or to be provided with copies of) documents whose contents comprise information processed for the purpose of management forecasting or planning – the more so if the premature disclosure of such information is likely to prejudice the conduct of the employer's business (*ibid* Schedule 7, paragraph 6).

Access to references?

21.17

Nor need an employer disclose the contents of a reference relating to an existing or former employee that he (or she) has sent in confidence to a prospective new employer. Nor need he reveal the contents of a reference sent to some other body or institution which is considering an employee for further education or training, or that relates to the appointment (or prospective appointment) of an employee to any public office; or that is given in respect of any service the employee hopes or intends to provide to another person or organisation (*ibid* Schedule 7, paragraph 1).

21.18

Although not obliged to disclose the contents of references sent to other employers, that same prohibition does not apply to references supplied by one or other of an employee's former employers. However, section 7 of the 1998 Act cautions that an employer should be wary of disclosing the contents of a reference supplied in confidence by a former employer unless it is possible to do so by deleting the name and job title of the person who wrote the reference as well as those of any other person named or referred to in the reference. Furthermore, in deciding whether it is reasonable to supply a copy of a reference without the consent of the person who wrote it (or that of any other person named or identified in it), the employer must pay due regard to any duty of confidentiality owed to the individuals in question; the steps that have been, or should have been, taken to obtain their consent; whether they are capable of giving their consent; and whether they have expressly refused to give their consent.

TRANSITIONAL PROVISIONS

21.19

The 1998 Act allows of two transitional periods. The first transitional period ended on 23 October 2001; the second ends on 23 October 2007. During the first transitional period, personal data held in automated or computerised filing systems was exempt from some but not all of the 1998 Act's provisions. The processing of data stored on computer must now comply fully with the 1988 Act. However, as is explained in the next paragraph, most employers have until 23 October 2007 to comply fully with the Act's provisions relating to manual or paper-based filing systems.

21.20

During the second transitional period, manual (or paper-based) files in existence before 24 October 1998, need not comply with the first data protection principle (save for the right of an employee to access personal data held on those files), nor with the second third, fourth and fifth data protection principles until the end of the second transitional period (that is to say, until 24 October 2007). Nor do employees have the right, during that second transitional period, to apply to the county court (or High Court) for an order requiring their employers to rectify, block, erase or destroy inaccurate data held on those files. In short, employers processing personal data held in manual files (set up before 24 October 1998) have some five years in all in which to 'put their houses in order' – by auditing and sanitising those files and putting the necessary compliance procedures in place.

21.21

What is not yet clear (and this has been the subject of some speculation) is whether personal data added to manual or paper-based files on or after 24 October 1998 'enjoys' the benefit of the same seven (now four) year transitional period or whether such data should now comply fully with the 1998 Act. In her *Introduction to the Data Protection Act 1998*, the Data Protection (now Information) Commissioner states that personal data about existing employees added to files that came into being before 24 October 1998 is 'unlikely' to alter the character of those files unless that additional material 'produces a different effect on the overall processing operation'. Further information about compliance with the 1998 Act (notably on this latter point) may be obtained by telephoning the data protection Information Line on 01625 545745. See also para. 21.25 below.

NOTIFICATION

21.22

Under the since-repealed Data Protection Act 1984, UK employers who kept personal data about their employees in a computerised filing system or by other electronic means (eg, in a mainframe, desk-top, lap-top computer, or on a floppy disc or CD), or who used the services of a computer bureau to store or process any such data, had no need to register that fact with the then Data Protection Commissioner if the data in question was held solely for the purposes of calculating and paying wages, salaries and pension monies. Even though registration was not required in the latter situation, the data stored on computer could not then (and cannot now) legally be used for any other purpose. Nor may it be disclosed to any other person except for the purpose of obtaining actuarial advice on pension issues or for use in medical research into the health and accident records of persons employed in particular occupations.

21.23

With the coming into force on 1 March 2000 of the 1998 Act, and the concomitant repeal of its predecessor, the former system of registration has been replaced by a new notification regime. Under that regime, employers who store and process personal data about their employees (whether on computer or in paper-based filing systems) need not notify the Information Commissioner of that fact (although they may choose to do so voluntarily) if the processing is done purely for staff administration purposes – eg, for recruitment and selection or payroll purposes or in connection with an employee's employment and career history, qualifications, experience, promotion, transfer or training, performance, health and attendance, conduct and capabilities, or related personnel issues. Nor is notification required if employers do not use computers for processing personal data about their employees. However, notification is required if personal data about an individual is processed on computer for pensions administration purposes. Further advice may be obtained from the Notification Helpline on 01625 545745 (Fax: 01625 545748 or e-mail: data@notiifcation.demon.co.uk).

EMPLOYMENT PRACTICES DATA PROTECTION CODE

21.24

In March and September 2002, respectively, the Information Commissioner published the first and second parts of a planned four-part *Employment Practices Data Protection Code*. Part 1 (*Recruitment and Selection*) and Part 2 (*Records Management*) may be downloaded from Web site www.dataprotection.gov.uk/dpr/dpdoc.nsf. Part 3 of the code (*Monitoring at Work*), in draft form, was published on 8 July 2002, and may also be downloaded from the same Web site. At the time of writing, a consultation draft of Part 4 of the code (*Medical Information*) had not yet been produced. It is as well to point out that the new code will not come into force until its four constituent parts have been formally agreed and published.

FURTHER INFORMATION

21.25

It is important to stress that the above is little more than a summary of the principal provisions of the 1998 Act and should not be relied upon by any reader as his (or her) primary source of information on the 1998 Act – the more so as the Act itself is not only lengthy and complex, but contains a great many 'ifs' and 'buts' which have not been explored in any detail in these pages. Copies of *The Data Protection Act 1998 – Legal Guidance* can be downloaded from Web site www.dataprotection.gov.uk or may be obtained (along with related publications, guidance notes and codes of practice) from:

Publications
Information Commissioner's Office
Wycliffe House
Water Lane
Wilmslow
Cheshire
SK9 5AF
Telephone: (01625) 545700

Transfer of undertakings

GENERAL INFORMATION

22.1

Far and away the most controversial piece of legislation to appear in the past 20 or so years is the Transfer of Undertakings (Protection of Employment) Regulations 1981. The purpose of the TUPE Regulations (so-called) – which came into force on 1 May 1982, implementing Council Directive 77/187/EC of 14 February 1977 (the 'Acquired Rights' Directive) – is to protect the rights of employees when the undertaking (company, firm, trade or business) for which they work (or part of that undertaking) is sold or transferred as a 'going concern' to another employer (the 'transferee'). Council Directive 77/187/EC, as amended by Directive 98/59/EC), has since reappeared in consolidated form in Directive 2001/23/EC, as to which, see paragraphs 22.43 & 22.44 below.

22.2

The Regulations apply to the transfer of a UK-based undertaking (or part of such an undertaking) from one person to another – whether effected by sale or by some other disposition (other than by the sale of shares), or by operation of law. Such a transfer (which may be effected by a series of two or more transactions, and may take place whether or not any property is transferred to the transferee by the transferor) is referred to in the Regulations as a 'relevant transfer'; and it is the meaning of that expression which has produced so many confusing and contradictory decisions in the courts (see *Meaning of 'relevant transfer'*, paras 22.30 to 22.41 below). The expression 'undertaking' includes any trade or business (Reg. 2).

The person selling or disposing of his (or her) business (the seller) is referred to as the 'transferor'; while the person to whom the business is sold (the purchaser) is known as the 'transferee'.

Note: If the receiver, administrator or liquidator of a company which has gone into receivership or liquidation (or which is voluntarily wound-up by its creditors) transfers the company's undertaking, or part of the company's undertaking, to a wholly-owned subsidiary of the company, the 'relevant transfer' will be deemed not to have been effected until immediately before the transferee company ceases (otherwise than by reason of its being wound up) to be a wholly-owned subsidiary of the transferor company, or until immediately before the relevant undertaking is transferred by the transferee company to another person, whichever occurs first. For the purposes of the TUPE Regulations, the transfer of the relevant undertaking will be taken to have been effected immediately before that date by one transaction only (Reg. 4).

TUPE REGULATION SUMMARISED

22.3
When a TUPE transfer occurs, the transferee (the buyer) inherits the contracts of employment of the persons employed by the transferor (the seller) immediately before the transfer took place. In short, those contracts of employment do not come to an end (as they might otherwise have done under the common law) but are treated in law as if they had originally been made between the affected employees and the transferee. So, if food manufacturer A sells one of his (or her) factories to food manufacturer B, as a going concern, food manufacturer B inherits the contracts of employment of every person employed in that factory (and their rights under those contracts) (*ibid* regulation 5).

22.4
A transferee who inherits the contracts of employment of persons employed in the undertaking immediately before the 'relevant transfer', (see paras 22.30 to 22.42 below) also inherits the transferor's rights, powers, duties and liabilities (including liability for redundancy payments, money in lieu of notice, compensation for unfair dismissal, subsisting allegations of sex discrimination, monies owed to employees, etc, but *not* any criminal liabilities) under, or in connection with, those contracts. Furthermore, anything done by the transferor *before* the transfer takes place, in or in relation to any such contract (or to a person employed in the undertaking in question), is deemed in law to have been done by the transferee.

22.5
Once a 'relevant transfer' has taken place it is not open to the transferee to presume to vary the contracts of employment of the transferred employees with a view to harmonising their working hours, rates of pay, holiday entitlement, etc with those of his existing workforce. Nor may the transferee insert fresh terms, such as a restrictive covenant, in the transferred employees' contracts (*Credit Suisse First Boston (Europe) Limited v Padiachy* [1998] IRLR 504, QBD; *Credit Suisse First Boston (Europe) Limited v Lister* [1998] IRLR 700, CA). This rule applies even if the employees in question are happy to accept any such variation in their terms and conditions of employment and are no worse off as a result of that variation (*Foreningen af Arbejdsledere i Danmark v Daddy's Dance Hall A/S* [1988] IRLR 315 and *Rask v ISS Kantineservice A/S* [1993] IRLR 133)). In the *Wilson/Bexendale* case (see next paragraph) Lord Slynn of Hadley opined (*obiter*) that any variation of the terms of an employee's contract, which is due to a TUPE transfer and for no other reason, is invalid. There can, however, be a valid variation, he said, for

reasons that are not due to the transfer. 'It may be difficult' he concluded 'to decide whether the variation is due to the transfer or attributable to some separate cause, but there may come a time when the link with the transfer is broken or can be treated as no longer effective'.

22.6

In *Wilson v St Helen's Borough Council/BFL v Baxendale & Meade* [1998] IRLR 706), the House of Lords held that a dismissal for a reason connected with a TUPE transfer (whether by the transferor or the transferee), while automatically unfair (unless for an ETO reason), is nonetheless legally effective and not a nullity – thereby overruling the Court of Appeal on that same point [1997] IRLR 505. An employee dismissed by a transferor cannot compel the transferee to employ him. Under English domestic law, said their Lordships, the dismissal of an employee by an employer brings to an end the working relationship between them. As a general rule, the English courts will not specifically enforce contracts of employment. If a dismissal is in breach of contract, the employee can claim damages for wrongful dismissal. If it is unfair, the employee may seek redress from an employment tribunal; in which event, the employer will be ordered either to reinstate or re-engage the dismissed employee and/or pay a substantial amount of compensation. But, save for the purpose of enforcing rights under it, the contract of employment is gone. As was indicated earlier, a transferee who does not take on the transferor's employees – because they have already been dismissed by the transferor or by the transferee himself – must, nonetheless, meet all the transferor's contractual and statutory obligations in relation to those employees, including a liability to pay damages for wrongful dismissal and/or compensation for unfair dismissal.

22.7

All of which suggests that the only way a transferee can legitimately vary the terms of conditions of incoming TUPE-transferred employees is to dismiss them all (which dismissals will be automatically unfair if not for an ETO reason involving changes in the workforce) and then offer to re-engage some or all of them on terms and conditions which they may or may not find acceptable. By any measure, this 'take it or leave it' option (and a willingness to pay compensation for unfair dismissal) cannot be in the interest of good industrial relations practice nor preferable to a negotiated and consensual variation in the terms and conditions of incoming employees.

22.8

In the joined cases of *Bernadone v Pall Mall Services Group & Others* and *Martin v Lancashire County Council*) [2000] IRLR 487, the Court of Appeal held that the liabilities inherited by a transferee under TUPE include any and all liabilities of the transferor in tort. Although tortious liabilities do not arise 'under' the contract of employment, they do arise 'in connection with' the contract, given that the employer's common law duty of care arises out of the relationship of employer and employee. In short, an employee injured in the course of his (or her) employment with the transferor (his former employer) may nonetheless sue the transferee (his new employer) for damages in negligence. However, the former employer's right to an indemnity under his (or her) employer's liability insurance policy also transfers to the new employer. In other words, it is the transferor's insurers, not the transferee's, who must pay any damages awarded by the court in such circumstances.

22.9

A transferee does *not*, however, inherit any term in an employee's contract of employment which relates to an occupational pension scheme as defined in section 1 of the Pension Schemes Act 1993 (although moves are afoot to remove this exception).

22.10

The phrase 'immediately before the transfer' is given a wide interpretation. It covers any person in the employ of the vendor who is dismissed in consequence of the proposed sale, whether or not negotiations for the sale had been completed or a buyer identified. It could apply where a liquidator trims the workforce before seeking purchasers to make a business more attractive, but not where he (or she) has run out of work and there is a true redundancy situation (*P Bork International A/S v Foreningen af Arbejdsledere i Danmark* [1989] IRLR 41, ECJ; *Litster v Forth Estuary Engineering Ltd* [1989] ICR 341, HL; and *Wendleboe v L J Music Aps* [1985] ECR 457, ECJ).

An employee's refusal to transfer

22.11

There is no transfer of a contract of employment (or of the rights, powers, duties and liabilities under, or in connection with, that contract) if the employee in question informs the transferor (or the transferee) that he (or she) objects to becoming employed by the transferee (*ibid* regulation 5(4A)).

22.12

An employee who refuses to work for the new owner of his (or her) former employer's business, for whatever reason, effectively brings his contract of employment to an end. In short, the termination of his employment does not amount to a dismissal in law and the employee has no right to complain of unfair dismissal, regardless of his (or her) length of service at the material time (*ibid* regulation 5(4B)) (*Katsikas v Konstantinidis* [1993] IRLR 179, ECJ).

22.13

However, a substantial and detrimental change in the employee's working conditions immediately before the transfer might well amount to so serious a repudiation of his contract as to entitle him to resign (with or without notice) and pursue a complaint of unfair constructive dismissal (*ibid* regulation 5(5)). That right would nonetheless be denied him if he had not been continuously employed for at least one year and was under normal retiring age at the effective date of termination of his contract of employment.

22.14

In *Hay v George Hanson (Building Contractors) Ltd* [1996] IRLR 427, the Employment Appeal Tribunal said that an employee who had expressed unhappiness about the prospect of working for the transferee could not be said to have objected to (or refused) the transfer. Although the TUPE Regulations are not specific on this point, an employee who refuses outright to transfer should inform his (or her) employer in clear and unequivocal terms (whether by word or deed, or by a combination of the two) that he refuses to work for the transferee.

Effect of transfer on collective agreements

22.15

If, at the time of the 'relevant transfer', the transferor has a collective agreement with a recognised trade union in respect of any employee whose contract is inherited by the transferee, the transferee inherits that collective agreement in respect of that same employee (and the rights and obligations that go with it) as if it had been made between himself (or herself) and the trade union in question (*ibid* regulation 6).

22.16

The transferee does *not*, however, inherit any term in a collective agreement as relates to an occupational pension scheme as defined in section 1 of the Pensions Act 1993.

Dismissal of employee because of relevant transfer

22.17

If, either before or after the 'relevant transfer', the transferor (or the transferee) dismisses any employee of the transferor (or of the transferee) for a reason in any way linked to the transfer itself, the employee in question will be treated in law as having been unfairly dismissed. The only justification for such a dismissal would be an 'economic, technical or organisational reason entailing changes in the workforce' – often referred to as an 'ETO' reason – which, if genuine, will be treated by an employment tribunal as having been for 'some other substantial reason' of a kind such as to justify the dismissal of an employee holding the position which that employee held (*ibid* regulation 8).

22.18

In short, an employer (transferor or transferee) will need to justify his (or her) decision to dismiss one or more of the employees affected by the transfer on grounds which have nothing whatsoever to do with the transfer (eg misconduct) or for a genuine ETO reason involving changes in the workforce. For example, it is arguably absurd (in a situation in which an undertaking or part of an undertaking is absorbed within the transferee's organisation) for the transferee to be left with a duplicated management team (two marketing managers, two chief accountants, two personnel managers, etc), and (say) a hundred or more production workers (when he only needs 60) without being able to make the appropriate organisational changes. If he (or she) has a highly sophisticated production process requiring far fewer workers, logic dictates that a number of workers will have to be made redundant. If the transferee can justify those redundancies (and the redundancy selection process) on purely business grounds (ie an ETO reason), the dismissals are likely to be held fair.

22.19

Curiously, an employee dismissed in consequence of a 'relevant transfer' does not qualify to present a complaint of unfair dismissal unless continuously employed for a minimum period of one or more years ending with the effective date of termination of his (or her) contract of employment and under 'normal retiring age' at that time (*ibid* regulation 8(5)).

Effect of relevant transfer on trade union recognition

22.20

If, after a 'relevant transfer' the undertaking (or part of the undertaking) transferred maintains an identity distinct from the remainder of the transferee's undertaking, any independent trade union recognised to any extent (or for any purpose) by the transferor shall be deemed to be recognised to that same extent (or purpose) by the transferee. If the transferred undertaking does *not* maintain an identity distinct from the remainder of the transferee's undertaking, but is simply absorbed within the latter undertaking, the recognition agreement no longer applies.

DUTY TO INFORM AND CONSULT REPRESENTATIVES

22.21

A 'relevant transfer' will inevitably impact on persons employed by both the transferor and transferee. Many will simply be concerned to know what effect the transfer is likely to have on their jobs, prospects or continued employment. To allay such concerns, the Regulations require both the transferor *and* the transferee, first, to inform the 'appropriate representatives' about the transfer and, second, consult them and listen to their representations.

First, the representatives must be informed of:

(a) the fact that the relevant transfer is to take place, when, approximately, it is to take place, and the reasons for it;

(b) the legal, economic and social implications of the transfer for all affected employees;

(c) the measures which the employer envisages will, in connection with the transfer, be taken in relation to those employees or, if it is envisaged that no measures will be so taken, that fact; and

(d) if the employer is the transferor, the measures which the transferee envisages he (or she) will, in connection with the transfer, take in relation to such of those employees whose contracts of employment he will inherit after the transfer or, if he envisages that no measures will be taken, that fact.

The information in (a) to (d) must be conveyed to the 'appropriate representatives' long enough before the relevant transfer to enable them to take an active part in the subsequent consultations. To that same end, the transferee must likewise give the transferor advance information about his (or her) own intentions under (d) above.

22.22

The term 'appropriate representatives' means employee representatives elected by the employees themselves or, if the employees are of a description in respect of which an independent trade union is recognised by the employer, representatives of that trade union (eg shop stewards). In an undertaking in which there are both employee-elected and trade-union appointed representatives, the employee must deal with those trade union representatives. If there is no trade union representing the interests of the affected employees (that is to say, the employees who may be affected by the transfer or may be affected by measures taken in connection with it) the employer must consult either with existing employee-elected representatives (who may have been elected for other purposes) or invite the affected employees to elect one or more of their number to represent their interests in consultations relating to the proposed transfer. If there are no elected employee representatives, the employers on both sides must invite the affected employees to elect one or more of their number to be representatives and give them sufficient time to carry out the election and to complete it *before* the information and consultation process takes place (*ibid* regulation 10 & 10A).

Note: When overseeing the election of employee representatives, the employer must do whatever is necessary to ensure that the election is fair. Although the employer has the right to decide on the appropriate number of representatives, he (or she) cannot presume to dictate which employees can put their names forward as candidates and which cannot. The employer must also allow the affected employees sufficient time to cast their votes *in secret*, and must see to it that the votes given at the election are accurately counted (*ibid* regulation 10A)).

22.23
Second, if either the transferor or transferee envisages taking (unspecified) measures in relation to any employees affected by the transfer, he (or she) must consult with the appropriate representatives with a view to seeking their agreement to those measures. During the consultation process, the transferor or transferee must (a) consider any representations made by those representatives, (b) reply to those representations, and (c), if he rejects any of those representations, give his reasons for doing so. Before, during and after such consultations, the employer in question must allow those representatives access to the affected employees and provide whatever accommodation and facilities they may need in that respect (eg an office, tables and chairs and, perhaps, use of a telephone).

Penalties for failure to inform or consult

22.24
An appropriate representative (or in the case of a trade union-appointed representative, the union in question) or one or more of the affected employees may complain to an employment tribunal that their employer had refused or failed to inform or consult them about the 'relevant transfer'. Such a complaint must be presented within the period of three months beginning with the date on which the relevant transfer took place. If the complaint is upheld, the tribunal will order the respondent employer to pay the complainant/s an appropriate amount of compensation; in short, such sum not exceeding 13 weeks' pay as the tribunal considers just and equitable having regard to the seriousness of the employer's failure to inform or consult. A complaint presented 'out of time' will not be entertained unless the tribunal is satisfied that it was not reasonably practicable for the applicant to have done so within that prescribed three-month period.

22.25
A failure to pay the compensation referred to in the preceding paragraph will lead to a further complaint to a tribunal and to an order directing the employer to pay the relevant amount (*ibid* regulation 11, as amended by the Collective Redundancies & Transfer of Undertakings (Protection of Employment) (Amendment) Regulations 1999 (SI 1999/1925)).

22.26
An employer may defend his (or her) failure to comply with the duty to inform and consult if he can satisfy a tribunal that there were special circumstances which rendered it not reasonably practicable for him to do so, but that he took all such steps towards the performance of that duty as were

reasonably practicable in those circumstances. However, it is no defence for the employer to argue (as transferor) that he (or she) was prevented from complying fully with his duty to inform the appropriate representatives because of the transferee's refusal or failure to provide the information referred to earlier in this section. If, on the other hand, the transferor has given notice to the transferee that he intends to show that fact, the giving of that notice will make the transferee a party to the proceedings (and liable in his turn to pay the whole or part of any award of compensation).

RESTRICTION ON CONTRACTING OUT

22.27
Any provision of any agreement (whether a contract of employment or otherwise) will be void in so far as it purports to exclude or limit the operation of the TUPE Regulations or to preclude any person from presenting a complaint to an employment tribunal arising out of an employer's failure to inform or consult the appropriate representatives about the transfer (*ibid* regulation 12).

22.28
In *Thompson & Others v (1) Walon Car Delivery, (2) BRS Automotive Ltd*, EAT/256/96, the EAT held that a 'compromise agreement' concluded with the transferor several days after a 'relevant transfer', and purporting to exclude the right of an employee to bring proceedings under TUPE, could not be relied upon by the transferee.

EXCLUDED CLASSES

22.29
Regulations 8, 10 & 11 of the TUPE Regulations do not apply to employees who, under their contracts of employment, ordinarily work outside the United Kingdom. A person employed to work on board a UK-registered ship is regarded as a person who ordinarily works in the UK unless the employment is wholly outside the UK or he (or she) is not ordinarily resident in the UK.

Note: Regulation 8 relates to the dismissal of an employee because of a relevant transfer; regulation 10, to an employer's duty to inform and consult the appropriate representatives; and regulation 11, to the consequences of an employer's failure to inform and consult.

MEANING OF 'RELEVANT TRANSFER'

22.30
There has to be a 'transfer from one person to another'. The European Court of Justice (ECJ) has held that the Acquired Rights Directive provides

protection where there is a change in the natural or legal person responsible for the running of an undertaking (*Landorganisationen i Danmark v Ny Molle Kro* [1989] ICR 330, ECJ), a view endorsed by the ECJ in (amongst others) *Dr Sophie Redmond Stichting v Bartol & Others* [1992] IRLR 366 and *Rask & Christensen v ISS Kantineservice A/S* [1993] IRLR 133.

22.31

There has to be a transfer of a 'going concern' or an economic entity, so that the purchaser can carry on the business without interruption. It does not matter that there are modifications. Goodwill is often included but is not essential. Where there was a change of tenants at a public house owned by a brewery it was held that continuity was preserved for an employee who worked there. The new tenant had been put in possession of a going concern and was running the same business as that run by his predecessor (See *JMA Spijkers v Gebroers Benedik Abbatoir CV & Another* [1986] 2 CMLR 296 ECJ; *Kenny & Another v South Manchester College* [1993] IRLR 265, QBD; *McLellan v Cody & Cody*, 7 October 1986, EAT Oct 7, 1986, EAT; and *Safebid Ltd v Ramiro & Others*, 3 May 1990, EAT).

22.32

But where a firm holding a catering concession prematurely stopped running the business, which was then carried on temporarily with a different sort of catering facility by the company that had granted the concession, the EAT held that this was not a 'relevant transfer' within the meaning of the 1981 Regulations (*Caterleisure Ltd v TGWU & Others*, 14 October 1991, EAT).

22.33

Where it is shown, on the other hand, that, shortly after the sale, the employees were re-engaged by the transferee, the Regulations would probably bite. A business was put out to tender. The company that previously ran it lost the contract to a competitor. That other company engaged nearly all the former employees who were previously engaged in the business. It was held that the 1981 Regulations applied (*Harrison Bowden Ltd v Bowden* [1994] ICR 186, EAT; and *Dines & Others v Initial Health Care Services Ltd & Another* [1994] IRLR 336, CA).

22.34

The possible permutations are endless, but there have been several important rulings on what is meant by and what are the consequences of the TUPE Regulations. The tribunals and courts must apply a purposive construction to the relevant provisions so as to achieve what they are manifestly intended to achieve (*Marleasing SA v La Comercial Internacional de Alimentacion* [1990] ECR 4153, ECJ).

22.35

It matters not how many transfers take place or between whom, provided that there is an economic entity in existence that the final employer carries on in some capacity, eg as purchaser of the business, or as franchisee or licensee (*Foreningen af Arbejdsledere i Danmark v Daddy's Dance Hall A/S* [1988] IRLR 315, ECJ; and *LMS Drains Ltd & Metro-Rod Services Ltd v Waugh*, 6 June 1991, EAT).

The 'Spijkers' test

22.36
In *Spijkers v Gebroeders Benedik Abbatoir CV* [1986] 2 CMLR 486, the ECJ held that the decisive criterion for establishing the existence or otherwise of a TUPE transfer (or 'relevant transfer') is whether the undertaking (or part of the undertaking) transferred retains its identity after the change of ownership. In other words, are the activities or the nature of the trade or business carried on (or resumed) by the transferee essentially or identifiably the same as those carried on by the transferor before the transfer took place. The ECJ in *Spijkers* listed a number of factors to be taken into account in deciding whether these conditions are fulfilled:

- the type of undertaking (trade or business) in question and the activities carried on by that business;

- whether or not tangible assets (including furniture and equipment, raw materials, stock in hand, finished products, and the like) were transferred to the new owner of the business;

- the value of intangible assets (such as 'goodwill') at the time of the alleged transfer;

- whether or not the majority of persons working in the business were taken over by the new employer;

- whether the new owner continued to do business with the same customers or clientele after the alleged transfer took place;

- the degree of similarity between the activities carried on before and after the transfer, and the period (if any) for which those activities are suspended.

Finally, it is for the national court to make the necessary factual appraisal, in order to establish whether or not a TUPE transfer had occurred.

22.37
The fact that an activity (i) was only ancillary, (ii) the business transferred only involved one person and (iii) there was no transfer of any tangible assets could not deprive an employee from the protection of the Regulations (*Christel Schmidt v Spar-undLeihkasse der früheren Amter Bordesholm, Kiel und Cronshagen, The Times*, 25 May 1994, ECJ).

The 'Süzen' and related cases

22.38

In *Rygaard v Stro Molle Akustik* [1996] IRLR 151, the ECJ held that a transfer must involve the transfer of a 'stable economic entity'. But, the 'cat was set amongst the pigeons' (so to speak) in *Ayse Süzen v Zehnacker Gebäudereinguing GmbH Krankenhausservice & Lefarth GmbH* [1997] IRLR 255, when the ECJ ruled that, in the case of a 'second generation transfer', an activity does not of itself constitute such an entity. There would, they said, have to be a significant transfer of assets and a transfer of the majority of skilled workers from one contractor to the next before such a transfer could be held to be a 'relevant transfer' within the meaning of the 1981 Regulations. In the *Süzen* case, a cleaner who worked at a school in Germany, was dismissed (along with seven of her colleagues) by the cleaning company by whom she was employed when the latter lost its cleaning contract at the school. The contract was awarded to another cleaning company. The ECJ held (following the opinion of the Advocate-General) that a change of contractors does not qualify as a 'relevant transfer' unless significant tangible or intangible assets (or a majority of the workforce in terms of numbers and skills) also transfers to the second (or new) contractor. In labour-intensive undertakings (such as contract catering or cleaning), where there are no significant assets, there will not be a transfer within the meaning of the TUPE Regulations unless a majority of the former contractor's workforce is taken on by the new contractor.

22.39

Following swiftly on the heels of the *Süzen* decision came the decision on 26 March 1997 of the Court of Appeal in *Betts v Brintel Helicopters Limited and KLM Era Helicopters* [1997] IRLR 361. In the *Betts* case, Brintel Helicopters had a contract to 'ferry' men and equipment to and from a number of North Sea oil rigs owned by Shell. When Brintel's contract expired, the contract was awarded to KLM Era Helicopters who did not (nor needed to) take on any of Brintel's staff or equipment. The Court agreed with *Süzen* and held that the changeover of contractors did not constitute a 'relevant transfer'.

22.40

Süzen was applied by the ECJ in *Francisco Hernández Vidal v Gomez Perez & Others* [1999] IRLR 132 and, again, in *Sanchez Hidalgo & Others v Asociación de Servicios Aser & Sociedad Cooperativa Minerva* [1999] IRLR 136. In the *Hernández Vidal* case, the ECJ held that a situation in which an organisation terminates its contract with a cleaning firm and decides to do its own cleaning would be covered by the 'Acquired Rights' Directive, so long as the operation is accompanied by the transfer of an economic entity between the last two undertakings. However, 'the mere fact that the maintenance work carried out, first, by the cleaning firm and then by the undertaking owning the premises, is similar, does not justify the conclusion that a transfer of such an entity has occurred'. And again: 'In certain sectors such as cleaning, the activity is essentially based on manpower. Thus, an organised grouping of wage earners, who are specifically and permanently assigned to a common task, may, in the absence of other factors of production, amount to an economic entity – a view repeated by the ECJ in the *Sanchez Hidalgo* case which was decided on a similar set of circumstances. In short, it is for the national court to determine whether the maintenance of the premises which awarded the contract was organised in the form of an economic activity within the outside cleaning firm before the firm awarding the contract decided to carry out the work itself.

22.41

However, in *ECM (Vehicle Delivery Service Limited v Cox* [1999] IRLR 416, the Court of Appeal (while distinguishing *Süzen* and cases like it, for reasons which are far from clear, given their similarity) held that an employer could not prevent the 1981 Regulations applying simply by refusing to take on the putative transferor's employees. Indeed, said the Court, an employment tribunal had every right to challenge those motives before deciding whether a TUPE transfer had in fact occurred.

COMMENT

22.42

Over the years, the tribunals and courts have delivered a number of seemingly inconsistent (it not wholly contradictory) decisions on the interpretation of the 1981 Regulations. The old adage holds true: that each case must be decided on its particular merits – which is, of course, of little comfort to employers who (short of seeking an opinion from a tribunal or court) are left to decide for themselves whether their activities (notably the termination or non-renewal of cleaning, maintenance and related contracts, or the outsourcing of some of their operations, eg, payroll services) fall within the scope of the TUPE Regulations.

For further references in this handbook to the TUPE Regulations (and there are many) please consult the Index.

RECENT DEVELOPMENTS

22.43

A consultation document published by the Department of Trade & Industry (DT) containing the Government's proposals for reform of the 1981 Regulations (including proposals for the transfer of occupational pension rights) was published in September 2001. Although the consultation period ended on 15 December 2001, the DTI advise that draft amending legislation is unlikely to appear (for further consultation) before the Summer of 2003. It should be noted that amendments to the 'Acquired Rights Directive' contained in Council Directive 98/50/EC (since repealed and consolidated in Council Directive 2001/23/EC) are optional in the sense that there are no 'time limits' for incorporation of those amendments into the domestic legislation of EU Member States.

22.44

The consultative document referred to above also includes proposals designed to enable employers contemplating the sale of their own (or purchase of another employer's) business or undertaking to obtain fast-track access to the employment tribunals for guidance on whether the intended purchase or sale is likely to constitute a 'relevant transfer' within the meaning of the TUPE Regulations. Copies of the consultative document may be accessed and downloaded from the DTI Web site www.dti.gov.uk/er/tupe/consult.htm.

Health and safety at work

EMPLOYER'S DUTY OF CARE

23.1
An employer has a common law, as well as statutory, duty to take reasonable care for the health and safety of his workforce. He must provide them with a safe working environment (including safe means of access to and from his premises), safe tools, appliances and equipment, and protection against any hazards associated with their employment.

23.2
An employee who is injured in the course of his (or her) employment may sue his employer for damages. To succeed in such an action, he will need to prove negligence on the part of his employer and that he was injured as a direct result of that negligence.

23.3
An employer cannot deny negligence on grounds only that he was not in breach of a statutory duty (eg, that he was under no obligation in law to guard a particular machine, or to provide an employee with this or that item of protective clothing or equipment). Liability at common law will still exist if the employer should have known of a particular hazard and did nothing to protect his employees from the possible consequences.

23.4
If, on the other hand, an employer has complied with a statutory duty to guard a particular machine (indeed, any duty under a particular statute or set of Regulations), he may be able to claim in his defence that he had fulfilled his common law duty of care to an injured worker. But, if a worker is injured in the course of his (or her) employment, in consequence of a defect in any machine or appliance provided by his employer, and the defect is attributable wholly or partly to the fault of a third party (usually the manufacturer or supplier of the machine or appliance in question), the employer will nonetheless be held liable for the employee's injuries and may face a civil action for damages in the ordinary courts. The expression 'injury' includes loss of life, any impairment of a person's physical or mental condition, and any disease. Any term in a worker's contract, which purports to exclude or restrict the employer's liability in such circumstances, is null and void. In

short, an injured worker may sue his (or her) employer for damages regardless of the existence or his acceptance of any such contract term (*Source*: Employer's Liability (Defective Equipment) Act 1969).

23.5
An injured employee may sue his (or her) employer on two counts: (a) that he was negligent and in breach of his common law duty of care, and (b) that he was in breach of a duty imposed by statute. Under the provisions of the Employer's Liability (Compulsory Insurance) Act 1969, an employer must insure against civil liability for damages arising out of personal injury sustained by his employees.

Duty to customers, clients, etc

23.6
In addition to his duty of care towards his own workforce, the occupier of premises owes a like duty to persons invited or permitted to be on those premises (such as guests, customers, patrons, clients, tradesmen, etc). This 'common duty of care' has been codified by the Occupiers' Liability Act 1957. In short, the owner or occupier of business premises may well be sued for damages if a member of the public is injured as a direct consequence of his negligence. Furthermore, he runs the risk of being prosecuted under the 1974 Act for failing to take all reasonably practicable steps to safeguard the interests of those members of the general public who have a valid or legitimate reason for being on or near his premises (*Source:* HASAWA 1974, s.3). If a customer, client, tradesman (or whomever) is killed or seriously injured while visiting or present in a shop, factory, warehouse, restaurant, office block , department store, or wherever, and the accident is (or appears to be) directly attributable to the manner in which that business was conducted, the owner or occupier must notify the 'relevant enforcing authority' immediately (in compliance with the Reporting of Injuries, Diseases & Dangerous Occurrences Regulations 1995, not otherwise discussed in this book).

HEALTH AND SAFETY AT WORK ETC ACT 1974

23.7
In addition to their common law duty of care, employers have a statutory duty, under section 2 of the Health & Safety at Work etc Act 1974 (HASAWA), to ensure, so far as is reasonably practicable, the health, safety and welfare at work of their employees. To that end, every employer must:

- provide and maintain plant, machinery, equipment, tools, appliances and systems of work which are, so far as is reasonably practicable, safe and without risk to health;

- arrange, so far as is reasonably practicable, that employees are not put at risk (or exposed to risk) in connection with the use, handling, storage or transport of dangerous articles and substances (such as chemicals, dusts, noxious fumes or vapours, etc);

- provide as much information, instruction, training and supervision as is necessary to ensure, so far as is reasonably practicable, the health and safety at work of his (or her) employees;

- ensure, so far as is reasonably practicable, that the buildings, offices, workshops, and other areas or places in which people are employed to work, are safe and without risks to health;

- provide and maintain safe means of access to (and egress from) all parts of the premises;

- provide and maintain a working environment (including facilities such as toilets, washrooms, cloakrooms, rest areas, and the like) which, so far as is reasonably practicable, is not only safe and without risks to health but also adequate in terms of heating, lighting, ventilation, and seating, etc.

(*Source*: HASAWA 1974, s.2.)

23.8
It is an employer's duty also to conduct his (or her) undertaking in such a way as to ensure, so far as is reasonably practicable, that persons not in his employment (contractors, tradesmen, etc) who may be affected thereby are not needlessly exposed to risks to their health or safety. That same general duty extends to other persons (members of the public, customers, guests, clients, etc) on the employer's premises who may be affected by the way in which he conducts his business (*Source:* HASAWA 1974, s.3).

23.9
An employer's duties under the 1974 Act are reinforced and supplemented by a variety of statutes and regulations – the latter now in the ascendancy as older statutes (such as the Factories Act 1961) are replaced by more up-to-date legislation, prominent amongst which are:

- the Electricity at Work Regulations (SI 1989/635);

- the Workplace (Health, Safety & Welfare) Regulations 1992 (SI 1992/304).

- the Health & Safety (Display Screen Equipment) Regulations 1992 (SI 1992/2792);

- the Personal Protective Equipment at Work Regulations 1992 (SI 1992/2966) (as amended);

- the Manual Handling Operations Regulations 1992 (SI 1992/2793);

- the Construction (Health, Safety & Welfare) Regulations 1996 (SI 1996/1592);

- the Fire Precautions (Workplace) Regulations 1997 (SI 1997/1840, as amended by SI 1999/1877);

- the Provision & Use of Work Equipment Regulations 1998 (SI 1998/2306);

- the Management of Health & Safety at Work Regulations 1999 (SI 1999/3242);

- the Chemicals (Hazard Information & Packaging for Supply) Regulations 2002 (SI 2002/1689); and

- the Control of Substances Hazardous to Health Regulations 2002 (SI 2002/2677).

Note: A list of current health and safety legislation (including a computer diskette) is available from HSE Books at the address given at the end of para. 23.14 below.

RISK ASSESSMENT

23.10

Regulation 3 of the Management of Health & Safety at Work Regulations 1999 (*qv*) imposes a duty on *every* employer (and on every self-employed person) to make a 'suitable and sufficient assessment' of the risks to which his (or her) employees are exposed while they are at work and of any risks to members of the public (customers, clients, visitors, guests, passers-by) who may be affected by the way in which he conducts his business or undertaking – the purpose being to identify the measures the employer needs to take to comply with the restrictions and prohibitions imposed upon him by or under contemporary health and safety legislation. That duty extends to assessing the risks associated with an outbreak of fire (per Part II of the Fire Precautions (Workplace) Regulations 1997); the risks confronting new and expectant mothers and women of child-bearing age; and the risks to inexperienced and immature young persons. Risk assessment is also mandatory under each of the Regulations listed above.

Meaning of 'risk assessment'

23.11

Risk assessment is nothing more or less than a systematic general examination of workplace activities, environmental factors and working conditions that will enable the employer (or self-employed person) to identify the risks posed not only by working methods, machines, tools and equipment, processes, noise, electricity, ionising radiation, flammable liquids and gases, dusts, fumes and vapours, and a seemingly endless list of prescribed hazardous substances (including lead and asbestos) but also by factors such as temperature, humidity, poor lighting and ventilation, the inadequacy of the means of access to (and egress from) premises, obstructions in corridors and walkways, the condition of floors, floor coverings, and so on. It is only when he (or she) has assessed the hazards and determined the degree of risk, that an employer can hope to take the steps he is required to take in law to eliminate or minimise those risks. Indeed, the whole tenor of the 1999 Regulations (and of the hazard-specific regulations listed above) is that employers (and self-employed persons) cannot realistically expect to comply with their general duties (to employees and members of the public) under the Health & Safety at Work, etc Act 1974) unless they *do* carry out a risk assessment and make a genuine effort to eliminate the risks uncovered by that assessment.

HEALTH AND SAFETY COMMISSION AND EXECUTIVE

23.12
The 1974 Act also established the Health and Safety Commission (HSC) and the Health and Safety Executive (HSE). The former is responsible for monitoring matters relating to health and safety, and the latter for enforcement (through the health and safety inspectorate).

23.13
Subordinate legislation provides for the appointment of one or more trade union-nominated *safety representatives* or (where there is no recognised trade union) the election of *representatives of employee safety*, whose functions include responsibility for monitoring health and safety issues at the workplace (*Cleveland CC v Springett & Others* [1985] IRLR 131, EAT) (*Source*: Safety Representatives & Safety Committees Regulations 1977 (SI 1977/500) and the Health & Safety (Consultation with Employees) Regulations 1996 (SI 1996/1513)).

CODES OF PRACTICE

23.14
Section 16 of the 1974 Act empowers the Health & Safety Commission (HSC) to issue approved codes of practice 'for the purposes of providing practical guidance with respect to the requirements of any provisions of sections 2 to 7' [of the 1974 Act] or of any of the *existing statutory provisions* – which latter expressions encompass all current and related health and safety legislation.

A failure to comply with any provision of a code of practice is not an offence *per se*; but, as is the case with a breach of the Highway Code, is admissible in evidence before a tribunal or court.

To date, the HSC has issued some 50 plus codes of practice, a complete list of which is to be found in the current HSE Books Catalogue available from: HSE Books, PO Box 1999, Sudbury, Suffolk CO10 6FS (Telephone: 01787 881165, or Fax: 01787 881165). For further information about HSE publications, readers can now access the HSE's on-line catalogue: www.hsebooks.co.uk

HEALTH AND SAFETY INSPECTORS

23.15
Health and safety inspectors, many of whom are local authority environmental health officers, are duty-bound to investigate and, where appropriate, enforce adherence to health and safety legislation in their separate areas of responsibility. They visit factories, offices, shops, roadworks, construction sites, hotels, restaurants, leisure complexes, schools, hospitals, etc (indeed, any premises in which people are employed to work) as often as may be appropriate (the more so if they have been formally notified of an accident or dangerous occurrence involving injury – or any serious risk of injury – to persons or property).

23.16
If an inspector discovers a contravention of the Act, he (or she) can either:

- verbally (and informally) advise the relevant employer of the contravention and caution him (or her) to set matters to rights before his next visit (eg inadequate ventilation, faulty power points, loose guard-rails, slippery floors, etc); or

- serve the employer with an Improvement Notice or (if there is a serious infringement) a Prohibition Notice formally advising the employer to take appropriate action either immediately or within prescribed time limits (usually 21 days); or

- institute criminal proceedings before a Magistrates' Court.

An inspector will not institute criminal proceedings unless satisfied that the employer in question has deliberately and persistently flouted the law or that the contravention was so serious (eg a dust explosion) as to warrant prosecution (*Source*: HASAWA 1974, s.33).

Improvement notices

23.17
An Improvement Notice is a document cautioning an employer that, in the inspector's opinion, he or she is contravening one or other of the *existing statutory provisions* (ie, Regulations made under, or saved by, the 1974 Act) ,

or has done so and is likely to do so again. The inspector must give reasons, and will require the employer to remedy the contravention within a period of not less than 21 days or within some other specified period (*Source*: HASAWA 1974, s.21).

23.18
The notice may be withdrawn by an inspector at any time before the end of the period specified. The period may be extended more than once, provided no appeal against it has been lodged. An employer can appeal to an employment tribunal on the grounds that it is not 'reasonably practicable' to comply with the notice, but must do so within 21 days of the service of the notice on him, or within such further period as is reasonable in the circumstances. The lodging of an appeal has the effect of suspending the operation of the notice until the appeal is finally disposed of. It may be by way of a hearing or a withdrawal of the appeal (*Source*: HASAWA 1974, ss 23 & 24. See also Schedule 5 to the Employment Tribunals (Constitution & Rules of Procedure) Regulations 2001 (SI 2001 / 1171).

Prohibition notices

23.19
An inspector may service a Prohibition Notice on an employer if, in his (or her) opinion, the activities carried on by the employer involve, or are likely to involve, a risk of serious personal injury. The notice must state that the inspector is of that opinion, specifying the matters giving rise to that risk, and identifying the relevant statutory provisions that are, or would be, contravened. It will also state that the activities must cease within the time specified in the notice and until the matters specified in the notice have been remedied. Where the inspector states in the notice that he believes that the risk of serious personal injury is imminent, those activities must cease immediately (*Source*: HASAWA 1974, s.22).

23.20
If a prohibition notice is not intended to have immediate effect, the inspector may withdraw it at any time before the end of the period specified in the notice. He may extend, or further extend the period provided no appeal has been lodged.

23.21
An appeal to an employment tribunal, against the service of a prohibition notice, must be lodged within 21 days of the date of service of the notice, although the tribunal may extend the time limit where it is satisfied, on an application made in writing to the Secretary to the Tribunals, that it is not or was not reasonably practicable for an appeal to be brought within that time.

However, the lodging of an appeal does not automatically suspend the operation of the notice. A separate application to do so has to be made to the tribunal (*Source*: HASAWA 1974, s.24(3)(b)).

Defence of not 'reasonably practicable'

23.22
In deciding whether it is 'reasonably practicable' to comply, it is necessary that 'a computation must be made by the owner, in which the quantum of risk is placed on one scale and the sacrifice involved in the measure necessary for averting the risk (whether in money, time or trouble) is placed on the other: and that if it be shown that there is a gross disproportion between them – the risk being insignificant in relation to the sacrifice – the [employers] discharge the onus on them' (per Asquith LJ in *Edwards v National Coal Board* [1949] 1 KB 704, CA).

23.23
Thus, an employer would have to show that the risks were small compared to the cost of carrying out the remedial work. For instance, an inspector might serve a notice on an employer requiring him to fit appropriate banisters to an otherwise dangerous or steep staircase. These might cost £10,000. If evidence is advanced to show that the staircase was very rarely used or that the risk of injury is small, the tribunal might well cancel the notice or approve a less expensive alternative (*West Bromwich Building Society v Townsend* [1983] ICR 257, DC).

Procedure on appeal

23.24
In proceedings, before an employment tribunal, the onus is on the employer to show that it is not reasonably practicable to comply with the terms of an improvement or prohibition notice. The tribunal may either cancel or affirm the notice. If the notice is affirmed, the tribunal may modify the notice to the extend that it deems fit (*Source*: HASAWA 1974, s.24(2)).

Costs

23.25
The tribunal may make an order that a party to the proceedings shall pay to the other party either a specified sum in respect of the costs incurred by that other party or, in default of agreement, the taxed amount of those costs. A tribunal will not generally exercise that power against a health and safety inspector unless satisfied that the improvement or prohibition notice should never have been issued on the information available to the inspector

at the material time. But, it is likely to make an order against an employer who brings an appeal that is lacking in merit or is otherwise hopeless (*Source*: Employment Tribunals (Constitution & Rules of Procedure) Regulations 2001 [*qv*] Sch. 5).

Proceedings in a magistrates' court

23.26
Employers served with an improvement or prohibition notice must either appeal to an employment tribunal, and avail themselves of the defence of 'not reasonably practicable', or comply with the notice. The offence lies in their failing to comply (*Dearey v Mansion Hide Upholstery Ltd* [1983] ICR 610, DC).

23.27
If proceedings are brought against an employer in the Magistrates' Court on the grounds that he (or she) has failed to comply with an improvement or prohibition notice, or with a notice which has been modified on appeal by the tribunal, the employer cannot raise the defence of not 'reasonably practicable', whether or not there are valid grounds for resisting the allegation. However, if proceedings are brought for a breach of a relevant statutory provision, the defence of not 'reasonably practicable' *is* available, but the employer must prove it, on a balance of probabilities (*Source*: HASAWA, ss 33(1) & 40).

Appeal to the High Court

23.28
An appeal from the decision of an employment tribunal, or from that handed down in a Magistrates' Court, lies to the divisional court of the High Court, which has powers very similar to those of the Employment Appeal Tribunal.

Penalties

23.29
The penalty for a failure to comply with the terms of an improvement or prohibition notice (including any such notice as modified on appeal) is a fine, on summary conviction, of up £20,000 and/or imprisonment for a term not exceeding six months. On conviction on indictment, the penalty is a fine of an unlimited amount and/or imprisonment for a term not exceeding two years (Source: HASAWA 1974, s.33(2A).

23.30
The penalty for a contravention of an employer's statutory duties under sections 2 to 6 of the 1974 Act is a fine, on summary conviction, of a maximum

£20,000 or, if the offender is convicted on indictment, a fine of an unlimited amount. For a breach of health and safety regulations, the penalty is a fine of up £5,000 or, if the offender is convicted on indictment, an unlimited fine.

Human Rights Act 1998

OVERVIEW

24.1

The Human Rights Act 1998, which came into force on 2 October 2000, gives 'further effect' to the rights and freedoms guaranteed to all citizens under the European Convention on Human Rights & Fundamental Freedoms made at Rome on 4 November 1950. The 1998 Act does not create any new statutory or common law rights. What it *does* do is impose a duty on 'public authorities' (government departments, local authorities, borough councils, the police, health authorities, and the like) to act in a way that is compatible with a Convention right. It likewise imposes a duty on the tribunals and courts (as public authorities in their own right), when determining a question which has arisen in connection with a Convention right, to take into account any relevant judgement, decision, declaration or advisory opinion of the European Court of Human Rights (ECHR); any opinion or decision of the European Commission of Human Rights; and any decision of the Committee of Ministers under Article 46 (as to the jurisdiction of the ECHR). Furthermore, without affecting their validity, continuing operation or enforcement, UK primary and subordinate legislation (eg, statutes, regulations and orders) must be read and given effect in a way that is compatible with the Convention rights (*ibid* s.3).

Practical guidance

24.2

It is important to bear in mind that the Human Rights Act 1998 has 'vertical direct effect' only. This means that while civil servants and public sector employees may sue their employers (government departments, local authorities, borough councils, the police and other public or quasi-public authorities) for damages arising out of an alleged breach of their Convention rights, that same option is not available to workers in the private sector. Private sector workers, who are pursuing complaints or claims against their employers before the tribunals or courts, alleging a breach of one or other of their statutory or contractual rights, may rely on (or pray in aid) a particular Convention right during the subsequent proceedings, but may not bring proceedings against his employer solely on the basis of an alleged breach of that right. They may, on the other hand, legitimately expect the tribunal or court entertaining their complaints or claims to interpret UK law in a way that is compatible with their Convention rights and to take account of any judgement or decision of the ECHR (and related Strasbourg-based institutions) which may have a bearing on the proceedings.

24.3
For example, an employee in the private sector, who has been dismissed for misusing his (or her) employer's facilities (eg, by playing computer games during working hours or for making too many private phone calls, or for accessing or downloading inappropriate material from the Internet), or for turning into work scruffily or scantily dressed, or for questioning his supervisor's judgement in a particular situation, and so on, may be prompted to pursue a complaint of unfair dismissal before an employment tribunal. But that same employee cannot institute proceedings before a tribunal or court solely on the ground that his employer's actions infringed his Convention right to respect for his private and family life (Article 8), or his right to freedom of expression (Article 10), and so on.

THE CONVENTION RIGHTS

24.4
Widespread speculation about the likely impact of the Human Rights Act includes the suggestion that employers should undertake a wholesale review of their job application forms and reconsider the propriety of asking questions about a job applicant's age or date of birth, marital status, sex, current and recent health problems, attendance record with a previous employer, or willingness to wear a uniform while on duty. There have been suggestions also that an employer's imposition of a dress code could infringe a worker's right to 'freedom of expression' under Article 10 of the Convention. Still others, that using CCTV surveillance and intercepting workers' telephone calls and e-mails without their knowledge, might also amount to an infringement of their Article 10 rights, unless wholly justified. What then are workers' rights under the Convention and how well-informed are such suggestions?

Many of the rights and freedoms guaranteed under the European Convention (listed in Schedule 1 to the 1998 Act), such as the right to life, the prohibition of torture (or of slavery and forced labour), have little relevance to the modern workplace. Those that are relevant or may have a bearing on the development of employment policies and procedures are Articles 8, 9, 10, 11 and 14.

Article 8: Right to respect for private and family life

24.5
In *Halford v United Kingdom* [1997] IRLR 471, the ECHR held that telephone calls from business premises may be covered by notions of 'private life' and

'correspondence' within the meaning of Article 8 of the Convention. Article 8 states that 'everyone has the right to respect for his private and family life, his home and his correspondence'. The European Court rejected the UK Government's submission that employers should, in principle, be at liberty to monitor their employees' telephone calls without their prior knowledge. The Court ruled (an important point) that, as Ms Halford was unaware that the private and business calls she made from her office were liable to be intercepted, she was entitled to assume that her right to privacy would be respected.

24.6

Employers, nonetheless, have every right to expect their employees to carry out their duties efficiently and productively, and not spend their working hours making or receiving private phone calls, misusing fax and e-mail facilities, or 'surfing' (or downloading inappropriate or illegal material from) the Internet for their own purposes. Indeed, employees caught misusing or abusing their employers' facilities in this way can expect to be disciplined and, in serious cases, summarily dismissed (eg, if caught e-mailing offensive, obscene, sexist, racist, libellous or defamatory messages or material to fellow employees or to clients, customers, friends or others outside the organisation).

24.7

The situation has since been regularised by the Telecommunications (Lawful Business Practice) (Interception of Communications) Regulations 2000 (SI 2000/2699), which came into force on 24 October 2000. The 2000 Regulations were made under section 4(2) of the Regulation of Investigatory Powers Act 2000, which latter imports the EU Telecoms Data Protection Directive (97/66/EC) into UK domestic legislation. Under those Regulations, employers may legitimately monitor or record all telecommunications transmitted over their systems, without the consent of the people using those systems, if that monitoring or recording is done to establish the existence of facts, or to ascertain compliance with regulatory or self-regulatory practices or procedures. They may do so also for quality control purposes, for the prevention or detection of crime, for investigating or detecting unauthorised use of the telecoms system, or for ensuring the effective operation of their telecommunications systems. Employers may also monitor (but not keep a record of) telephone calls or e-mail transmissions to check whether the communications in question are relevant to the employer's business.

24.8

Employers must nonetheless 'make all reasonable efforts' to inform employees that their phone calls, e-mail transmissions, etc may be intercepted. This can best be achieved by posting notices to the like effect on (or adjacent to) telephones and PC's cautioning employees that unauthorised use might well result in disciplinary action or dismissal. It is as well to add that employers are under no legal obligation to inform third parties (ie, outside callers) that their calls or incoming e-mails may be monitored or recorded.

24.9
Employers should take appropriate steps to inform new recruits and existing employees that their telephone calls, e-mail transmissions and use of the Internet are likely to be monitored and/or recorded. So far as job applicants and new recruits are concerned, this is best done at the pre-employment interview and during induction training. The same applies to CCTV surveillance of sensitive work areas, body searches, sick visits, and random drug testing. Staff and works handbooks should clearly state the employer's policy on such matters, reinforced (especially when CCTV cameras are present) by suitable notices posted about the workplace.

24.10
In keeping with their Article 8 rights, employees should not be denied the opportunity to make and receive private phone calls when there is an urgent domestic crisis (eg, a sick or injured relation, a death in the family, a gas explosion at home, a burst water pipe, and the like) which requires their immediate attention. Most reasonable employers will permit a limited number of private phone calls from the office or workshop (either with or without the prior permission of supervisors); while others provide pay phones for the use of employees when an emergency arises. It is all a question of balance (balancing the legitimate interests of the employer against those of the workforce). An employee who is dismissed for abusing the right to make private phone calls may pursue a complaint of unfair dismissal before an employment tribunal and may rely on Article 8 of the Convention if convinced that his or her employer had acted unreasonably in taking the decision to dismiss.

Other Article 8 issues

24.11
The notion advanced by some commentators, that it is an infringement of an employee's (or would-be employee's) human rights to require a job applicant to complete a job application form stating his (or her) date of birth, marital status, ages of children, current and previous health and attendance records, criminal convictions, disabilities, and the like, is absurd. The need for such information can be justified on a variety or practical and legal grounds. For instance, an employer will need to know an employee's date of birth to ensure compliance with (amongst others) the National Minimum Wage Act 1998, the Management of Health & Safety at Work Regulations 1999, and legislation prohibiting or restricting the employment of young persons and school age children in certain occupations. Such information is also necessary in order to

calculate an employee's entitlement to a redundancy payment, and for pension and actuarial reasons. Information about an employee's disabilities, or current and previous health record, is necessary to enable the employer to make the 'appropriate adjustments' to the workplace and to ensure that the person in question is not unwittingly engaged in work involving exposure to dangerous, chemicals, processes or substances or in any work calculated to exacerbate an existing disease or medical condition.

24.12

In some industries, employers are liable to prosecution if they knowingly employ a new or expectant mother, or a woman who is breastfeeding, in work that is likely to pose a risk to her own health and safety or to that of her new or unborn child. There is a body of UK health and safety legislation which specifically prohibits the employment of such women (indeed, in some circumstances, any woman of child-bearing age) in work involving exposure to physical, biological or chemical agents that are either embryo toxic or regarded as agents causing foetal lesions or likely to disrupt placental attachment. Regulation 18 of the Management of Health & Safety at Work Regulations 1999 allows that an employer need not alter the working conditions or hours of work of a woman (or suspend her from work on maternity grounds) if she has refused or neglected to inform him, when asked to do so, that she is pregnant or breastfeeding or has given birth within the previous six months. Given the possible ramifications, it is a nonsense to suggest that it is an invasion of a woman's Article 8 right to privacy to ask such questions.

24.13

An employer who refuses to permit a woman to return to work in a part-time or job-sharing capacity, after she has given birth, may be able to justify that decision on wholly objective grounds, notwithstanding the *prima facie* infringement of her Article 8 right to respect for her private and family life (see *Home Office v Holmes* [1984] IRLR 299). However, in all such cases, the burden of proof rests squarely on the shoulders of the employer (see also *Kidd v DRG (UK) Limited* [1985] IRLR 190 and *Clymo v Wandsworth London Borough Council* [1989] IRLR 241).

24.14

An employment tribunal will not willingly gainsay an employer's prerogative to reorganise the pattern of working hours (or to introduce a system of shifts) in the interests of greater business efficiency or profitability. However, when contemplating any such reorganisation, employers should nonetheless consult with the affected employees and take into account any attendant disruption to their family and domestic commitments. In short, they should act, and be seen to have acted, 'reasonably'. In *United Bank Limited v Akhtar* [1989] IRLR, an employee with a sick wife and two small children was held to have been constructively dismissed (notwithstanding a mobility clause in his contract) when he found it impossible to comply with his employer's unreasonable request to transfer to another branch of the bank within the next six days.

Article 9: Freedom of thought, conscience and religion

24.15
Article 9 of the Convention allows that 'Everyone has the right to freedom of thought, conscience and religion. This right includes freedom to change his religion or belief and freedom, either alone or in community with others and in public or private, to manifest his religion or belief, in worship, teaching, practice and observance'.

24.16
In *Ahmad v ILEA* (1981) EHRR CD 168, an employer refused to allow a Mr Ahmad, one of his employees and a devout Muslim, to take 45 minutes off work every Friday to attend prayers at his local mosque. Mr Ahmad, a primary school teacher, resigned in protest and subsequently presented a complaint of unfair constructive dismissal to an employment tribunal. In evidence, it was revealed that his employer had offered to reduce Mr Ahmad's working hours from a five-day week to one of four-and-a-half days; but he had refused to accept that offer on the grounds that he would suffer a loss of pay and benefits. By a majority decision, the tribunal held that, notwithstanding Article 9 of the European Convention, Mr Ahmad had no legal or contractual right to take time off work for religious worship, whether paid or otherwise. Mr Ahmad's attempts to pursue the matter before the ECHR were ruled inadmissible by the European Commission on Human Rights. They held that Mr Ahmad's employers had properly considered his Article 9 rights by offering to reduce his working hours to enable him to attend the local mosque in his own time.

24.17
In a not dissimilar case, that of *Stedman v UK* (1997) 23 EHRR CD 168, a Ms Stedman, who was contracted to work on Sundays, was dismissed when she refused to do so. Such work, she said, offended her religious sensibilities. The European Commission on Human Rights decided that it was Ms Stedman's refusal to comply with her contractual obligations, not her religious beliefs, that had led to her being dismissed. She was well aware, when she applied for the job, that she would be required to work on Sundays. If she did not wish to do so, she should not have applied for the job in the first place.

24.18
Save for Northern Ireland, it is not yet unlawful in the UK to discriminate against job applicants or existing employees because of their religious beliefs or affiliations. With the coming into force of the Human Rights Act 1998, any

employee who is dismissed or forced to resign, either for observing or promoting his (or her) religious duties or beliefs or for persistent bullying or harassment at the hands of unsympathetic or bigoted colleagues and supervisors, may pray Convention Article 10 in aid of his contention that he had been unfairly dismissed – the more so if the evidence shows that the employer had done little or nothing to put an end to such treatment or abuse. The employee may also bring an action for damages arising out of his employee's breach of the duty of trust and confidence implicit in every contract of employment.

Article 10: Freedom of expression

24.19
'Everyone', says Convention Article 10, 'has the right to freedom of expression'. While employees undoubtedly have the right to propound their views on a variety of topics, they do not have the right (certainly not in the workplace) to create an unhealthy atmosphere or to disrupt the smooth and efficient running of their employer's business by making critical remarks to (or in the presence of) clients or customers. Nor can they expect to escape disciplinary action or dismissal if they make rude, offensive, racist or sexist remarks to fellow employees.

Standards of dress and appearance

24.20
In spite of suggestions to the contrary, the long-standing right of employers to prescribe minimum standards of dress and appearance amongst their employees is unlikely to be affected by the Human Rights Act 1998. Case law has long since endorsed (and will continue to endorse) the right of employers to dismiss or discipline workers who stubbornly refuse to dress smartly or decently, or who fail to comply with accepted standards of personal cleanliness and hygiene. There is legislation, for example, that prohibits eating, drinking or smoking (not to mention the use of cosmetics) on health and safety grounds (eg, the Control of Substances Hazardous to Health Regulations 2002). Under the Food Safety (General Food Hygiene) Regulations 1995, 'food workers' must comply with certain hygiene standards when handling 'open food'; and so on.

Uniforms and protective clothing

24.21
It is not open to the employment tribunals to undermine or challenge the right of employers to run their businesses efficiently and profitably (*Schmidt v Austicks Bookshops Limited* [1977] IRLR 360; *Boychuk v Symons Holdings*

Limited [1977] IRLR 395). If employees are required by their contracts to wear uniforms or protective clothing while at work (in order to convey a corporate image, or in the interests of health, safety or hygiene), they can expect to be disciplined or dismissed for refusing to do so; and are unlikely to receive a great deal of sympathy when they allude to a supposed infringement of their Article 10 rights when pursuing complaints of unfair dismissal before the employment tribunals.

24.22
Flight attendants, waiters, chefs, ticket collectors, bus conductors, security guards, receptionists, cashiers, shop assistants, postal workers, housekeepers in hotels, etc are likewise unlikely to persuade a tribunal (let alone the European Court) that the uniforms they are required to wear under their contracts infringe their right to 'freedom of expression' under Article 10 of the Convention. Nor is a tribunal likely to accept the contention that wearing a uniform is unnecessary on the grounds that it has no effect whatsoever on an employee's ability to carry out his (or her) duties efficiently or safely (*Burrett v West Birmingham Health Authority* [1994] IRLR 7). In *Smith v Safeway plc* [1996] IRLR 456, the Court of Appeal held that a male employee had been fairly dismissed for refusing to cut his long hair, even though the same requirement did not apply to female workers. In *Panesar v Nestlé* [1980] ICR 144, a Sikh was held to have been justifiably rejected for employment as a food worker because of his refusal to shave off his beard on religious grounds.

24.23
However, notwithstanding *Schmidt* (*qv*), an employer's arbitrary refusal to allow a woman to wear tailored trousers to work, instead of a skirt, is nowadays likely to be challenged as amounting to unlawful discrimination under the Sex Discrimination Act 1975 (*Owen v The Professional Golfers Association* (1999), unreported).

Tattoos, body piercing, etc

24.24
An employer's rules relating to unsightly or offensive tattoos, facial and body piercing, outrageous hairstyles, and the like, may, of course, be challenged before the tribunal courts in support of a complainant's contention that his (or her) dismissal for failing to comply with such rules was not only unfair but an infringement of his rights under Convention Article 10. Such a challenge would be unlikely to succeed if the employee's duties involved work with 'open food' or routine and face-to-face contact with members of the general public. However, a consistent approach is important. In *Harris v McDonalds* (COIT 1392/25), a female employee, with barely noticeable tattoos on her fingers and arms, and whose work brought her into direct contact with customers, was held to have been unlawfully discriminated against when it

was revealed in evidence that her employers had not taken similar action against male employees with clearly-visible tattoos on their forearms.

Article 11: Freedom of assembly and association

24.25
Article 11 states that 'Everyone has the right to freedom of peaceful assembly and to freedom of association with others, including the right to form and to join trade unions for the protection of his interests.'

24.26
The right of a worker to be or not to be, or to refuse to join or remain, a member of an independent trade union, or of any trade union, and the concomitant right of such a worker not to be discriminated against, disciplined, dismissed or selected for redundancy for exercising that right (or for participating 'at an appropriate time' in the activities of an independent trade union) has long since been entrenched in UK domestic legislation (notably, the Trade Union & Labour Relations (Consolidation) Act 1992). Indeed, any employee who is dismissed or selected for redundancy (or otherwise discriminated against) because of his (or her) membership or non-membership of a trade union may complain to an employment tribunal and is likely to be awarded a substantial amount of compensation if his complaint is upheld (as to which, please turn to Chapter 5, para. 5.26 and Chapter 6, paras 6.2 to 6.12).

Article 14: Prohibition of discrimination

24.27
Article 10 of the Convention cautions that 'The enjoyment of the rights and freedoms set forth in this Convention shall be secured without discrimination on any grounds such as sex, race, colour, language, religion, political or other opinion, national or social origin, association with a national minority, property, birth or other status.'

24.28
UK domestic legislation currently prohibits discrimination on grounds of sex, marital status, gender reassignment, race, colour, nationality, national or ethnic origins, disability, and trade union membership or non-membership. In Northern Ireland only, it is unlawful to discriminate against job applicants and existing employees because of their political opinions or religious affiliations. Article 10's prohibition of discrimination on 'any grounds' suggests that the list is by no means exhaustive and could be said to encompass discrimination on grounds of age, religion and sexual orientation. Whether or not workers can pray Article 14 in aid of their contention that they had been unfairly or unlawfully dismissed (or discriminated against on such grounds)

remains to be seen – the more so as Article 10 is not a free-standing right but merely provides that 'the enjoyment of the rights and freedoms set forth in [the] Convention shall be secured without discrimination on any ground...'. Regrettably, there is little, if any, relevant ECHR case law on the subject.

24.29

It is as well to note that, with the publication on 2 December 2000 of Council Directive 2000/78/EC 'establishing a general framework for equal treatment in employment and occupation', the UK and other EU Member States have until 2 December 2003 in which to introduce domestic legislation outlawing discrimination in employment on grounds of age, religion or belief, disability or sexual orientation. Article 18 of the Directive nonetheless allows that, in order to take account of particular conditions, Member States may, if necessary, have an additional period of three years, from 2 December 2003, to implement the Directive's provisions on age and disability discrimination. It is not yet clear whether the UK Government intends to take advantage of the latter derogation.

FURTHER INFORMATION

24.30

The Home Office has published an introductory guide to the Human Rights Act titled: *Human Rights Act – An Introduction*, and a more detailed *Study Guide*, copies of which may be obtained by telephoning 0845 600 1151 or Minicom 0845 600 0347.

24.31

The reader is also commended to the Data Protection Commissioner's *CCTV Code of Practice* and a related document titled *Telecoms Guidance*, either or both of which will be supplied on request by telephoning the Commissioner's Office on 01625 545745. The documents may also be downloaded from Web site: www.dataprotection.gov.uk.

Index